ST.   AND LIBRARY
W9-BWF-248   MARYLAND

REPUBLIC OR RESTORATION IN FRANCE?

1794-7

REPUBLIC OR RESTORATION
IN FRANCE?

1794–7

The Politics of French Royalism,
with particular reference to the activities of
A. B. J. d'André

W. R. FRYER, *B. Litt., M.A.*

MANCHESTER UNIVERSITY PRESS

© 1965, W. R. FRYER

Published by the University of Manchester at
THE UNIVERSITY PRESS
316–324, Oxford Road, Manchester 13

Printed in Great Britain by Butler & Tanner Ltd, Frome and London

2/276

Contents

Illustrations

Preface

ON a brilliant and carefree day in July 1949, I called at a second-hand bookshop in Orléans and bought a handsome copy of the three essays published by Paul Thureau-Dangin, under the title, *Royalistes et Républicains* (1874). My reading of the first of the three essays (*La Question de Monarchie ou de République du 9 thermidor au 18 brumaire*) set my mind upon a track of interest which has led me at last to produce the following monograph.

I had been interested since before my undergraduate days in the history of France during the years between Robespierre and Napoleon. My studies under J. M. Thompson at Magdalen further deepened that interest, and I returned to the period without reluctance. The study which has taken shape in the following pages is a modest contribution to the cultivation of this period of French history in England, a cultivation which appears to have been very much neglected. I make no claims to have dealt with all aspects of French history, even of French political history, during the few years which my subject embraces. I am not even under the illusion that I have dealt definitively with the matters upon which I have written. I hope, however, that I may have written enough, and widely enough, to encourage a greater interest in the period.

*   *   *

Wickham's papers contain about sixty letters, memoranda and notes written by D'André to Wickham himself or to Wickham's secretary Leclerc, between the spring of 1796 and the *coup d'état* of Fructidor. Most of those which were written while D'André was residing in Switzerland are originals. The handwriting of D'André is not very elegant and not particularly easy to read. His use of accents is rather eccentric, and so, occasionally, is his spelling. Wherever I have quoted, either in the text or in notes, from his original letters I have done my best to reproduce both their curious use of accents, and their spelling. From the time when D'André removed himself to France to take personal part in the movement which he was trying to promote, his original letters to the British legation at Berne are practically illegible, and in some instances have apparently not survived at all. The reason is

that their real contents were written in an invisible ink within
an ostensible text written in ordinary ink; the ostensible text consisted of a jargon usually in the style of business letters, and the
invisible text was brought to light on reception by the application
of a liquid which subsequently became more or less hopelessly
confused, both with the invisible ink of the real text, and with the
ordinary ink of the false text. The place of these unreadable or
missing originals is filled by fair copies made in Wickham's office.
In these, both the use of accents and the spelling are rather more
orthodox than the practice of D'André himself in those matters.
In quoting from them, I have followed the usage of the copyist.

The same principles have guided me in the use which I have
made of documents in this correspondence written by Wickham's other French connections. As for the writings of Wickham
himself from which I have quoted, here I have had the benefit, in
almost all cases, of having in front of me the envoy's own original
drafts. It will be seen that I have in a few valuable instances been
able to make use of expressions in his drafts to Lord Grenville,
which he subsequently deleted from the text as sent, either because, on reflection, he thought it better to leave his innermost
thoughts, or details of his conduct, unexpressed, or because a care
for security bade him avoid particulars. It will be noted that
Wickham sometimes drafted letters, even to his French correspondents, in English. I have tried to reproduce his spelling and
use of capitals in English. Where his texts are framed in French,
whether in his own hand or in that of a secretary, I have followed
the same procedure as with the texts of his French correspondents, by attempting to copy the usage as to accents and to spelling which occurs in the drafts or copies in question. It will
appear that Wickham expressed himself fairly well in French: his
use of the accents however, though less eccentric than D'André's,
is not unnaturally a little below the standard with which we are
familiar.

Among published works, I have made relatively little use of the
large memoir literature of the period. This is partly because much
of it is of little particular importance for the subject in hand. I have
of course used some of the few memoirs which could not be
described in these terms, such as those of Thibaudeau and de la
Rue. In contrast, I have quoted extensively from the published
correspondence of Mallet du Pan. This is not because I think Mallet

a plenary or infallible authority on French politics at this period, but simply because he illustrates so copiously and so forcefully the field of facts, alleged facts, and interpretations of those facts, which were of significance to Frenchmen of the time who did not love the Republic or its rulers.

In writing about the general movement of political history, within which the activities of D'André, and of the other Royalist or pro-monarchist politicians with whom I am concerned, took place, I have tried to refer to authorities who should be fairly accessible, reliable for their purposes, and, so far as the case permitted, recent. Since I am not attempting a complete political history of the years covered by my subject, I have not thought it desirable to go at any great length into the history of, or the literature about, many features and episodes of French political life which extend far beyond, or lie outside, the main line of interest which I have tried to follow. On the other hand, at one or two points I have had to argue at some length that the evidence available in Wickham's papers suggests the need to correct some of the statements and inferences about matters immediately concerned with my subject made by such important authorities as Meynier and Lefebvre.

It may be observed that I have not included any reference to the valuable new study by M. Godechot, *La Contre-Révolution: Doctrine et Action.* My own study was completed when this appeared, and I thought it best not to try to benefit, at that late point, by what M. Godechot had written.

*   *   *

I have a number of great obligations to acknowledge, and I turn to this task with deep gratitude to all those concerned. Professor A. C. Wood of the Department of History at Nottingham, and Professor J. S. Roskell of Manchester University, gave me sympathetic encouragement throughout. The important collection of printed works on the history of the French Revolution and of the first Empire, formerly belonging to the Earl of Crawford and Balcarres, and now in the possession of the University of Nottingham, considerably facilitated my reading in the subject; and the Librarian of the University and his staff have throughout been indulgent and helpful.

I owe an expression of particular thanks to Lady Bonham

Carter, the present representative of the family of William Wickham, and the owner of the private papers of that important contributor to the political movements which I have tried to explain. Lady Bonham Carter has not only allowed me the full use of those papers, but has shown me great kindness and hospitality. Mrs Cottrill, the County Archivist at Winchester and at present the custodian of the papers, made it a real pleasure to sit and make transcripts from them in her friendly and well managed office. The Senate and Council of the University of Nottingham have given me generous assistance towards the costs of publication, and this constitutes an obligation which I am especially happy to acknowledge. My colleagues and friends at Nottingham, Professor H. G. Koenigsberger and Dr J. A. S. Grenville, did me further great kindness by reading, and most helpfully discussing with me, much of what I have written. I record also my thanks to M. Roman d'Amat, the present editor of the *Dictionnaire de Biographie française*, who has placed at my disposal his invaluable bibliographical knowledge. The Manchester University Press have shown me every possible consideration since the day I sent them my manuscript.

Most of all, however, I remember in this connection my tutor, J. M. Thompson. Though I was no longer working with him when I planned and started work on this study, it is, however inadequate, the fruit of his influence upon me. Assuming, not without misgivings, that the work has any merits at all, it is to him that I largely ascribe them; and, if it does not appear unduly presumptuous, I would like to offer this book to his memory.

W. R. F.

Nottingham,
April 1964.

Introduction

BETWEEN the summer of 1796 and the *coup d'état* of Fructidor in the following year, elaborate attempts were made to promote counter-revolution in France by the use chiefly of 'legal' methods. The object was to capture the political machinery of the Republic by ostensibly Republican activities, but for ultimately Royalist ends. It was hoped to mobilize the support of all those sections of opinion in the interior which, whatever their ulterior preferences might be, were agreed at least in their hostility to the rule of the old Conventional majority, and in their anxiety over the prospects of a regime which still resembled, too closely for their comfort, the Jacobin dictatorship. The plans for counter-revolution by 'legal' means commanded impressive and increasing support, both inside France and without. By the period of the Germinal elections of year V, when the second *tiers* of the legislative body was renewed, these projects had the active support of numerous deputies already sitting in the two Councils, as well as that of the Pretender and of the exiled Bishops. They had the approval of General Pichegru as well as that of the Pretender's Agents in France. William Wickham, the British Minister at Berne, was placing all his hopes upon their success, and he was lending them important financial assistance besides supplying overall direction at the highest level. These designs enjoyed, no less, the support of Mallet du Pan. Their promoters had, indeed, achieved the seemingly impossible, by bringing together representatives of the *royalisme de l'intérieur*, which had always scouted the idea of a restoration of the old regime *in extenso*, and champions of the 'pure' Royalist emigration who had always stood out for nothing less.

These plans enjoyed other apparent advantages besides. They were attempted in a country which had every reason to dislike the existing personnel of its government and to welcome the prospect of a more stable, more respectable, less exacting and, up to a certain point, more conservative political system. The final intention behind the plans was sufficiently imprecise to permit people of rather diverse sympathies to support them; everyone was free to hope that the solution which would ultimately be reached would correspond with his own particular views as to how far the new reaction towards the right ought to go. The leaders of the undertaking were well aware of the need for caution and delicacy in its further development. They knew that a crushing defeat for the Directorials in the Germinal elections would not alone suffice to overturn the Republic. They meant to exploit whatever opportunities those elections brought them with patience and subtlety. Avoiding any premature declaration of their purpose, they hoped to work by slow and combined stages, leading the legislative body, the administrative authorities, and a carefully indoctrinated mass of public support step by step towards the impeachment of the Republican leaders and then finally towards a legislative enactment in restoration of the throne.[1]

These apparently brilliant prospects were soon overcast: the event of Fructidor decisively reversed all the hopes which the outcome of the Germinal elections had raised so high; and the great project of restoration by 'legal' means was relegated to the lumber rooms of history. But the student of history may find profit, as well as the pleasures of curiosity, in its lumber rooms; and it is chiefly in the hope of contributing to a better understanding and appreciation of this episode of French political life in the difficult years between the Jacobin and the Napoleonic dictatorships, that the present study is undertaken.

I formed the impression very early in my reading on this period of Revolutionary history that it was in the correspondence of William Wickham, the British envoy at Berne,[2] that I would most

---

[1] For general treatments of the political developments briefly referred to here, see G. Lefebvre, *Le Directoire*, 1946, pp. 56–67, 85–90; G. Pariset, *Hist. de France contemporaine* (ed. Lavisse), tome II, 1920, pp. 325–46; A. Meynier, *Les Coups d'Etat du Directoire: Le 18 fructidor*, 1928, pp. 11–20 and p. 183 f. A more detailed study of the whole movement appears in chs. III–X below.

[2] See William Wickham in *D.N.B.* and *The Correspondence of The Rt. Hon. William Wickham*, ed. William Wickham (grandson of the diplomatist), 2 vols., 1870. Wickham twice filled the position of British Minister to the Swiss Cantons. His first mission to Switzerland, with which we are concerned in this book, began in December 1794 (when, after a special and unofficial visit there, as Lord Grenville's personal representative for a particular negotiation, he was appointed British *Chargé d'Affaires*) and ended in autumn 1797 (when the French Directory, shortly after its successful *coup d'état* of Fructidor against the legislative majority, exerted pressure on the Cantons to secure Wickham's recall to London). During this period of three

probably find materials of the greatest importance for the better understanding of the politics of opposition. There, and perhaps only there, might one hope to discover the means to answer with any degree of exactitude the question, how far the political reaction of 1796-7 was in fact dependent upon British assistance, as its Directorial enemies declared it to be. There one might hope to trace the story of the rapprochement, which evidently took place, between the spokesmen of the *royalisme de l'intérieur* and the court of the Pretender who had issued the Declaration of Verona. There one might expect to find informative factual details and instructive comment from the papers of a man who, if not impartial in his judgements of French affairs, had at least the advantage of a detachment of feelings such as no child of France, Republican or Royalist, diehard reactionary or moderate liberal, was likely to have enjoyed. And there, also, one might expect to find a converging mass of observations and suggestions from Frenchmen representing different elements in the coalition of opposition forces with which the British envoy worked. The selection of Wickham's correspondence, published by the envoy's grandson in 1870,[1] raised a strong suggestion that all these hopes would be fulfilled by reference to the whole mass of the papers from which that selection had been made. I was fortunate enough to discover that Wickham's papers still existed intact in the custody of the lady who now represents his family, and to find that their owner was most kindly prepared to lend me every facility and assistance for my proposed investigation. It is upon the evidence arising from Wickham's papers, during the period of his first mission in Switzerland, that this study is chiefly based.

As I pursued my task of reading those papers, I found my early suppositions of what I might find there were abundantly fulfilled. But it also became my object to arrange the materials which I was

---

years, Wickham had in fact been employed in espionage and intrigue against the French Republic, rather than in the ostensible business of his legation.

[1] Wickham, op. cit. Over five hundred pages of this work were devoted to selections from Wickham's correspondence during his mission of 1794-7; but the editor, as he explains (vol. I, p. 20), did not think it necessary to print any correspondence with French Royalists, of which the substance was subsequently retailed by Wickham to Lord Grenville. This rule of course excluded any representation of the more detailed observation and discussion, which that part of Wickham's correspondence included.

gathering for publication around one individual figure. The individual in question is not the British envoy, though this is not to suggest that the part played in the drama by Wickham is in any sense lacking, either in intrinsic importance, or in human interest. It is rather that the British envoy himself identified another person as the principal leader of the policy, and had good grounds for so doing. It appears clearly from Wickham's papers, that though Wickham was, so to speak, the sponsor and producer of the plan, the more directly active function of executive manager was left in the hands of this other person, and that Wickham very largely deferred to his advice in all that concerned both the elaboration and the operation of the plan.

This second person, who thus assumes a position of central personal interest in our study, is a character by no means unknown to the history of the Revolution, though fame of the wider sort has certainly evaded him: Antoine-Balthasar-Joseph d'André.[1]

D'André[2] was an almost exact contemporary of Robespierre,

[1] For the career of D'André generally, see the *Notice sur M. Antoine-Balthazard-Joseph d'André*, 1827 (two years after D'André's death) by A. F. de Silvestre (Bibl. nat., Ln. 27. 378); the various funeral orations pronounced over him (Bibl. nat., Ln. 27. 31256); the articles on him in Robinet *et al.*, *Dict. historique et biographique de la Révolution et de l'Empire*, 1889, tome I, p. 35, and in Robert & Gougny, *Dict. des parlementaires*, 1889, tome I, p. 68. See also Octave Teissier, *Députés de Provence à l'Assemblée nationale de 1789*, 1897. D'André's role in the Constituent Assembly is illustrated by Aulard in his *Orateurs . . . Assemblée Constituante*, 1905; his contribution to the Feuillant reaction of 1791 is traced in G. Michon, *Adrien Duport, Essai sur l'histoire du parti feuillant*, 1924. In my introduction I have also made use of D'André's letter of submission to Louis XVIII (18 March 1796), a copy of which is filed in Wickham's Papers. (This document is considered in its proper context in ch. V below.) D'André himself left two short pieces dealing with certain aspects of his Provençal activity (Bibl. nat., Ln. 27. 377 and 8 Le 29. 1174). I am indebted to M. Roman d'Amat, Editor of the *Dictionnaire de Biographie française*, for several of these references.

[2] D'André appears always to have written his name with the apostrophe, according to the usage of the old regime. Sometimes, at least, he seems to have used a capital D. The usage of Revolutionary times was of course to write it without the apostrophe: Dandré. Contemporary historians of the period (Pariset, Meynier, Aulard, Lefebvre) follow, for this as for certain other names, the usage of Revolutionary times. I have shown the name, except when I first mention it with the addition of D'André's Christian names, as *apostrophized and with the capital D*. This represents a compromise between the normal usage of the old regime, which would have been to put the *d* in a small character, except at the beginning of a sentence, and the

and like him had been a member of the Estates-General, at an age
far below the average. Seigneur de Bellevue and *conseiller* in the
Parlement of Aix en Provence, he represented the Nobility of
Aix.[1] He began as one of the liberal nobility, and went on to
earn for himself a position of great prominence (in the eyes of
contemporaries) among the *patriotes*; but, like his more celebrated
fellow countryman Mirabeau, he had within him the makings of
a champion of order and moderation, as well as the ideals of a
liberal. Again like Mirabeau, he early sought a private approach
to the Court. At the end of 1789, he accepted a mission from the
government to his native Provence, and subsequently claimed
credit for a resolution of the Marseille Commune, calling for the
effective restoration of the King's executive authority.[2] In the
Assembly he tried to concert measures with the Ministry, and
his inevitable reward was to be accused of compromising his
patriote principles for a share in the good things of the Civil
List.[3] Nevertheless, he three times occupied the chair of the
Assembly.

In summer 1791 he played a prominent part in the defence of
the interests of 'order' and of the monarchical principle. His plea
that 'a great example' should be made of the democratic agitators[4]
was gratified when fire was opened on the demonstrators of the
Champ de Mars on 17 July. He was a founder member of the
Feuillant Club,[5] and he took an energetic part in the efforts of the
Feuillants to bring about a stiffly conservative revision of the
constitution. Circumstances thus brought him into alliance with
the 'triumvirs', Duport, Barnave, and the brothers Lameth,[6]
who, having so long led the Left Wing of the Assembly, now took

usage of the contemporary historians. Whether the compromise is a happy
one is for others to judge.

[1] A. Brette, *Les Constituants*, 1897, p. 162.

[2] D'André's letter of submission to King Louis XVIII.

[3] See the chapter on D'André in Aulard, *Orateurs*.

[4] Quoted by Aulard, *Hist. pol. de la Rév. franç.*, 1901, p. 105.

[5] Michon, *Adrien Duport*, p. 273, n. 3.

[6] As Goodwin points out (*French Revolution*, p. 110 n.), the term 'Triumvirs' is a misnomer, for in the group in question Charles de Lameth was
almost as influential as his brother Alexandre, and the 'triumvirate' thus
included four men. In the years to which this book is devoted, yet another of
the Lameths (Théodore) was concerned in an interesting attempt to revive
the policy of the Feuillants.

the lead of a very different policy, and sought to impose themselves, as the apostles of moderation, not only on the Assembly
but also on the hapless Louis XVI.

D'André later professed contempt for the more famous politicians with whom he was thus thrown into a new and close
association. He declared their latter-day Royalism insincere, the
product of mere ambition.[1] Whether or not he thought this from
the beginning, it is likely enough that he regarded these latest
self-appointed mentors of the King with jealousy and illwill; for
he stood towards them in the same relationship as the Elder Son
to the Prodigal. For himself, he thought of an elective post in the
new administrative system. Already he had been beaten by
Robespierre in the election for the post of *accusateur public* of
Paris; and he had refused the consolation prize of acting as
Robespierre's *substitut*. If the Triumvirs could now have succeeded in bringing about his election to the great office of *pro-
cureur-général-syndic* of the Department, D'André's feeling towards
them might have taken a different course. But the Triumvirs
failed; La Fayette, who professed the same general principles as
his old opponents now maintained, was at heart still estranged
from them, and had his own candidate for this post. It was La
Fayette's candidate, Roederer, who was elected.[2] D'André had no
better success in his hopes of the mayoralty of Paris. He thus
missed all his chances of playing a *beau rôle* as champion of the
constituted authorities during the troubled months which preceded the fall of the throne. One can only speculate on what he
might have done in the place of Roederer, or of Petion. After these
successive failures, if not before, D'André told the King that no
good was to be expected from the efforts of the Triumvirs,[3] and
turned his own thoughts towards emigration.

[1] In his letter of submission to Louis XVIII, D'André wrote, apparently
with reference to the time of the Feuillant reaction, and to the activities of
the 'Triumvirs', 'Lorsque je vis des hommes qui n'avoient attaque l'autorité
royale que pour s'en emparer monter au Gouvernail, je jugeai que je
devenois inutile.' It seems clear that contemporaries of all shades of opinion
were shocked by the too obvious contrast between the conduct of the
'Triumvirs' down to about the end of 1790, and their warm championship of
Royal authority in summer 1791.

[2] Michon, op. cit., p. 349.

[3] In his letter of submission to Louis XVIII, D'André claims (giving no
precise date): 'Je me résolus, apres avoir dit franchement ma façon de penser,
sur le peu de bien qu'on pouvoit espérer de ces hommes, a sauver du moins

D'André now all but disappears from the history of public affairs for many years. Only at the time of the great attempt, in 1796-7, to capture the machinery of the Republic for Royalist ends, does he reappear in the story of the revolutionary period, and even then, hitherto, only faintly. His plans and doings at that point have, indeed, received brief attention from certain well-known modern French historians—Pariset, Meynier, and Lefebvre.[1] Their knowledge of these was apparently derived in part from memoranda composed by D'André himself, to describe his efforts and to account for their failure.[2] In the present study an attempt will be made to fill out, and in some degree to amend, their treatment of D'André's contribution to that famous failure.

After the *coup d'état* of Fructidor, the twilight once more descends on the career of D'André. If the victorious Directorial party were not unaware that he had been one of their most influential and resourceful opponents, they must nevertheless, for whatever reasons, have been willing to let the curtain fall upon him. In the official Report on the great conspiracy, presented to the expurgated remnant of the Council of the Five Hundred by the government's spokesman J.-Ch. Bailleul,[3] the honours of villainy are attributed to Pichegru, the deputies Lemerer and Mersan, and the King's Agents; D'André is not even mentioned. He was not arrested. Wickham's papers show that he escaped the troops of Augereau on the fatal day and made his way safely back to Swiss soil, on which he had been residing when his part in the great adventure began.

Wickham's papers also show that D'André kept up for some time his connections with the British diplomat, and was once more active in Anglo-Royalist combinations at the time of Wickham's second mission in Switzerland during the war of the second

---

ma personne pour mes enfans et mon pays.' Silvestre, op. cit., recalls that at the time of Petion's success in the mayoral election D'André's house had been pillaged, and charges of correspondence with the émigrés raised against him.

[1] Pariset, op. cit., pp. 329-30, 332, 343-4, 346; Meynier, tome cit., pp. 188-90, 193; Lefebvre, op. cit., pp. 56-7, 88.

[2] The historians concerned do not give detailed references.

[3] Printed in Buchez & Roux, *Hist. parl. de la Révolution*, tome 37, 1838, pp. 388-437.

B

coalition. According to D'André's biographer Silvestre, the ex-Constituent at this point gained not only the acquaintance but the confidence of the Archduke Charles, now once more leading the Habsburg armies against the Republic; and thanks to this happy chance, he gained an honourable refuge for himself at Vienna, when the Royalist cause seemed utterly extinguished amid the triumphs, both domestic and international, of the First Consul. The Austrian sovereign raised D'André to the honours of a barony and appointed him president of the Imperial Society of Agriculture, which D'André had played an important part in promoting.

With the Restoration of 1814, D'André at last returned to the public life of his own country. The sometime *patriote* had made his peace with Louis XVIII in the spring of 1796, before his part in the great attempt to subvert the Republic from within had begun. Although he had failed in that attempt, he had subsequently rendered further loyal service to his titular sovereign, and had established himself lastingly in the King's regard. More fortunate than many others who had rowed with him in the hard galley of Royalist politics, he now reaped the rewards which his labours, his talents and his fidelity had deserved. A grateful sovereign appointed him *directeur-général de la police*, with Ministerial status.[1] His new fortune was indeed momentarily clouded, when he was criticized for failing to procure timely information of Napoleon's return from Elba; and he lost his new post even before the King lost his capital to the usurper.[2] But he had not forfeited the personal favour of the sovereign; and on the second Restoration he received, besides the Legion of Honour, another great appointment, the intendantship of the Royal Forests and Domains. He lived to correspond again, this time in the vein of mutual congratulation and reminiscence, with his old British patron and admirer Wickham; and he died full of honours, while Charles X sat, to all appearance firmly, upon the throne, and Villèle presided over the Council, being thus spared the sight of the final downfall of the regime which he had once worked so hard and so ingeniously to restore.

This is all that need be said here of D'André's career as a whole. What will concern us henceforward is his contribution to the

---

[1] Recorded in Testu's *Almanach Royal*, 1815.

[2] See, e.g., Lamartine, *Hist. de la Restauration*, tome III, 1851, p. 90.

restauration manquée of the Directorial period. Before we can approach this, however, we must establish the background of the whole episode. We must begin with a discussion of the shades and prospects of French Royalism between Thermidor and Vendémiaire.

PART I

ROYALISM IN SEARCH OF A POLICY
1794–6

I

The Prospects of Restoration

IN THE TWELVE MONTHS FOLLOWING THERMIDOR

WHEN the Robespierrists went to the guillotine and the structure of the revolutionary government began to disintegrate, the first French Republic arrived at a critical moment. It was the end of a phase; might it not also have been the 'beginning of the end' of the Republic? The French people could never again have been brought to accept Royalty as the exiled French princes then conceived it. But, if the French people's true wishes could then have been elucidated, there are grounds for thinking that they would have favoured a return to the traditional kingship, defined and limited by some new agreement between the old dynasty and the renewed nation. It is true that Louis XVI had largely lost his credit before he lost his head; it is also true that the act of regicide had destroyed, and not enhanced, the mystique of the monarchy. For all this, kingship was deeply rooted in French tradition; and the Republic could claim neither a true popular mandate, nor the subsequent acquisition of wide popularity. The Jacobin dictatorship and the Terror had saved France, but had hardly endeared the Republic to it. If the Republic was now relieved of these reproaches, others promptly took their place. Inevitably the Thermidorian reaction involved a relapse into economic and administrative anarchy, which brought fresh miseries to millions. For undertaking this change from Jacobin hot water to Thermidorian cold, the Convention certainly reaped no reward in popular favour; the load of reproach which it had to bear was merely doubled, and the public credit of its members sank steadily. The deputies who made up the supreme, almost the sole, constituted authority of the regime had little chance, as they moved through their third year of office, to attract lustre either to their own reputations or to the Republic which they represented.

It would no doubt be rash to claim that any high proportion of the French people at this time entertained any views for the future so positive as a conscious ambition for a moderate and sensible restoration. But it was clear that the country disliked and despised the system under which it lived, that it was perforce hankering for something better, and that it had, in its recent experience, the appealing ideal—never as yet adequately realized, but still possessing great attraction—of a polity in which the monarchical tradition was to be reconciled with some expression of popular consent, with the rule of law, and with enlightened administrative techniques. These were facts, which, in the minds of many people both within the territory and in exile, pointed in a clear and hopeful direction. Those who held such a view included some of the leading spirits of moderate liberalism in the days of the Constituent Assembly, and also some of the more realistic opponents of the Revolution even in its earlier phases. Men of these two kinds now converged, across the barriers of old animosities and across the frontiers which in many cases physically separated them, to hope and work for a restoration on sensible and moderate terms. Old constitutional royalists hoped to engage leading members of the Convention to support the project of enthroning the young Louis XVII and of constituting a regency to govern in his name under defined legal conditions. It seems that their hopes were not entirely baseless. Deputies of note were reported to favour such a solution, and some of these deputies were members of the Convention's Commission of Eleven, appointed to prepare a revision of the now tacitly repudiated Constitution of 1793.[1] The general idea behind such projects was regarded with sympathy and hope by such distinguished critics of the Revolution as Calonne, the Archbishops Boisgelin and Champion de Cicé, and Mallet du Pan.[2] All these men believed that a restoration was now within the bounds of possibility, but they also agreed in thinking that it could only be realized in the medium of constitutional monarchy. None of these men had any very good opinion (to say the least) of the vanished constitutional order of 1789-91, or of the politicians who had identified themselves with the effort to create and maintain that order. But they believed that the system of 1789-91 could now provide an initial basis for negotiation between the nation and the Crown, from which it might well become possible to advance towards a more

[1] Cf. G. Lefebvre, *Les Thermidoriens*, 1946, pp. 137, 164.
[2] Ibid., p. 137.

substantial reconstruction of Royal power. Mallet du Pan, at least, also believed that the surviving representatives of the party which had stood for the regime of 1791 had a necessary part to play in creating the conditions requisite for this negotiation and reconstruction.

Such enlightened conservatives thus looked beyond the basis provided by the work of the Constituent Assembly, and proposed to use it, and to ally with its defenders, only as a means to a more thorough-going restoration. They thought, however, that even in the more substantial restoration to which they looked forward, the Crown must adopt some of the more practical and generally accepted achievements of the revolutionary period, and must carefully eschew any intention to revive the most generally unpopular features of the old regime.

At this point we may naturally refer to the diagnoses of French affairs which Mallet du Pan was submitting to the Court of Vienna in the earlier months of 1795. The famous Swiss journalist was neither impartial nor infallible, but the sobriety and good sense of his appraisals at this juncture are surely beyond question. In his note of 8 January 1795, Mallet gave it as his opinion that not more than a quarter of French people were convinced adherents of the republican regime, and that the number of those who were, in some shade and degree, convinced adherents of monarchy was considerably larger, perhaps one-third of the whole.[1] These royalists were, indeed, by no means homogeneous in their outlook. The remnants of the aristocracy, and many of the bourgeoisie who had long since bitterly repented of the revolution, made up the pure Royalists, who would gladly participate in a return to the old regime. But this section of opinion was not only depleted in its leadership and deeply intimidated, it was also an unpopular minority, without support of any kind except in the Western areas of insurrection.[2] The pure Royalists would never

---

[1] Most of the text of this Note of 8 January 1795 is printed in A. Sayous, *Mémoires et Correspondance de Mallet du Pan*, 1858, tome II. The passage in question here falls on p. 127 of that volume. Michel's edition of the *Correspondance inédite de Mallet du Pan avec la Cour de Vienne*, 2 tomes, 1884, gives a more complete version of the text, and incidentally supplies the date of the Note, which Sayous omitted.

[2] Sayous, op. cit., tome II, pp. 128–9. 'Pure' royalists inside France or with the emigration, upheld the claims of the lawful heirs of Louis XVI on the traditional basis of the Monarchy. They stood, just as much, for the

achieve anything except in conjunction with the representatives of the constitutional-royalist phases of the Revolution. These latter were also, as yet, a suppressed and powerless body. But, unlike the pure Royalists, they had once enjoyed, on broad issues, the support of most of the country; and a large following, particularly among the substantial propertied classes, could be expected to rally to their banners as soon as circumstances made it safe for them to do so.[1]

Mallet went on to say that the constitutional royalists had other very important advantages besides their possession of wide potential support. They had useful intellectual affinities with other, and more immediately influential people, the 'moderates' of the Thermidorian Convention and the surviving so-called 'federalists': men who had themselves been involved in the Revolution much more deeply even than the constitutional royalists, but who now had little or no faith in the future of republicanism, and were interested to find a decent and tenable position upon which to retreat.[2]

In the same note Mallet developed the view that the bases laid down by the Constituent Assembly provided in any case a necessary first stage towards that more substantial reconstruction of the French monarchy which he considered to be the destined end of the whole process.[3] He argued that the old constitutional royalists not only offered, so to speak, a half-way house ready made, but would themselves assist in the further retracement of steps; they would all accept, without difficulty, a revision of the text of 1791 along the lines once favoured by the *monarchiens*, and he believed that many of them would be willing to make modifications of a still more drastic kind. They would be prepared, even, 'à sacrifier la plupart des institutions populaires'—provided only that they could be assured they had nothing to fear from the anger and folly of the pure Royalist emigration and could look forward with confidence to 'le pardon, la sûreté, la considération personnelle et la vanité'.[4] The conduct and projects of the 'Triumvirs'

---

restoration, so far as possible, of the old social order. In either respect, they were far removed indeed from all those who had accepted 1789, not to mention 1792.

[1] Ibid., p. 129.   [2] Ibid., p. 130, cf. pp. 118–24.
[3] Michel, op. cit., tome I, pp. 46–7.
[4] Sayous, op. cit., tome II, p. 130; Michel, op. cit., tome I, p. 48.

and other leading Feuillants in 1791-2 certainly went far to authorize Mallet's predictions on these points.

In other passages of his correspondence, Mallet laid great emphasis on the point of caution, that this substantial restoration of monarchical authority, which he thus believed to be attainable, would nevertheless depend entirely upon the Crown's realizing the need to remain clearly and resolutely aloof from all pretensions to restore the old order in all its particular features. He exhausted his considerable resources of language to make the point that the restoration of the old regime in that sense was for ever out of the question:

...personne en France n'a la plus légère pensée ni le moindre désir du retour à l'ancien régime. Le gouvernement d'autrefois est aussi effacé dans l'opinion que celui de Clovis: il en est de même de la féodalité, du pouvoir et des biens de l'église.

Il est aussi impossible de refaire l'ancien régime que de bâtir St-Pierre de Rome avec la poussière des chemins.[1]

Side by side with these passages we may place a letter written by Mallet to Wickham, at the time of the envoy's original (unofficial) mission of investigation to Switzerland towards the end of 1794. The purpose of Wickham's journey was to look into certain interesting but not very substantial propositions then being made to the British cabinet by three of the old Feuillants (Théodore de Lameth, Brémond, and Mathieu-Dumas). The details can readily be referred to, and need not delay us here.[2] All that we need notice about these propositions is that Mallet du Pan himself and Mounier had acted as intermediaries to bring them to the notice of London. Wickham had arrived in Switzerland and had held discussions with the proposers under the chairmanship, so to speak, of Mallet and Mounier; and when the British agent broke off these discussions, perhaps with some expressions of impatience and disgust, Mallet du Pan sent to him this most interesting statement of the reasons why, in Mallet's judgement, the British Government should not impatiently abandon, but should rather cultivate and pursue, these relations with the old constitutional royalists, despite their immediate

[1] Michel, op. cit., tome I, pp. 115-16; Sayous, op. cit., tome II, p. 142.
[2] Hist. MSS. Comm., *Dropmore Papers, Fortescue,* vol. II, pp. 637-8, 649, 651-2; Wickham, *Correspondence,* vol. I, pp. 9-16; Sayous, op. cit., tome II, pp. 93-109.

uselessness, and despite the unsatisfactory character, as both
Mallet and the British regarded it, of the party from whence the
proposals came.[1]

M. Moun... et moi avions l'un et l'autre considéré les ouvertures que
nous transmettions à Londres comme infiniment plus importantes par
les circonstances qui les fesaient naître, que par le caractère ou par les
liaisons déjà formées des gens qui s'adressaient à nous. On employe en
médicine le mercure et la cigue—malheureusement on est forcé
aujourd'hui de réduire ses espérances à une théorie de contrepoisons.

Mallet went on to argue that the British Government should
welcome and persist in the negotiation with the old constitutional royalists in the same spirit in which he and Mounier had
tried to promote it. The drift of political developments in France
was placing these old Feuillants, through no merit of theirs, in
an all important strategic position. The fortunes of the Thermidorian Conventionals, of the French nation, and of the Allied
Powers were being placed in their hands. Their system provided
the necessary and only bridge whereby the nation, and, even more
pertinent, the politicians who now ruled over it, might achieve
their general objective, which was to retire from the unending
horrors of revolution. If this should prove impossible, these men
and their sympathizers in the country would be invaluable allies
of any politicians who might try to resist either of the two grand
calamities to which the drifting state stood exposed, a revival of
terroristic Jacobinism or the triumph of the extreme reactionaries.

Les constitutionnels... sont placés sur la ligne qui avoisine le plus tout ce
qui voudra, dans un tems ou dans un autre, abjurer la République...
que la Révolution continue à retrograder, ou qu'on tente de revenir
au régime de la terreur, le jeu des constitutionnels a une infinité de
chances; chaque pas de recul rapproche d'eux et de la Monarchie la
grande masse de la nation; la même affinité... fereit combiner leurs
résistances à un nouveau systeme d'oppression et de guillotine... Tout
parti dans la Convention qui aura le besoin... de... changement y
employera les constitutionnels: ils ont de commun avec les Révolutionnaires actuels la crainte de retomber à discretion sous la monarchie
absolue, gouvernée par les Princes et les Emigrés.

The application of all this to the interests of the British Government, Mallet considered, should be obvious. The Allies could not

[1] Wickham Papers, 16 November 1794.

hope to promote a restoration of the French Crown without the support of a powerful party inside France; and this party was not to be found except among the old constitutional royalists and those who, in their revulsion from the experiences of the past two years, were likely to seek a solution in principles similar to theirs. The Allies could expect nothing from the friends of the old order pure and simple.

Ce parti, il faut le chercher non dans les cendres de l'ancienne monarchie, mais dans les moins mauvaises dispositions de ceux qui, après avoir concouru à la renverser, voudront un jour en refaire les éléments.

Ce serait prolonger dangereusement les illusions qui ont gouverné les Cabinets, que de leur offrir aujourd'hui le secours des aristocrates de l'intérieur, celui d'une guerre civile ou d'un révolte; tout cela est moralement impossible.

Mallet went on to warn the British agent in emphatic terms, that unless his government grasped in time the chance to 'jetter les fils d'une grande connexion intérieure' with the constitutional royalists, it would run the risk of losing all chance of better things to come; these men had, he thought, only an imperfect sense of loyalty to the Crown, but (even if only from selfish motives) they had a very deep sense of the evils of extreme reaction; and unless the Allies lent some encouragement to their hopes of a compromise between the nation and the old monarchy, this party might well abandon all hopes for a restoration, and take up with any conciliatory offers which the ruling politicians, themselves involved in the same difficulty, might offer them.

As the earlier months of 1795 progressed, Mallet had no reason to congratulate himself upon any evidence that the British authorities were giving due weight to these arguments. But he had what he thought good reason to believe that the movement of opinion inside France was continuing to develop as he had judged and hoped. In Notes to the Austrian Government, dated in May and early June, he reported a great development of specifically Royalist feeling in the interior, and the emergence of a positively Royalist group inside the Convention, including Lanjuinais and his friends from one quarter, and the less reputable Tallien and his from another.[1] All these, he asserted, were thinking of the

[1] Michel, op. cit., tome I, pp. 204–5. These assertions of Mallet about the movement of notable contemporary politicians towards the young King find interesting partial corroboration in a draft despatch of Wickham to Lord

Constitution of 1789–91, revised in a conservative direction. As a first step in this direction, they were hoping to persuade moderate republicans to accept the principle of a single person at the head of the executive branch with powers similar to those possessed by the President of the United States.[1]

Mallet laid great emphasis on the point that it was only on some kind of constitutional basis that these politicians of the Republic were prepared to contemplate a restoration. They had abandoned, if they ever possessed, faith in the future of the Republic; but they would not hear of the pure Royalist solution;[2] and their distrust of the exiled princes made them very uneasy even at the prospect of admitting one of these to a Regency, albeit of strictly limited powers, on behalf of the young King. Some of them preferred to contemplate the alternative of an elected Council of Regency, or (an interesting echo of an old sympathy) favoured an appeal to Prince Henry of Prussia. Mallet obviously shared the feelings which he thus attributed to these men, that the prince to whom, by the laws of the old monarchy, the Regency was certainly due, had shown little sign of his fitness for the office in the circumstances which then obtained.[3]

The Royalism thus adopted by certain leading deputies was clearly very far indeed from Royalism as the princes defined it: it was calculated, conditional, and suspicious. Yet, as Mallet took pains to emphasize in his reports to the Viennese cabinet, this was the best that could as yet be expected from any large part of French opinion. If the country was turning towards its traditional institutions, it was only in this very mitigated and eclectic spirit. Any return to certain other institutions of the past was, he

---

Grenville, of considerably later date (Wickham Papers, 14 May 1796, 'Private and Separate'.) In this despatch, Wickham was commenting on the poor quality of the information about developments at Paris, which he had been receiving in the previous year from his then agent, Vincent. He added: 'however, there certainly was *some* foundation for the report he had sent me, of the disposition and intention of several members of the Convention to place the young King on the throne in the month of May, and that Tallien was beginning to enter into the plan. *Marginal Note:* 'I have since learnt from undoubted authority that Tallien was at that moment in correspondence with the Austrian general Seckendorf.'

[1] Michel, op. cit., tome I, p. 225.
[2] Ibid., p. 219.
[3] Ibid., p. 206.

reiterated, quite unthinkable: 'on ne veut point du régime des dîmes, de la gabelle, des parlements, des intendants, de la féodalité.'[1]

While Mallet du Pan was composing these notes, the young Prince, about whom his hopes and those of so many others had gathered, was abandoning his struggle with an intolerably harsh destiny. He died on 8 June, and it is in retrospect clear beyond dispute that the projects for a reconciliation between the nation and the traditional kingship, which despite his death continued to attract attention, were fatally compromised by this event. The present study is largely a commentary upon that fact.

Monsieur, who had been so unwelcome to the interior as Regent, was now, by legitimist principles, King. It was indeed the case, as Mallet du Pan had reflected, that, gifted as he was, Louis Stanislas-Xavier had done nothing to earn the esteem of his fellow countrymen. He had already done much to deprive himself of their esteem for ever. Leaving aside any reference to his conduct between his departure from France in June 1791 and the execution of the King, we will refer to the official statement of policy which he issued on 28 January 1793, immediately after that event, when he assumed the Regency for his nephew Louis XVII.

This *Declaration to the French People* announced a most uncompromising attitude towards the erring subjects of the Crown. It stated plainly that, save for the correction of certain only vaguely specified administrative abuses, the Regent intended to re-establish the old regime in its full extent, and also that he proposed to punish with condign severity all the crimes committed in the name of the Revolution. There was nothing in the document which suggested a temper of clemency, still less of compromise, towards either the principles or the persons of those whose errors had become manifest at any date later than August 1788. By contrast, the titular Regent tacitly if not expressly identified the interests of the Crown with those of the privileged revolutionaries of the immediately preceding years. Instead of the principles of Calonne or Lamoignon, he offered the country the remedies of Fréteau or Sabatier de Cabre.

Je m'emploierai premièrement à la liberté du roi (*Louis XVII*), de sa mère, de sa sœur, et de sa tante, et simultanément au rétablissement de

---

[1] Ibid., p. 226.

la Monarchie, sur les bases inaltérables de sa constitution, à la reforma-
tion des abus introduits dans le régime de l'administration publique,
au rétablissement de la religion de nos pères dans la pûreté de son culte
et de la discipline canonique, à la réintegration de la magistrature..., à
la réintegration des Français de tous les ordres dans leurs droits
légitimes et dans la jouissance de leurs propriétés envahies et usurpées,
à la sévère et exemplaire punition des crimes...[1]

Between the date of that Declaration and the death of the
young King there had occurred two and a half years of dismal
misfortune for the cause of the Regent. Had the passage of this
time brought about any change in his policy? There had been
signs that his private temper was becoming more dispassionate,
that he was becoming more disposed to clemency; but none that
he was resigning himself to compromise on matters of principle.
Any possibility of doubt about this was dispelled by the famous
Declaration from Verona, which, in his new capacity as King of
France, he presented to a hostile or indifferent world on 24 June
1795.

This new Declaration can without absurdity be represented,
from one point of view, as a moderate and conciliatory document.
This is, needless to say, the point of view of its Royal author. He
himself regarded it with complacency as a work of great moderation and breadth of view. He thought that in it he had conceded
everything which it was in his power to concede, consistently
with those traditional principles to which he considered himself
to be irrevocably committed.[2] From this point of view, three
features of the Declaration deserve particular notice.

First, though Louis XVIII in this document claimed the Crown
by divine hereditary right, he repudiated with apparently complete sincerity any pretensions to despotism. He emphasized
rather that the Royal prerogative was limited by the 'ancient and
venerable Constitution' of the realm. This, in his judgement, had
been substantially corrupted long before 1789; but he was just as
determined to restore this, in its integrity, as he was to restore
himself.

With regard to the French Constitution [wrote Lord Macartney, the
British representative at Verona, a few months later], it is regarded,

---

[1] E. Daudet, *Histoire de l'émigration*, 3me edit., 1907, tome I, pp. 218–19.
[2] Paul Thureau-Dangin, *La Question de Monarchie ou de République, du 9
thermidor au 18 brumaire*, in the volume *Royalistes et Républicains*, 1874, p. 48.

Qui oseroit se venger

quand le Roi pardonne ?

PLATE I

Louis XVIII, shortly after his (titular)
accession to the throne of France

'Qui oseroit se venger quand le Roi pardonne?'
This reassuring phrase was used by Louis himself in his Declaration
of Verona

particularly by the King, with the same fondness as the Common Law was contemplated by my Lord Coke, as the wisdom of ages, the perfection of reason, etc... he admits that many serious abuses had crept into it... (*but*) none of the abuses does he look upon as making any integral part of the real constitution itself, which in his opinion is as little despotic as our own.[1]

In the Declaration of Verona, the new Pretender gave some, though not a very complete, account of the ancient and venerable Constitution of the realm. According to him, the constitution entrusted to the King the plenitude of both the legislative and the executive power. On the other hand, the consent of the Estates-General was necessary for the imposition of new taxation and for additions to existing taxes. The Estates-General also enjoyed of right the important function of presenting the grievances and expressing the wishes of the nation. Though, according to the Pretender, the Crown alone had the power to determine the convocation and dissolution of these Estates, and there was no provision for any regular meeting of their assembly, he certainly granted that the King lay under a real obligation to obtain the assent of the Estates-General before making any taxative changes, and to attend seriously to any recommendations which might be expressed there. In addition, the Declaration recognized the claims of the Parlements to act as depositories and guardians of the laws; and thus, to some rather uncertain extent, it limited its own assertion of the King's plenary legislative power.[2]

Secondly, the Pretender now put forward what can certainly be described, so far as the terms of the document go, as a liberal offer of amnesty. With the only exceptions of the regicides and the terrorists, he was now willing to receive all his subjects into grace, provided that they would for the future accept the claims and precepts of the lawful King. Although some of his own actions seem oddly out of accord with the spirit of this offer, and although it is quite obvious that he allowed his adherents to contradict him, it seems certain, in retrospect, that the Pretender was quite sincere in making this gesture. As Lord Macartney noted at the time, the 'King of France'

professes the utmost moderation, and integrity, and those who have

---

[1] Lord Macartney to Wickham, 15 October 1795; Wickham, *Correspondence*, vol. I, pp. 181–2.

[2] Cf. Daudet, op. cit., tome I, p. 287.

had opportunities of knowing him best seem persuaded of his sincerity.... He speaks of the principal persons concerned in the Revolution without any appearance of rancour, and of the revolution itself with a degree of calmness and dispassion that one would scarcely expect.[1]

Pausing here for a moment, it is not hard to understand why, despite these ostensibly moderate and reasonable features, the new Declaration failed to make any but the most unfavourable impression on opinion in the interior, including that part of opinion which consciously favoured a return to some kind of monarchical government. It was in vain that the Pretender renounced any claims to despotic authority, for the limitations of a constitutional kind that he admitted were such as to offer satisfaction—a partial satisfaction—to the privileged constitutionalism of 1787–8. They offered none to the aspirations of the national party of 1789, and, evidently, none to any of the more advanced formulations of popular principle which had followed on. Wedded as he was to the 'ancient and venerable Constitution', the Pretender would admit of no new contract between the Crown and the nation, neither that which had been drawn up by the Constituent Assembly nor any revised version of it. The Estates-General to which he referred was evidently the assembly comprising the three separate orders, into which the nation, like its representative body, was to be solemnly forced back. It was all of a piece with this that he should admit the pretensions of the Parlements. On all this part of the ground, the new Declaration represented no significant advance on the positions taken up by the Declaration of 28 January 1793. It flew in the face of the facts, proclaimed in vain by Mallet du Pan and many other observers by no means friendly to the Revolution, that the old apparatus of privilege was far more abhorrent to the French people than the Royal despotism which the Pretender was so anxious to disclaim, and that the restoration of orders and Parlements and so forth was a simple impossibility.

In its offer of amnesty, the Verona Declaration certainly marked an advance on that of January 1793. But, if this were the only feature of improvement, then clearly it could not be enough to effect the reconciliation of Crown and people. As Mallet was shortly to point out to the cabinet of Vienna, the new statement

[1] Macartney to Wickham, 15 October 1795, cited above.

was sadly lacking in incentives to the old constitutional royalists and to all those who shared their point of view; the only satisfaction it offered them, in concrete terms, was a very negative one, 'une amnistie qui les réduit à n'être point pendus'.[1]

Here we reach the third point. Is it really the case that the Declaration offered no positive improvements on the old regime? It has to be said that it offered very little. We have already noted its undertaking that the nation should not be taxed without its own consent. Apart from this, the Declaration repeated the Pretender's earlier promise to investigate and correct 'abuses' in the administration. This was all; and it was bound to impress the country as extremely thin and unsatisfactory. Taxation by consent was more than outbalanced by the proposed restoration of orders and Parlements. The abuses of the old government had been swept away, and the promise to correct them was, in the strict meaning of the word, impertinent. For the rest, the Declaration was more eloquent in its silences than in its promise of practical reforms. Even without lending countenance to any of the theoretical principles of the Revolution, the Pretender might have expressed his intention to retain and honour innumerable practical reforms and improvements, to confirm many practical and established results of revolutionary legislation. He did not do so. Most especially, there was nothing in the Declaration of Verona to reassure the purchasers of nationalized properties; and, by insisting on the re-establishment of the Church, as well as of the orders, it implied that no such reassurance was intended.[2]

The professed moderation of the Declaration was thus void of useful effect upon the interior. But the wording of this new announcement was not the only evidence upon which the attitude of the Pretender could be judged. Some of his own contemporary actions, and the character and doings of other exiles, to whom he now as in former times showed complacency, or at least tolerance, provided evidence which was still less reassuring.

One celebrated act of the new titular Sovereign was bound to suggest the gravest doubts, to all those who had been in any degree whatever concerned in the Revolution, whether even the Pretender's offer of amnesty had any serious significance. This was

---

[1] Mallet du Pan to the Court of Vienna, 13 September 1795; Michel, op. cit., tome I, p. 308.

[2] Cf. Daudet, op. cit., tome I, p. 287.

his dismissal of the Prince de Poix from his position as Captain
of the Guard. This act suggested that what the Pretender had in
store for all those who had been at all favourable to the popular
cause of 1789 was not even the coldest sort of pardon, but, to
some extent, punishment. For the only apparent offence of M. de
Poix was that in 1789 he had favoured the union of the three orders
in the Estates-General; and all his subsequent record of devotion
to Louis XVI could, it seemed, avail nothing to save him from the
abrupt disgrace which now fell upon him.[1]

Meantime other members of the Pretender's entourage and
party were allowed without risk of displeasure to go on using the
most frantic language of revenge and repression against all the
men and the measures since the opening of the States-General.
D'Antraigues and Oultremont were proclaiming the need to hang
or shoot the surviving members of the Constituent Assembly,
and all the purchasers of nationalized properties. Comte Ferrand,
destined to be one of the Ministers of the Restoration in 1814, at
this time declared that the counter-revolution must be attended by
forty-four thousand executions—one in every commune. Such

---

[1] See the comments of Mallet du Pan on this unhappy gesture in Michel,
op. cit., tome I, p. 309. The British Government was equally unhappy over
this affair, and Lord Macartney made anxious enquiries about it at Verona.
The Pretender in his reply did his best to explain away the unfortunate implications. 'As to the Prince de Poix', related Macartney, 'he (*the Pretender*) had
so little resentment towards him, he should not be unwilling to employ him
in various situations suitable to his rank; but in a confidential place, as Captain of his Guard, he could not in justice to himself consent to it. He owned
that it would have been more politic to have concealed for a time his intention
of discharging him, but his heart revolted at any kind of duplicity, and he
hoped that the frankness of his conduct in this instance would recommend
him to every honest man, however it might be disapproved by others.' Lord
Macartney added that all others at Verona, to whom he had spoken about
this matter, thought it 'disastrous', and said that the dismissal had been made
'against their opinion' (Macartney to Wickham, 15 October 1795, printed in
Wickham, op. cit., vol. I, pp. 182–3). The circumstances of the subsequent
disgrace of the Maréchal de Castries were to afford further early evidence of
the apparently ungenerous spirit behind the Pretender's professions of mildness. De Castries was actually the Chief Minister in the exiled Government.
His offence was that he protested against the maintenance of a corps of
Guards round the titular Sovereign, on the grounds that 'c'était le faste qui
avait renversé le trône'. This, it seems, was sufficient to bring about his
departure and replacement by the duc de la Vauguyon, at the beginning of
1796 (Daudet, op. cit., tome I, pp. 288–9).

men apparently found special satisfaction in treating to their worst contumely and threats the politicians of the old constitutional royalist parties; these, they urged, were more guilty than the men of the Republic, for they were the original authors of all the misfortunes of the last six years.[1]

It is a relief to discover that other members of the *aristocrate* emigration creditably protested against such views, and declared that counter-revolution on these terms would be worse than the Revolution itself: 'Vaincus, nous ne sommes que malheureux; vainqueurs, nous deviendrons scélérats.' [2] But such protests were nowhere accepted as typifying the outlook of the pure Royalist emigration; and it is easy to appreciate, in particular, the dilemma upon which the survivors of the Feuillant party, and all those landed and propertied elements whom they had once tried to lead, now again felt themselves to be thrown. In 1791-2, the Feuillants had tried, in their terror of the democrats and Republicans, to moderate the course of the Revolution, and to reconcile, under their own leadership, the Royal house, the émigrés, and the Church with the principles of 1789 (suitably diluted). Between Thermidor, year II, and the French elections of year V, such plans were revived, by surviving leaders of the old Feuillant party or by their former disciples inside France. But every effort to promote this policy of 'no enemies to the Right' was fatally embarrassed by the resurgence, in more or less identical shape, of the difficulties which had confronted the 'Triumvirs' and La Fayette in 1791-2. The princes would accept no compromise with the principles of

---

[1] See, for instances of this kind of behaviour, Lefebvre, *Thermidoriens*, p. 137; Daudet, *Emigration*, tome I, p. 285; Thureau-Dangin, op. cit., vol. cit., pp. 50-2. See further the indignant comments of Mallet du Pan, in his letter of 16 July 1795, on the untimely new edition of D'Antraigues' *Observations sur la conduite des puissances coalisées* (Sayous, op. cit., tome II, p. 173). In a much later letter, Mallet was to retail a now famous remark of D'Antraigues, which epitomizes the attitude of that nobleman towards all who had been in any way implicated in the revolutionary movements: 'Montlosier me trouve implacable, il a raison; je serai le Marat de la contre-révolution, je ferai tomber cent mille têtes, et la sienne la première' (Sayous, op. cit., tome II, p. 291). We may also refer here to a letter of Mallet of February 1796 in which he singles out certain of the old *parlementaires* as being among the most ferocious of these émigré extremists, and points to a recent *parlementaire* publication which reserved its most bitter animosity for the *monarchiens*, the *anglomanes*, and the old constitutionalists (Sayous, op. cit., tome II, pp. 211-12).

[2] Cited by Daudet, op. cit., tome I, p. 286.

1789, however much diluted; their émigré supporters would not only not compromise with the Feuillant policy, but insisted on their intention to punish the Feuillants, and all who had shared their errors, with every weapon at their command. It is not surprising that few Frenchmen who had held the opinions of the Feuillants, or anything like them, could ever bring themselves to be reconciled with Louis XVIII on the only terms he would accept for that purpose (unconditional submission). Even those who went this length could never forget that this step availed nothing towards their reconciliation with the D'Antraigues and the Ferrands. As for the far more numerous pro-monarchist moderates who would not pay this price, it is quite comprehensible that they should go on dreading the possible victory of the pure Royalist émigrés almost or quite as much as they dreaded the Jacobins.

The princes and their adherents, moreover, still evidently believed that the restoration of the old order must be pursued by methods which (it should have been obvious) were as unpalatable to the nation as the system itself. 'La contre-révolution absolue et violente', as Mallet du Pan expressed it—that was their intention still. They persisted in cherishing plans to inflict upon their fellow countrymen further foreign invasions and fresh civil wars, as the only practicable means of overthrowing the republican tyranny, and of giving back to France the institutions, which, in their view, the nation was really longing for. In this respect, at least, there was no difference whatever between the Pretender and the most intransigent of his party. The heads of the Princes and their entourages were filled by such projects as the much canvassed plan of an Anglo-Royalist descent on the Western coasts, the efforts of Condé, Précy, and Imbert Colomès to foment new Royalist insurrections in the Franche Comté and at Lyon, and the still more ambitious design to gain over Pichegru and his whole army. For the levying of insurrection inside France, they relied on the secret Agence Royale de Paris, then headed by Le Maître, and soon (February 1796) to fall under the direction of the Abbé Brottier: as also on the similar but separate Southern Agence under Précy.[1] But they hardly hoped to win final success simply through

[1] Cf. Lefebvre, *Thermidoriens*, pp. 138–9. The temper persistently displayed by the most thoroughgoing exponents of the Royalist *manière forte* at this time finds capital illustration in one of the pieces filed among Wickham's

the efforts of French Royalists, even if it became possible to include in the number of these the troops of a Republican commander suborned into the service of the Crown. It was outside of their own nation that they still hoped to find the decisive reinforcements; it was in the military, naval, and above all financial resources of the Coalition, or what remained of it, that they placed their final trust.

For evident reasons, it was on British policy that the Pretender and his adherents chiefly calculated. Austria's attitude towards them and their cause was cold, and in any case it was only British subsidies which kept the Habsburg war machine on a war footing. The active intervention of Russia was a matter on which the imagination of the exiles dwelt fondly; but it was destined to remain, what it had hitherto been, a subject of anticipation.

The attitude of the British Government towards the ideological issues of French politics about this time can be very interestingly illustrated in the correspondence of Wickham. When Lord Grenville first despatched Wickham to Switzerland in the autumn of 1794, to appraise the offers which Théodore de Lameth and other

---

unpublished correspondence (Wickham Papers, Bundle 64, Bayard to Wickham, 29 August 1795). Here, a young agent (Bayard) who served both the Pretender and the British envoy, retails to Wickham the contents of a letter just issued to all the municipal officers of the French area concerned, by a Royalist insurgent commander (Besignan) then raising his standard in the name of Louis XVIII. The insane ineptitude, arrogance and optimism displayed by this champion of the old order in arms are such as to deserve full citation: 'N'allez pas croire, Messieurs, que je vous reconnaisse dans une place légitime, parce que je m'adresse à vous aujourd'hui; ce n'est absolument que pour vous rendre responsables de l'exécution des ordres du Roi, mon Maître, qui est aussi le vôtre.

Ma lettre reçue, vous ne ferez pas faute de publier et afficher dans toute l'étendue de votre commune le manifeste que je joints ici; vous devez être assez las du Règne du crime pour accueillir avec empressement celui de la justice; s'il en était autrement, vous devriez vous attendre à une punition exemplaire; épargnez moi cette douleur, et par votre zèle à remplir les vues de sa majesté, travaillez plutôt à lui gagner les coeurs de tous ses sujets, qu'il mérite a tant de titres.

Inutilement prétendriez-vous cause d'ignorance, je prendrai toutes mes précautions pour que chaque commune reçoive son paquet; mais s'il en était autrement, la chose sera trop publique pour que vous puissiez vous justifier de négligence; le Drapeau blanc flottant de toute part dans vos environs doit être le ralliement général; et on doit bien s'attendre que sa majesté regardera comme ses ennemis ceux qui ne se décideront promptement pour elle...'

old constitutionalists were then making, he gave Wickham elaborate instructions, which included a lengthy definition of the
Government's attitude towards the political issues which continued to divide the French.[1] This shows that, in spite of all the
discomfitures which the Allied cause had suffered after two years,
more or less, of warfare with the Republic, the British Government was still rigidly adverse to treating with the Republic, and,
what is more, was deeply reluctant to tolerate any attempted
settlement of French affairs, other than a settlement on the basis
proposed by the exiled princes.

Lord Grenville began by professing, much in the terms of the
British Declaration at the time of the occupation of Toulon
twelve months before, that:

The King has never desired to interfere for the purpose of giving to
France any particular form of Government, further than became
necessary for his own security and that of the rest of Europe. . . .

The qualification thus introduced is then at once used to rule out
all question of British acceptance of the republican regime in any
form. 'All the Republican parties in France . . . have uniformly
professed' principles which would be fatal 'to all civil society in
Europe' if the government of so powerful a state as France should
become permanently identified with them. Grenville then con-
cludes, naturally enough from these premises, and at first in
rather cautious and general terms, that only 'a legitimate Principle
of Government' in France could offer Europe the necessary
security, and that this principle could only be found in 'the restoration of a monarchy' 'in the person of the undoubted Heir of
that throne' (referring of course, at that date, to the young Louis
XVII).

Lord Grenville then passes on to consider a restoration of the
constitutional monarchy. Regard for the interests of Britain and
the rest of Europe leads him to treat this with undisguised reluctance. He does not go quite the length of saying that Britain would
not tolerate such a solution, but he certainly protests that Britain
could tolerate it only under elaborate conditions. The object of
these conditions is, apparently, to provide securities for the international good behaviour of France; but the conditions themselves
all bear upon domestic issues inside the country.

[1] These instructions are printed in Wickham, op. cit., vol. I, p. 9f.

'The constitution of 1789–90' had contained 'in itself the seeds of its own ruin' and had 'led . . . to all that has since happened'. 'No approbation can therefore ever be expressed from hence of any government founded on that Basis.' But, he continues, this constitution which Britain could not be expected to approve, she might nevertheless contrive to tolerate—always provided that 'a just security could be held out to foreign Nations against . . . attempts to destroy their governments'.

This 'just security' would seemingly be obtained by the fulfilment of the conditions which follow. Grenville's conditions have little to do with the machinery of government in France. They are chiefly concerned to ensure that the restored constitution of 1789–91 should be placed in the hands of its deadly enemies, the exiled princes and their adherents. On these terms, Britain would allow the French to live under it, if they were so unwise as to wish to do so.

Grenville's first condition is that 'the restoration of monarchy' (even in constitutional form) 'if really intended, must necessarily imply the recall of the Princes and the vesting the powers meant to be left to the King in the hands of some person intended to maintain and support them'. A mere proclamation of the young King, under conditions which left the exercise of his authority during his nonage in the hands of any of the prevailing politicians, would be no real change of system at all; there must be an individual Regent, with a mind of his own and able to act independently of any of the recent masters of France. And, continues Lord Grenville, this individual Regent with a mind of his own must not only be able to communicate with the princes, he must be one of them; he must, in fact, be *Monsieur*. 'No personal objection may justly be made to Monsieur, and any other plan is full of insurmountable difficulties.' The British refusal hitherto to grant formal recognition to the claims of *Monsieur* as Regent of France, then, was by no means inconsistent with the warmest inner regard for his pretensions.

Grenville went on to advert to the fears which filled the minds of the constitutional royalists, regarding 'the disposition of the Princes towards systems of revenge and proscription'. Not only, he says, had the British Government always pressed upon the princes the need for 'conciliation and moderation', but the princes, on their side, had 'uniformly given to this Government the most express assurances' of their intentions to that effect. However, he adds, 'sufficient securities might easily be provided'.

The Foreign Secretary passed on to insist upon other 'indispensable' features of 'any plan for the re-establishment of a quiet and well ordered government'. Apart from 'the repeal of all Laws of banishment, Proscription and Confiscation', he emphasizes the need to re-establish the Church and to provide in some way (he does not commit himself to any particular method) for the financial support of its clergy. As for the nationalized properties which had already been sold, he suggests that some kind of compromise would have to be arrived at.

It is only fair to add that Lord Grenville proposed to wish upon the restored princes a very liberal interpretation of their promises of 'moderation' so far as persons were concerned. An amnesty ought to be granted, to cover even those guilty of regicide and massacre, provided that they would now 'render distinguished service' in bringing about the return of the monarchy.

But when we turn to reflect on the general bearings of the text which we have now analysed, we feel that there is little enough of real moderation, or even of common sense, in Lord Grenville's remarks. He begins by claiming that Britain did not wish to interfere in French political affairs, beyond the point dictated by her own vital interests. But this apparently sensible principle is then worked out in such a manner that it ceases to have much relation to reality. Britain must disallow the French liberty to choose, not only a republican form of polity, but even the constitutional monarchy, except with the most restrictive, and indeed contradictory, conditions. Britain will tolerate the re-establishment of the constitution of 1789-91—provided that the French will hand over its supreme executive direction to a prince who openly detests that constitution; provided, again, that they will entrust themselves to his promises of clemency, which even his own most ardent followers refuse to take seriously; provided, again, that they will readmit all the émigrés, reopen the question of the lands, and re-establish the Church.

It is surely not too much to say that all this amounts to something completely chimerical. The interior deeply distrusted the exiled princes, not so much, perhaps, in their character merely as opponents of popular representative institutions, but most certainly because it regarded them as bent on measures of revenge and proscription, and as devoted to features of the old regime which the country detested far more deeply than the mere principle of strong monarchical government. It seems needless to say more.

The greatest objection to Lord Grenville's proposed response to the offers of the constitutional royalists, however, still remains to be noticed. Even if his conditions had been less unpalatable, and indeed impracticable, than they were, their acceptance would have been imperilled by the mere circumstance that they represented an interference by a foreign state, a traditional national enemy, in the most intimate domestic concerns of France, and an interference backed by the implicit sanction that, if the British stipulations were not met, war between Britain and France must continue.

Behind all Lord Grenville's cold and clumsy attempts to toy with the constitutional royalists' offers stands the fact, which this paper of instructions does not discuss but rather assumes, that what the British Government really wished to see in France was a restoration of the monarchy on the basis of pre-Revolutionary conditions. The British Ministers did not, indeed, think it desirable to insist on a restoration of the old order in detail, still less to gratify the craving for vengeance which so many of the pure Royalist émigrés made no effort to conceal. No doubt, too, they would not have thought it a matter for objection if the restored Royal government had conceded, on its own terms, certain constitutional provisions to the nation. But beyond question they desired to see the monarchy restored, in the first instance, on the traditional basis, without obligation to either the principles or the personnel of the first revolutionary constitution. In this solution, and in this alone, did they think to find adequate security against any resumption of the unhappy experiences which the European order had undergone since the French declaration of war on 20 April 1792.

In conformity with this preference, while they had been willing on occasions to collaborate with French opponents of the Republic of very various shades, they had always expressed, in their actions if not in their formal pronouncements, a partiality for the alliance of the pure Royalists; and this partiality is clearly revealed in Lord Grenville's instructions to Wickham, not, as we have seen, in what is actually stated, but in what the terms of the paper tacitly assume.

This was the British attitude when Louis XVIII ascended his paper throne, and in the weeks that followed the British Ministers expressed that attitude perhaps more clearly than ever before, by addressing to his court a representative of high rank[1] and by referring to the Prince who issued the Declaration of Verona, and whom the constitutional royalists of the interior regarded as impossible, as the King of France. In appointing Wickham, moreover, to the interim and finally to the official position of British Minister to the Cantons, Lord Grenville was investing a very special degree of confidence, in all that related to French affairs, in a man who made no secret of his warm sympathy for the pure Royalists, his devotion to the interests of the princes, and his abhorrence and contempt for the principles, if not for the persons, of the constitutionalists.

Thus Britain was apparently committed, if not to 'la contre-révolution absolue' in the full extent of the words, at least to the basic features of that policy. It remains to reflect that Britain was also quite prepared to take part in promoting 'la contre-révolution violente'. The landings at Quiberon were soon to be attempted, while Wickham busied himself to promote a rising in the Franche Comté in collaboration with Condé, and to encourage similar projects in other areas.

We need not dwell, at this stage, on the obvious unwisdom of such a policy on the part of the British Government. It is more to our purpose to point out that, for all the grave and indeed fatal weaknesses which marked it, the policy of England was in certain respects a good deal more conciliatory and indeed more realistic than that of the French princes and their party. Even in the summer of 1795, when British relations with the new Pretender appeared so cordial and when Quiberon was being prepared, certain divergences of approach and method in the conduct of ideological warfare can be perceived to distinguish the British from their pure Royalist allies. These divergences were destined to become wider. British policy towards the French interior, following the line of more realistic appraisal which has just been referred to, finally moved into the great design of a coalition of French opponents of the Republic, working by political rather than by military methods. This design was, of course, in the end a failure. But it had better prospects of success than the

[1] Lord Macartney, famous for his mission to China.

policy of uncompromising pure Royalism and methods of violence which the princes and their adherents cherished; and it was
largely due to British pressure that the Pretender eventually came
into line with it, and lent it a certain minimal support, without
which it could not even have been attempted.

One sign of a difference of attitude between the British and
their pure Royalist allies in the summer of 1795 can be seen in
the matter of the amnesty to be granted by the restored French
monarchy. Grenville's instructions to Wickham illustrate the
anxiety of British Ministers to convince all those in France who
might be concerned, that a liberal amnesty would in fact be
granted. The Foreign Secretary was obviously concerned to make
the most of such professions of clemency as the princes had so far,
though unofficially, held out, and to promise to obtain securities
for the due fulfilment of such an undertaking. He himself, in those
same instructions, sketched the terms of a suitable amnesty in
language rather more generous than Louis XVIII was to use,
when he finally committed himself on this subject in solemn form
in the Declaration of Verona. The princes, on the other hand, down
to the date of the Declaration of Verona, had been more than a
little ambiguous on this topic. Whatever impressions of clement
intentions they had allowed their British allies to collect from
them, they had certainly not been at pains to convince their fellow-
countrymen that they cherished any such intentions. *Monsieur's*
Declaration, as Regent, in January 1793 spoke, as we have seen,
of punishment, not of easy oblivion. The princes had throughout
permitted, and even after the Declaration of Verona they still permitted, any of their supporters who chose to do so, to utter the
most terrifying threats of proscription. The conduct of the Pretender, in the affair of M. de Poix, suggested to an incredulous
world—wrongly, no doubt, but still naturally—that the very man
in whose name the Declaration of Verona ran cared little for the
professions of clemency and moderation, to which that document
had, so far as its words went, committed him.

The British attitude in this matter was dictated not by any sympathy for the constitutional royalists, still less for partisans of the
Republic, but by simple business-like expediency in the interests of
the pure Royalist cause itself. The British authorities were anxious
to promote the recruitment of new supporters for the pure
Royalist party. They thought the times propitious; they thought

that many people in France, disillusioned with the Revolution in all its aspects and phases, would be willing to accept, even to assist, the return of the princes on their own terms. In taking this view, the British Ministers were certainly taking a dangerously oversimplified view of the problem. It may have been the case, as Mallet du Pan also believed, that even the former champions of the constitution of 1789–91 had little interest left in such matters as representative government and would accept, in principle, a substantial reconstitution of Royal authority. It was, however, quite another thing to suppose that France in general was tired of the whole Revolutionary experience in such a sense that she would accept back all the paraphernalia of the old order, as the Pretender promised from Verona; and it was a wilder thing still to believe that France would suffer, or even make common cause with, renewed civil war and fresh Allied invasions, in order to reach this desirable goal. Yet British policy displayed at least this mark of common sense: its authors realized plainly enough that, if Frenchmen who had taken any part whatever in Revolutionary politics were to return to the fold of true political orthodoxy, it was absolutely essential to convince them that generous terms of oblivion were held out, and what was more were sincerely and seriously held out.

This was sufficient, in itself, to create a difference, and some degree of tension, between the British authorities and the pure Royalists in the summer of 1795. Wickham's correspondence shows the growing misgivings which forced themselves upon the mind, both of Wickham himself and of other British representatives, in this regard. It shows how they came to feel that the pure Royalists were continually damaging their own and Allied interests, by their failure to offer to former adherents of the Revolution, even though they were now prepared sincerely and completely to repent, any *convincing* prospect of pardon and of consideration for their self-respect.

On 25 May 1795, Wickham addressed a report[1] to the Foreign Secretary which offers a useful illustration of the manner in which he was then working to procure the conversion to the princely cause of important former supporters of the Revolution, and of the difficulties which he discovered. The despatch describes an interview which Wickham has recently had with a person who

1 Wickham Papers, Wickham to Grenville, draft despatch, no. 37 of 1795.

could claim some standing in the Franche Comté. This was the former Feuillant minister, Terrier de Monciel. It appears that Monciel was one of those who were prepared, despite all the obvious embarrassments of such a course, to purchase escape from the republican regime by accepting the claims of the princes, and by working to induce others to do the same. He was ready to help in bringing about an object very dear to the British envoy, 'an union between the leading proprietors and persons of respectability of every description' in the Franche Comté, with the particular purpose of raising an insurrection in support of the thrust into the province which was planned by Condé.[1] Monciel had already committed himself to this effect in his confidential understanding with another Comtois gentleman, a man of good pure Royalist character, M. de Champagne. It seems that Champagne was intelligent and humane enough to be willing to welcome such recruits as Monciel, without spoiling the game with hints of a threatening or scornful nature. Monciel, however, for all his readiness to work for the pure Royalist cause and for all his confidence in Champagne, was gravely concerned lest his repentance should be in vain after all; he had a very strong impression that however reasonable Champagne might be, Condé and his entourage regarded ex-constitutionalists like himself as utterly beyond the pale. Champagne believed that Condé ought to give assurances of a serious and convincing kind to Monciel and all those in a similar position, that the princes would accept their services in good faith and with a good grace; and with the object of gaining such assurances, he took Monciel to see Wickham, on whose good sense and influence with the Prince he was prepared to rely.

Wickham explains in the despatch how he received the minister of 1792. He retailed to Monciel the dishonest conduct (as Wickham regarded it) of Monciel's old allies, Théodore de Lameth and others, at the time of the abortive discussions arranged by Mallet du Pan in the previous autumn; and having thus done his best to face Monciel with the fact that constitutional royalism was a bad business, he bluntly asked the ex-Feuillant:

if he himself and the other leading members of the party with which he had acted were disposed to make their submission in due form to

---

[1] Cf. Wickham, op. cit., vol. I, p. 136 (Wickham to Sir Morton Eden, 6 August 1795).

their own Princes?—in using the word *submission* I told him I meant to use it in its true sense and in the full extent of the term.

Wickham added:

There must be no idea of treating upon an equality, but a fair acknowledgement of their wrongs, made with all the expressions of Decency and Respect that would have become them at other times.

Monciel replied that his fear was, that any formal submission offered by such men as himself 'would be rejected with contempt'. The envoy retorted, in all apparent seriousness, that the French princes had already given

assurances of a disposition on their part to act in every case that regarded their unhappy country with all that temper and moderation which the circumstances of the moment seem particularly to require.

He readily undertook to sound the princely reaction to the particular case of Monciel, however; and he took the opportunity to urge upon Monciel that the 'Clemency and Moderation' of the princes was such, that the former Feuillants would find it also their best resource for the solution of a rather different problem, about which Monciel seemed to be deeply concerned, namely the liberation of La Fayette and his fellow prisoners from Allied captivity.

In all this, Wickham shows no signs whatever that he as yet realized any of these all-important facts: that few Frenchmen who had ever shared, in any degree at all, in the hopes and efforts of the Revolution, would be willing simply and unconditionally to submit to princes who had plainly identified themselves with all the most characteristic features of the old regime; that such men had fair reasons for doubting whether submission would avail to save them, after the throne was restored, from punishment for their former offences, or, at best, would avail to save them from contempt, suspicion, and surveillance for the rest of their lives; and finally, that their pride, self-respect, even vanity, would hold them back from such a course even if conviction, or fear of subsequent proscription, did not.

But it is only proper to add that Wickham's political education was to make rapid progress from this point. The very day after drawing up the despatch quoted above, the envoy reported to Lord Grenville a conversation which he had had with Condé on these subjects.[1] This conversation perhaps sowed in Wickham's, mind serious doubts about the political sanity of the French princes. To us, certainly, the language held by Condé on this occasion is significant of the complete lack of all real generosity, even of responsibility, which lay behind such promises as the princes were prepared to make. Condé assured Wickham of his 'most ready' agreement to a 'general Amnesty, with the sole exception of Regicides and Assassins', and added that 'himself and the other Princes had always holden the same language'. Apparently the Prince did not comment on the very different language which was tolerated from numerous adherents of the princely party, including many of his own officers. Nor did he say anything to relieve the widespread fear, that even though an amnesty of wide scope were in fact granted, it might be a protection against the rope, but still no protection against scorn and insult, isolation and suspicion. Indeed, Condé added some words on the subject of La Fayette, which showed how very superficial—even when the temptations of real power were still far away—were the professions of welcome to the erring sheep made by at least one member of the Royal family:

Upon the subject of La Fayette, as was indeed most natural, he seemed deeply affected. He admitted that it would not be possible to make an exception for him out of the . . . amnesty, but added that he must never set his foot in France, as it was certain he never could keep the first Promise alone.

On 16 June 1795, Wickham drafted a report to London[2] which shows that the envoy had now learned at least this much about the subject, that the British Government's belief in the clemency and moderation of the princes was shared by hardly anyone besides. The report also makes it clear that Wickham was seriously alarmed about the possible consequences. Wickham urges upon Lord Grenville that he feels the need of 'an actual Assurance' by the new Pretender, that he would in fact grant an amnesty of the wide scope envisaged by Grenville in his instructions to Wickham during the previous autumn. 'I have been told repeatedly',

[1] Wickham Papers, Wickham to Grenville, draft despatch, no. 39 of 1795, Mulheim, 26 May.
[2] Wickham Papers, Wickham to Grenville, draft despatch, no. 51 of 1795, Bern, 16 June.

explains the envoy, 'that no one would believe such a thing possible, unless they were to see it under his own handwriting.'

Only a few days after Wickham wrote this, Louis XVIII published from Verona his determination to grant an amnesty on terms which were fairly liberal, so far as the words of the offer went. Wickham did not doubt the sincerity of the Pretender's word; but Lord Grenville, who shared his anxiety over the implications of all this, seems to have felt that the offer ought to be made with greater emphasis, and ought to be rested explicitly on 'a desire to unite all Parties'.[1] Wickham certainly had no occasion to lull himself into a belief that the mere utterance of the oracle from Verona would convince the erring nation that the road to unconditional submission was now safe and easy. Facts soon forced themselves upon his notice which convinced him that the words of Verona, even liberally interpreted, would carry no weight at all unless the words of other Royalist spokesmen, and the conduct of the Princes themselves, were brought into closer alignment with the ostensible meaning of the offer of amnesty. In writing to Lord Macartney, the recently appointed British agent at the court of the Pretender, on 4 October 1795, Wickham adverted to the small effect as yet produced on the interior by the Verona Declaration, and pointed out that the notorious disgrace of the Prince de Poix, still unreversed, was alone more than sufficient to counterbalance the paper clemency of the Pretender:

The conduct of the King in taking away the appointment of the Prince de Poix has made a deep impression, not only on this side of the country but more particularly at Paris, where I know it is made use of with the greatest effect, not only by the Republicans but by the ill disposed leaders of the Constitutional Party such as Montesquieu (*sic*): and even in this country, if ever I venture to say, what no one will believe, that the conduct of the Emigrants and particularly that of the

---

[1] Grenville to Wickham, no. 19 of 1795, 6 July; printed in Wickham, op. cit., vol. I, pp. 113–15. In this despatch, the Foreign Secretary replies to Wickham's despatch no. 51 of 16 June. He announces to Wickham the forthcoming establishment of a British Mission to the Court of the new 'King of France' (the Mission which was to be headed by Macartney) and adds: 'One of the objects of this Mission will be to recommend, in the strongest manner, some public Declaration of Forgiveness, and a desire to unite all Parties; and I will instruct the Person who will be sent, to request that some Means may be found for enabling you to hold the same Language, as coming directly from the King.'

Royal family will be very different from what the imprudence of their language seems to threaten, I am constantly answered by that fact, to which it is impossible to make any reply.[1]

And even supposing it could be clearly established that men who had adhered to the earlier phases of the revolutionary movement had, in fact, nothing to fear from the King's return so far as concerned their lives and property, such men might be brought practically no nearer to making immediate submission, or to collaborating actively in the cause, unless they could also be persuaded that submission would be not only, in that sense, safe, but also easy. At the time of the Declaration, and for far too long afterwards, this point was covered in an obscurity quite as deep as the other. By January 1796, Wickham had discovered that the obscurity concealed nothing very reassuring:

Your Lordship will perceive, by a letter from His Serene Highness (the Prince de Condé) enclosed in my No. — that I cannot persuade that Prince to answer a very decent letter written to him by M. de Moncil (sic) . . . because it does not contain an explicit avowal of his former wrongs. I fear, indeed, that there still exists in the minds of all the French Princes an invincible repugnance to treating with any of that party on any other terms than such as would be too humiliating for any person to submit to, who had the least sense of Honour or of decent pride remaining.[2]

This paragraph is of interest as evidence of the movement of Wickham's own ideas, as well as because it reveals something about the state of mind of the French princes. We remember that in May 1795, Wickham had himself urged the same Monciel to make 'a fair acknowledgement of his wrongs'; now the envoy regards it as highly unreasonable of Condé to refuse a kind response to Monciel on the very grounds that he had not made this 'explicit avowal'. He now protests against such rigour in the name of a decent generosity of attitude. Perhaps a growing impression that this rigour was politically harmful had even more to do with the change in the envoy's attitude than his reflection that it was inhumane.

It was not only in these respects that the British Government

[1] Printed in Wickham, op. cit., vol. I, pp. 177–8.
[2] Wickham Papers, Wickham to Grenville, draft despatch, no. 4 of 1796, 5 January.

and its agents displayed a difference with their princely protégés. Though the British entertained a strong preference for the pure Royalists, and though their first hope, with respect to the former constitutional royalists, was to recruit these men to the banners of the princes, the fact remains that British policy was not confined to first preferences exclusively. If any promising body of French-men were prepared to throw effective weight into the scales against the rulers of the Republic, the British were quite prepared, in principle, to encourage and support this, even though it were not done in the interests of pure Royalism; and they would not scruple to urge the pure Royalists to collaborate with such move-ments without raising awkward stipulations in advance as to the form of polity to be set up in France if such a heterogeneous coali-tion contrived to bring the Republic down. This further and larger manifestation of British opportunism was bitterly condemned in the pure Royalist camp. Wickham's correspondence in summer 1795 includes interesting illustrations of this difference also. On 26 June 1795,[1] Colonel Crauford retailed to Wickham the latest projects of Condé for an armed irruption into the Jura, and thence onward to Lyon. Crauford explained that the only support in the interior, to which Condé proposed to offer any welcome, would be that of persons prepared to show 'unequivocal support of the Royal cause in what he calls its ancient purity—that is, without modification'. The Colonel then continued:

You see, my dear Sir, how difficult it is to make use of these arch-Royalists in the manner we could wish. They are always suspicious that we incline to retrench their Prerogative. The Prince evidently suspects Lyons of an inclination towards the constitution of 1791 and He is very much afraid of taking any step that may appear to commit him as an indirect supporter of any principles excepting those of pure Royalism. It is impossible almost to make them understand that their great object should be to get a firm footing upon any terms, and that they will have an opportunity of arranging things according to cir-cumstances. In short, you know all this history better than I can explain it.

Crauford's letter reflects not only the soreness of pure Royalist leaders towards what they regarded as British opportunism, but also the irritation of a British agent over what to him appeared the impracticability of the pure Royalist attitude. Wickham himself

[1] Crauford to Wickham, in Wickham, op. cit., vol. I, pp. 103–7.

echoed and even underlined the reaction of Crauford in this conjuncture in a despatch home dated 10 July:

I can readily understand the Prince's feelings, and I by no means take
upon myself to blame his Conduct on this occasion, but it is *unfortunate*
that His Serene Highness could not have been persuaded to have acted
otherwise. Much useful time will be lost, the enemy in the meantime
will adopt *in principle* the measure that I would have recommended to
the Prince, and Your Lordship will observe from Doulcet's Report that
the Convention, sensible of its own danger, is now determined to
accept the services of every party, the pure Royalists only excepted.[1]

Yet another subject of tension between the Anglo-Royalist
allies at the same time concerned the conduct to be adopted by
the Royalist troops, of Condé in particular, whenever they
achieved the much canvassed offensive deep into French territory.
The head of the Royal house of course professed on paper only
the most mild and conciliatory intentions towards all his erring
subjects. Condé himself, in conversation with Crauford, declared
that the conduct of his army on entering France should be as innocent of punitive measures against the lately rebellious populations
on the spot, as the restored Royal government was to be throughout the country:

the most conciliating clemency shall mark his progress . . . he has not
the most distant idea of vengeance, nor will he permit any person under
him to discover, in word or deed, such a Sentiment.[2]

But, despite these august disclaimers, the British agents could not
but recur to the notorious fact that the personnel of Condé's
army were, at this very moment, still promising the interior
nothing better than the rope and the sword, and could not fail to
appreciate how damaging it was for the whole prospects of civil
war against the Republic, that the interior accepted only too
readily, as true predictions of what would happen on the morrow

[1] Printed (from Wickham's draft) in Wickham, op. cit., vol. I, pp. 115–16.
In the passage quoted, Wickham refers to the well known appeal, made in a
speech to the Convention by Doulcet de Pontécoulant on 1 July (four days
after the Anglo-Royalist landing at Quiberon). The appeal was directed to *all*
Frenchmen who had in any sense supported the Revolution ('Républicains,
Anglomanes de 89, Constitutionnels de 91'), and urged them to unite now,
behind the Convention and under the *tricolore* against émigrés at war on French
soil to restore the old regime.
[2] Crauford to Wickham, 26 June 1795; Wickham, op. cit., vol. I, p. 104.

of important Royalist successes, the threats of the Royalist officers. The British officials deeply regretted these deplorable indiscretions and tried, more or less vainly, to have them both silenced and discountenanced; but the main result of their efforts was that the adepts of intransigent pure Royalism turned away from Wickham and his colleagues as being little better than traitors to the cause.

The tone and manner of the Prince's army, wrote Wickham to Lord Grenville on 15 June, 1795, is (sic) . . . very different from what it ought to be at this moment. It is difficult to conceive the style of their conversation without having heard it. It must however be entirely changed before they enter into France, or it will produce the most serious mischief. The Prince is well aware of this but has not the courage to attempt to check it.[1]

On 10 July, Wickham reverted to this subject in the course of a rather despondent report home about his efforts to win over influential waverers to the Royal cause. He explained that such waverers were themselves dismayed by the prospect of an émigré invasion under these auspices; and that the hot heads of Condé's entourage, so far from seeing the folly of their own conduct, were actually doing all they could to blacken in Condé's opinion the waverers whom Wickham was trying to convert, and even trying to set the Prince against the British envoy also:

. . . in general all persons of any Influence, who have remained in this part of France, dread the return of the Emigrants almost as much as the revival of the power of the Jacobins, and I am very sorry to say that the conduct of many of those whom I have seen does but too well justify these apprehensions.

The Prince cannot be persuaded of the truth of this fact, and it is very much to be lamented that His Serene Highness should suffer himself to be deceived by the misrepresentations of those persons to whom he ought not to listen for a moment. . . . It is impossible for me to see any person whose principles have not always been those of pure Royalism, without his being immediately denounced to the Prince of Condé as a dangerous Man capable of giving me very bad advice and misleading me; and I am represented as entering into all his views.[2]

---

[1] Wickham to Grenville, draft of this date, Wickham, op. cit., vol. I, pp. 99-100.

[2] Wickham to Grenville, draft of this date, Wickham, op. cit., vol. I, pp. 115-16.

We have illustrated, at some length, the various respects in which British policy towards the problems of France thus already displayed a greater measure of liberality, and indeed of realism, than was to be found in the attitude of their pure Royalist allies. But let us not exaggerate these differences. If the British attitude was more realistic and more generous it was still by no means realistic and generous enough. The British were placing, though not their sole reliance, yet their chief reliance, on efforts to restore the exiled princes upon their own conditions. The British sought to realize this policy by methods which differed in no way from those favoured at Verona. Like the leaders of the Royalist cause, they thought in terms of inflicting upon the distressed fatherland of Louis XVIII further experiences of foreign invasion, internal insurrection, and treason within the French Army.[1]

It has to be said, therefore, that the *substance* of British policy on this great issue was, as yet, as hopelessly unsound as the policy of the Pretender and his adherents.

Suitable support for this emphasis can readily be found in the correspondence of Mallet du Pan about the time of the Pretender's nominal accession. Here the great publicist denounces, with unforgettable vigour and earnestness, the ineptitude of both the Princes and the Allies in their treatment of the interior.

A first instance may be taken from his reply to the question asked by the court of Verona, what effect the change of titular

---

[1] It is only fair to say that Wickham early became aware of the difficulties involved in promoting the cause of the monarchy by the invasion of *foreign* troops: 'Foreigners of every description, particularly the Austrians in Alsace and the English in Provence, are universally feared and detested' (Wickham to Sir Morton Eden, 6 August 1795, printed in Wickham, op. cit., vol. I, p. 135f.; the quoted words appear on p. 137). Hence Wickham's great efforts to secure a footing on French soil for Condé's Army, which had at least the advantage of being French.

It is also only fair to remark that the British authorities were not absolutely blind to the possibilities of different methods of action on the problems of France. Grenville and Wickham were considering in May 1795, the prospects which might be opened if the primary assemblies of France, whose convocation in the near future was to be expected, in connection with the establishment of the new constitution, could be induced to record a want of confidence in the republican regime and raise, in a free and peaceful way, the issue of a return to the monarchy (Grenville to Wickham, 5 May 1795, Wickham, op. cit., vol. I, p. 38). But such ideas formed as yet only a minor element in the make-up of British policy towards the French interior.

sovereigns might have upon the fortunes of the Royalist cause. Mallet's unflinching rejoinder was:

cette perte (*de Louis XVII*) est une calamité; elle a fait ajourner la monarchie, et sert de base à la coalition à laquelle on travaille entre les républicains et les constitutionnels. S.M. ne comptait pas comme régent; on la redoute comme roi.[1]

In writing to the court of Vienna, Mallet had already explained more fully his views on this issue. The most common inclination, he said, among the French people was towards a limited monarchy; but for the young King's death, this principle would have continued to gain ground, and certain members of the Convention would have favoured its progress. But none of the many moderate pro-Royalists of the interior could now be expected to make any efforts for a King who had publicly identified himself with the pure Royalism of the emigration.[2]

A note to Louis XVIII himself expounded the basic difficulty in the plainest possible terms:

La grande pluralité des Français ne veut pas l'ancien régime... La grande pluralité des Français ne se rendra jamais à discretion à l'ancienne autorité et à ses dépositaires.[3]

Elsewhere, Mallet dwelt on the attitude of the peasants. The abolition of tithe, and their liberation from the manorial regime: these were 'deux avantages positifs que leur a procurés la révolution'. They could never, he thought, be brought to accept the re-establishment of tithe; and to induce them to resume the redemption of manorial incidents was nearly as far from possibility.[4]

The methods adopted by both the Pretender and the Allies were as inapposite, Mallet argued, as the Pretender's professed objectives. No *spontaneous* insurrection in France, in the interest of

---

[1] A. Sayous, op. cit., tome II, p. 166. Cf. the opinion expressed by Wickham on the same point and almost at the same moment: 'More I see and hear of the public opinion in this country, more I am satisfied that the death of the young King will prove a fortunate circumstance for the cause of Royalty' (Wickham, op. cit., vol. I, p. 102). Wickham, at this stage, had still a great deal to learn, and to unlearn, about French affairs.

[2] Mallet to the Court of Vienna, 27 June 1795; Michel, op. cit., tome I, pp. 239-40.

[3] Mallet to the exiled French Court, 3 July 1795; Sayous, op. cit., tome II, pp. 157, 150.

[4] Ibid., p. 164.

pure Royalism, need be expected. Insurrections of a local character could certainly be *fomented*, but would never justify themselves
by results, if only because everyone in France, outside of the
common people, feared new disturbances above everything else.
The Vendée, Mallet predicted, would provide no real exception,
for it was so much identified with the cause of the old regime; and,
he declared,

tant que la Vendée se présentera en armes pour reconquérir l'ancien
régime, l'universalité de la France la combattra de gré ou de force, et
finira par l'étouffer.[1]

Mallet proceeded to argue that any hopes which might be
built upon the policy, and the military undertakings, of the Allies
would be equally vain, unless indeed the Allies began to fight the
Republic in a manner very different from their efforts hitherto.

Rien n'égale le mépris qu'on porte en France aux armes et à la politique
des alliés, si ce n'est la haine non moins générale qu'ils ont inspirées.
Ces sentiments sont aussi prononcés chez les monarchistes que chez les
républicains.[2]

The Allies were despised, because hitherto they had fought without evidence of serious determination, and also, very obviously,
without success. They were hated in addition, because they not
merely levied war against France, but aspired to filch French ter-
ritories and to interfere in French domestic concerns. If the Allies
seriously wished to advance the cause of Royalty in France, their
conduct must undergo a drastic change; they must prosecute the
war with far greater vigour, but on the other hand they must convince the French that their ulterior purposes were both honourable and reasonable:

qu'elles ne prétendent attaquer ni à l'intégralité, ni à l'indépendance
législative de la France, mais qu'elles sont prêtes à donner la paix et à
rouvrir les portes du commerce et de l'échange, au moment où l'on
sera revenu à la monarchie quelconque.[3]

Mallet urged the Pretender to recognize, and to set himself
seriously to break down, the enormous mass of hostility which
existed in France against him and against his present adherents.
To state this more positively, Louis must bring about 'the moral

[1] Ibid., pp. 150, 155, 157.
[2] Mallet to the exiled French Court, 3 July 1795; Ibid., p. 151.
[3] Ibid., pp. 151–2.

resurrection of the King'.[1] This would involve his making a new, and this time a more reasonable, public appeal to the nation; it would also involve his publicly repudiating 'tous ces brochuriers incendiaires, tous ces frénétiques massacrants qui parlent comme Gengis-Khan ne parlait pas à la tête de deux cent mille Tartares'.[2] Moreover, Mallet contended, the King ought to appoint representatives who might seriously attempt the opening of negotiations with the moderate monarchists of the interior.[3] These moderates, he insisted, were still hoping and working for the return to the monarchy in the only sense that was possible. Their great object, in the summer of 1795, was to induce the electors, at the early expected summoning of the primary assemblies, to record a vote in favour of the *chef légitime de la nation*.[4] The outcome of that vote would not be unconditional surrender to the pure Royalist emigration, but a public recognition of the King's right, *in principle*, to reign over France; the terms and circumstances of the restoration would have to be settled in subsequent discussions.[5]

It hardly needs to be said that all this advice was, at the time when it was given, quite wasted. Neither the exiled Court, nor the British Government, displayed any substantial evidence of a change of mind. In the latter half of 1795, the policy of the Royalists and the British, assisted at least in name by the Austrians, moved through the dismal phases of Quiberon, the abortive project of Artois's descent upon Saint-Malo, the revival of the guerilla war in the West, the long-winded and futile intrigue between Pichegru and Condé, and the equally futile plan for the betrayal of Besançon to Condé. But in the meantime, the French nation was passing through the exciting political experiences which culminated in Vendémiaire.

---

[1] Ibid., pp. 164, 158.   [2] Ibid., pp. 159, 164.
[3] Ibid., pp. 152, 154-5, 160.   [4] Ibid., p. 158.
[5] On this last point, see a letter of Mallet du Pan of 10 January 1796 (ibid., p. 204) in which he urges that it is hopeless to expect that the 'foule de gens revenus à la monarchie' will ever unconditionally invite the King to return; 'tout ce qu'on peut espérer, c'est qu'ils adressent au roi leur capitulation, et traitent avec lui, en le reconnaissant comme héritier légitime de la couronne',

II

Vendémiaire and the elections of year IV

THE advent of Louis-Stanislas-Xavier to the headship of the
Royal cause not only discouraged the numerous moderate
pro-Royalists of the interior, it also deprived them of any early
possibility of help from the pro-monarchist deputies in the Convention. Those deputies now joined their Republican colleagues
to enact the constitution of the year III (23 June—22 August
1795). The new constitution of course reconsecrated the Republic, though it did so with an unmistakeable inclination in favour
of the propertied classes and the interests of the central government. It may be the case that some of the deputies whose personal
sympathies were for monarchy still cherished the hope that at a
later stage the executive power, now entrusted to a Directory of
five, might be transferred to a constitutional king. But such a
prospect offered no present satisfaction to the moderate Royalists;
and in the meantime, the Anglo-Royalist incursion at Quiberon
fell as a fresh blow upon them.[1]

A majority of the Convention went on to take the fateful
decision to prolong the monopoly of power in the hands of men
who belonged to their own number. It was declared that two-
thirds of the membership of the new legislative Councils must be
chosen from among the sitting members of the Convention. Not
surprisingly, the immediate effect of this 'law of the two thirds'
was to give new strength to the movement favouring a moderate
monarchical settlement. It gave to that movement both fresh incentives, and the prospect of fresh supporters. It did not, of
course, in any degree tend to rescue the moderate Royalist cause
from the embarrassment in which the attitude of Louis XVIII
placed it. But it greatly strengthened the already intense dislike
which was so widely felt for the old governing personnel; and
thereby it encouraged all those who shared this dislike to look
for an alternative political direction, and to feel that if only the

---

[1] The landings at Quiberon were effected on 27 June; the Republicans
drove the émigrés from their bridgehead on 20–21 July. 'Qui que ce soit',
wrote Mallet du Pan on 16 August, 'ne pouvait ni n'osait parler de royauté
lorsque les émigrés coalisés avec les Anglais en parlaient en Bretagne les
armes à la main' (Sayous, op, cit., tome II, p. 178).

public disapprobation of the Convention could be effectively organized and expressed, somehow or other a workable alternative system would be brought into being by the very pressure of the demand for it. Such a situation played directly into the hands of moderate Royalists. They had an alternative system already to hand, and theoretically at least it was workable and reassuring. If opinion in the country could now be rallied to their theoretically acceptable solution, surely it would impose itself upon events and acquire the one virtue which as yet it lacked—practicability; the legitimist claimant would be brought, by irresistible incentives, to see reason, or another constitutional king would somehow be discovered. At all events, there was nothing to prevent them from leading a very practical movement of protest against the immediate menace—the prospective prolongation of Conventional rule—while uniting with this the suggestion that, if the present incubus could only be removed, the ideal of a kingship limited by law might then somehow be reduced to practice.

The new phase of opposition began before the law reached the statute book. The law was ill regarded by certain members of the Convention itself: fifty or sixty reputed monarchists, joined by such important figures as Boissy d'Anglas, Thibaudeau, Pelet, and Rabaut, who were themselves suspected by Mallet du Pan of casting their eyes, especially since the Declaration of Verona, towards the Duc d'Orléans.[1] Whatever the truth about this, it is certain that, once the need for 'union' behind the Convention had been removed by the failure of Quiberon, signs of the general public detestation of the Convention began to reappear in abundance, and the Law of the Two Thirds inevitably gave it a great new impetus. A vociferous opposition to the law, and a rather vaguer expression of dislike for the Republic, soon became the dominant notes, both in the Paris sections and in the metropolitan press. The sentiments which were expressed were described by Mallet du Pan as Royalist in an '89'-ish sense.[2] Those

---

[1] Mallet to the Court of Vienna, 13 September and 4 October: Michel, op. cit., tome I, pp. 305, 306, 327. It is well known that several members of the Convention were subsequently accused of complicity with the Parisian insurrection of Vendémiaire, particularly Boissy d'Anglas, Henry-Larivière, Lanjuinais, Lesage, Rovère, Saladin and d'Aubry. See Meynier, op. cit., p. 5.

[2] On 16 August Mallet reported that 'Cet incident terminé (*i.e. Quiberon*)... les esprits ont repris leur essor,... les sections leur résistance, la presse sa liberté, les honnêtes gens courage... Dans les sections... les quatre-vingt

who expressed these sentiments were outspokenly bitter against
the new legitimate claimant and the militant émigrés. Some of the
89-ists canvassed for an Orleanist solution,[1] others regarded the
identity of the monarch as an open question, to be settled by
deliberation in the future. Mallet du Pan believed that the Pretender should make haste to announce his willingness to accept
the Crown on such a basis as this party was likely to think acceptable, and that it was only in the context of such an announcement
that the movement would display any interest in the claims of the
legitimate ruler. Failing any such gesture of compromise on his
part, the 'patriotes de 1789' would turn their attention to the
collaterals, or to a new monarchy.[2]

Not the least impressive feature of these developments was the
fact that some known partisans of pure Royalism made common
cause with the movement. This was, perhaps, partly because, like
so many of their contemporaries, they wished to avert the prolongation of Conventional rule, but disliked, as strongly as the
'patriotes de 1789', the idea of falling under the rod of the
militant pure Royalists of the emigration.[3] By supporting this

neuvistes... dominent de plus en plus, et ont à eux les trois quarts des feuilles
publiques. La haine pour les horreurs de la révolution se prononce chaque
jour davantage, et l'on comprend ouvertement le 10 août 1792 et le 21 janvier
1793' (Sayous, op. cit., tome II, p. 178-9). In his Note to Vienna, 13 September,
Mallet speaks of the Parisian movement against the Convention as being led
by 'anciens constitutionnels, patriotes de 1789...' (Michel, op. cit., tome I,
p. 305).

[1] On 16 September, Mallet du Pan observed that 'Les monarchistes se
défendent en ce moment contre la Convention pour échapper à la tyrannie,
beaucoup plus que pour refaire la royauté. On la désire sans dévouement,
et l'on a fait au dehors tout ce qui était nécessaire pour en éteindre les
semences. Le duc d'Orléans, son jeune frère, gagnent des partisans; mais le
roi perd chaque jour des siens' (Sayous, op. cit., tome II, p. 182). For the
question of contemporary interest in an Orleanist solution to the problem of
the regime see pp. 65-8 below.

[2] Mallet to the Court of Vienna, 20 September, Michel, op. cit., tome I,
p. 316; Mallet to Ste Aldegonde, 23 September, Sayous, op. cit., tome II,
pp. 183-4; Mallet to the Court of Vienna, 4 October, Michel, op. cit., tome
I, p. 326. Cf. also a passage in Michel, I, p. 308.

[3] In his note to the Court of Vienna, 13 September, Mallet associates with
his remarks about the 'patriotes de 1789' the further denomination 'tous les
royalistes qui n'ajoutent foi à une contre-révolution par les armes' (Michel,
op. cit., tome I, p. 305). In his Note of 20 September, he speaks of 'tout le
monde, même les royalistes par naissance' as 'craignant les émigrés et ne
voulant absolument de leur influence' (Michel, op. cit., tome I, p. 316).

movement, they perhaps hoped to bring pressure on their king, to abandon, not indeed his principles, but his reliance on the militant émigrés. All of them, it may be, felt that in so far as the movement tended towards the destruction of the Republic—by methods which did not involve invasion and insurrections—it must deserve pure Royalist support; there was nothing to prevent any pure Royalist from hoping that, when the Republic was finally overthrown, it would be his own party, and not the 'patriotes de 1789,' who would then seize control and determine the character of the Restoration.[1]

It is a point of some interest, that this spontaneous coalition between Royalists in rather different senses of the term constituted already a partial and tentative execution of the tactic of a 'union of Parties', so much favoured by the British authorities. Here was precisely what the British Government never tired of prescribing: an immediate alliance against the Republic, without need for too much anxiety, at this stage, over what was to be erected in its place. As such, the Parisian sectional movement of Vendémiaire was to be a curtain-raiser for the more elaborate design of 1796–7.[2]

By the time the primary assemblies met, moreover, this coalition of enemies of the Republic had received further development. The clergy widely threw its influence in favour of the new opposition.

The opposition which was thus forming against the Convention had, on the other hand, important weaknesses. Except to some extent, at Paris, it had no organization;[3] it was an army, or rather a mob, of individuals, united in a common negative aim indeed, but wanting not only in agreement upon ulterior objectives, but also in leadership and in party machinery.

For all this, it achieved formidable successes at the primary assemblies of Paris and the surrounding departments. The Paris sections were practically unanimous in their repudiation of the Law of the Two Thirds. A majority of the primary assemblies in nine adjoining departments took the same line.[4] The Parisians

[1] Cf. the remarks of Mallet du Pan on the attitude of the Parisian pure Royalists in Michel, op. cit., tome I, pp. 308, 318–19.

[2] Ibid., p. 319.   [3] Cf. Lefebvre, *Thermidoriens*, pp. 181–2.

[4] Lefebvre, op. cit., pp. 184–5, gives a general summary of the voting in different parts of the country, and points out that nineteen departments, in all, rejected the Law. See the comments of Mallet on the voting in Sayous, op. cit., tome II, p. 184, and in Michel, op. cit., tome I, pp. 312–14.

returned, as electors responsible for the subsequent choice of the metropolitan deputies to the new legislature, a body of men whose sympathies obviously lay in the direction of constitutional monarchy: Lacretelle, Peuchet, who had succeeded Mallet du Pan as editor of the *Mercure*, General Mathieu-Dumas, Quatremère de Quincy, and many others whose temper was reflected in their past activities as members of the right wing of the old Legislative Assembly, or of the earlier Commune of Paris.[1]

The correspondence of Mallet du Pan at this stage reflects the hopes then cherished by the Parisian leaders, that the country as a whole would record a similarly decisive verdict against the Law of the Two Thirds, and that it would also accept the Parisian proposal to adopt arrangements whereby the newly appointed electors would be empowered to choose not simply one third, but the whole, of the new legislature.[2] In fact, the Parisian leaders lacked the time, the means, and even the patience to exploit these or any similar possibilities. The Convention was soon in a position to publish a very lame, but still a sufficient, affirmative result on the referendum about the Law of the Two Thirds; and this led directly to an open quarrel between the Convention and the Parisian opposition about the authenticity of the verdict. The Convention took precautionary measures in case the sections resorted to force, and these in fact precipitated the insurrection of Vendémiaire, which, by its failure, settled decisively for the immediate future all the issues affecting the government of France.[3] 'Nous voila retombés dans un abîme sans fond,' wrote Mallet du Pan. 'Mon découragement est au comble.'[4]

Mallet had deprecated, before he knew of the event, any appeal to force by the sections, and he bitterly deplored it afterwards. 'On doit observer,' he wrote, immediately before the news, '...qu'une opération de force est indispensable à la Convention, si

[1] Mallet du Pan to Ste Aldegonde, 23 September, in Sayous, op. cit., tome II, p. 184; to the Court of Vienna, 26 September, in Michel, op. cit., tome I, pp. 319–20, and 4 October, in Michel, I, p. 328. Note his striking reflection: 'C'est un autre monde: en un mois on a rétrogradé de cinq ans.'

[2] To Ste Aldegonde, 23 September, in Sayous, op. cit., tome II, p. 184; to the Court of Vienna, in Michel, op. cit., tome I, pp. 301, 304–5.

[3] The stages of the struggle between the Convention and the sectional opposition are clearly outlined in Lefebvre, *Thermidoriens*, pp. 185–9.

[4] Mallet du Pan to Wickham, 13 October 1795, in Wickham Papers; same to Ste Aldegonde, 28 October, in Sayous, op. cit., tome II, p. 187.

elle veut conserver son pouvoir ébranlé, au lieu que les sections n'ont besoin, pour triompher à la fin, que de se maintenir dans la révolte passive où elles persistent depuis un mois.'[1] After the tidings of disaster were known, he observed that while the sectional movement had been efficiently organized for political warfare, it was not organized at all for military operations;[2] and he therefore expressed the deepest regret for the bad judgement of the opposition leadership:

Un zèle vif et nul concert, la meilleure volonté et point de chefs, aucun plan militaire par l'impossibilité d'en former un qui ne fût divulgué...[3] Les sections ont succombé parce qu'on les a fait battre avant le temps... elles jouaient une partie d'échecs, emportant une pièce chaque jour; avec ou sans les deux tiers, leur force restait entière après la formation du nouveau corps législatif; il suffisait de se faire craindre, sans donner sa mesure à coups de fusil; mais l'impétuosité nationale ne sait rien attendre.[4]

It was, however, not only the unwise bellicosity of the sections which Mallet found to blame in this affair. He blamed also the incomprehension and stupidity of the exiled Court and of the Allied Powers, which should have understood that this whole movement by the interior against the dictatorship of the Conventionals offered them their only substantial chance of bringing to an end the nightmare of the Revolution, and should have lent it every kind of aid, but in fact responded to it with nothing but contempt or indifference. Thus, in the midst of the proceedings at the primary assemblies, the Parisian leaders, despite their resentment against the Pretender and the Powers, were constrained to seek financial assistance from without in order to promote their campaign, and applied to Mallet, among others, for assistance in their quest. Mallet wrote bitterly of his entire lack of success in obtaining such aid for them.

Avec un million d'écus, un million de livres, on décidait de haute lutte la victoire des sections. On m'a fait de Paris des instances réitérées à

---

[1] Note to the Court of Vienna, 11 October, in Michel, op. cit., tome I, p. 331.

[2] Note to the Court of Vienna, 24 October, in Michel, op. cit., tome I, p. 340.

[3] Mallet du Pan to Wickham, 13 October, Wickham Papers.

[4] To Ste Aldegonde, 4 November 1795, in Sayous, op. cit., tome II, p. 190.

ce sujet. Mais que puis-je? J'ai sollicité, remontré des ministres, des grands seigneurs: pas un liard. On perdra des milliards à se faire battre; mais pas un écu pour se sauver.[1]

The French princes and their entourage could not have assisted the movement financially, but they failed to respond to it even by such gestures as were within their power. Their attitude was well expressed in an article published shortly before the insurrection by the abbé de Calonne, in which the struggle at Paris was described as being little, if anything, more than a quarrel between different sorts of Republicans.[2] And, if certain of the pure Royalists of Paris, acting on their individual responsibility, worked with the movement, the conduct of the King's Agents at Paris was very different—as we shall have occasion to illustrate at a later stage.[3]

It is, however, a fact of some importance in this study that the movement of the interior against the Convention had not risen and fallen without attracting a little more favourable regard, even assistance, from without, than these words admit; and the same Mallet du Pan who wrote the condemnatory words quoted immediately above was presently to write in different strain, acknowledging an offer of material assistance (though belated) to the sectionalists. These gleams of light in the generally dark surrounding scene came from the quarter of Great Britain.

The response of the British authorities to the situation created by the Law of the Two Thirds was certainly not, by the standards of Mallet du Pan, an adequate one; but at all events it was very different from that of the princes and their company. The attitude of the Foreign Secretary, early in September, is shown in the

[1] To Ste Aldegonde, 23 September, in Sayous, op. cit., p. 184.

[2] Mallet du Pan to Ste Aldegonde, 4 November 1795, in Sayous, op. cit., tome II; the reference to the abbé's article is on p. 190.

[3] Chapter III below, pp. 88-9. On the other hand, the young agent Bayard, though an ardent pure Royalist, deeply regretted the fall of the sectional movement. His attitude towards it may not be unconnected with the fact that he believed it to be under, or at least to be coming under, the influence of men whose own sympathies were pure Royalist; but at least it displays an intelligent appreciation of the point that the success of the movement would have destroyed the Convention and opened an immediate way to large new possibilities. See his report to Wickham, undated, but clearly composed on the morrow of the insurrection, and very shortly after Bayard's return to Switzerland from an extensive mission to France, including Paris: Wickham Papers, paper headed: *Coup d'œil sur l'état actuel de la France, et sur l'état de Paris en particulier.*

E

following passage of one of his despatches to Wickham, where, after his comments on the existing state of the projects involving foreign force and insurrection, he reflects on the alternative prospects, which now seem to have arisen, of promoting the overthrow of the Revolution by electoral methods:

Some Expectations are formed here from the Discontent which has been excited by the Decree for continuing the present Conventionalists as members of the new Legislature. But our Accounts of the Country at large, in this respect, are not sufficiently extensive to enable us to judge with much Certainty on this Point. It would certainly be in every View an Object of much Advantage, if the Primary Assemblies were to reject the Decree, and to elect the full number of Members, especially as it must be hoped that these Elections would, in many Instances, fall on those Royalists who have already introduced themselves into the Municipal Offices. It is hardly necessary for me to say that this latter Object is of course to be forwarded, by any means which may be in your Power.[1]

While it is clear, from the whole context of Lord Grenville's correspondence at this time, that he did not regard political action within the interior as offering the only, or even the principal, prospect of encompassing the fall of the Republic, and that, in this sense, his view of the French situation still lacked clarity and depth, this passage is sufficient proof that he was not wholly unaware of the possibilities in that field which were now arising.

The envoy to whom Grenville addressed these remarks was watching the new developments in France with great attention, and, at least by the later stages of the crisis, reached an intelligent appreciation of its importance and of some of its implications. It is not unfair to say that he did not as yet reach a completely clear view of the French question, and that his own contribution to the crisis was too little, and too late, to be of much use. But his reactions deserve to be displayed here, for this among other reasons, that they show stages in the growth of his thought and policy which eventuated in the great design of 1796-7.

The measure of success which Wickham had in his efforts to understand and appraise the situation can be judged from an interesting note which he addressed to Lord Macartney at the exiled Court in the opening days of October.[2] Here Wickham states his

[1] Grenville to Wickham, 8 September 1795.
[2] Wickham to Macartney, 4 October 1795. Printed (from Wickham's draft) in Wickham, op. cit., vol. I, pp. 176-80.

conviction, based upon a 'great many' letters which he had received or seen on the subject, that the Parisian opposition deserved to be treated as a serious new factor in the situation, and
that it pointed in particular to the need for a real change of attitude
on the part of the Pretender and his servants:

It appears to me very clear that the Sections are well conducted
and . . . have able persons at their head, that they are determined to
resist the Convention, that they have the means of doing so, and, what
is of no less importance, that both parties are so committed that they
cannot now recede . . .

Among the Electors named there are certainly *some* who are known
to be true and determined Royalists, but it cannot be disguised that by
far the greater part are persons who either still *are*, or *have been*, friends
of some one of the different governments and parties by which France
has been so long distracted, and that though the Royalists are extremely
active at this moment and appear to gain, yet that all the power and
authority of the Kingdom, in case the Convention should be legally
overthrown, would rest in the hands of persons of the above description.

What the event of the struggle will be it is impossible to foresee, but
it seems certain that the crisis is such as that the fate of France, for some
years to come, must necessarily be decided in the space of a few weeks.
This is surely, therefore, the moment for the King to endeavour to
conciliate the different parties by some more active and direct means
than any he has yet adopted, and to relax from that extreme rigour,
which I believe to be as contrary to his own principles and feeling as
it is to his own interests and those of his Kingdom.

Wickham proceeded to urge upon Macartney that 'the King's
correspondents at Paris should be immediately charged and
authorized to speak directly in his name to the leading Persons at
Paris. . . .'

Wickham then went on to argue that the King, by thus con-
descending to seek the alliance of the interior, would secure that,
if the Convention were disposed of, the leaders of the victorious
opposition would openly identify themselves with his cause. If
that could be brought about, things would probably turn out in
exact correspondence with the Pretender's wishes.

If the Leaders of the Sections should once encourage the cry of Royalty
at Paris, I am satisfied that the natural extravagance and enthusiasm of
the nation would again show itself and that the movement would be
too prompt and too rapid to admit of their giving any direction to it.

But, on the other hand,

if . . . the cry of Royalty should not immediately become general, I tremble for the consequences. The new Assembly will be composed of able and ambitious men, who will certainly do nothing in his favour without making their own conditions, which will be more or less humiliating according to the line of conduct he shall have personally adopted. They certainly will never suffer the power to go out of their hands—consequently the King will find himself in the very awkward situation, either of renouncing the Crown altogether, or of involving the country again in all the horrors of a civil war, or of retracting openly his own Declaration which has been issued with so much solemnity.

In the same letter, Wickham urged that the Pretender, besides himself offering friendly advances to the Parisians, should also move them to 'throw themselves into the arms of Charette', thereby giving further effect to the policy of a 'reunion of Parties' (of the need for which Charette was now convinced) and bringing additional resources of physical force to the Parisian cause.

Clearly it would be unwise to celebrate too solemnly the clarity and wisdom displayed in this letter. Wickham's strong partiality for the pure Royalist cause is very obvious; so is his belief that it may still be brought to victory, despite all the machinations of the constitutionalist leaders of the new opposition. His notion that the Parisian moderates would accept—and at the instance of Louis XVIII—the alliance of Charette, even of Charette converted to the 'reunion of Parties' seems, to say the best of it, dubious. Again, unlike Mallet du Pan, he seemed to regard the prospect of a decision by force between the sections and the Convention without reluctance. Yet, for all this, Wickham did grasp some of the implications of the fact that the struggle now on foot at Paris might well decide the whole political destiny of France for a long time to come, irrespective perhaps of what the Allies or the Pretender might desire or attempt to the contrary. He saw that the Pretender must therefore take steps, without delay, to conciliate the interior; and he openly inferred that hitherto the Pretender had not done enough to conciliate it. Again, it must be admitted that Wickham speaks only in the vaguest terms of the extent to which the Pretender should be willing to carry concessions; and we notice that the envoy seems to think that whatever concessions the Pretender makes at the expense of his own Royal preroga-

tives need be only temporary; so that he is really advising the
Pretender, not so much to make terms with his people, as to
deceive and over-reach them. But at least Wickham now appreciated the truth that the Pretender must be prepared in some sense
to court the favour of the interior, and that it was not enough
simply to give the law to the whole French nation, from an aloof
eminence.

Wickham's advice to the Pretender was given too late, as it
happened, to promote any of the objects which the envoy had in
view. But good advice was not the full extent of Wickham's contribution to the anti-Conventional movement. Wickham's was
one of the doors on which Mallet du Pan had knocked in his
quest of financial aid for the movement. Grenville had urged
Wickham to lose no opportunity of supporting the election activities of the French opposition; and when Mallet announced, in the
words which we have cited, that all doors were closed to his
entreaties, he was unaware that Wickham's door was just about
to open. It opened, indeed, too late, and too little to affect the
proceedings at the primary assemblies. Nevertheless, it opened.

The very same day as Mallet wrote the savage words quoted
above, Wickham drafted a letter to Mallet. He said that Mallet's
'friends' at Paris might consider themselves at liberty to make a
direct approach to the British Government; and he added:

In the meantime I will readily advance you the sum you want in
assignats, c.a.d. 100 mille frs. suppose we say 100 Louis which is something more, and if you can present to me any immediate object which
would justify me in taking such a measure upon myself I would without difficulty advance a much larger sum. But it would be necessary
that I should be informed very accurately of the quality and Character
of the Persons to whom it would be entrusted, their political opinions
and connexions and the steps by which they hope at length to carry the
point we all so much desire.[1]

Mallet promptly drew up for Wickham a statement of the political character which he attributed to the principal leader (unidentified by name) of the sectional movement.[2] He lost no time, moreover, in forwarding to Paris the one hundred Louis which had

[1] Wickham's draft to Mallet, 23 September 1795, Wickham Papers.
[2] Mallet du Pan to Wickham, dated 25 September 1795, in Wickham
Papers. A somewhat shortened version is printed in Wickham, op. cit.,
vol. I, p. 170f. Mallet describes this leader as a former member of the first

been made at once available by the British envoy. But the whole negotiation appears to have made no further effective progress before it was interrupted by the event of the insurrection. By that date, as Mallet later advised the British Minister, most of the one hundred Louis had been spent, and Mallet then authorized the use of the balance 'en petits secours à ceux de nos affidés que la nécessité de fuir ou de se cacher peut mettre dans le besoin'.[1]

The victorious Convention now presided over the secondary stage of the elections, fully able to ensure that the principle of the Law of the Two Thirds would be enforced, and enjoying the additional advantage that its most advanced and most courageous opponents were silenced and scattered. Yet the proceedings at the secondary stage reflected none the less the profound and by no means alleviated dislike of the country for the Conventional majority. It was, and is, possible to argue over the question, whether the electors expressed a positive preference for candidates who were, in one or other sense of the term, Royalists; but there has never been any room for doubt that they recorded, as clearly as their circumstances permitted, their condemnation of the existing national leadership. Compelled as they were to conform to the Law of the Two Thirds, they showed marked favour to the most moderate deputies of the old Assembly; and the deputies who had been accused of complicity with the sectional movement received an especially great share of their favour,[2] as is exemplified by the election of Boissy d'Anglas, Lanjuinais, and Henry-Larivière in more than thirty departments in each case.[3] Paris elected several of the deputies of this complexion, and incidentally eliminated entirely what was still left of the deputation which it had returned in 1792. The efforts of the electors generally, to return to the new legislature only the less unpopular members of the Convention, brought it about that only 379 of the old Assembly were actually re-elected in the constituencies; it was then left to the 379, sitting together in the capacity of a special electoral college (*Assemblée électorale de France*) to fill the rest of the five hundred

---

Commune of Paris, who, however, had parted company with the Revolution in October 1789, and had consistently taken his stand on the cahiers and the Royal Declaration of 23 June 1789.

[1] For all of this, see Mallet to Wickham, 13 October 1795, Wickham Papers.   [2] Meynier, op. cit., *le 18 fructidor*, p. 5.

[3] Lefebvre, *Le Directoire*, 1946, p. 20.

reserved places from among the remaining members of the Convention. Thereby numerous Republicans, who would otherwise have had no chance of it, were able to prolong their legislative careers, and to stand guard, in the new Assemblies, over the operation of the new constitutional order of the Republic.[1]

The political character of the two hundred and fifty new deputies, whom the electors were free to choose outside the ranks of the Convention, and who made up, in the new legislature, what contemporaries called the *nouveau tiers*, is a matter of considerable importance to us here. It has, however, always been a subject of controversy. Perhaps we ought, in attempting a fresh discussion of this point, in the first place to go behind this and say what can be said about the intentions of the electors, before considering those of the elected.

The well-known Conventional moderate Thibaudeau discussed these matters in his memoirs. He made the claim, often subsequently repeated by historians of Republican sympathies, that it was not the Republican regime, but the Convention, against which the electors on this occasion voted.[2] It is, however, surely a somewhat doubtful distinction which this claim involves. In 1792, the Republican regime had been foisted upon a country which, on the whole, was certainly not ready for it. Since then, the Republican regime had become identified with the successful defence of the territory against foreign invasion, and with the resistance of the country to the forcible restoration of the old order. These were no small assets. But the regime had won no other titles to merit in the eyes of most of its citizens; as was observed above, the case was very much to the contrary. Whatever appeal we may think was made to Frenchmen in 1795 by the political ideals of Republicanism, at all events they knew that the Republic had never hitherto respected those ideals; and the Law of the Two Thirds suggested that those ideals would not be respected much better in practice, even under a definitive constitution. Frenchmen must have found it very difficult to distinguish, in any meaningful sense, between the regime and the Conventional politicians who had been, and who evidently meant to go on being, identified with it. This means that the French people had to judge the Republic

[1] Ibid.

[2] A. C. Thibaudeau, *Mémoires sur la Convention et le Directoire*, 1824, tome II, p. 12.

in the light of the Jacobin dictatorship, in time past, and of Thermidorian leadership more recently. But—it needs no emphasis—
the national attitude to the Jacobins was one of open detestation;
towards the Thermidorians, as had been clear enough even before
the Law of the Two Thirds and Vendémiaire, it had long since
been turning into one of disgust, dismay and derision.

In the light of these reflections, it seems hard to evade the conclusion that when the electors of year IV condemned, so far as lay
in their power, the old Conventional majority, they were also, in
intention as well as in effect, condemning the Republican regime.
It is possible to contend that they were not necessarily condemning the Republic *as a bare theory* or speculative ideal; but any such
contention is not only questionable in fact, it is also really insig-
nificant, for masses of men do not vote in accordance with abstract preferences and platonic ideals. The only real Republic was
the Republic created, and still dominated, by the Conventionals;
and this Republic the French had no reason to wish to preserve.

To say this is not to infer that the nation had, in the autumn of
1795, any clear positive alternative to the regime which the Convention had created for it. The indications seem indeed to be that
the national mind was little nearer to this than it had been in the
autumn of 1794. The inference which does emerge is that the
electors cannot have been deterred from returning any candidate
simply on the grounds that he lacked, or might prove to lack,
loyalty to the Republican system. And from it follows the further
inference, that we cannot afford to reject out of hand suggestions
that the deputies of the *new third* were not only hostile to the old
Conventional majority, but also hostile to the Republic.

Thibaudeau himself admitted that the greater number of the
new deputies were 'not irrevocably attached to the Republic, nor
even to the Revolution'.[1] He went on, it is true, to claim that most
of them were nevertheless capable of being won over to sincere
acceptance of the regime of year III, provided that this were
honestly and wisely administered.[2] But, in the opinion of the same
Thibaudeau, this condition was never fulfilled, and on the lines
of his argument it seems to follow that the new deputies must have
remained at the best neutral in their attitude towards the regime.

Mallet du Pan formed the impression that about three-quarters

[1] Thibaudeau, *Mémoires sur la Convention et le Directoire*. 1824, tome II, p. 12.
[2] Ibid., pp. 13–14.

of the new members were, in some sense of the word, Royalists.[1]
The opinions of Thibaudeau and of Mallet are not really incompatible. All that we know of these men leads to the conclusion
that the attitude of most of them towards the Republican regime
was and throughout remained, at the best, ambiguous. The old
Conventionals who dominated the operation of the Republican
order used their power in a manner which the new deputies felt
to be detestable. The new deputies, with some aid from a minority
of the old Conventionals, reacted by adopting an attitude of
opposition, not, ostensibly, to the regime, but certainly to the
persons and policies of those who claimed to monopolize it. And
they identified themselves, in the process, with proposals which
plainly endangered, not only the ruling party, but the survival of
the Republic itself.

We could not properly argue, from these facts alone, that the
new deputies as a whole entertained any positive proposals for a
moderate monarchical system, and still less that they deliberately
acted towards any such end. But we can and must assert both of
these things regarding a number of them, and these some of the
most active and conspicuous of them. Against these, the reproach,
early brought against them by the friends of the government, that
they were *Royalistes cachés*,[2] was not brought in vain.

Let us mention firstly the Feuillant group of General Mathieu-
Dumas and his friends: Dumas himself, Barbé-Marbois, Dupont de

---

[1] Mallet du Pan to Ste Aldegonde, 4 November 1795, in Sayous, op. cit.,
tome II, p. 191. '(*Le*) nouveau tiers, dont les trois quarts sont des royalistes.'
The description 'royalistes' must be taken as qualified by the comments
which Mallet had made about the character of the anti-Conventional movement generally; e.g. on 28 October he had described the new *corps législatif*
as 'le monstre d'Horace: on y verra l'aristocrate siégeant à côté du Jacobin,
le constitutionnel auprès des auteurs du 10 août' (Sayous, op. cit., tome II,
p. 188); again, on 13 September he had advised the Viennese government
that the constitutional monarchists had been robbed of any clear forward
policy on the question of the regime by the attitude of Louis XVIII (see the
passage in Michel, op. cit., tome I, p. 308, already referred to above).
According to Wickham, the pure Royalists ('really attached to the antient
Government') among the new deputies numbered 'eight or ten.' Some of
these, such as Madier de Montjau, he declared to be actively working for the
return 'not of a constitutional Royalty but of their old Government' (Wickham, op. cit., vol. I, pp. 206-7, 357). Wickham is not likely to have under-
stated the number of deputies holding views of this kind.

[2] Cf. Buchez & Roux, op. cit., tome 37, p. 112.

Nemours, Tronçon-Ducoudray and Lebrun in the Council of the
Elders, with Siméon, Dumolard and Gibert-Desmolières in the
Council of the Five Hundred.[1] (It was under the roof of the last
named, in the rue de Clichy, that the famous 'club' of opposition
members came into existence.)[2] Dumas in his *Mémoires* admitted,
what his own past record and that of several of his friends inevitably suggested, that his group cherished 'opinions monarchi-
ques'; but the disclaimer which Dumas also made—and which
certain of his collaborators echoed—of the charge that they actually 'served the Royal cause' during their time in the Republican
legislature, is a rather serious oversimplification.[3] It is true that
these men feared the return of the princes and the émigrés un-
fettered and secretly bent on revenge, as much as they dreaded
the revival of Jacobin terror; and they more than once tried to
bargain with the Directory. But, as Wickham's papers show, at
other times they explored the possibilities of an understanding
with Louis XVIII; in particular, at the time of the elections of year
V, they entered into activities which, they well knew, were intended to promote a restoration. They still did not wish to see
Louis restored on his own terms, and they soon repented of the
activities upon which they were embarked; but after this they
could no longer say with real truth that they had never served the
Royal cause.[4]

Others of the new *tiers* also earned notoriety for their opposition and for their reputed Royalism. Such were Portalis, of the
Council of the Elders, Lemerer, Jourdan (des Bouches du Rhône),
de la Rue, Couchery, Pastoret, André (de la Lozère), Mersan and
'Job' Aymé in the junior Council.[5] One or two of these, and other
deputies who have not yet been mentioned, such as Valentin-
Duplantier, in any case had connections in the Dumas group. As
will appear later, Wickham's papers show that the charges of
Royalist conspiracy brought, at the time of the *coup d'état*, against
Lemerer and Mersan, were fully justified. Wickham's papers also

---

[1] Meynier, op. cit., *le 18 fructidor*, pp. 5–6, citing Mathieu-Dumas,
Mémoires, tome III, p. 75.

[2] Pariset, op. cit., tome II, pp. 296, 326–7.

[3] The disclaimers of Mathieu-Dumas and of Barbé-Marbois were cited,
and, indeed, accepted, by Meynier, *le 18 fructidor*, pp. 6, 185.

[4] For the evidence see ch. VI, VII, below.

[5] Cf. Buchez & Roux, op. cit., tome 37, p. 112,

show that Royalist sympathies found some active expression in the cases of Portalis, Jourdan, Pastoret and Duplantier.

It is true enough that these *Royalistes cachés* all, sooner or later, severely disappointed the expectations built upon them by D'André and by Wickham. And, avoiding any details here, it is indeed the case that the whole record of the new *tiers* of 1795, even after it was reinforced, at the elections of year V, by a second new *tiers* just as bitterly anti-Conventional as itself, must appear feeble and frustrated by whatever standard it is judged. The opposition did not succeed in unseating its enemies from the place of power in the Republic; still less did it bring about, as the *Royalistes cachés* wanted, a restoration of monarchy in any form whatever; it ended in complete political disaster. But the opposition's dismal record can be explained, though it can hardly be glorified; and without entering here into any reference to its conduct after the elections of year V had so greatly strengthened its apparent chances, we may usefully point out the general reasons for its rather poor showing during the earlier part of its career.

The chief difficulty which the opposition encountered did not arise on the score of numbers in the legislative chambers; though the new *tiers* was by definition a minority, it could expect important aid from those members of the old Convention whose attitude more or less closely resembled its own. The opposition suffered rather from lack of cohesion; it never established an agreed leadership, able especially to overcome the diffidence which divided the new deputies from their potential allies among the ex-Conventionals.

A further important difficulty arose from the fact that under the new constitution there was an executive power enjoying a real measure of independent existence, and able to exert great influence over the whole conduct of politics. The opposition could not prevent the old majority from dictating the choice of the Directors, and thereafter the Directors were able, from an independent position, not only to take their own line in matters outside the competence of the chambers, but to hold together a majority favourable to themselves within the chambers.

Finally, the *Royalistes cachés* who included in their number the men most fitted to provide leadership for the new *tiers* were inhibited from taking what would have been, for themselves, the clearest and most encouraging course. Their incentive to force the issue against the Republic, even to undermine the existing Conventional ascendancy within the Republic, was weakened by the fact that there was no candidate for the throne who could convincingly proclaim the programme of a moderate and enlightened monarchy. They tried, though intermittently, and inadequately, to keep up an opposition while vainly hoping for the emergence of a clear middle way between evils.

At the time when the elections of year IV were completed, all of this lay in the unknown future. But the list of the new *tiers* was itself enough to cause the Convention grave new alarm. The past records, alone, of these men were in too many cases disturbing. If the next legislative elections, when another third part of the chambers would be renewed, were marked by any large number of similar choices, the Republicans and the Republic alike would be in mortal danger. It was bad enough, from the standpoint of the old majority, that Dupont de Nemours, Mathieu-Dumas, Laffon-Ladébat, Muraire and Lecoulteux de Canteleu had all been prominent among the defenders of the constitutional monarchy, that Tronchet had been counsel for Louis XVI and Tronçon-Ducoudray counsel for the Queen. There were other returns which boded worse still. Barbé-Marbois, according to Tallien, had been one of the authors of the policy of Pillnitz; Madier de Montjau, an ex-member of the Constituent Assembly, now enjoyed the reputation of having 'uniformly spoken and voted in favour of the old government from first to last'; Job Aymé on the morrow of the elections appeared as one of the organizers of a *chouan* insurrection in the South.[1]

The Convention drew the conclusion that it must enact, before it separated, whatever fresh measures it could to ensure that no further electoral slide towards reaction should occur; and it supposed, not without reason, that among the causes which had favoured, and unless removed would continue to favour, the reaction were the facilities which the Thermidorian policy had given to returning émigrés and to the non-juring clergy. It therefore carried the famous *lois d'exception* of 3 brumaire, year IV

[1] For the point on Barbé-Marbois, see Buchez & Roux, op. cit., tome 37, p. 112; the words quoted about Madier are those of Wickham in a letter to Sir Morton Eden, 17 November 1795; Wickham, op. cit., vol. I, p. 206; on Job Aymé, see Lefebvre, *Thermidoriens*, p. 213, and *Directoire*, p. 21.

(25 October 1795). These laws reiterated the prohibition of the exercise of public functions by any émigré, even though he had been *provisoirement radié*, or by his relatives; they pronounced a similar prohibition against all who had promoted 'seditious motions' at the time of the recent elections; and they revived the laws of 1792–3 providing for the deportation of non-juring clergy.[1] Next day the Convention furthermore enacted a general amnesty in respect of 'all acts relating simply to the Revolution'; but this amnesty did not affect the incapacities enacted on the previous day, nor repeal the other laws against the émigrés, nor, finally, did it cover the past activities of clerics who had neither accepted the civil constitution nor the more recent declaration of submission to the Republic and its laws.[2]

The ruling party soon adopted a number of other measures, of a less negative kind, and calculated to reinforce its immediate grasp on the country. When the new legislative chambers were formed, they were dominated clearly enough, at the outset, by the old majority, which of course also dictated the composition of the new executive Directory. Working closely together, the legislative majority and the Directors lost no time in improving their situation in several important respects. The electors had hardly had time to fulfil their duties of choosing the personnel of the new local administrations and of the courts of law; but many of the appointments which they had made in those fields reflected the same anti-governmental, perhaps anti-Republican bias as the new deputies. There were, however, many of these places still to be filled, and a new law now empowered the Directory to fill them, *pro hac vice*, by nomination. The Directory not only made energetic use of this new prerogative, but also exploited in a similar spirit

[1] Lefebvre, *Thermidoriens*, p. 193; *Directoire*, pp. 10–11; Meynier, *le 18 fructidor*, p. 4. One of the effects of this legislation was presently to bring about the exclusion from the legislative body (in pluviôse, year IV) of two of the *royalistes cachés* who had been newly elected to it: Job Aymé and Mersan. For details of the debates which occurred on this issue, particularly in the case of Aymé, see Buchez & Roux, op. cit., tome 37, pp. 143–6. Mersan, if not himself capable of being described as a *chouan*, was in connection with the Royal Agents at Paris (as was Lemerer) and with the baron de Marguerit, a Royalist adventurer who was planning a *coup de force* at Paris during the months following Vendémiaire. Pariset, op. cit., p. 302.

[2] Pariset, op. cit., p. 293; Lefebvre, *Thermidoriens*, p. 190. Text in Buchez & Roux, op. cit., tome 37, pp. 88–9.

its undoubted constitutional right to dismiss unsatisfactory administrators; and it filled the new vacancies thus created by the procedure of nomination authorized by the new law.[1]

Both in making these new appointments and in other respects also, the government at this time displayed marked favour towards the Jacobins. This was inevitable; the object throughout was to trim the balance against the monarchists, and this involved of necessity an alliance with the democrats, just as the Thermidorian reaction against the Jacobins had formerly required the aid, and promoted the interests, of conservatives and of all the shades of Royalism.[2] In now showing such favour to the Jacobins, the ruling party was only carrying on the policy which it had already begun, even before the elections and the sectional crisis; for its fears that reaction was travelling too fast and too far in the country had been aroused considerably earlier than that time. When the Directory entered office, the Jacobins had already benefited by the repeal of the Thermidorian decrees providing for the disarming and supervision of the terrorists, and by a wide policy of dismissals and reappointments in the army, intended to increase the numbers of active officers with left wing sympathies, and to diminish the numbers of those of opposite opinions.[3] The amnesty of 26 October had also had significance in this respect. The terrorist leaders already sentenced to penal deportation were indeed expressly excluded from the amnesty, as, on the other side, were the émigrés; but the amnesty cleared all other agents and supporters of the Jacobin regime from all fear of future proceedings. They were left in full enjoyment of the civic rights which were now once more emphatically denied to all those whose political sins lay too far to the right of the ruling constitutional orthodoxy. To these advantages for the Jacobins, the Directory now added a large distribution of local patronage,

---

[1] Lefebvre, *Directoire*, p. 24.

[2] Mallet du Pan aptly expressed the situation of the regime in his note of 4 June 1796 to the Imperial Court: 'Le nombre des républicains non-jacobins est trop petit,... trop peu actif, pour soutenir à eux seuls cet édifice monstrueux contre les agitateurs anarchiques ou contre les monarchistes' (*édifice monstrueux* = the 'middle class' republic) (Michel, op. cit., tome II, p. 92).

[3] Lefebvre, *Thermidoriens*, pp. 187, 190; for the earlier measures in favour of the sansculottes and the Jacobins, beginning at the time of Quiberon, see the same work, pp. 162-4.

facilities for opening clubs which tolerated, or even expressed, their point of view, and subsidies to assist their propaganda.[1]

In this conjuncture of affairs, we should expect to find the outlook of the new *tiers*, and of those who sympathized with them in the country, extremely depressed so far as the immediate prospect was concerned. In the more distant future, they had the hope that the next legislative elections would bring decisive changes; though even this hope was clouded by the obvious animus of the laws of brumaire, and by the obvious consideration that the ruling majority would take whatever further measures it could to stave off the danger which those elections would involve for its cause. But for the immediate future, it might well appear that the opposition had to contemplate only a scene of unrelieved gloom. The indications are, however, that during the opening weeks of the new governmental order the opposition, both in the legislature and among the public, was in very good heart. It seems to have been only towards the turn of the year 1795–6 that a period of acute discouragement began for those who inclined to the right of governmental orthodoxy. It will be suitable to bring this chapter to a close, by accounting for and illustrating the brave show which the opposition first attempted, and by similarly explaining its early relapse into despondency.

At the inauguration of the new system, the opposition regarded it as self-evident that it must spare no efforts to bring about the repeal of the laws of brumaire and the rupture of the alliance between the government and the Jacobins. With respect to the laws of brumaire, indeed, the opposition had a certain motive for caution: the laws were directed against the émigrés, the relatives of the émigrés, and the refractory clergy; few of the regime's opponents would have wished to make the way too easy for those émigrés and clergy who wanted the restoration of the old order in its fullness, and revenge on all those who had ever supported the new. But for all this, the moderate Royalists of the interior were

[1] Lefebvre, *Directoire*, pp. 26–7. The official favour thus bestowed on the Jacobins, together with the Directory's rather high handed interpretation of its own prerogatives, raised among the legislative opposition, and indeed among the *honnêtes gens* in general, the fear that the regime was already moving, and would soon fall entirely, back into the methods and character of the Revolutionary government. These fears were echoed by Mallet du Pan and by Wickham: Mallet to Wickham, 5 January 1796, Wickham Papers. Cf. Wickham to Grenville, draft despatch no. 2 of 1796, 5 January, Wickham Papers.

nevertheless clear that this risk must be taken, and the laws repealed. Little as they liked, much as they dreaded, the émigré extremists, they needed whatever support they could find to defeat
the government at the next elections, just as the government
feared but nevertheless tried to use the Jacobins; and moreover there were very numerous émigrés and clergy who were not
extreme reactionaries and who appeared as the natural and safe
allies of the moderates of the interior. As for the alliance of the
government with the Jacobins, the opposition regarded this not
only as a curb, but as a real threat, to themselves; it was widely
feared that the ruling party would itself fall under the domination
of the democrats whom it was trying to use, and that the country
would relapse under the yoke of terrorism.[1]

But how could the opposition dream, in the autumn of 1795,
that it could realize either of these objectives? Firstly and mainly,
because it thought it had reasons for hoping that the ruling party's
grip on the legislative chambers was much less secure than
appeared. The opposition knew that certain very important deputies, whose own adherence to the Republican form of government
was not in doubt, themselves objected to the laws of brumaire,
as inconsistent with the regime of strict constitutional legality
which, they thought, would alone offer to France the means of
emerging from the bitterness of the revolutionary conflicts and
of recovering national unity under the Republican aegis.[2] The
opposition also knew that many other ex-Conventional deputies,
formerly of the Plaine, were disposed to join in any attack on
the current policy of the ex-Montagnard Directors, if only because, having so long trembled before the Jacobin regime, they
were anxious to make the men in office tremble before themselves.[3] With aid from these quarters, the opposition thought it

[1] On the attitude of the constitutional monarchists, and of the *honnêtes gens*
in general towards these issues, see Lefebvre, *Directoire*, pp. 12–13; the documents quoted in the previous note also have relevance here.

[2] Such as Thibaudeau, Doulcet de Pontécoulant, and Cambacérès, mentioned by Lefebvre, *Directoire*, p. 21, and also Mailhe, mentioned by Meynier,
le 18 fructidor, p. 7. Thibaudeau discusses his own attitude to the laws of 3
brumaire in his *Mémoires*, tome II, pp. 62, 67–8.

[3] Cf. Meynier, *le 18 fructidor*, pp. 5 and 11, 'les anciens trembleurs de la
plaine qui voulaient faire trembler à leur tour.' In opening its campaign against
the governing party, the opposition did not as yet make any concerted attack
on the laws of 3 brumaire, though a proposal for their repeal was attempted,
unsuccessfully, by the former Conventional Fayolle (Thibaudeau, *Mémoires*,

could place the majority in doubt and force the ruling party to compromise, even to disarm itself.

These hopes appear exaggerated, and indeed they proved to be so. But there were other circumstances, outside the governmental precincts, which made them appear far from absurd. The ruling party had latterly, in several decisive respects, imposed its will by force. But the force of opinion, even on the morrow of Vendémiaire, was heavily on the side of the opposition, and it was not wholly unreasonable to think that this could be exerted as a very heavy means of pressure on the government. The government and its legislative supporters had inherited all the unpopularity of the Convention, and to maintain a conscious public hostility to their rule was not difficult, on these grounds alone; certainly not difficult at Paris, where, on the very morrow of the insurrection, Royalists of various shades practically monopolized all the means of expression. The newspapers, the tone of the theatres and the doings at the Café de Valois all witnessed to this fact.[1]

tome II, pp. 61–2). The opposition concerned itself rather to test the balance of the chambers by challenging the government on the general state of the country, the conduct of the finances, the principles involved in governmental nominations to vacant local appointments, and the progress of the Jacobin resurgence. The issue of the laws of brumaire to some extent raised itself, in so far as the verification of the deputies' powers was meantime in progress, and the laws obviously affected the legal right of certain deputies to exercise their mandates. By the end of 1795 the opposition had failed to carry the houses on any of these issues, though the question as to whether certain deputies should be excluded or suspended still remained to be finally decided. See Buchez & Roux, op. cit., tome 37, pp. 109–46.

[1] Lefebvre, Directoire, p. 25; Meynier, le 18 fructidor, p. 5. At this point we may refer again to the Coup d'œil which Wickham's agent Bayard composed immediately after the insurrection. It includes a review of the state of public temper at Paris, which, though marked by the illusions of a pure Royalist, is not without intelligence and insight. Bayard admits that it is not the case that 'tous les Français veuillent un Roi, et un Roi Bourbon'; nevertheless, he maintains, 'ils ont plus de disposition à en venir à un gouvernement différent de celui qui a fait si longtems leur opprobre: ils se réunissent tous pour le détester, et cette haine a passé sur la masse de la Convention... le parti Royaliste est si fortement prononcé aujourd'hui que les constitutionnels ont pris le parti de dire que leur sistème était le premier échelon nécessaire aux Royalistes et que c'était pour eux le moyen infaillible de parvenir à leur but.' Bayard passed on to suggest, as the chief reason for the revival of the old loyalty, the painful contrast between the standard of living which the Parisians had enjoyed under the old regime, and that which they suffered under the Conventionals.

F

Building on these foundations, Mathieu-Dumas and his friends in the chambers, applauded from the wings, so to speak, by the Feuillant elder statesmen Adrien Duport, Théodore de Lameth and Montesquiou, not only indulged the hope of forcing the government to large immediate concessions, and of compelling it, in fact, to stand by with folded arms while the opposition prepared conditions for a decisive victory in the next legislative elections, but even thought it worth while to embark on the political re-education of the Pretender. In a draft to Lord Grenville early in January 1796, Wickham, referring back to this time of great expectations, says of the Feuillants and their friends in active politics:

Whilst their own party appeared to be gaining a momentary influence at Paris . . . the King was daily threatened with the loss of his throne unless he entered actively into their views and called all their leaders into his counsel. He was alarmed with the origin of a new faction called *Royalist of opinion* which was said to be composed of a reunion of all the moderate persons of every party, whose leaders were determined to have a King, but one of their own choosing, and over whom they could have a decided influence; and that they had allready fixed their views upon another person in case the legitimate sovereign should refuse to accept the Crown on their conditions.[1]

Yet all this optimism and briskness had faded by the end of the old year: why? The respectable public might read opposition papers, and profess moderate opinions. But Vendémiaire had not been without its effects. This public was unwilling to risk, not only another armed collision, but anything which could possibly give excuse for further acts of rigour.[2] Inside the chambers, the

[1] Wickham Papers: Wickham to Grenville, draft despatch no. 4 of 1796, 5 January.
[2] Mallet du Pan pointed out to Ste Aldegonde, 28 January 1796, that though 'grand nombre de bourgeois, de rentiers, de lettrés', at Paris in particular, were now 'bons royalistes', they were also thoroughly cowed and discouraged by the events of Vendémiaire and by the activities of the government and of its Jacobin auxiliaries. Mallet urged his correspondent not to believe those who maintained that the common people had come back to Royalism; Mallet's editor, Sayous, quoted a letter addressed to Mallet which put this point even more strikingly than Mallet himself: 'le peuple crie misère, il sacre contre la république, mais parlez-lui raison, dites-lui qu'il fut jadis heureux, etc., il répond qu'il ne veut plus de maître, et que les aristocrates voudraient lui faire demander un roi par la faim et la peine, mais qu'il

moderates found it difficult to build up an effective combination against the governing party; and the Pretender seemed to be equally unmoved. The world seemed hostile to all their calculations. Hence Mallet du Pan's observations to Wickham:

Toutes mes informations de Paris se réunissent à constater la nullité totale où sont tombés pour le moment les Constitutionnels, les Monarchistes, les Indépendants, les Royalistes de toute couleur. Leur situation est parfaitement semblable à celle du côté droit de la 1ère. législature en 1792. Ils ne savent ni former un Parti, ni établir un Plan... effrayés, décousus, ils n'osent lutter que dans les questions purement personnelles, où leur sûreté propre est directement attaquée...[1]

Les deux conseils [added Mallet to another correspondent], sont deux bureaux de renvois où l'on enregistre les lois d'après la volonté des cinq... Un grand tiers n'y assiste plus, le reste des opposants se tait et approuve tout.[2]

Wickham was sending to Lord Grenville further evidence to the same effect. The dejection of the constitutionalist leaders, he declared, was attested

by private letters from Dumas to Theodore Lameth, by the language of Mme. de Stael who is just arrived here from Paris, by the conversation of ye persons with whom I know Montesquiou to be in correspondence, and by the letters of Lameth to his friends in Franche

---

mangera plutôt les pavés.' Mallet concluded that for this reason the *bas peuple* would always support the régime against the monarchists of the respectable classes, and that the latter, however good their sentiments, were, in those circumstances, a broken reed to lean upon: 'tout cela ne vaut pas cinquante sans-culottes. Celui-ci compte sur ses bras; le royaliste, sur son voisin. Celui de Paris espère dans les départements, celui des départements espère dans Paris' (Sayous, op. cit., tome II, pp. 207–8).

[1] Mallet du Pan to Wickham, 5 January 1796, Wickham Papers.
[2] Mallet to Ste Aldegonde, 28 January, Sayous, op. cit., tome II, p. 208. In fact, when at the beginning of January 1796 the legislative commissions for the verification of the powers presented reports proposing the exclusion of several deputies in accordance with the terms of the brumaire laws, the opposition, despite the discouragement into which it was falling, put up a considerable struggle in the Five Hundred to resist the proposals. This reached its end only in February 1796. It cannot be said that the opposition was wholly unsuccessful, since the final decision was to exclude Aymé and Mersan only; a number of others were merely suspended (Buchez & Roux, op. cit., tome 37, p. 146).

Compté, some of which have lately fallen into my hands, full of lamentations on the present state of things.[1]

Wickham added that Théodore de Lameth now felt so far from elated over the prospects of his party, that he felt his friends must 'throw themselves into the arms either of the Jacobins or of the Royalists' (that is, presumably, either of the Directorialists or of the pure Royalists). In his original draft, the envoy continued, though he later deleted the phrase, 'in which dilemma, he seems to me rather disposed to adopt the former'.

In that same despatch, Wickham enclosed to Lord Grenville a memoir of which he had just contrived to possess himself. He believed this writing to be the work of Duport and his circle. A copy of it had been sent to Verona. The tone of this memoir, so far as it related to Louis XVIII, commented Wickham, was very different from that which the party had used when it thought it could threaten the King with the loss of his throne: 'Now .. they no longer hold out any menaces *as from their own party* but on the contrary the evil consequences which they represent as likely to follow in case their proposals be refused are stated to be common to themselves as well as to the King and all the purer Royalists.' In other words, the Feuillants were reduced from threats to entreaties.

So matters stood at the outset of the year 1796. In the battle for the control of France which had now for long been in progress between the Republican minority and the friends of a moderate monarchical settlement, no decisive advantages had as yet been secured on either side. The Conventionals had forcibly imposed on the country an extension of their own rule; yet the elections, in so far as they had been allowed to express the national wishes, had registered real successes for the opposition, and the latter had even been able to hope that there need be no halt in their onward movement to complete victory. Those hopes had now been disallowed. But the discouragement of the opposition, which we have just illustrated, marked only a lull in the confused and ill-defined encounter. The moderates of the interior had by no means renounced for ever their ambitions to escape from the prison in which the old Conventional majority had enclosed them.

*   *   *

[1] Wickham to Grenville, draft despatch no. 4 of 1796, 5 January, Wickham Papers.

The question of an Orleanist or other non-legitimate monarchy in France

At several points between Thermidor, year II, and Fructidor, year V, reports were current which related to the growth of interest in, and to plans for the development of, a new constitutional kingship under the branch of Orleans, or under some foreign prince. These reports won serious attention in various quarters. They were not in all respects well founded, but the attention which they attracted had serious practical consequences. The whole matter calls for general discussion at this stage.[1]

Broadly speaking we may say that in so far as these reports alleged the growth of interest in projects for a new constitutional monarchy, they had some real foundation; in so far as they asserted that organized activity to that end was in progress, they deserve little credit. At the time, however, they gained a more undiscriminating reception.

The general idea of an Orleanist, or other non-legitimate monarchy was certain to make a more or less favourable impact on the minds of those who had supported the earlier phases of the Revolution, but who had throughout regarded the Republican regime with distaste. To them, it offered a thinkable alternative to the unpromising princes of the main line, who identified themselves with the old order and sought to reimpose themselves on the country by force, and whose supporters preached revenge

---

[1] Aulard, in *Hist. pol. de la Révolution* (1901), pp. 640–41, has a useful brief review of the rumours and realities of the Orleanist interest at this period. Mallet, in January 1795, believed that both a certain number of the Thermidorians, and also many of the partisans of limited monarchy in the country, were inclined towards an Orleanist solution, or favoured the election of some foreign prince: Michel, op. cit., tome I, p. 51, and Sayous, op. cit., tome II, p. 122. We have already referred to some of Mallet's statements about Orleanist preferences among some of the Parisian opponents of the Convention at the time of the plebiscites and elections. Wickham's despatch to Grenville, 26 May 1795, gives an interesting glimpse of the anxiety of the princely party about the possible rivalry of the Orleans branch, and shows that Condé, at least, treated the constitutional Royalists as identified with the Orleans interest. Reporting a discussion with Condé on relations with 'the constitutional party', Wickham quotes him as remarking: 'if any of their leaders should be disposed to make a submission, he wished that the young Duke of Orléans might be the first' (Wickham Papers, Wickham's draft to Grenville, no. 39 of 1795). Further developments of this question are detailed in the following chapters.

on the men of 1789. This kind of solution was said to make some appeal to moderates even before the death of the young prisoner in the Temple, and such assertions may well have been true; Louis XVII, even if he survived long enough to reach the throne, was of minor age, and his installation would raise the difficult, even hazardous business of a Regency. After his death, and the passing of the legitimate inheritance to Louis-Stanislas-Xavier, the appeal of an Orleanist or similar solution was no doubt much increased in the minds of this party. Then secondly, the same kind of solution was reported as appealing to other men of a very different stamp, politicians who had identified themselves, from self-interest rather than from conviction, with the Republic, but who had since come to despair of the Republic's survival. In consequence, it was said, they now turned, for their own safety if not for the good of the nation, to the idea of a new monarchy, contrived by themselves, which might obviate the danger which any Restoration of the legitimate claimant, conditional or unconditional, would involve for them. Certainly reports asserting that men such as Tallien or Barras were actually *working* to set up a monarchy in favour of the Duc d'Orléans or a member of the Spanish Royal House cannot be accepted without great caution; but they no doubt reflected a real fact, namely that these politicians were indeed anxious for their own future safety and would have been quite capable of embarking on such a project if any real opportunity had occurred.

In the event neither the frustrated admirers of 1789, nor the despondent and anxious Republican politicians were ever able to pursue very far the hopes of this kind which they may well have cherished. The best possibility of a monarchy of this kind no doubt lay with the princes of the Orleans line. The young Louis-Philippe might have succeeded in rallying a large part of French opinion behind him. He represented in 1795, as much as he did in 1830, both the traditional reigning family and also the patriotic glories of 1792. He could have accepted the principles of 1789 without having to carry any of the burden of reproach and personal discredit which had lain so heavily on his father. Strict legitimists and convinced Republicans would have had nothing to do with him, but the large mass of French feeling which was identified with neither of those groups might well have accepted him with relief. Whatever his motives, Louis-Philippe gave no opportunity

to those who might have proclaimed or welcomed him. After his
emigration in April 1793 in the train of Dumouriez, he resided
quietly for about two years in Switzerland, whence he seems to
have made no effort to exert any influence, however discreet, on
French affairs. In 1795 he removed further from the scene, travelling first to Hamburg, thence to Stockholm, and finally, in January
1796, to America. He now permitted the circulation of a letter
which had been addressed to him by his old governess, Mme de
Genlis, in which she had exhorted him not to listen to any
offers to raise him to a new-fangled kingship on the ruins of the
Republic in whose defence he had won glory. By publishing this
letter, the Duke seemed to imply that it was loyalty to the
Republic, rather than deference to the elder branch of the Royal
family, which led him to evade offers of the Crown; it was, at all
events, clear beyond dispute that he was evading them.

His younger brothers, the Ducs de Montpensier and de Beau-
jolais, were meantime actually in France, but as prisoners of the
Republicans. In autumn 1796 they were allowed to sail for America
in the wake of Louis-Philippe. They all remained in the New
World till the time of the Consulate.

Both before and even after these departures, an Orleans monarchy attracted the sympathy, and may to some degree have
attracted the active interest, of certain elements in France. But
it was a vain sympathy, and a useless interest. Despite the many
contemporary reports on the subject, and the wide credence
which those reports received, there is no reliable evidence that
any Orleanist party, or any concrete design for an Orleans monarchy, ever came into existence; and in the circumstances which
we have described, this is in no way surprising.

As for the reported projects for the installation of a Spanish
Bourbon or some other foreign prince, these relate to something
which can hardly have emerged from the realm of vague specula-
tion and discussion. It was one thing for frustrated constitutionalists and nervous Republican adventurers to wish for the
appearance of a tractable and popular foreign personage; quite
another thing to agree upon who it was to be, to persuade him to
accept, and to secure his acceptance by the country.

Nevertheless, the persistent reports of activity in these directions have a great and direct importance for our study, for they
helped to bring about the great design of 1796-7, by forcing into

alliance some of the most important elements which took part in it. The Pretender and his party, who would of their own initiative do nothing to reconcile the new France to the old monarchy, nevertheless became in the course of the year 1796 seriously worried over the supposed possibility that a bastard monarchy, Orleanist or other, would shortly be set up in France, foreclosing, perhaps for ever, the way to a legitimist Restoration. This fear was one of the causes which finally compelled the Pretender, reluctant and unrepenting, to give his support to the 'coalition of Parties' for the capture of the machinery of the Republic for what he still hoped would be pure Royalist ends. Again, many of the moderates also at that time became seriously worried by the possibility that an Orleanist monarchy, or some other new-fangled system of kingship, would be proclaimed; not that hopes for such an outcome had not been cherished by some of themselves, but that they feared it was now to be attempted by, and for the sole profit of, some of the most unsavoury survivors of the Revolution, foreclosing, perhaps for ever, all hope of a regime devoted to the interests of the *honnêtes gens*. This fear was one of the causes which was to lead the deputies of the Mathieu-Dumas group, and others besides, to try the way of collaboration with Louis XVIII—though still essentially opposed to their ideals—in the same coalition. Finally, that same fear lent added impetus to the efforts of Wickham to build up and sustain that coalition. He feared that a new French monarchy, erected and controlled by the regicides, would persist in and perpetuate that system of external aggression and domination which was removing all the landmarks of British foreign policy, and placing his own country in mortal danger.

III

Starting Points of the 'Great Design'
1796

AT the beginning of the year 1796, the opposition in the French
Councils and the Feuillant leaders who had applauded them
from the wings were alike in deep dejection. But the discomfiture
of these champions of the (modified) ideals of 1789 brought no
substantial comfort to the princes and their party. That the constitutional monarchists had been brought to the depths of disappointment did not mean that they were any nearer surrender at
discretion to the pretensions of Verona. It might mean, rather,
that they would turn finally towards a substitute monarchy; and if
important members of the ruling party in France chose to agree
with them on this line, the end of the Republic might occur in conditions which placed the hopes of the Pretender not nearer to, but
indefinitely further from, realization. It might be true, as Royalist
agents reported, that pure Royalism, rather than any variety of
constitutional Royalism, was the ascendant force in Parisian opinion. But what, in existing conditions, was such opinion worth?
What seemed certain was that the favourite methods of the pure
Royalist emigration, whereby such opinion was to be mobilized
for decisive action, were as far from success as ever. Invasion, conspiracy, internal insurrection, were equally barren of results.

It seems that in the winter of 1795–6 the princes and other members of their circle were fitfully, confusedly and on the whole very
unrealistically considering whether they should, to some modest
extent, reappraise their presentation to the interior. Should they
not begin to woo the interior by a more conceding attitude on
circumstantial issues? They were still far from admitting the need
for, or even possibility of, a change of attitude on the issue of
principle. It cannot be said that much of importance immediately
came of this; nor did the princely change of front, slight as it was,
find any early means of expression to the world. Nevertheless, we
see here the first and very hesitant signs of that real, though still
only superficial, change of policy which finally brought the Pretender to give his heavily qualified blessing to the great project
which failed in Fructidor, year V.

As early as November, 1795, Lord Macartney reported to his colleague at Berne that

the King of France has been gradually relaxing in some points, and is now nearly brought to the disposition that was to be wished. I have not failed to reiterate to him at every favourable moment those sentiments of conciliation which are so necessary to his interests, and I believe he has taken some pains of late, to convince people that he sincerely entertains them.[1]

Of course this did not mean that Louis was thinking of compromising his principle; from the pen of a British diplomat at this time, such phrases only connote that the Pretender was less unfriendly to the British policy of gathering a coalition of anti-Republicans, agreed to attack what they all disliked, but not agreed about the regime which was to displace it; and, more generally, that the Pretender was willing to give a more substantial interpretation to his own promises of clemency and welcome to persons. Even so, the most significant word in the passage just quoted is 'nearly'; and it is a certain fact that, for a whole year after this, the world at large remained quite unaware that any change, however limited, was occurring in the policy of the titular King.

In January 1796, even Mallet du Pan was unaware of any such change. At that time, Mallet reiterated to his friend Ste Aldegonde the views which he had expressed about the need for a change in Royal policy at the period of the elections and the sectional crisis. Mallet had in mind changes considerably greater than Lord Macartney contemplated; he wanted the Pretender to consider any propositions which might be made to him by the interior, provided only that their makers would recognize, on their side, that Louis was (however his government might later be constituted) the lawful head of the French state; he wanted Louis to let this be known by appointing new agents in the interior, empowered to negotiate for him on this basis, and he wanted Louis to prove his good faith in this, among other ways by changing the membership of his 'shadow' government.[2] But he certainly did not know, when he wrote in those terms, that the Pretender's attitude now offered any hope, however faint, of his coming to accept that programme.

[1] Published in Wickham, *Corresp.*, vol. I, pp. 195–6.

[2] See his letter to Ste Aldegonde, 10 January 1796, in which he recapitulates many of his earlier observations on these points, in Sayous, op. cit., tome II, p. 204.

He believed, on the contrary, that there was nothing to be done with Verona, and he rejoiced in reports that glimmerings of sense had now appeared in the head of the Comte d'Artois; that the younger brother had first seen the need for a 'système de rapprochement'.[1] Friends in London, who shared Mallet's general approach to the great issue, promptly wrote to disabuse him; the court of the younger brother, they declared, was no different from the court of the elder; if it had recently played with ideas of a new and moderate policy, this was only a chance result of the deep discouragement which supervened on the failure to disembark *Monsieur* on French soil; but when, a little later, the younger court had received reports that Louis-Stanislas-Xavier was mortally ill and that Artois was soon to become Charles X, then, Mallet was told, it was easy to see what all their *velléités de modération* had been worth:

C'était une joie parmi tous ces messieurs... on faisait mourir le pauvre homme en moins de trois mois... et puis l'on verrait quelle différence de son frère à lui! C'était celui-là qui serait Henri IV! Si vous saviez comme toutes les velléités de modération disparaissaient![2]

At the end of January 1796, Mallet believed that, so far from either of the Royal brothers providing a new direction for their cause, many of their staunchest aristocratic supporters were now deserting them in despair, and throwing in their lot with the constitutional royalist exiles of Hamburg.

Les émigrés royalistes qui affluent de plus en plus dans le nord de l'Allemagne [wrote Mallet in a hitherto unpublished letter to Wickham's secretary Captain Leclerc], se jettent dans les bras des constitutionnels, qui ont à Hambourg un comité dirigeant très actif... Vous serez bien étonné si je vous citais ceux des Aristocrates panachés... qui se sont jettés dans le Patriotisme de 1789... Je reconnais là... le résultat du détestable plan de conduite qu'on fait tenir au Roi.[3]

Mallet indeed felt alarmed, as well as vindicated, by this development. He thought that the pure Royalists ought to reach a reconciliation with the great mass of opinion in the interior whose

[1] Ibid.

[2] Lally-Tollendal (in London) to Mallet du Pan, in Sayous, op. cit., tome II, pp. 200–1; cf. a contemporary letter of the Chevalier Panat to Mallet, Sayous, tome II, pp. 196–7.

[3] Mallet to Wickham's secretary, Captain Leclerc, 26 January 1796: Wickham Papers.

views were roughly represented by the old Feuillant leaders; but he did not approve of or trust the old Feuillant leaders themselves, and he did not wish to see leading pure Royalists rushing out of one futile extreme, only to place themselves too uncritically in the hands of men whom he felt to be selfish careerists first, and only by accident spokesmen for a system best suited to the needs of the country.

Despite these apparent false starts, the Royal reappraisal was destined to continue, though still in far too half-hearted and obscure a fashion. Perhaps the reported desertions of the cause by Mallet's 'aristocrates panachés' helped to give it a new impetus. In February 1796, the Comte d'Artois had abandoned whatever hopes he had cherished of his early succession to the Royal title, and was trying to convince his brother of the need for a very considerable change in Royalist strategy. The substance of his advice to the Pretender was that he must try to rally in one common front all sections of French opinion which feared and hated Jacobinism; this reunion would acquire real unity of outlook in so far as its different members learned to work and sacrifice together; the Pretender must solemnly promise that he would adopt whatever forms of government this united party finally agreed upon.[1] Meantime, *Monsieur* spoke with emphatic respect of Mallet du Pan, and even asked for his help with propaganda.[2] At Verona, despite inevitable resistance from die-hards of the last ditch, there was now a slight sympathetic response,[3] though the elder brother and his advisers were still unprepared to go by any means so far. What the Pretender did was to authorize a proclamation, dated 25 February 1796, to be issued, it would appear, by his Agents in the interior when they judged the moment ripe. When we have pointed out the context and contents of this document, it will be clear that it deserves very little applause for freshness or breadth of view. It offers—need it be said?—no concession on grounds of principle. It was apparently associated with new instructions to the Paris Agency, which clearly imply no intention to give up the policy of

---

[1] Mallet to Ste Aldegonde, 7 February 1796, Sayous, op. cit., tome II, pp. 210-11.

[2] Ste Aldegonde to Mallet, 28 February and —(?) March '96 in Sayous, op. cit., pp. 214-15, 221.

[3] Mallet to Ste Aldegonde, 7 February 1796, and Ste Aldegonde to Mallet, 28 February 1796, in Sayous, op. cit., tome II, pp. 211, 214.

civil war in the West. There is no suggestion, either in the proclamation or in the instructions, that the Pretender had now renounced the hope of winning back an unconditional throne by force. But there is, in the proclamation, an expression of the King's good feelings towards his subjects, which is worded in the warmest terms and which embodies a promise of an amnesty, from which this time not even the regicides are excepted. All appeals to the claims of severity, and even to the requirements of justice, are pointedly laid aside, and the King is made to hold the language of pure forgiveness and indulgence.[1]

This language presumably represents an effort, such as Lord Macartney must have approved of, to show that the King was indeed inspired by genuinely conciliatory intentions towards persons. But the sense of the proclamation had no immediate effect whatever. It was not published; it was intended for publication, it would seem, only when the Agents had the internal situation— thanks to force as much as to propaganda—entirely at their disposal. Unfortunately this moment was never likely to arrive. In any case, an unpublished proclamation was not likely to bring it nearer.

It seems that Louis XVIII attempted nothing further, as yet, in the way of a more attractive approach to the interior. His better disposition, such as it was, remained entirely hidden from the public eye. He made no more effort to display himself in an attractive light, than he made to display his cause, and he did nothing to disavow, or even to offset, the odious follies for which the more militant of his supporters had long been notorious. At the beginning of March 1796, Mallet du Pan wrote about it all to the court of Vienna in terms which imply that he now disbelieved in any repentance, however partial, at Verona, and which display the most heartfelt contempt for the Pretender and all his active adherents:

On cherche en France un chef qui ait force et sagesse, et l'on trouve un roi enseveli à Verone, passant ses jours dans l'abandon et la nullité..., une division militaire entre les mains d'un prince du sang... dont l'esprit absolu et le dessein d'une contre-révolution par les armes font reculer les trois quarts des partisans de la monarchie... des agents obscurs et imbéciles, employés... pour exposer sans utilité ceux qui, dans l'intérieur, seraient tentés de les écouter; l'obstination à... penser

---

[1] Buchez & Roux, op. cit., tome 37, pp. 186–7 (Proclamation), pp. 187–8 (Instructions).

séduire la France par de misérables attaques de détail, par des conspira-
tions de comédie, par des chouans qu'on laisse faire une guerre exter-
minatrice à tous ceux qui n'ont pas pris le panache de Coblentz.[1]

Thinking in this way, Mallet obviously could have no faith in
the reports that pure Royalism was winning ground inside France.
On the contrary, he insisted, it had to be said in the spring of
1796, just as it had had to be said in the summer of the Verona
Declaration, that the true King was losing adherents daily. The
Royalists who still alone mattered in the interior were the 'Royalistes de 89'; they could only dread Louis XVIII, and 'les expédi-
tions des chouans, et tout ce que disent ou font de mauvaises
têtes au dehors, ne sont pas propres à les détromper'.[2] It is not surprising that when, towards the end of March, Mallet had a request
from the court of *Monsieur* that he should make every effort to
spread in the interior the news of a change for the better in the
Royal policy, he replied in tones of wounded indignation:

j'aurais beau faire cent fois par jour ce que j'ai déjà fait, c'est à dire
rassurer les esprits sur les sentiments des princes; qui voulez-vous qui
me croie, en les voyant constamment sur la ligne qu'ils tiennent depuis
cinq ans, sans que le moindre fait vienne appuyer mes rémontrances et
me donner crédit auprès des Français?[3]

Yet while Louis and his immediate advisers thus made ludi-
crously little progress in their ostensible attempts to reappraise
their policy, a wider circle of more powerful forces was already
forming and was destined to shape for the Pretender's cause a vast
and skilful strategy which he and his entourage would surely never
have originated. The first of these outer and more powerful forces
which will now be considered arose from important changes
which occurred during the earlier months of 1796 in the unstable
pattern of politics inside France.

About the turn of the year 1795–6, the alliance between the
Directorial party and the Jacobins began to break down. This
breakdown occurred almost inevitably, because the leading Jacobins were not prepared to acquiesce indefinitely in the position of
tolerated and subordinate partners, which was after all the utmost

[1] Michel, op. cit., tome II, pp. 21–22.
[2] Mallet du Pan to the Imperial Court, 5 and 17 March 1796: Michel, op.
cit., tome II, pp. 23, 35.
[3] Mallet to Ste Aldegonde, 27 March 1796, in Sayous, op. cit., tome II,
p. 222.

that the Directorials could afford to concede to them. The Jacobins thought that the final crescendo of inflation, and the deep popular unrest which of course went with it, offered them an opportunity to strengthen their grip on the regime, perhaps the chance to re- cover supremacy. Their attitude to the government became one of challenge. The Directorials veered abruptly away from them, as the Thermidorians had once veered abruptly away from their sub- ordinate but ambitious allies to the right: moderates, *muscadins*, and *émigrés*. Before February 1796 was over, the government had shown that it was ready and determined to deal firmly with the challenge. It had closed the club at the Panthéon; it had not only discontinued the conferment of patronage on the Jacobins, but had started to remove Jacobins from the offices they held. Driven by ambition or vexation, the Jacobin leaders plunged into con- spiracy. The government, prompted chiefly by Carnot, who re- garded with particular hostility this revival of democratic pres- sure, took all possible measures to avert a Jacobin attempt against the regime. In mid-May, Cochon, Carnot's nominee as Minister of Police and incidentally a Republican of very shaky loyalty, was able to arrest all the individuals concerned. Barras, and part of the Directorial majority led by Sieyes, were anxious to make as little as possible of the business, for fear of inducing a stampede of ner- vous property owners towards the political right, such as would once more endanger the moderate Republic, this time to the bene- fit of the monarchist parties. Carnot, however, supported by the rest of the Directorials and by the moderate Republican press, in- sisted on severe and ostentatiously public measures of repression —intended, seriously enough, to convince the property owners both of the reality of the new Jacobin peril, and also of the com- petence and good faith of the existing government in putting it down. Carnot and his friends hoped thereby to consolidate not only the property owners generally, but even the moderate monar- chists, in loyal support of the established regime. Why, indeed, should all these people hesitate to throw in their lot with a Repub- lic which was thus to show itself as capable and as resolute in the defence of the *honnêtes gens* as any monarchical government? It was a calculation worthy of Thiers, and it offered its authors a prospect of fitting rewards: all the ideological doubts which still hung over France would be cleared away, since the *ralliement* of *honnêtes gens*, propertied men and moderate Royalists would crush for all time to come the spirit both of the true counter-revolutionaries and of the Jacobins.

The views of Carnot and his supporters prevailed, and it seemed for a time that events were justifying their expectations. The conciliar opposition were willing enough to join the government in severities against the Jacobins. They made no difficulties over authorizing domiciliary visits or over the trial of the civilian, as well as the military, conspirators by a military court. The adhesion of the new *tiers*, and of all that the new *tiers* represented, seemed to have been secured by Carnot, when, on a famous occasion in June, several leading members of the conciliar opposition accepted an invitation to dine at the Luxembourg.[1]

In fact, however, Carnot's calculations were doomed to failure. By the time of the famous dinner, the leaders of the right wing in the legislature were indeed enjoying the turn which events had

---

[1] For the developments in French politics sketched here, see Lefebvre, *Directoire*, pp. 27, 33, 36, 38–40. Mallet du Pan in mid-February 1796 understood that at that point Barras and Letourneur, supported from without by Tallien and other Thermidorians in the corps législatif, were still very reluctant to break with the Jacobins; and that they stood in opposition to the three other Directors, Carnot, Reubell and La Revellière, who were on very bad terms, if not with the Jacobins, at least with those of their own colleagues who still favoured the Jacobins (Mallet to the Court of Vienna, 20 February 1796, in Sayous, tome II, p. 218). Mallet is clearly correct in reporting that the Thermidorians who were anxious to put an end to what they regarded as the very dangerous alliance of the regime with the Jacobins had from an early point the support of the numerous '89-ist' Royalists (Mallet to the Court of Vienna, 5 March 1796, in Michel, op. cit., tome II, p. 23), and, as the government's quarrel with the Jacobins deepened, had the support also, in the legislature, of leading members of the new *tiers* (Mathieu-Dumas, Barbé-Marbois, Pastoret, Lemerer) as well as of the old Conventionals who had sympathized with the sectional movement in autumn 1795 (Boissy d'Anglas, Henry-Larivière, Pelet). Mallet to the Court of Vienna, 3 April 1796, in Michel, op. cit., tome II, pp. 43–4.

In a note to Vienna, 11 June 1796, Mallet reported the dinner given at the Luxembourg to Mathieu-Dumas, Muraire, Dumolard and Pastoret (Michel, op. cit., tome II, pp. 95–6).

It is a point of considerable interest in view of the fortunes which actually befell Carnot's policy of courting the *ralliement* of all these anti-terrorists, moderates and constitutionalists, that Mallet as early as 3 April 1796 declared that the opposition deputies (who were then so willing to urge the government on against the Jacobins) were not only anti-Jacobin, but implicitly acting against the government itself (Mallet to the Imperial Court, 60th Note, Michel, op. cit., tome II, pp. 43–44).

taken since the new year, and were once more full of hope and activity. But gratitude and obligation to the government of the moderate Republic had little, if any, share in their thoughts. They were both more ambitious, and more rancorous, than Carnot supposed. They would not be content to bless from a respectful distance the triumph, even the triumph in a good cause, of ex-Jacobins such as Carnot and Reubell. Long before the arrest of the *Babeuvistes*, they had formed the hope of refloating their political fortunes on the rising tide of respectable anti-Jacobin opinion. They had hoped to use this, not merely to secure the final elimination of the Jacobins, but also to capture the system from the Directorials themselves, whom they regarded as little preferable to the Jacobins, and whom they were still not in the least prepared to accept as partners. At an early stage, they had contemplated an elaborate programme to give full effect to these ambitious views: not only the repeal of the laws of 3 brumaire, but (following the proscription of the immediate conspirators) the drastic pursuit of all the terrorists of earlier years; a move for immediate peace on the basis of the old frontiers; finally, the reconvening of the primary assemblies and fresh elections, which would obliterate the effects of the Law of the Two Thirds. In cherishing such ideas, they no doubt enjoyed the sympathy of the large section of opinion which was 'Royaliste de 89' and even of the pure Royalists, with the exception of the few who found nothing objectionable in the methods of violence employed by the princes.

When the Jacobin conspiracy turned the governmental majority into sharper hostility to the Jacobins, the legislative opposition was indeed prepared to support and encourage the government in a repressive policy; but it was not safe to assume, as Carnot assumed, that the opposition could be won over to act as a new satellite in the Directorial system. The new anti-Jacobin offensive had given the opposition a much needed stimulant. Its leaders were determined to use the opportunity, in one way or in another, to resume their own bid for the reality of power. They were not willing to be cajoled by the Directorials into accepting a junior partnership with the governing party. Carnot's attempts during the summer of 1796 to pursue this policy of cajolery won only illusory successes.

It seems very possible that Mathieu-Dumas and the other opposition leaders who attended the famous dinner were temporarily and superficially impressed by the friendly attentions of the ruling group. But, even taking this possibility at its highest, Dumas and his allies were nevertheless expecting, in return for their support against the Jacobins, extensive concessions in favour of the *honnêtes gens*, concessions such as would, in fact, place the governing party at their mercy. Carnot indeed made many concessions to them; he made amply enough to reinforce their ambitions, and then he, or his colleagues, refused enough to justify their inevitable return to open hostility.

Every concession which the government made could be used against its interests in all that related to the great contingency, which imperilled the whole future of the government and of the regime itself—the elections, legislative and administrative, which must, by law, be held at some time within the year V. The approach of these elections would doubtless have revived the hopes and spirit of the legislative opposition, even if the Jacobin question had not revived these at an earlier date. As it was, the government's *rapprochement* with the opposition, and its efforts to cement that *rapprochement* by concessions to the *honnêtes gens*, could hardly have failed to strengthen the will of the opposition to employ those elections for the downfall of the ruling party; and, even if Dumas and his friends had at first been fully sincere in accepting Carnot's alliance, it seems morally certain that the approach of the elections would have brought them irresistible temptations to break away again, and to use the government's concessions against the government.

Thus, even so far as concerns the effect of his policy on Dumas's group, Carnot was, for all his vastly different intentions, leading the Republicans into an impasse. But Carnot's policy was not only to this extent a dangerous illusion; to an even greater extent it was a simple failure. Other opposition leaders, and probably the greater part of the opposition public, never accepted the government's olive branch at all, but persisted in treating the ruling party as quite beyond the pale. When Dumas and his friends, in the autumn of 1796, severed their connections with the Luxembourg, they only rejoined a large company of opponents who had never been even superficially or temporarily converted to agreement with the bourgeois Republic.

From the early summer of 1796, in some cases, and from the autumn in others, the leaders of the opposition groups planned and worked for decisive victory in the elections of year V. They were enjoying not only a revival of their self-confidence and combative spirit, but many material advantages presented to them by Carnot's concessions. And, to make success sure, they tried to arrange that there should be no enemies, no neutrals even, on their Right. In other words, they planned for a 'coalition of parties'. The *omnium gatherum* which British policy had favoured for civil war and insurrection could be used for the more promising operations of the hustings. The émigrés, whom the government, in its redressment against the Jacobins, had once more allowed to return—the non-submissive clergy, against whom pressure had been relaxed—the White Terrorists whom the government had once more allowed to emerge in the South: all these elements were to be employed to clinch the decisive defeat of the ruling party. But could such an *omnium gatherum* have a positive programme on which to remain united when victory was won? If not, it was always possible to argue that it would be the constitutional moderates who would finally dominate the scene.[1]

But certain very prominent opposition deputies were not prepared to leave the fortunes of the coalition to such calculations. Partly with a view to the better conduct of the elections, but partly also from other motives which will have our attention later, they tried, in summer 1796, to bring the Pretender himself into the alliance. Their approaches to him were made in a very different spirit from the whimpers which marked the last days of 1795. They now urged him to adopt their own constitutional principles. If he did so, then the other right wing elements whose alliance they sought would seemingly have no alternative but to follow his line, and the coalition would from the outset reflect only their own point of view. What is more, they seemed to assume that the Pretender would now indeed accept them on their own '89-ish' terms. And when, somewhat later, Mathieu-Dumas and his friends resumed the road of opposition to the Directory, they too proposed alliance, not to the Pretender directly, but to the former Feuillant D'André, whom they understood to be now working for Louis XVIII in a conciliatory spirit, and to have connections already with certain members of the opposition.

What is more, all these deputies looked for assistance to the representative of England. All of them hoped for his aid in developing the 'coalition'; Dumas and his friends hoped for England's

[1] For the last five paragraphs above see, e.g., Lefebvre, *Directoire*, pp. 40–3; Meynier, *le 18 fructidor*, pp. 7–14.

support, if need arose, in bringing the titular King to reason. In seeking English help, none of them were revealing any unlimited complacency towards the national enemy; they were primarily concerned to induce England to play their game, and some of them were far less inclined than others to help England's interests in return.[1]

Such, in its barest outlines only, for the present, was the pattern of events and ambitions at the origin of the 'great design' on the side of the interior. We can now attempt a brief sketch of the efforts which were being made, simultaneously but independently, by men whose sympathies had not hitherto been with the '89-ish' Royalists of the interior,[2] to bring about a great change of policy from the side of the Pretender and his Court. In spring and summer of 1796, then, a number of the Pretender's avowed adherents, men who represented a wide variety of experience in the pure Royalist cause, were converging to press upon the exiled Court the need for a new approach to the problems of the interior. They did not all give the Pretender precisely the same advice; but they all, with whatever differences, united to urge him in a general direction which would certainly bring him significantly nearer the wishes of the moderates and sensible pro-monarchists in France. Some pressed the Pretender to meet the interior on the issue of *methods* of political warfare; others to make concessions of *principle*

---

[1] We shall illustrate (ch. VI, VII, IX) the dealings of some of these men with England. It will be seen that Lemerer's party and his associates, whom Wickham describes as 'the friends of Mr D'André', were, or became, under the influence of D'André, (in theory) warm towards English interests, while Dumas and his group never overcame their deep animosity to England, even though at one point they solicited English aid. Wickham appears to have been deeply impressed by the profound hostility, or at best suspicion, with which almost all the French, whether pure Royalists, moderates, or Republicans, regarded the British Government, however much some of them might be induced by necessity to dissemble it. See his Private despatch no. 28 of 1796. There is nothing, from our perspective, very surprising in the fact that Frenchmen of all parties loved England no better for her calculated, humiliating and costly 'generosity' to the Royalists. In chapter VI we shall describe the curious suspicions which Dumas and his group entertained about English intentions towards France at the time of their *rapprochement* with D'André in autumn 1796.

[2] I give here a statement in very general terms of the character of several simultaneous efforts by professed adherents of Louis XVIII to bring about a change in his policy.

and agree to rule as a constitutional King. Some urged him to dis-
card the use of forceful methods, or at least to supplement them by
authorizing his supporters to join with the monarchist moderates
and the rest of the *honnêtes gens* in peaceful, 'legal' and parliamentary efforts to capture the Republic from the Republicans; others
looked to the further future and asked him to admit that the
Crown could only be restored on the basis of, as well as with the
aid of, the constitutional monarchists.

In fact, the first of these lines of general suggestion logically
implied the second also; and the suggestion that force should no
longer alone be relied upon logically required to be taken to the
more thoroughgoing conclusion that force should be wholly abandoned, at least until electoral and parliamentary action had wrested
control of the Republic's constituted authorities out of Republican hands. The various suggestions now made required to be
brought together, each being adjusted and developed in the light
of the others, and the whole reduced to a coherent synthesis. But,
from one quarter and another, the exiled Court was being presented at least with the raw materials for a large-scale restatement
of its policy.

In presenting these partial but valuable sketches for a new
policy, the important Royalists now in question were actuated by
two common general motives. The first of these sprang from their
growing realization that the system of invasion, conspiracy and
insurrection, upon which the militant pure Royalists had hitherto
built their hopes, had uniformly yielded results so disappointing
that an inference of great and permanent importance irresistibly
emerged. They drew that inference, as has been intimated above,
with varying degrees of clarity and courage. They all, however,
saw at least that force could no longer be expected alone to solve
the problem; that it must be, if not given up, then supplemented
by more conciliatory methods of appeal. The best and most complete form which such suggestions could assume was the adoption
of election warfare, to the exclusion, at least until the final stages
of the struggle, of all methods of force, and the mobilizing of all
sections of opinion which detested the government upon a basis
which represented the greatest measure of agreement among
French people.

The second motive which influenced the makers of a new policy
for the exiled Court coincided with one of the considerations

which also influenced the leaders of the legislative opposition in making approaches to the Pretender from their own side. In the present chapter, we have as yet only glanced obliquely at this. What both these groups of people had in common was the suspicion that the Directorials were planning to erect an Orleans monarchy. The ruling party, they supposed, feared that their bourgeois Republic, having lost the support of the Jacobins, would be unable, with its own few proper supporters, to withstand another slide of incalculable length towards the right. A bastard monarchy was believed to be the Directorials' only possible refuge. For, under the nominal rule of a prince identified with Revolutionary principles, the regicides would still effectively govern; and the country would be pacified by the semblance of a return to Kingship, of a kind, however, innocent of any designs in favour of the old regime. It is easy to see why both the leaders of the conciliar opposition and the wiser adherents of the Pretender felt that this reputed design of the regicides must at all costs be resisted. To the legislative opposition and to the opinion in the interior which they represented, an Orleanist solution would be detestable, not so much on dynastic grounds as because it would be attempted precisely to re-establish, under a plausible disguise, the real mastery of the old Conventional majority. To pure Royalists, the Orleanist policy threatened not only this evil, but the final ruin of the legitimate line and also of all their hopes (whatever in different cases they amounted to) of turning back the clock of the national life.

In this common peril, the moderate monarchists of the interior and the legitimist claimant were natural allies, despite all the mutual hostility and bitterness which had lain between them for so long. The Orleanist danger, in which so many now believed, would of itself have promoted some kind of *rapprochement* between the exiled Court and the 'royalisme de 1789' even if no other forces had been working, on one side and on the other, in the same direction. For, if the legislative opposition was to trump the king whom it expected the regicides to produce, then the only card it could convincingly play was the 'real' King—somehow converted, of course, to sense and reason. Therefore the opposition had to attempt agreement with the 'real' King, while at the same time it had powerful arguments to make him enter the alliance on the interior's own terms: accept the throne on our conditions, or

resign yourself to being supplanted, perhaps for ever, by a substitute Royalty. And the Pretender had equally strong motives, on
these grounds alone, for joining himself with the legislative opposition: if the Directorials meant to make an anti-King, he had
a new and powerful reason for trying to overthrow the Directory,
and overthrow it quickly; what means so likely as entering the
electoral lists against the ruling party? and what hopes of winning
the elections except through an alliance with the moderate monarchists of the interior?

Among the avowed adherents of the Pretender who united,
from somewhat different directions, to give him advice which
converged along the line which we have now tried to explain, we
must mention Précy, Frotté, Pichegru, and the Agents at Paris. Such
also was the policy moved by D'André, whose formal submission
to Louis XVIII was made in March 1796.[1] In subsequent chapters,
we shall consider in detail the activities of D'André, both at this
and at later stages of the 'great design'; in what remains of this
chapter, we propose to discuss the suggestions for a revision of
Royalist policy which were first made by Pichegru and by the
Royal Agents at Paris.

These suggestions are worth particular discussion in their own
right: for one reason, that they illustrate the first and groping
stages of the attempt to construct a new and better policy for the
Pretender, and their obvious imperfections are in themselves instructive. Another reason, in the case of the Paris Agents, is that
there occurs here not only a partial coincidence of thought, but a
direct and friendly contact, between old adherents of the Pretender
and members of the legislative opposition in the French Chambers. We see men on both sides not only trying to plan the con-
vergence of their respective movements, but at an early stage
already converging to construct the plan.

But we embark on this discussion also because it will help to
pave the way for the consideration of D'André's part in all these
matters, a part which, thanks largely to the special interest and

[1] The attitudes of Précy and of Frotté at this time are noted by Pariset,
op. cit., p. 329. To the persons mentioned in the text we may add, as a belated
convert to the new line which they represented, another prominent exponent
of the Royalist *manière forte*, Comte Joseph de Puisaye, head of the Agence
de Bretagne, and instigator of the ill-fated Quiberon campaign. Puisaye is
referred to in this sense in a letter from the Paris Agence to Wickham, 24
October 1796: Wickham Papers.

support of Wickham, was to produce a greater practical effect upon the policy of the exiled Court than the more or less similar advice which flowed into it from other quarters.

Pichegru finally lost command of his army in April 1796.[1] It took him no long time to discover that his moral influence over the troops formerly his would not long survive his resignation. The effect of this discovery, together with the impression produced on his mind by an immediately subsequent visit to Paris, where he took some pains to gauge the state of public feeling,[2] led him to announce to the British and Royalist representatives with whom he had connections the need for a large reappraisal of Royalist policy towards the interior. Wickham reported to his principal on these issues in the following terms:

Pichegru had not been able to obtain the confidence of his army to the point that he had hoped or expected . . . his dismission had occasioned very little sensation there . . .; he now sees no prospect whatever of employing it in favour of a counter-revolution . . . On his arrival at Paris, he there also found things in a very different situation from what he had expected . . . He now sees no hope for the Royal family but in the acceptance, at least for a time, of a limited or constitutional Monarchy . . . it is by no means to be wondered at that he should have become an entire convert to (*that opinion*) and should have determined to act in future upon that principle only, as the only one capable of being carried into execution. Be that however as it may, it is most clear

---

[1] The comments of Mallet du Pan on the final end (as it proved) of Pichegru's career with the army are worth quotation: '10 avril 1796... Pichegru est nommé ambassadeur en Suède; c'est une manière honnête de le dépayser et de l'écarter... Il est étonnant qu'on s'en soit tenu à sa démission, après la connaissance qu'a le Directoire des principes de Pichegru, de sa correspondance de l'année dernière avec M. le Prince de Condé, des espérances que l'émigration française avait formées sur lui, et qu'elle avait soin de répandre dans tous les cabarets' (Michel, op. cit., tome II, p. 52). A little further in this correspondence, Mallet reports Pichegru's refusal of the offer of the embassy to Sweden: Michel, tome cit., p. 58.

[2] Wickham, in his Private despatch no. 12, 4 May 1796, which is partly published in Wickham, *Corresp.*, vol. I, pp. 356–8, mentions Pichegru's connections with constitutional Royalists of various shades, with 'at least *some* members of the Directory', and with the Minister Bénézech (who, according to Wickham, had himself offered to serve the interests of Louis XVIII if these were relieved of identification with the old regime). Mallet du Pan in his correspondence with Vienna reports that Pichegru on his visit to Paris was 'fêté et accueilli par le parti modéré' (Michel, op. cit., tome II, p. 58).

that he has actually adopted that principle, and that he has renounced all hope of acting through his army.[1]

There are grounds for thinking that when Pichegru thus began to urge the exiled Court to adopt, at least provisionally, the programme of constitutional monarchy, he was speaking out for a solution which he had privately favoured since a much earlier time. Mallet du Pan, in a note to the Viennese Court dated 10 April 1796 (it announces Pichegru's nomination, abortive as it proved, to the Republic's embassy in Sweden) had adverted to the supposed well known fact that Pichegru, like his friend and military successor Moreau, favoured a limited monarchy; and the Royalist Agent Duverne de Praële had reminded Wickham at the time of Vendémiaire that the 'monarchiens' had been boasting of having Pichegru 'dans leur manche'. But even if the General had long privately cherished constitutional monarchist convictions, it was an event of much importance when he moved the Court to admit that it was only on this basis that the King could hope to erect his throne.[2]

Pichegru's proposed reappraisal, for all its clarity and good sense on this single point, appears to have been in other respects as ambiguous and as apparently confused as we might expect from the personage in question. We level these criticisms, not against Pichegru's suggestion that the King would have to acquiesce in limited monarchy 'at least for a time' (for, as has been seen, many contemporaries, with far greater knowledge of politics than the General, believed that a Royal Restoration, even made on a constitutionalist basis, might be supplemented by further recoveries

[1] The portion of Wickham's Private despatch no. 12 of 1796 which contains these lines is published in Wickham, *Corresp.*, vol. I, p. 356 f.

[2] Michel, op. cit., tome II, pp. 52, 58; Duverne de Praële to Wickham, 13 October 1795, in Wickham Papers, bundle 105. It may therefore appear that Pichegru should not have been included, in the text above, p. 80, as one of those adherents of the Pretender, men 'whose sympathies had not hitherto been given to the 89-ish Royalists of the interior', who now united to press for a change of Royalist policy. Pichegru was, however, a very different man in the eyes of different people. The high reputation he already enjoyed at the exiled Court rested in part upon the Court's belief that he was a Royalist of the true type. Wickham's despatch no. 52, 14 May 1796 (published in Wickham, *Corresp.*, vol. I, pp. 361–5) reported to Lord Grenville that the General's new advice to compromise with constitutionalism 'had given them (*the exiled Court*) more pain even than the certainty of his being unable to assist them with his army'.

of Royal prerogatives, and Pichegru's suggestion is only a version of this general idea)—but rather against his proposals for bringing about the Restoration. Abandoning his original idea of using his army, directly, in a *pronunciamiento*, Pichegru commits himself to plans which are even more impracticable, and quite as much redolent of the mentality of deception and force as his earlier plans. Not for him the long-winded civilian methods of hustings and parliamentary majorities. All that he suggests is that the Austrians may supply the incentive which he now admits that he himself directly cannot supply. Let the Austrians now unleash a bold and persistent offensive from the East—against *Pichegru's own former comrades* and *his own friend and successor* in the command, Moreau. He believed, or professed to believe, that his army would give way under the pressure; the government at Paris would collapse in the consequent crisis, and he himself would be reinstated in command of a now tractable army, with Full Powers in the name of the Republic to treat with the enemy.[1] He would declare for the King, and play the part of Monck; all that the interior, and also the pure Royalists of the interior, would apparently have to do was to applaud from the auditorium. Needless to say, all this was an empty dream, based on the worthless assumptions that Austria had the will or the leisure to mount such a large-scale offensive on the French Eastern front. The subsequent development of the campaigns of 1796 was to place, not the Republic, but the Austrian Monarchy in dire straits.[2]

Pichegru's plans for the future of Royalist policy were thus by

[1] Pichegru's plans to this effect are outlined in Wickham's despatches; see the drafts published in Wickham, *Corresp.*, vol. I, pp. 368–9, 374–8.

[2] When Pichegru was sketching these plans for a sharp Austrian offensive against the Republican army of the Rhine and Moselle, which he expected, in its admittedly denuded and discontented state, to break under the pressure, his hopes had already been fatally compromised by the movement of events. Wickham commented bitterly in his despatch no. 12 (Private) of 1796, 4 May (portion not published in Wickham's *Corresp.*) that his own hopes of action against the Republic that season had been 'chiefly founded on the defence of Italy, the active and immediate *prosecution* of hostilities on this side by the Austrians, the throwing the Prince of Condé into France, and above all the gaining (not Pichegru but) Pichegru and his whole army', but that (*he subsequently deleted the following words*) 'judging from what has lately happened . . . not one of those events will probably now take place'. Wickham might well say so; and developments in the summer of 1796 abundantly justified his pessimism. Austria, plunged as she was in disaster in Italy, and compelled

no means entirely wise, or even coherent; and an even harsher judgement would have to be passed on their morality. But the central idea which they enclosed—that the Crown must come to terms with the 'royalisme de '89'—was not only correct, but, proceeding from such a quarter, also very important.[1]

We turn now to the changes in Royalist policy suggested by the King's Agents at Paris. Wickham's papers illustrate these more fully than they do the new ideas of Pichegru. They throw interesting light, especially, on the reasons which prompted the Agents to make such suggestions.

Lefebvre seems to have thought that what particularly alarmed the Agents, in the spring and summer of 1796, and brought home to them the futility of the policy which the Pretender had hitherto pursued, was the apparently large success of Carnot in his efforts to rally the moderate monarchists and the *honnêtes gens* as a whole to the support of the bourgeois Republic. The Agents, he seems to suggest, could not close their eyes to the fact that the King's most important potential supporters, so far from returning to his fold, were visibly drawing further away from it, even to the point of reconciling themselves to regicide rule. Lefebvre also suggests that the Agents were worried about the apparently growing chances of Orleanism; and he seems to think that what especially worried them about it was that (in their estimation) many of the constitutional monarchists were also being attracted in this direction. These people, the Agents considered, being allied with the government today, and contemplating a final settlement in favour of the younger branch tomorrow, were giving double evidence of their profound antipathy to the policies of the lawful King. The Agents, then, concluded that this section of opinion must be won back, at nearly any price, to the side of the King.[2] There was no time to be lost if the complete and perhaps final supersession of his claims were to be avoided; and it was better that Louis XVIII

---

to fight a simultaneous and dubious struggle on the German side of the Rhine, was never within sight of the brilliant offensive against France which Pichegru had envisaged.

[1] Pichegru's standing in the esteem of the exiled Court successfully survived both his failure to bring over the army and his repeated proffers of advice that the Pretender should agree to 'pass through' a phase of constitutional monarchy. See Wickham's letter to Drake, 21 July 1796, in Wickham, *Corresp.*, vol. I, pp. 431–2.

[2] *Directoire*, p. 56.

should return as King on the hitherto despised principles of the constitutionalists, than that he should not return at all.

The impressions given by the Agents themselves, in their correspondence with the British Minister,[1] of the motives which led them to propose the King's surrender to the claims of the constitutional monarchists are, to an important extent, different from the account which we have just presented. This will become apparent from a brief review of certain parts of that correspondence.

This correspondence, or the surviving parts of it, contains about a hundred pieces. The letters begin at the period of the sectional crisis, in the last week of September 1795, and run on to the eve of the arrest of Brottier and Duverne by the government at the end of January 1797.[2] The original subject matter of the correspondence had to do with Royalist armed action in the interior, and with the provision of British financial aid for this. The outlook of the Agents upon the political issues of France is at first exactly as we should expect. Thus at the time of the sectional crisis the Agents express only faint and rather contemptuous interest in the fortunes of the anti-Conventional movement; they reserve their enthusiasm for the pure Royalist insurgent bands. In a letter written a week after the event of Vendémiaire, Duverne observes on this event with unalloyed satisfaction. His attitude is exactly the same as that of the émigré extremists so much detested by Mallet du Pan: the anti-Conventional moderates were unwelcome competitors of the pure Royalists, in character no better than the Convention, and worthy of contempt as well as of hatred, since they are wielders of the pen, and not, like the stalwarts of insurrection, men of the sword:

La déconfiture des sections a fait tomber le parti monarchien, constitutionnel, etc.—ils ont l'oreille très basse, on se moque d'eux... les royalistes au contraire y gagnent autant. Les femmes, les prêtres, tout est content du triomphe de la Convention parce qu'on ne craint rien tant que les constitutionnels, et il faut bien se garder de croire qu'ils aient beaucoup de moyens et d'influence, d'abord ils n'en ont point dans la partie armée des royalistes, où les prêtres en ont assez pour déterminer l'opinion à être entièrement exclusive. Ils n'en ont que dans les

---

[1] Wickham Papers.

[2] There is, indeed, one further letter from Duverne to Wickham, 23 May 1797, in which the hapless Agent complains, in tones not lacking in a certain dignity, of his being abandoned by those whose interests he had tried to serve.

acquéreurs des biens nationaux et dans ceux qui ont tiré quelque profit de la révolution... mais ces gens là sont nuls en caractère et en courage... la seule force des constitutionnels est dans leurs écrits, mais nous touchons au moment où l'on ne voudra plus rien lire, et où l'on ne voudra entendre que des coups.[1]

In a memorandum[2] which he wrote for Wickham, apparently in November 1795, Duverne lengthily expressed the view that the Royalist cause in the interior lacked only one thing needful; and that one thing was nothing so realistic as a change of outlook, or even a change of method. According to Duverne, what was needed was the appointment of an effective commander in chief—preferably a Prince—to overcome the jealousies and disagreements which were rife among the partisan leaders. This memorandum does, however, contain one indirect admission of uneasiness over the current activities of the insurgent bands, and one unwilling concession to the demands of common sense: an admission that the 'bouleversements partiels' which individual partisan leaders can produce will never, of themselves, bring nearer the Restoration.

In a letter of December 1795,[3] occurs the first reference in this correspondence to the subject of the Orleanist design. Writing in the style of a despondent Republican, Duverne advises his friend in Switzerland that the Republic which they both love is once more under attack from both sides. On one side are the Royalists proper; on the other, the 'partisans de la branche Orléans'. But it is not to the monarchist moderates that Duverne attributes Orleanist intentions, it is to the Jacobins! And there are no signs that the Agents at this stage regarded Orleanism as a danger to their own proper cause; Duverne seems to regard it as an embarrassment to the Directorial Republican party, and as nothing more.

Until a point far into the year 1796, the Agents continued to write to Wickham without any sign of misgiving about the efficacy or the ultimate success of the policy of armed action which they were trying to administer. Duverne recurs to his suggestion that a princely generalissimo for the interior ought to be appointed, and expresses the hope that an Austrian offensive on the frontiers will

---

[1] Duverne to Wickham, 13 October 1795: Wickham Papers.
[2] Undated, but filed with papers dated in November 1795, and consistent with ascription to this time.
[3] Undated, but inscribed by Wickham 'Paris 16th Frimaire 1795'.

supply the needed complement to the efforts of the insurgent bands within the territory.[1] He thus admits again, by implication, that the insurgents need better military co-ordination, and even that they could not hope to drag down the Republic without Allied co-operation from other quarters. But he does not suggest that the methods of internal civil war are in themselves futile, or even that their efficacy is on the decline. On the contrary, late in the month of March and again at the beginning of April,[2] he claims that the Republic is staggering under the blows of the Royalist operations in the interior, and that the cause of Louis XVIII is in the ascendant. In his letter of 1 April, he refers again to the Orleans party, which he again associates with the Jacobins. Here he suggests that the party has little following, and distinctly asserts that it is not very dangerous.

In the later weeks of May, however, comes evidence of a very drastic change in the attitude of the Agents. Brottier admits to Wickham that the *chouans*, operating as they are without effective overall command and without supporting pressure from the frontier, cannot hope to shake the Republic, and are, on the contrary, themselves a waning force. He reluctantly confesses the progress made by Hoche in his efforts to stifle the Western Royalists. He complains that the clergy, an indispensable element in the *chouan* movements, is now flagging in its zeal for the cause. Even more important, he admits, in an indirect and glancing fashion, that underlying all these particular weaknesses is the fact that *chouan* methods have failed to gain any real purchase on public support for the Royal cause.[3]

In a letter dated 10 June, Brottier shows that the Agents had not only become very despondent about their own operations, but

[1] Duverne to Wickham, 17 February 1796 and 20 March 1796.

[2] The letter of 20 March, just referred to, and a further letter dated 1 April.

[3] The source referred to here is a very lengthy paper in Duverne's hand, headed by him *Extrait des dépêches de M.Br. en datte du 15 au 25 Mai 1796*. It is evidently the Agence's 'copy to Wickham' of communications primarily addressed to the exiled Court. The elements of despondent appraisal which it contains, and which are mentioned in the text above, are combined, inconsistent as it may seem, with proposals for the more vigorous organization and conduct of the insurgent warfare, a plan for a *coup de main* by *chouan* forces in Paris against the Government itself, and a project (which will be examined in the text at a later point) for gaining the assistance of one of the Republican commanders. It is clear that if Brottier had by this date become a sadder man, he had not in all respects become a wise one.

had meantime become anxious over the possible competition of the Orleanist movement. Brottier's impression is that the bourgeois Republic and the true Royalists may well alike find themselves brushed aside by a sudden initiative in favour of the younger branch. The Orleanist danger has quite abruptly become a very real one in the eyes of the Agents. On this occasion, however, Orleanism is not attributed to the Jacobins; such an association could not at this date be made, for the Jacobin leaders had been arrested by the government about a month earlier. Nor is Orleanism imputed to the monarchist moderates, who are indeed not mentioned. It is imputed to ambitious Thermidorian Republicans, who despair of their own work and are seeking any way out of an impasse:

Ce moment est très intéressant à observer et à suivre. Le gouvernement n'a a ni argent ni crédit. Tallien fait tout pour se soustraire à la haine et au mépris qui le poursuivent. Syes (sic), qui n'est pas moins haï, intrigue. Le fils du duc d'Orléans pouvait paraître et se mettre sur le trône, si nous lui laissions prendre la place.

In the light of these admissions and anxieties we are quite prepared for some announcement of a reappraisal of Royalist policy by the Agents. It comes dramatically enough in one of Brottier's letters near the end of May,[1] thus anticipating, by a couple of weeks, Brottier's admission that he was now perturbed about the Orleanist challenge. The proposed change does not involve the abandonment of the policy of force, as the context of the same letter shows. But it does involve something of quite fundamental importance, the tearing up of the Verona Declaration and the adoption by Louis XVIII of a constitutional-Royalist platform. This is represented as the necessary condition of an alliance with the legislative opposition in the French Councils, which Brottier claims to have arranged. Brottier seems to be at pains to suggest that such an alliance was what his principals, and, as he puts it, 'Mr Wickham especially' had long been seeking. Whatever the sense in which this was true, it certainly could not be said that Louis XVIII and his Ministers had ever wanted an alliance with constitutional Royalism on terms such as these. Brottier was proposing nothing less than the complete surrender of his party to the long despised and detested 'Royalisme de 1789'.

[1] *Extrait des dépêches de M.Br. en datte du 15 au 25 Mai 1796.* The original addressee was the Pretender or his Minister. A copy was sent to Wickham.

Nous avons enfin réussi à arriver au terme si désiré de nos commettans, et de M. Wickham surtout. Nous avons à nous un chef de faction, qui dispose de plus de 150 membres dans le Conseil des Cinq-Cents et de la majorité de celui des Anciens; qui par ses moyens et son influence peut acquérir une majorité transcendante dans tous les points, et nous livrer une des armées. Ce chef de parti, qui se donne à nous, et qui traîne à sa suite une armée entière, dont le chef lui est dévoué, est ce qu'on appelle constitutionnel de 1791, Monarchien, Bicamériste en un mot. Il demande, il veut, les deux chambres: et il ne se livre qu'à cette condition, qu'il ne sera point contrarié dans cette vue.

Nous avons tout promis au nom du Roi et de M. Wickham, parce que nous convenons qu'il faut exister avant de raisonner sur les formes. Que le Roi ne repousse pas les idées de notre chef de parti! Jamais il ne trouvera une plus belle occasion de s'en faire un puissant dans l'interieur; et jamais il ne pourra y reparoître sans cet heureux concord. Enfin, nous croyons qu'il faut tout sacrifier pour obtenir son prompt rétablissement sur le trône.

We must observe, firstly, that it is perfectly clear that the Agents had become convinced that the King must win over a far larger body of support in the interior if he wished ever to reign in France, and that violent wooing of his subjects would never of itself bring him this wider support; it could be won only by far-reaching concessions on the ground of principle. Secondly, it seems implicit in all that Brottier writes, that the King has not unlimited time in which to reach this understanding with the interior. There is danger that some other system will consolidate itself and consign the legitimate cause to outer darkness. The bourgeois Republic is not the King's most serious rival, for it is itself in precarious fortunes; it is the prospect of an Orleans monarchy which seems to provide the cause of their anxiety. But, thirdly, though Brottier obviously implies that the moderate monarchists of the interior might rally to this compromise, and thereby ensure its success, he does not assert, or even suggest, that the leaders of the legislative opposition are themselves promoting, or, more passively, as yet accepting, this alternative. On the contrary, the movement in favour of Orleans is attributed only to such desperate moderate Republicans as Tallien and Sieyes; the legislative opposition leader who claims to speak for practically all— or more than all!—the opposition is anxious to give himself, and his party, to the true King, if only the true King will now accept a constitutional monarchy. If we had no evidence beyond these letters of Brottier, we should be inclined to risk the inference that Brottier understood the opposition to be just as anxious to avoid a sudden *fait accompli* in favour of Orleans, as he was himself.

The risk is practically removed, however, by reference to expressions used by Wickham in his private despatches to Lord Grenville. Wickham at several points in the middle and later months of 1796 apprised his principal of advances by members of the legislative opposition to the legitimate King. He also informed Grenville of the movement which he, like so many other contemporaries, believed to be occurring in favour of the Duc d'Orléans. But, like the Agents at the point now under consideration, he does not attribute Orleanist gestures to the legislative opposition, but only to the Directorials, and he too implies, more directly than Brottier, that the legislators whom he reports as making approaches to the true King are as anxious as the pure Royalists to avert an Orleanist solution. The following passage especially, from his drafts to Lord Grenville (16 July 1796), seems pertinent:

It is notorious that the whole Directory is disposed to the party of the Duke d'Orleans, and that they will be supported by Tallien, Sieyes and all those who have voted the King's death. It is nothing but the persuasion of this truth that has induced so many persons of late to turn their thoughts towards the lawful sovereign.[1]

In this passage, it seems natural to interpret 'so many persons' as referring, at least among others, to the legislators whose approaches to the Pretender he several times mentions in despatches of this period.

There are other points in Brottier's proposed reappraisal which also call for observation. We notice that his projected alliance with the constitutional Royalists does not, at this stage, involve any adoption of electoral methods. It is a curious attempt, as curious as Pichegru's, to link together constitutional principles and military methods. In both cases, the plan includes the use of a Republican army, led by a general devoted to constitutional Royalist principles. In this form, Brottier's plan was destined to be as barren of results as Pichegru's; but the ideas of the Agents were to undergo further development, and in the later months of 1796

---

[1] Wickham to Grenville, Private no. 34 of 1796: Wickham Papers, 16 July.

H

they gave some attention to the prospects offered by the elections of year V.

Meantime, we must clarify, as well as we are able, the picture which has now emerged, as yet only in the vaguest outlines, of Brottier's plan in its original form. Who was the master-politician who had promised, on his own terms, such powerful aid to the King? Who was the General prepared to place his army at this politician's disposal? There is clear evidence that the reputed master-politician was Gaspard-Roland Lemerer, deputy (Cinq-Cents) for the Ille et Vilaine, one of the new *tiers* of year IV, and destined to be one of the victims of Fructidor.[1] It is also clear that Lemerer did not, in fact, enjoy the unquestionable leadership, even inside his own immediate group, and still less over hundreds of his colleagues, which Brottier seems to attribute to him. It is no doubt true that he took, if not the sole, at least the chief part in this business with the Agents. The confessions later made to the Directory by Duverne indicate that only one other person, from the side of the legislature, was associated with Lemerer in the negotiations; this was Denis-François Mersan, deputy elected in year IV by the Loiret, but deprived of his seat at the verification of the powers in the early days of 1796.[2] But Lemerer, though he appeared to the Agents to be the leader of a party, and perhaps boasting of being such, was in fact acting as one of a small informal committee of deputies, which was at this same time negotiating also with D'André. In this latter negotiation, Lemerer did not occupy any specially leading position.[3]

---

[1] In a letter to Wickham, 24 October 1796, Brottier identifies the party which he had won over as 'la faction Lemerer.' Wickham to Grenville, Private no. 30 of 1796, 10 July (in Wickham Papers), informs the Foreign Secretary that 'the leading person among the Abbé Brottier's friends is Lemerer.' On Lemerer, see the detail given in A. Kuscinski, *Les Députés au Corps Législatif... de l'an IV à l'an VII* (Paris, 1905), p. 375.

[2] On Mersan, see the detail in Kuscinski, op. cit., p. 379.

[3] Even though he was not a 'chef de parti' in the sense attributed to him by Brottier, it appears to be the case that Lemerer enjoyed a reputation for ability, forcefulness and daring in the politics of opposition. Mallet du Pan describes him as 'Lemerer de Rennes, homme d'un talent distingué' (Mallet to the Imperial Court, 3 April: Michel, op. cit., tome II, p. 43). Bailleul, in his report (from the point of view of the Directors and their party) on the events leading up to the *coup d'état*, looks back on Lemerer in interesting terms: 'Ce Lemerer avait tout juste la figure de Robespierre. Des royalistes disaient que parmi tous ces coquins, il n'y en avait qu'un qui allât droit au but, c'était

It is equally clear that the General of whom Brottier spoke was Moreau, the friend and successor of Pichegru, and like him already reputed in some quarters to be a constitutionalist.[1]

Did Lemerer really claim to be able to dispose of Moreau and his army, and if so had he any right to such a claim? We cannot answer these questions with any confidence. Nor do we know how the Agents supposed that the two elements in their new design, the legislative opposition in the existing Councils and Moreau's army, were to work together with the militant pure Royalists of the interior to bring about the Restoration. The natural inference from Brottier's words is that the armed Royalists, reorganized, as he still proposed, under an effective high command, and now enjoying the moral support of moderate public opinion, would converge to attempt a *coup* at Paris; Moreau would make a *pronunciamiento* from the frontier, with preparations to interfere directly if needed; there would then be a sort of fructidor in reverse, and the existing Councils, purged of their Republican members, would be left to lend legislative form to arrangements for the return of the King on constitutional terms.[2]

In making these proposals, the Agents were entering upon a long period of anxiety and disappointment. It was not only that nothing ever came of the hopes which they built upon Moreau and his army. In addition, they incurred insuperable difficulties in their attempts to persuade their King to accept the basic condition of their proposed alliance with Lemerer and his party; and having long and vainly pursued this indispensable Royal consent, they had the further mortification of finding that Lemerer and his party had far less influence, even inside the Councils, than they had

---

Lemerer, et que Dumolard n'était auprès de lui qu'un bavard peureux' (Buchez & Roux, op. cit., tome 37, p. 419, note).

[1] Brottier to Wickham, 24 October 1796. 'Les revers de Moreau n'empêchent pas qu'on ne doive mettre du prix à ce Général.... Nous avons plus d'accès auprès de lui, parce qu'il est très-lié avec le chef de notre faction', Wickham Papers. (The immediate reference here is to the failure of the invasion of Germany undertaken by Moreau and Jourdan. At this date, Moreau was just completing his (successful) retreat back to Alsace.) 'Le général Moreau, successeur de Pichegru... n'est nullement républicain: il tient au système de la monarchie limitée,' Mallet du Pan to the Imperial Court, 10 April 1796, in Michel, op. cit., tome II, p. 52.

[2] These inferences are collected from the *Extraits des dépêches de M. Br.* (15 au 25 Mai, 1796) in Wickham Papers.

originally claimed. So, at least, Duverne afterwards alleged to his Directorial captors.[1]

The legislators in question seem to have been equally disappointed in the Agence de Paris. The Agents' disenchantment with them resulted in part, at least, from their adoption of deliberate reserve in dealing with the Agents. D'André was, independently of the Agents, in touch with a group of opposition deputies more or less identical with those whom Wickham calls 'the friends of Mr Brottier'.[2] About the time when Brottier and Duverne were arrested, D'André had an interview, in Switzerland, with a personal emissary of Louis XVIII on the subject of his connections with members of the legislative body of Paris. He told this emissary that the legislators in question had become completely disgusted with the Agence:

As to the agents at Paris, his friends there had so poor an opinion of their talents, their means and above all of their discretion, that they were ashamed of the connection . . . and that for the good of the cause they had avoided introducing them to any more members of the two councils. . . .[3]

In taking up a discussion of the proposals of the Agence for a change in Royalist policy towards the interior, we thus seem to have embarked on a poor and futile contribution, which made, and deserved to make little impression on the world. But, admitting all that in this respect has to be admitted, it remains true that the Agents, like Pichegru, had made a real contribution to their cause, if only by urging upon the Pretender the need to make radical concessions to the opinion of the interior. Even though the Pretender would not accept their advice to adopt a constitutionalist basis, this advice nevertheless became one of the factors which induced him at length to make certain real changes in his policy.[4] And this was not all that the Agents contributed towards

[1] Duverne told his judges that 'le parti étant beaucoup plus faible qu'il ne s'était annoncé, a relâché de ses prétensions' (he added, it is true, 'sans pourtant y renoncer entièrement'), Buchez & Roux, op. cit., tome 37, p. 443.

[2] Wickham to the Duc de la Vauguyon, 16 January 1797 (Wickham Papers, bundle 94): 'Le Comité de M. d'André est le même qui s'etoit addressé à M. Brottier . . .' Cf. Wickham to Grenville, no. 102 of 1796, 11 December, in Wickham, Corresp., vol. I, pp. 485–6.

[3] Wickham to Grenville, no. 12 of 1797, 24 May, in Wickham Papers.

[4] Such a change of front, on the part of men who had of course figured as pure Royalists de choix, could not but have made a deep impression on the

the 'great design', though it is all that has been included in the present chapter. Waiting in vain for Moreau, and becoming disappointed even in their legislative allies, the Agents, in the later months of 1796, were driven by the mere circumstances in which they found themselves to grasp the point that the best way of advancing the Pretender's cause was to unite with all who opposed the government to secure an anti-Directorial majority in the councils at the elections of year V.[1]

Further still, the Paris Agence provided a centre from which another Royalist agent, Des Pomelles, began in the later months of 1796 to develop a new resource, of great potential value in any design for capturing the Republic by electoral methods. This was, of course, the famous *Institut philanthropique*, a secret organization

---

exiled Court, even though the Court remained adverse to the particular line of policy which the Agents had now recommended. The impression was all the more profound, as the Agents insisted that if their advice were not accepted they would throw up their appointments. (Note the remarks of Wickham upon their attitude in his no. 70 of 1796, 16 July: Wickham, *Corresp.*, vol. I, p. 416.)

[1] The Agents' communications to Wickham in the later months of 1796 show that, without abandoning their reliance on methods of a military nature, they were giving an increasing share of their attention to the prospects of progress by political methods first; they finally reach a point at which they distinctly envisage the defeat of the Directorials at the elections of year V as a necessary prerequisite for the realization of their plans. It seems likely that three considerations progressively affected their ideas during these months. First, that their allies in the legislative body were much less powerful there than the Agents had first believed, and themselves gave the Agents to understand that final victory could not be anticipated before the elections had reversed, as it might be hoped, the Directorial majority in the Councils. Second, that they were losing hope of an early and decisive *chouan coup* at Paris which their allies in the legislature were (they had supposed) to validate after the event. Wickham was now advising his Government to refuse further funds for *chouan* movements, in which he had lost all confidence. Third, their hopes of gaining Moreau, though not given up, were receding into the future. On both the second and third counts, the Agents may well have felt that they could only gain, in the interval until force became available, by activities promising to strengthen the hands of the reaction by nonviolent means.

It is a further point of importance in their correspondence with Wickham at this time, that while the Agents waited in vain for the King's consent to their plans, for the chance to attempt the *chouan coup*, and for Moreau to commit himself, their anxiety on the score of the Orleanist menace was steadily increasing.

of propaganda and enlistment on lines roughly similar to those later adopted by the Carbonari. To enlist opponents of the government and to mobilize them for election purposes was one of its main objectives.[1]

It must be said, then, in justice to the Paris Agents, that in the closing months of their activity they considerably improved upon their first crude idea of coupling the adoption of a constitutionalist platform with an early appeal to *chouan* companies and to Moreau's army. Their plans to mount an election campaign against the Directorials, and the project of the *Institut* for which they provided a base, were to bear important fruit, and to carry the 'great design' many stages further, in the spring of 1797. But by that time, Brottier and Duverne were to be languishing in a Republican prison, and D'André had entered into the direction of the plans on which they had resolutely but fumblingly embarked.

[1] There is a considerable literature in France on the subject of the *Institut philanthropique*. Without giving detailed references here, we may refer to the brief sketch of its origins and methods offered by Meynier in *le 18 fructidor*, pp. 186–8. It seems clear that it was Des Pomelles who planned it and submitted his ideas on the subject to the British Government (August 1796) with a view to obtaining financial support for it. The Paris Agents do not seem to have played any part in its inception, and although Des Pomelles proceeded with his plans under their general direction, at a time when they were evidently becoming more interested in the possibilities of the elections, they seem to have lacked the will, the time, or the authority to take any great part in prosecuting this design. It is notable that their communications to Wickham between August 1796 and their arrest in January 1797 contain no reference (or, at least—having regard to the cryptic style and occasional illegibility of these pieces—no discernible reference) to the *Institut*.

IV

A new Royalist Policy?

THE ATTITUDES OF THE FRENCH PRETENDER AND THE
BRITISH ENVOY

WE have seen that from the middle months of 1796 the exiled French Court was being pressed, both by opposition deputies at Paris and by some of its own close adherents, to change the basis, or the methods (or both) of its approach to the problem of the recovery of the Kingdom; to form new connections, and to collaborate with, instead of ignoring or defying, the wishes of the interior. We have discussed the form which some of these proposals took, at least in their original lines. Before proceeding further into the subject matter of this study, it will be well to observe rather more closely the reactions of the Pretender and his circle to these suggestions, and to describe, what we have not yet even glanced at, the attitude adopted by the British Minister, whose views were likely to be so influential in the development of the legitimist movement. Wickham's papers offer us copious and interesting details on both these topics.

We have already seen the line of advice offered by Pichegru after his final departure from his military command. The General's intimation that the King would have to resign himself to some kind of bargain with politicians who still professed to stand by the earlier ideals of the Revolution came as the first of a series of painful shocks to the Pretender and his circle. In a despatch home, Wickham described what passed in his presence at a Royal council held at Riegel early in May, when Louis XVIII, with Condé, La Vauguyon, d'Avaray and Jaucourt considered the latest news and advice from the disloyal Republican officer upon whom they had built hopes so high:

The opinion of Baptiste as to the necessity of the King's passing through the hands of *some* at least of the persons now in power and place had given them more pain even than the certainty of his being unable to assist them with his army. . . . I submitted to them, however, that it would be wise to say in general terms to Baptiste that he might assure his friends at Paris that the King's views were entirely moderate and conciliatory, and that he was ready at all times to make such personal sacrifices as should be found consistent with the real good of his people. Less objection was taken to this proposal than I had expected, the word *real* being considered by all the persons present as leaving them at full liberty to put their own constructions hereafter on whatever might be proposed as *really* advantageous to the people.[1]

Here, at the very outset of our present discussions, we have a fair indication of the line generally adopted, by the Pretender's entourage on the one side, and by Wickham on the other, to any suggestions that the Court should resign itself to compromise on the issue of principle. The Court's own immediate reaction is always one of *non possumus*; the British Minister (as we might expect) is anxious to refuse no offers from any quarter which will join in attacking the conquering Republic. Wickham had never had any love for the constitutional Royalists or for their principles; even at this stage he does not press the Pretender simply to accept Pichegru's suggestion; but he willingly takes up a line of ambiguous phrases and is prepared to treat the final issue of principle with a gesture of postponing opportunism. To close no door, to leave final questions for settlement in the future, to consider any method of making head against the Republic—these are the characteristic reactions of the British envoy. And he is ready to clothe these general ideas in voluminous language of a mild, comprehensive and mystifyingly vague character, intended to soothe and in a sense to hoodwink both the French Court and the French interior.

Wickham felt by no means sure that his counsel had really satisfied the Pretender and his entourage on this occasion; and about a fortnight later he drafted a very carefully worded letter on this subject to the Comte d'Avaray, whom he regarded, not without justification, as possessing far more personal influence over Louis than his nominal Minister La Vauguyon.[2] Wickham considered that d'Avaray, though 'honourable and amiable', was by no means as wise as he was influential. But he also believed that d'Avaray might be led in the right direction ('capable of re-

---

[1] Wickham to Grenville, no. 52 of 1796, 14 May, in Wickham, *Corresp.*, vol. I; the passage cited falls in pp. 362–3. 'Baptiste' is the well-known code name of Pichegru in his dealings with the Royalists and the British.

[2] Ibid, p. 364.

ceiving the best impressions') and in that hope he treated the Count
to a drench of skilful, if deafening, verbiage, in which warm
flattery both of d'Avaray and of the Pretender is joined with
delicate pleas to admit that sensible men cannot always refuse the
second best:

Let me earnestly intreat of you, My dear Sir, as you value your Master,
your country, and your unhappy countrymen . . . that you will let pass
no opportunity of cultivating those humane and moderate sentiments,
by which the natural character of H.M. seems to be particularly distinguished. It is in your power, my dear Sir, to do much for your own
Country, much perhaps also for the rest of Europe. The King will have
need to be supported on many occasions by the mild and temperate
Councils (*sic*) of a *real friend*, who will advise him not to be apprehensive of following the dictates of his own excellent Judgement. As long
as he takes *that* for his real guide, and does not suffer himself to be misled by the ill-timed fears and apprehensions of a class of persons whose
understanding is infinitely beneath his own, I am sure that everything
will be done for the best.

I am induced to speak to you thus earnestly, because, among other
events of Importance, it is more than possible that the ideas holden out
by Baptiste may soon be realised. Should that be the case, let me con-
jure you most earnestly to reflect, before any sudden resolution be
taken, of what infinite consequence it might prove, that an opportunity of that kind once offered, *though not precisely of the nature that
could have been wished*, should not be suffered to slip by.[1]

It seems that Wickham's letter to the Royal favourite made no
more profound impression on the views of the exiled Court than
his suggestions at the Royal Council. The Court remained still
quite unprepared, either to bury a difference of principle in
ambiguous phrases, or, even more so, to resign itself to a second
best. This was strikingly shown when, not long after the unpalatable advice of Pichegru, the circle of the Pretender received a yet
more unwelcome suggestion from the Agents. The General had
proposed acceptance of a constitutional settlement 'at least for a
time'; the Agents advocated unconditional surrender to the
'Royalisme de 1789'. The *non possumus* of the exiled Court rang
out again, with a resolution which surprised Wickham completely;
the envoy had been so much convinced that the Court must give
way—had given way—to the dictates of events and the wisdom of

[1] Wickham to D'Avaray, dated 30 May 1796, in Wickham, *Corresp.*, vol. I,
pp. 370-2.

his own appraisal that he had quite misjudged its real state of mind.[1]

In mid-July, Wickham retailed to Lord Grenville in these vigorous terms the reaction of the Pretender and his entourage to the Agents' suggestion of an alliance with Lemerer and his friends:

> ... the propositions sent to the King by the Abbé Brottier from Paris have been declared wholly inadmissible; and ... it has been laid down as a fundamental principle, that the Declaration of Verona cannot be departed from in any respect.
>
> It was a leading point of the Abbé's propositions that the Monarchy should be Limited in some shape or other ... This is the article that is considered as vitiating the whole.[2]
>
> I have procured for your Lordship's perusal a copy of the King's answer sent to his agent at Paris, as well as of Mr de la Vauguyon's instructions that accompanyd it. It is there peremptorily laid down that the Propositions sent from Paris are *inadmissible*, and the agent is referred to his original instructions, and censured for having departed from them. The leading feature of those instructions here alluded to is this,
>
>> that the King is disposed to make any reasonable sacrifice, that can be grafted on what is called the *antient constitution*, but that nothing should be accepted or *listened to* that might tend to establish a permanent representation.
>
> —that is, that the King will listen to no terms of accommodation whatever with his people, that shall not have the *principles* of the antient Government for their Basis.
>
> Mr Duvergne was so penetrated with the danger of sending such an answer to Paris at this moment, that he wrote a very strong ... remonstrance to the King and to the Duke de la Vauguyon ...
>
> At the very moment that it was about to be sent off, the Duke himself arrived, and Mr Duvergne immediately repeated to him the whole of what he had written, but was not able to make any impression whatever.[3]

[1] Wickham's surprise at the attitude taken by the Court on this occasion is considered more fully later in this chapter.

[2] Wickham to Grenville, no. 70 of 1796, 16 July, in Wickham, *Corresp.*, vol. I, pp. 416–17.

[3] Wickham to Grenville, no. 71 of 1796, 18 July, in Wickham, *Corresp.*, vol. I; the passages quoted fall in pp. 423–4. Duverne de Praële was at this time at Berne visiting Wickham.

Wickham added his own remonstrations to those of Duverne. It cannot be said that he had no success at all. He obtained from La Vauguyon what seemed to him at the time to be a possibly important concession. The Paris Agents should be permitted not to *reveal* the outright Royal refusal to the deputy with whom they had been in touch (Lemerer) and also to tell the deputy 'that the King would be glad to discuss the matter . . . with any person that they should think proper to send to him . . .' Wickham hoped that the outcome of such a discussion would be an agreement between the King and the opposition deputies, including, if not the Pretender's acceptance of a constitutionalist basis, then at least an ambiguous formula leaving each side to hope that in the end it would be able to secure the triumph of its own principles. Agreement at nearly any price was the envoy's object, and to this end the great point was to keep the parties in touch: 'by this measure', commented Wickham on his proposal for a direct discussion, 'time at least will be gained, no unfavourable impression will be given . . . and the correspondence will be kept open'.

If Wickham clutched at this concession hoping that it would result, sooner or later, in something positive, the Royalist Prime Minister granted the concession equally resolved that it should result in nothing at all. The Duke, Wickham declared, told him

distinctly . . . that the King's mind was entirely made up upon the subject; that he would do nothing that might have, in the smallest degree, the appearance of encouraging or even listening to a proposal of the kind; and that should the matter ever come to a point, he would rather relinquish his Crown than accept of any conditions that were not grafted on the basis of the antient Government.[1]

Hard upon these discussions came another message to the exiled Court from Pichegru. In it, the General repeated very earnestly the advice he had given in the spring. Wickham rejoiced that Pichegru had returned to the attack so opportunely for the Agents; soon he believed that under the united pressure of Pichegru, the Agents, and himself, La Vauguyon was inclining to a more conciliatory attitude, and that a compact with the opposition deputies, if not on their terms, at least in terms of amiable *double entendre*, might indeed be arranged. Wickham was not unwilling to accept, or to press the Royalist Minister to

[1] Wickham's no. 71 of 18 July: Wickham, *Corresp.*, vol. I, p. 424.

accept, Pichegru's reiterated argument that the King must acquiesce, not at all necessarily in a *final*, but rather in a *temporary* surrender to the ideals of '1789'. The envoy clearly thought that Pichegru's prognostication of a constitutional Restoration, followed by a progressive slide into virtual, if not formal, prerogative government offered both a credible, and also a very suitable outcome. He would, perhaps, have been delighted to see the exiled Court pin its faith to that prognostication, even though he himself had had no regard for it and no confidence in it; his great object at the moment was to bring to the Pretender's side the additional support in the interior which the deputies claimed to represent.

Baptiste [reported the envoy to his principal] has sent a message again to the King, to desire he would not be discouraged, notwithstanding the defeat of the Austrians. He says that this unfortunate circumstance will only occasion a delay, but that he (= *Louis XVIII*) will certainly succeed *at last* provided he will consent to *enter* France under some form of constitutional government.[1]

Pichegru, added Wickham in another despatch of the same time, was counselling the King to 'take some pains' in the interval 'to gain the leaders of the different factions' by giving them solemn assurances 'that he was ready to make every sacrifice that would not carry with it the establishment of a weak and turbulent government'. The King might feel certain that in this case 'as soon as he had the reins of government in his hand . . . the torrent would become irresistible, and the Royal Prerogative would have no bounds but in his own wisdom and moderation'.[2]

The envoy declared himself 'happy to say that his (*Pichegru's*) advice and opinion had had a strong effect on the Duke de la Vauguyon' and that he himself had 'passed these last three days with that Minister very much to my own satisfaction, and, I hope, to the service of the common cause'.[3] But Wickham's incipient satisfaction was premature. For months to come, the Pretender declined to take any step significantly closer to the lines recommended by his various importuners.

[1] Wickham to Grenville, no. 76 of 1796, 21 July, in Wickham, *Corresp.*, vol. I; the quoted passage falls at p. 430.
[2] Wickham to Grenville, 23 July 1796, in Wickham, *Corresp.*, vol. I, pp. 434–5.
[3] Wickham's no. 76 of 21 July: Wickham, *Corresp.*, vol. I, p. 430.

The letter in which the Pretender had already informed Brottier that the propositions made by Lemerer and his group were 'wholly inadmissible' [1] calls for careful study here. It expresses the attitude from which the claimant refused to recede, in terms which are impressive, not only in their firmness, but also for their subtlety. It unmistakably rejects the propositions of the deputies. But it does so in a manner which, in one sense at least, deserves to be called masterly. It bears, indeed, a delusive resemblance to the message which Wickham persuaded La Vauguyon to agree to, while really saying something quite different.

The Pretender had placed his own construction on the thought which others besides Pichegru had conveyed to him: that a constitutional Restoration might be used not as a platform but as a slope towards a progressive recovery of the lost prerogatives. He argued, it would seem, that if the moderates of the interior were indeed willing, at bottom, to recede much further from the principles of the Revolution, and maintained them only provisionally and from motives of precaution against the danger of reprisals and excessive reaction—then it would be well, for the Crown and the nation too, to eliminate in advance all prospect of having to pass through so clumsy and hazardous a political comedy as a temporary compromise with Revolution. His true policy, he thought, must be to convince the moderates of the interior that such a comedy was quite superfluous. He must persuade them that there were no good grounds for fearing a Restoration such as he had always planned it; far from converting him (provisionally) to constitutional monarchism, they merely required gracious and solemn personal explanations from their Prince to turn them into immediate and true adherents of his own cause. There need be no purgatory to turn the sons of Belial back into children of light; still less need the King go to purgatory himself. Now when he received the proposals of Lemerer and his friends, the Pretender assumed, without apparent question, that these people must be representatives of this supposedly large section of opinion which sought constitutional monarchy as a first move back to better things; and he proceeded to deal with them accordingly.

Hence we find that the Pretender's reply to the deputies

[1] Wickham Papers, bundle 105, paper headed 'Copie de la lettre du Roi à M. Brottier'. The letter is dated: Dillingen, le 11 juillet.

(through Brottier), though a very positive refusal *of what they had suggested*, is by no means a refusal *of them as persons*. On the contrary; it offers the deputies a personal contact with the King, and for purposes of discussion. The peculiarly admirable feature of the letter is, however, that it offers a discussion of something really quite different from what the deputies had proposed, and offers it in terms of warm paternal welcome such as any Pope might be delighted to authorize for the perusal of his lost children of the Protestant world.

Je suis touché jusqu'au fond de l'âme [writes Louis to his Agent] des sentimens que me témoigne celui dont vous êtes l'interprete, beaucoup moins parce qu'il m'offre l'espoir prochain d'occuper mon trône, que parce que la seule consolation que mon cœur puisse gouter est de voir mes enfans revenir dans mes bras paternels. Tous les Français le sont... [Nevertheless, he continues] le moyen qu'on me propose me paraît entièrement inadmissible. L'auteur de la proposition le regarde lui-même comme vicieuse, et le rejetterait, s'il ne croyait que c'est un échelon necessaire pour parvenir au but auquel il tend aussi bien que moi. La juste estime qu'il m'a inspirée... me fait ardemment desirer de le ramener au meme sentiment que moi... je desire donc et je regarde comme indispensable qu'il m'envoye quelqu'un qui soit digne de toute sa confiance, afin d'avoir avec lui la discussion la plus importante peut-être qui fut jamais.

Only in the light of this text and of the preceding comments can we fully grasp how far the Pretender, in July 1796, still stood from all those who were urging him to adopt some change of policy, and how stubborn yet also subtle was the reception which he gave to those who urged one upon him. So far from preparing to contemplate what the Agents suggested, he will not make even the purely transitional agreement with the 'Royalisme de 1789' which Pichegru was urging; even the vaguer gestures, so much recurred to by Wickham, involving discussion without binding commitments, find no favour with him. He will admit no Royalists but pure Royalists. Yet it would be inadequate, even misleading, to say that his attitude is 'unconciliatory'.

From this time onwards till near the end of the year, the Pretender on his side, the Agents and the Lemerer group from theirs, were engaged in a double series of futile appeals. Louis, so Duverne later told his Republican judges, from that moment onwards 'persisted in asking' that the deputies should send to him 'un fondé de pouvoir'.[1] This plenipotentiary was, however, not sent; and the Agents sooner or later abandoned any attempt to secure that he should be sent. Why this failure? Duverne explained that Lemerer and his friends proved to have far less weight in French politics than they had first claimed, and that their enthusiasm for the Restoration declined in proportion. But he himself admits that they never entirely abandoned the line they had taken, and he adds a further explanation which is perhaps more pertinent. The Agents, he says, realized that if the King were indeed to be restored with the aid of the French Councils, these would inevitably be in a position to impose their own conditions on the King; so they 'did not insist' upon the despatch of an emissary from Lemerer and his friends.[2] An interesting and perhaps important admission, carrying the implication that the Agents did not believe, as the King did, that the moderate monarchists of the Councils were, actually or potentially, pure Royalists at bottom. The Agents, it would seem, thought rather that, even if the King were able to talk Lemerer and his friends into accepting plans for Restoration immediately on a pure Royalist basis, they would still by no means carry the mass of the moderate Royalists. They believed, in short, that the King was cherishing a fatal illusion in persistently offering to discuss with the deputies something which there was no point in discussing.

That we are correct in drawing these inferences is to some extent confirmed by the certain fact that the Agents for long continued to press the King, through Wickham, to accept the alliance of Lemerer and his group *on their own original terms*. They would not be deterred by the Royal *fin de non recevoir*—not, at least, if they could hope to add the persuasions of the British Minister to their own. A letter of Brottier to Wickham, dated in late October, gives eloquent expression to their conduct on this point:

Les sentiments de... la faction Lemerer... sont bons, sont excellens, mais exigent qu'on pactise avec les nouveaux principes. Nous allons envoyer auprès du Roi un ami intime de La Vauguyon... qui se flatte de faire gouter nos idées. Je désire que celui-ci (*La Vauguyon*) goute les raisons de ce nouvel envoyé, et se départe de la rigüeur de ses principes. Qu'il y pense bien! nous pouvons encore rallier au Roi une faction

---

[1] 'Le roi... demanda... qu'il lui fût envoyé un fondé de pouvoir; depuis lors il n'a cessé de le demander...' (Buchez & Roux, op. cit., tome 37, p. 443).
[2] Ibid.

puissante. Nous la manquerons, au contraire, si nous nous montrent trop exigeants.[1]

We need not seek far for reasons to explain why the Agents should have remained determined, in the teeth of their King's and his Minister's disapproval, to stand by their new-fangled policy of alliance with constitutional monarchists on constitutional terms. They were convinced, not only that this alliance could not be gained for the King on any other terms, but also that the menace of a non-legitimist monarchical solution was looming ever closer, and that the King had, to say no more, simply no time to waste in arguments with those who were prepared, even if only on hard conditions, to support his claims.

The Pretender, however, had said his last word on these particular proposals. At no stage of his struggle against the Revolution did he consent to compromise on the 'true principles' of the Monarchy. Only in an indirect sense did these suggestions of Pichegru and of his Paris Agents finally influence his policy; and when they did so, the concessions which he actually made were very different from those which they had urged upon him. There was no further reference to principles, and the Pretender still hoped to bring his own principles to final victory. What he accepted was a policy of concession, not on principles, but on methods. He agreed to authorize his party to join an *ad hoc* coalition to attack the Directory by electoral and parliamentary means. This represented a success, *so far as it went*, for Wickham rather than for either Pichegru or the Paris Agents. Wickham would have been very much gratified if the exiled Court had accepted the suggestions made from those quarters, and was, as has been seen, by no means pleased when it took up a line of firm refusal. But Wickham had not *insisted*, as a matter of necessity, on their unconditional *acceptance*; his great object was to *avert* their unconditional *refusal*: to gain in some way, and preferably by the very vaguest of undertakings, the alliance of the moderate monarchists. The ambiguous and opportunistic policy of a 'coalition of parties', united only in negative objects, and postponing the shaping of the final settlement till after the defeat of the immediate enemy—this was at least as accordant with the outlook and temper of the British Minister as the proposals of

[1] Letter to Wickham, 24 October 1796, in Wickham Papers.

PLATE II

The Right Honourable William Wickham

Pichegru and of the Agents, and may indeed be said to bear his characteristic stamp.

It is time that we should turn our attention more directly to the part played by Wickham at the period of these first suggestions for change in Royalist policy. Incidentally, something has already been said about Wickham's attitude, in previous pages of this chapter. But there is more than has yet been seen, and its exposition will help considerably in setting the stage for the activities of D'André, in which Wickham was more intimately involved than in these affairs, and in which he was governed by the same motives.

As emerges from previous parts of our study,[1] Wickham had embarked on the difficult seas of French politics very sympathetic to the hopes of the princes, and with nothing but adverse feelings to the constitutional Royalists and their principles. He believed, like his chief in London, that the return of Louis-Stanislas-Xavier on the basis of his own principles offered by far the best prospects of a settlement satisfactory to the interests of England, of the French nation itself, and of the whole of Europe. Nevertheless, as has also been seen, Wickham from the beginning of his mission interpreted the practical implications of pure Royalist policy rather differently from the exiled Court, and in particular he (again like his principal in London) considered that the princes should be prepared, not only to welcome to their own party, with genuine magnanimity, men who were now anxious wholly to break with the Revolution, but also to work for immediate ends with men who had still not entirely renounced the Revolution. The reluctance of the Pretender and his followers to admit, or at least to act upon, the British interpretation of what pure Royalist interests required had, by the end of 1795, produced in Wickham's mind a growing distaste and uneasiness.

During the struggle between the Convention and the sections, Wickham meantime developed further convictions as to what the French problem called for. He came to see that the Pretender not only should, but must 'conciliate the different parties' in the country 'by some more . . . direct means' than the 'rigour' of his existing policy permitted. Not only must there be a 'coalition' of all those elements of public opinion which agreed in opposing the existing ruling party, whatever their disagreements as to further

[1] Chs. I and II.　　　　[2] Ch. I above.

I

objectives, but the Pretender must be prepared to facilitate this (Wickham seems to have meant) by some large concessions, not excluding concessions on matters of 'principles'. In proposing such developments, Wickham was not receding from his preference for a pure, as opposed to a constitutional Royalist solution. He was not even confessing that a pure solution must be regarded as unattainable and an inferior system accepted as second best. He was still concentrated on the question of method, rather than on that of final aims. He had formed the impression, rather, that the *current* dispositions of the bulk of French opinion did not permit an *immediate* persistence in the line of pure Royalist policy. If the King would show some willingness now, however, to meet the anti-Conventionals of the interior half way, and thus secure that they would acknowledge (in some sense) his claims, there was a great possibility that once the Convention was overthrown and a Restoration (in some sense) effected, the King would be able to reap rich rewards for his calculated generosity. With trust and popularity behind him, he would be able to advance rapidly to a more thoroughgoing reconstruction of Royal power.[1]

On this appraisal of the needs of the time, it is quite understandable that Wickham should have regarded with much indifference the question, what concessions exactly the King should offer. His own mind, as his correspondence makes clear, readily expressed itself in large and vague verbal generalizations about these matters. It was, for him, a matter of creating a *temper* of rapprochement rather than of working out a detailed and lasting treaty between the King and the nation.

In noting these points, we are, again, only recapitulating and commenting upon developments which have already been dealt with. But, of course, so far as concerned the fortunes of the sectional movement, in the midst of which he offered this advice, Wickham offered it in vain. What, then, was Wickham's attitude during the period of roughly six months which followed Vendémiaire?

There is evidence that Wickham continued to give attention to possibilities of bringing about a *rapprochement*, on whatever terms, between the Pretender and the moderate pro-monarchists of the interior. He did not rely only upon the method of general

[1] Cf. ch. II, above.

exhortation, but tried himself to create opportunities for such an approximation. It seems probable that the Paris Agents, in persevering with the negotiations with the opposition deputies even at the cost of bringing their master's principles into debate, were fortified by the expressed wishes, even by the promptings, of Wickham. Again, in the New Year season, as will be made out more fully below,[1] Wickham exerted himself to bring together, on Swiss soil, two carefully chosen members of the Constituent: the Abbé Lacombe, who had belonged to its right wing, and who, at this later time, was actively in touch with the court of Verona, and, on the other side, D'André. Wickham regarded D'André as being able to speak for, and as having influence with, other constitutional, or former constitutional, royalists. The 'result' of their conversation was forwarded by Lacombe to Verona, and Wickham expressed lively interest in the reception it might get. Evidently this conversation had to do with Wickham's design that there should be 'conciliation' between the King and 'the different Parties'. In the spring of 1796, as will also be explained later, Wickham induced this same D'André to make his submission in due terms to Louis XVIII, and joined with D'André in a design to communicate the Pretender's very gracious reply to certain opposition deputies at Paris, with whom D'André had connections. Leaving aside here all the details of this affair, the envoy's design to promote 'conciliation' between the 'parties' is clear enough. In the case of D'André it will be noted that his object seems to be to turn the ex-constituent, and his friends the deputies, into pure Royalists rather than to induce the King to accept them as constitutional Royalists. But this is characteristic of Wickham's highly flexible approach to the whole matter. 'Conciliation' is his great objective; its terms are a matter of opportunity.

This last point, indeed, must in no way obscure the further fact, which is of more general importance, that Wickham was convinced of the need for the King to extend a welcome *also* to the larger number who were not, at that stage, prepared to accept the King on his own terms—even on his own terms widely and graciously interpreted. He felt that whenever openings could be arranged in which the moderates of the interior might offer to promote the return of the King on some kind of constitutional

[1] See ch. V below.

conditions, these stipulations must at the least not be met by absolute refusal. These openings might be made under auspices very far from ideal, but they must be developed and exploited with every refinement of good feeling and emphasis upon common ground.

Undoubtedly it was made easier for Wickham to hold and develop this line, that the King must agree to be all things to all monarchists of whatever shade, in so far as he was very willing to believe that, if the King would only follow this line, matters would turn out sooner or later exactly as he wished; it would be pure Royalist principles which won in the end. We have already noticed Wickham's opinion to this effect at the time of the sectional crisis. When, in the spring of 1796, Pichegru produced his advice for a policy involving the King's acceptance of constitutional monarchy 'at least for a time', Wickham not only exerted himself to ensure that the exiled Court should at least *not reject* this out of hand, but, for his own part, finally accepted this as the only realistic policy which remained. He accepted it with the less reluctance, since he was, like Pichegru, able to take refuge in the belief that the compromise need be only temporary. 'I am decidedly of opinion', he advised his colleague Drake in a letter dated 21 July, 'that some form of constitutional monarchy must be *passed through*. This can never be done but by a coalition of Partys. . . . Baptiste, with whom my correspondence is still both active and direct, is of the same opinion.'

In the spring and early summer of 1796 there were particular considerations in the envoy's thought which powerfully strengthened the appeal of such a policy. When Vendémiaire had removed all immediate possibility that the interior was to settle, by its own sole action, the destinies of France, Wickham had perforce fallen back on the other means of combating the ruling party. In addition to the military power of Austria, there were the resources of militant Royalism. Condé's army and the Royalist insurgents of the interior were fighting for the King on his own terms. Wickham went back to his efforts to make something of these elements in the struggle against the Republic; and no doubt, if the militant Royalists could even now have succeeded in gaining, with the collaboration of the Allies, important advantages against the Republic within French territory, Wickham and his principals would have been pleased enough to promote a consequent effort to secure the Pretender's triumph on his own terms. On his own terms, sensibly and generously interpreted, no doubt; even, on his own terms vaguely and delusively interpreted. Wickham still hoped that if such successes could be gained, if the victors would clothe their intentions in suitably mild language, and if they would shape their conduct accordingly, the interior would clutch at the chance to escape from its tyrants, and would facilitate the final violent overthrow of the Republic.

Wickham was also able, after Vendémiaire, to fall back on the *prospect* of another and larger means of armed action: the prospect of decisive action, on the Pretender's side, by Pichegru, or by other suborned Republican commanders, with large and disciplined formerly Republican forces well in hand behind them. If this prospect could have been realized, again we may say that Wickham and his government would have been only too pleased to hail the final success of the pure Royalist cause. (No one concerned, at that stage, doubted that it was for the pure Royalist cause that Pichegru intended to declare.) Once again, Wickham and his principals would have been concerned to insist that the pure Royalists should construe their programme in a mild, or even a vague, manner. But we cannot doubt that they would then have hoped for, and expected, the complete acquiescence of the interior, and even for its active support.[1]

In either of these cases, Wickham would have found no need to recur to his advice that the French King should resign himself to a compromise of principle, albeit provisional, with the constitutional monarchists. But in fact, during the spring and early summer of 1796, Wickham was steadily driven to the conclusion that all these possibilities were receding beyond the bounds of hope. The Austrians, it became clear, would attempt nothing on the Rhine front. In April, Bonaparte attacked their positions in Italy. In June, the Republicans took the offensive across the Rhine. If, in mid-July, some hopes were cherished that the Archduke Charles would be able to halt this French thrust into Germany, and then turn the tide back on to French soil, Wickham did not share these hopes. The prospects of decisive action from the

---

[1] Wickham's interest in these methods of action against the Republic, during the period now in question, is amply illustrated in despatches to Lord Grenville. Since this book is not directly concerned with these aspects of his activities, detailed references are not offered here.

militant Royalists were meantime also failing. It became clear that the successes of Hoche, early in the year, against the Western insurgents, had been fatal not only to the hopes of militant Royalism in that quarter, but to their prospects in the whole interior. Even the pure Royalists of the interior were giving up all hopes of success by insurrection. In April came the end of all the hopes pinned upon Pichegru's ability to carry his army over to the King. Finally, Wickham was driven to see that the interior would have nothing to do with any of these methods. The country detested its existing government and had no faith in its endurance. But, whether from dislike of a pure Royalist solution, or from determination to take no further risks of violent upheaval, or from both of these considerations, the French people were obstinately averse from all such remedies.[1]

For Wickham, therefore, the conclusion was emerging with increasing clarity that, if the struggle against the Republic were to be carried on inside French territory at all, it would have to be carried on both by different methods and on different principles. It would be necessary to wage it by means in which the moderates of the interior would take part; and moreover they would not take part in any efforts against the Republic, in conditions such as these, except with the conviction that their own preferences regarding the future form of government would be complied with. Pure royalism could no longer supply the force, therefore it could no longer dictate the terms. It would not be enough even to interpret the 'pure' programme in a less unbending spirit, or to swathe it in benevolent generalizations. The King must be prepared, if not to adopt, provisionally, a constitutional basis, at least to let the interior hope that he intended to work on that basis.

Thus Wickham came to accept, what Mallet du Pan had pointed out long ago, that 'an absolute and violent counter-revolution' was impossible. And, in the midst of all this, a new anxiety began to press itself on the envoy, as upon so many other enemies of the Republic: the fear that the Directorials would make a throne of

---

[1] See Wickham's despatches Private no. 12, 4 May 1796 (unpublished portion); Private no. 16, 26 May (unpublished); Private no. 17, 29 May and Private no. 28, 4 July (the latter is published in R. Hist. MSS. Comm. *Dropmore*, III, p. 616f.); Private no. 34, 16 July (unpublished); Private no. 35, 18 July, and letter to Drake, 21 July (both in Wickham, *Corresp.*, vol. I); no. 75 of 1796, 20 July (unpublished).

their own devising for the Duc d'Orléans.[1] Like others who shared this fear, he thought that this would probably perpetuate the rule of the adventurers who had proclaimed mortal war, both on the social structure and on the international system of Europe. The implication was, once again, perfectly clear: Louis must win the moderate monarchists over to his cause, before both they and he —indeed all Europe in addition—found themselves saddled with a new version of regicide government, all the more stable and permanent for being disguised as an Orleanist constitutional monarchy.

It is only when we estimate the weight with which these various considerations collectively pressed on Wickham's mind in July 1796, that we can at all fully understand the shock and anger which he now experienced at the conduct of the exiled Court. That Court, presented, in this seeming extremity of its fortunes with the chance of an alliance with the legislative opposition of Paris, greeted the offer with a blank rejection. The envoy's discomfiture was total. His chagrin was all the greater, moreover, because (strange as we must think it) Wickham was quite unprepared for the Court's reaction. No doubt—this had already been suggested—Wickham had been thinking that the Court was already mentally resigning itself to an alliance with the legislative opposition (or with the public which it represented) on constitutionalist terms, for the same reasons as appeared so obvious and so convincing to himself. The fact that the Court had eventually professed approval of the temporizing reply, which he had suggested in the case of Pichegru's first plea for an alliance with constitutional royalism, probably helped to satisfy him that the King and his circle were indeed inclining, even though with a

---

[1] See his remarks in two despatches, 16 July 1796: Private despatch no. 34, and no. 70 in the public series, the latter being published in Wickham, *Corresp.* In the former, after expressing his amazement that the exiled Court could not see how 'wonderfully changed' conditions were since the days of the Verona Declaration, Wickham went on: 'It is notorious that the whole Directory is disposed to the party of the Duke d'Orleans, and that they will be supported by Tallien, Sieyes and all those who have voted the King's death.' In the latter he added: 'I have never had, till now, any serious alarm about the Duke of Orleans, but unless the French King and Princes (*can be induced*) to relax somewhat of their pretensions and particularly to recede from the Declaration of Verona—I am persuaded that everything is to be apprehended' (*Corresp.*, vol. I, p. 417). (Both cited more fully below, pp. 117–18).

decent reluctance, before the verdict of events. Wickham appears, indeed, to have become so confident of the Court's willingness to adopt his own point of view, that between May and July he forgot that it had ever been so deeply committed to the 'intolerance as to principles', which in fact still distinguished it as much as ever. Such a statement may well appear incredible, and even very foolish, but it seems to offer the only means of explaining the extremity of surprise and indignation which Wickham displayed on learning the Court's reaction.

Thus woefully unprepared in mind, Wickham faced the fact that the one point in the new plan of the Agence which he considered indisputably sound and desirable was the very point which the exiled Court branded as 'wholly inadmissible', and against which, as La Vauguyon told him, 'the King's mind was entirely made up'. The envoy reported his discoveries to Lord Grenville 'with infinite pain',[1] and with the comment, which seems so astonishing, that this attitude on the part of the Pretender was something that 'he never could learn before'.[2] But, disconcerted though he obviously was, Wickham grasped, firmly if belatedly, the size and importance of the obstacle which confronted him, and he moved swiftly and strongly against it.

We have already seen how the envoy threw himself into the remonstrations which his visitor Duverne made to the Royalist Prime Minister. We can now show, from passages in his original draft of the same despatch—phrases which he wrote, but then abandoned unfinished and omitted from the text which he finally sent to London—that he did more than remonstrate with La Vauguyon: he threatened him plainly that the Allies would abandon the Royal cause completely if the Court's obduracy continued. Thus, after the paragraph in the despatch which ends: 'The Duke persists that the King is not to be shaken in his resolution',[3] Wickham's draft originally continued:

And upon my asking him whether he expected that the powers of Europe would be justified in spending their blood and treasure any longer in fighting with the Republick . . . [at this point the sentence breaks off, and is cancelled].

---

[1] No. 70, 16 July (*Corresp.*, vol. I, p. 416).
[2] No. 71, 18 July (*Corresp.*, vol. I, p. 424).
[3] In Wickham, *Corresp.*, vol. I, these words fall on p. 424.

And another broken and cancelled passage in the draft indicates
that La Vauguyon admitted the force and reason, from the
British point of view, of such a menace. Indeed, if La Vauguyon
during the next few days showed signs of greater complacency
towards the policy of compromise, this was perhaps quite as
much due to Wickham's warnings as to the influence of Pichegru's
reiterated appeal for a provisional acceptance of the compromise.

In a private despatch to the Foreign Secretary, Wickham had
already poured out at some length and with much vehemence his
feelings about the King's refusal, taken in conjunction with the
gloomy fortunes which, in that summer, so darkly clouded the
prospects of the Republic's enemies. He commented on the high
improbability that the Archduke Charles would be able to withstand the weight of the Republican thrust on the Upper Rhine, the
likelihood that Germany would be 'entirely lost', the probability
that Prussia as well as Spain would go over to the Republic, and
the disastrous effect which Austrian reverses in Germany must be
expected to have on the struggle in Italy. Then he turned to the
situation of French affairs. The interior, he pointed out, desired
peace above everything else and had no stomach to try conclusions with their apparently all-powerful rulers.

In the midst of all this [he went on] the Conduct of the King makes me
tremble. The orders to M. Brottier are *peremptory* (?) to abide by his
original instructions and the King's declaration. How will they not
see that things are wonderfully changed since that epoch? It is notorious
that the whole Directory is disposed to the party of the duke d'Orleans
& that they will be supported by Tallien Sieyes and all those who have
voted the King's death. It is nothing but the persuasion of this truth
that has induced so many persons of late to turn their thoughts towards
the lawful Sovereign.[1]

With the conclusion of this passage we may compare what
Wickham wrote in the public despatch, of even date, in which he
announced that Brottier's proposition had been branded as
'wholly inadmissible'.

I have never had, till now, any serious alarm about the Duke of Orleans, but unless H.M. (*King George III*) have sufficient influence with
the French King and Princes to induce them to relax somewhat of
their pretensions and particularly to recede from the Declaration of

[1] Private no. 34 of 1796, 16 July: not published in Wickham's *Corresp.*

Verona—I am persuaded that everything is to be apprehended. This is the opinion of every thinking and well informed man who is at all acquainted with the real opinion of the interior.[1]

What gave Wickham greater pain than even the Royal refusal of the proposals of Brottier was, what he now clearly saw, that 'Mr D'André's offers would of course meet with a similar fate'.[2] For, as we shall have to show at a later stage, Wickham had far greater confidence in D'André than in the Agence, whom he complained of at this time as being both inefficient and indiscreet;[3] and he set far higher value on the plans of D'André and his associates than he did on those of the Agents, and even than on the suggestions of Pichegru. The valuable feature of the plans advanced both by the Agents and by Pichegru, in Wickham's opinion, was their common proposal that the King should resign himself to the constitutional exigencies of the interior and thereby, in the only way now possible, win for himself the alliance of a large mass of his subjects. The other features of these plans were such as the envoy could now place little if any reliance upon. Both plans projected the co-operation of a Republican army; the Agents wanted to associate with this the good old method of Royalist armed action also. Wickham's faith in all these notions had been severely shaken, if not destroyed.[4] He himself had come

[1] No. 70 of 1796: Wickham, *Corresp.*, vol. I, p. 417.

[2] Ibid.

[3] Wickham's mature judgement of Brottier and Duverne is illustrated in his (unpublished) Private no. 40, 2 September 1796. Wickham there refers to his reiterated complaints that they were timid and unenterprising in espionage, and had handled badly both their financial and their personal dealings with various insurgent leaders. He says that he has, after much effort, prodded them into more efficient habits in some respects; but it is clear that he still regards them without enthusiasm. Wickham does not accuse them of *indiscretion* in the more specific sense of being bad keepers of important secrets; but D'André and the opposition deputies who had dealings with them raised this charge against them also.

[4] Here we have the explanation of the fact, which clearly emerges in the Agents' letters to Wickham during the later months of 1796, that for all the envoy's persistence in urging the exiled Court not to reject Brottier's propositions, he nevertheless left the Agents with the impression that the British Government cared little for their policy of alliance with the Lemerer group. In fact, Wickham was determined to bring about a 'coalition' on terms which the moderate monarchists could accept; but he had no faith left in the other developments which the Agents proposed to associate with this, nor, for that matter, in the competence of the Agents to direct such a policy. He pre-

to the view that there must be not only a means of 'conciliating the different parties' and the construction of a 'coalition' of all the more conservative elements of the interior, but also a system of action which made it possible to combat the Directory in ways with which the interior would be willing to co-operate. This, he felt, pointed away from methods of force, at least until very substantial changes in the situation of French affairs had been realized. The only possible method of carrying on the struggle against the Directory on French soil, in existing circumstances, was therefore the method of electoral and parliamentary operations.[1] D'André, working with the same group of deputies as the Agents had also approached, but had probably in part misunderstood, was offering precisely what Wickham thought the needs of the time required. Impressing Wickham at once by his prudence, his character and his experience of Revolutionary politics, he also proposed, not only a 'coalition of Partys' but its operation by methods of 'legal' action within the institutions of the Republic.

It was, therefore, with a clear view that he had to save, not so much the *plans* of the Agents and of Pichegru, in all their details, but rather the one all important *principle* which their plans embodied—that the King must take whatever steps were needed to win over the constitutional monarchists—that Wickham now faced the 'pride and prejudice' [2] of the exiled Court; and in facing it he knew that unless he could overcome it on this critical point, unless he could bring the Pretender, if not to embrace constitutionalist ideas 'for a time', then at least to be all things to all sorts of monarchists, the better plans associated in his mind with D'André were as still-born as those of the Agence and of the General.

We have seen at an earlier stage how Wickham hoped for a moment that he had prevailed upon La Vauguyon, and how, in fact, whatever the Prime Minister really thought, the Pretender

---

ferred to promote their general principle by other means, and to work through other men.

[1] See, for a particularly clear and full expression of Wickham's views to this effect, his letter to Drake, 21 July (published in Wickham, *Corresp.*, vol. I, pp. 430–3).

[2] Wickham's Private despatch no. 34 of 1796, 16 July (not published in Wickham's *Corresp.*) uses this expression regarding the entourage of the Pretender.

had then already committed himself to the very different line, to which he was to stick for several months, of treating the opposition deputies as good pure Royalists at heart and trying to bring them to an explicit acceptance of his own position. The envoy, however, was now forearmed against any such further disappointment; seeing now clearly all that was at stake, he was resolved to persevere in the struggle until the old Court finally gave him its blessing. On 21 July, immediately after his conversations with La Vauguyon, he wrote in the following terms to his colleague Drake:

The period you mention (*the election of the new third part of the assembly*) appears to me to be that which we must all look to. It is unfortunately still very remote. I am also decidedly of opinion that some form of constitutional monarchy must be *passed through*. This can never be done but by a coalition of Partys, which partial insurrections tend more than anything else to prevent. I have been labouring (hitherto in vain) to bring certain persons who formerly resided at Verona to the same way of thinking. It has been peremptorily declared to me that the King would rather resign his Crown altogether than come to any agreement with his People, the conclusion of which should be what they call a permanent representation . . . I do not, however, abandon on that account either my own opinion or my hopes, if not of bringing the others to think as I do, at least of making them act, to a certain degree, as I should wish them . . . They see and feel that our Government will support its Ministers . . . and they find by experience that I am not to be shaken in my resolution of giving no funds for any partial purposes. A conduct of that kind persevered in with sufficient obstinacy cannot, I think, fail in *the end* of producing its effect.

Baptiste . . . is of the same opinion. He has repeated it several times to the principal Person concerned; and as great reliance is placed on his future services this opinion of his has not failed to make a serious impression.[1]

---

[1] These passages of the letter fall on pp. 431-2 of Wickham, *Corresp.*, vol. I.

PART II

D'ANDRÉ AND THE 'GREAT DESIGN'

1796–7

V

The origins of D'André's contribution to the 'Great Design'

JANUARY TO AUGUST 1796

WE may now turn our direct attention to the views and activities of the ex-Constituent whom we have already identified as providing the chief centre of personal interest in this study. When and in what circumstances did D'André become involved in the projects whose origins we have now tried to illustrate?

Meynier believed that D'André, at the time when these plans were being formed, was already a regular servant of the exiled Court, 'chef de la circonscription militaire de Paris'.[1] Lefebvre understood that, in the original efforts of the Agence de Paris to open friendly discussions with representatives of the moderate monarchists of the interior, D'André acted as intermediary.[2] There is certainly no question but that D'André was, at this time and from the beginning, a determined opponent of the Republic. But Wickham's papers dispose entirely of any suggestion that he had as yet an official position of whatever kind in the Royalist movement, or any connection at all with the Agence de Paris. D'André's own correspondence with Wickham and with Wickham's secretary Leclerc[3] shows clearly that between March 1796 (to go back no further) and February 1797 the ex-Constituent resided continuously in Switzerland.[4] It also shows that he was, at least for much the greater part of this time, quite without personal knowledge of, or direct relations with, the Royal Agents at Paris. Further still, it shows that it was only in March, 1796 that D'André made his submission to Louis XVIII.[5]

On the other hand it emerges with equal clarity from Wickham's papers that the ex-deputy for the Noblesse of Aix had enjoyed connections with the British Minister in Switzerland from

---

[1] *Le 18 fructidor*, p. 188.   [2] *Le Directoire*, p. 56.
[3] Wickham Papers.   [4] At Morges, on the lac Léman.
[5] Wickham Papers include a fair copy of D'André's letter of submission, 18 March 1796.

a time considerably earlier than the spring of 1796,[1] and that his part in the Royalist political activity of the period with which we are concerned emerged solely from his relations with Wickham. His own letters to Wickham and to Leclerc show that, from the very beginning of his activities in these Royalist politics, the British envoy was something far more than his friend and confidant: Wickham was his political patron, who exerted great personal influence over the development of his action, and also provided him with his means of access, whether to the Pretender or to adherents of the Pretender's cause in Paris. It is quite true that, from spring 1796 onwards, D'André was working to bring into better relations the Pretender and his adherents on one side, and representatives of the 'Royalisme de 1789' on the other. But he was not attempting this as the colleague, or even as the intermediary, of the Agence de Paris; his was an independent effort of mediation, under the encouraging eye of Wickham, who provided his approach to the pure Royalist elements, while D'André himself enjoyed direct connections with the persons who stood for the moderate monarchism of the interior.

It seems that it was in or about the New Year season, 1795–6, that Wickham, already concerned as he was to promote a 'coalition' of the more conservative elements of French political life against the Republic, took the first of the steps whereby, in the end, he launched the well-known ex-Constituent into the career which we now have to examine. In a letter to Lord Macartney, dated 19 January 1796, Wickham reported as follows:

The Abbé de la Combe, a member of the *right side* of the Assemblée constituante, has lately communicated to Verona, the result of a conversation that he has had with the famous M. d'André, a member of the *côté gauche*. I should be very curious to know the opinion that has been formed upon it, by the King and the persons about him. Having been, in some measure, the means of bringing about the meeting, and of disposing each party to meet the other graciously, I am anxious that this opportunity that the two parties have found of talking together, may not be altogether thrown away.[2]

---

[1] The earliest reference to D'André found in the Wickham papers occurs in a letter of 30 January 1795, addressed by an unidentified writer to Wickham's agent Bayard. This letter refers to D'André as a person well known to Bayard. There is evidence of communications directly between D'André and Wickham as early as the summer of 1795.

[2] Wickham, *Corresp.*, vol. I, p. 247.

BALTHAZARD JO.^{PH} D'ANDRÉ
Conseiller au Parlement
Né à Aix en Provence en 1759.
Depute de la Sénéch.^{ssée} d'Aix
à l'Assemblée Nationale de 1789

Perrin del.   Courbe Sc.

A Paris chez le St Dejabin éditeur de cette Collection
Place du Carrousel. N.°4

PLATE III

D'André, as a Member of the
Constituent Assembly

Wickham was not content, however, simply to bring so important a former representative of the old constitutionalists into friendly conversation with a spokesman of pure Royalism. He regarded D'André with a more active interest, as being, like Terrier de Monciel, one of the Feuillants who were ripe for complete conversion to authentic Royalism, if only they could be completely assured of a sincere and honourable welcome.[1] Recognizing, as by this date he did, that the Pretender's adherents, as not the Pretender himself, made the fulfilment of this condition in practice far more difficult than the Court's fair general promises announced,[2] Wickham was still anxious to do whatever he could to bring about such complete conversions. Such a man as D'André might, indeed, in any case become one of the promoters of a 'coalition' between men who did, and men who still would not, accept the Pretender without constitutional stipulations. But this possibility need not necessarily rule out the further chance, that D'André himself might accept something more than the principle of the 'coalition'. Such a man would be an even more precious recruit in the struggle with the Republic if he were definitively turned into a pure Royalist. His example might progressively encourage others to do likewise. The *ad hoc* coalition against the Republic might, by such means, be transmuted, while it was yet being built, into something still better—a great 'monolithic' party of true Royalists.

The envoy therefore 'took great pains' 'to induce Mr D'André, the famous member of the Constituent Assembly, to write to the King and make an offer of his services'.[3] In bringing this to pass, he incurred 'many difficulties, arising chiefly from the conduct of the Prince of Condé with respect to Mr Monciel.' [4] In so expressing himself, Wickham implies that D'André found little trouble in renouncing, in principle, the political ideals of 1789, but a great deal in considerations of a more practical kind. Wickham, after

---

[1] See above, ch. I.   [2] See above, ch. I.

[3] Wickham's despatch no. 66 of 1796, 3 July, the text of which, as corrected from the rough draft by Wickham himself, is printed in Wickham, *Corresp.*, I, pp. 401–4; at this point, Wickham's original draft (Wickham Papers), reads, not, as in the version printed, 'great pains were taken . . . to induce Mr D'André to write . . .,' but, 'I took great pains', etc.

[4] Wickham's no. 66 of 1796. These words are cited from Wickham's original draft. He omitted them in the text finally despatched, and printed in the *Corresp.*

K

his experience of the case of Monciel, and the somewhat analogous case of the Prince de Poix, was quite willing to take such difficulties seriously.[1] In pressing D'André, he did not overlook the importance of exhorting also the other party to the proposed reconciliation. 'Nothing was left undone that might tend to secure him a favourable answer.' [2] At last Wickham's efforts were rewarded; on 18 March, D'André addressed his letter of submission to the legitimate King.[3] In due course, that Prince replied in those terms of gracious personal welcome and confidence, in the expression of which he was so great a master.[4]

[1] Wickham's remarks on the case of the Prince de Poix are quoted above, ch. I.   [2] Wickham's no. 66 of 1796.

[3] The text of the fair copy of D'André's letter to the Pretender, contained in Wickham Papers, is as follows:

'Sire,

Appelé à 29 ans aux Etats Généraux j'y suis venu avec les idées naturelles à cet âge dans un homme qui avoit été témoin de bien des abus.

Envoyé par S.M. Louis XVI en Provence je profitai du moment ou Votre Majesté se rendit à sa Section; et d'après les mêmes principes qui l'y conduisirent, je fis prendre à la Commune de Marseille le 12 Janvier 1790 une délibération pour demander le rétablissement de l'autorité Royale. Cette délibération fameuse dans le tems, provoquée, rédigée et signée par moi, me valut de violentes dénonciations de la part des Jacobins et une approbation honorable du feu roi.

Revenu à l'Assemblée, je fus le constant ennemi des Désorganisateurs. Je n'entrerai dans aucun detail. Le tems de Votre Majesté est trop precieux. Il me suffira de lui exposer que le feu Roi m'honnorât d'une confiance particulière, que mes motions furent concertées avec le Gouvernement, et étoient la suite d'un système qui devoit amener un meilleur état de choses.

D'autres plans furent adoptés. Lorsque je vis des hommes qui n'avoient attaqué l'autorité Royale que pour s'en emparer monter au Gouvernail, je jugeai que je devenois inutile. La profession que j'avois embrassé d'après le consentement, je dirois presque par les ordres de Sa Majesté m'exposoit à mille dangers. Je me résolus, après avoir dit franchement ma façon de penser, sur le peu de bien qu'on pouvoit espérer de ces hommes, à sauver du moins ma personne pour mes enfans et mon pays.

Ma personne, c'est tout ce qui me reste. Je viens la mettre aux pieds de Votre Majesté. Elle aura connu sans doute des détails qui doivent la convaincre que si l'age, les circonstances, le caractère, m'ont entrainé dans quelques erreurs, mon attachement à l'ordre public, et mon dévouement au feu Roi, ont été sans bornes. Je m'estimerois heureux que Votre Majesté voulut accepter l'assurance que ces sentiments (sic) n'ont point varié, et que je suis prêt à employer tous mes moyens à son service.

Morges 18 Mars 1796.'

[4] The text of the Pretender's reply can be seen in the copy enclosed in

D'André's letter to the titular King is itself the product of considerable literary skill. In it, he apologizes with an almost naive gracefulness for his share in the 'errors' of the opening years of the Revolution; at the same time he insists at some length on the efforts which he made, despite these errors, on behalf of the prerogative, and offers himself at last quite simply and without any undue self-humiliation, as a man who had always 'had the root of the matter in him', to the service of the King. He suggests no conditions to the King. He implies, by his reference to the 'abuses' which had helped to lead him and so many others into error, that all that was really required was the repudiation of such abuses; and Louis XVIII had already promised, readily enough, to meet the just complaints of his subjects on the score of the evils included in this vague term. This, in short, is the letter of a man prepared to accept Louis XVIII on the latter's own terms; and it is clear from the Pretender's reply that he accepted it as such.

It is a point of much interest to us in this matter that D'André in his letter of submission did not apply to the King for any particular appointment in his service, nor did he suggest to the King any fresh development of Royalist policy. The Pretender, in his brief reply, made no offer or suggestion to D'André. D'André, with the help and encouragement of Wickham, was already planning to work for the King in his own way, independently both of the exiled Court and of the King's Agents at Paris. At a later stage, if not from the beginning, this preference for an independent line of action was justified by the ex-Constituent on the grounds of his distrust, both of the wisdom and of the discretion of the official servants of the King.

What D'André and Wickham had in mind was that D'André should communicate his own experience of reconciliation with the legitimate King to 'several members of both assemblies' at Paris, showing them copies of the gracious welcome which Louis had written to him, and adding 'the most positive assurances that the King was really actuated by the most moderate

---

D'André's letter of 15 April: 'J'ai reçu, Monsieur, votre lettre avec une véritable satisfaction; mais j'en ai bien davantage à vous dire que les erreurs dont vous faites un si noble aveu, sont désormais entièrement effacés de ma mémoire. Je ne me souviens plus que de vos talens, et je suis bien sûr que vous ne les emploierés jamais qu'à la défense des vrais principes de la Monarchie.
Comptés aussi, Monsieur, sur tous mes sentimens pour vous.'

principles, and the strongest exhortations to his friends to exert themselves'.[1] It seems that the two men regarded these legislators, with whom D'André had means of connection of his own, as probable converts to pure Royalism, who only needed an impressive and happy example, such as D'André could now supply; or who would at the least be encouraged by his example to participate in the building of a coalition of parties, agreed to work for a Restoration, even if not fully agreed as to the forms it should assume. A specially interesting feature of this new departure, occurring in April 1796, is that it shows Wickham to have been giving serious attention to promoting the cause among the French legislators, long enough before he gave up all hopes of progress by military methods. Though there is insufficient evidence to warrant confident statement, it seems possible that in first selecting D'André for such careful attention and such warm encouragement, Wickham had already turned his mind towards the electoral and parliamentary lines of action, to which a few months later he was to commit his hopes entirely. For D'André was not only a distinguished former member of the Feuillant party, he had made his reputation specifically in the field of parliamentary activities, and his connections at Paris, which he was now to exploit, were pre-eminently with men of the legislative chambers, men of political and not of warlike significance.

D'André communicated his news and his exhortations to the deputies at Paris, not in person (he had reason to fear the attentions of the authorities) but by two carefully chosen messengers.[2]

---

[1] Wickham's no. 66 of 1796, referred to above. The passage including the words 'the most positive assurances . . .' *etc.*, was subsequently deleted by Wickham from his draft. Wickham added, after the words 'to several members of both assemblies' the amplification 'particularly to Messrs. Portalis, Durand Maillane, Simeon and Dupont de Nemours'. Perhaps all these were indeed approached. But whether their mention by name reflects Wickham's impression of their outstanding importance or goodness of disposition, or whether it reflects D'André's, is not clear. Wickham, as will be seen, was liable to become confused among all these politicians.

[2] In a letter to Wickham at the time when this approach was being arranged (16 April 1796) D'André wrote: 'D'après tout ce que j'ai appris, je n'hesiterois pas à aller moi-même, persuadé que je suis, combien je ferois plus d'un mot que lui (= *his intended messenger*) dans un jour. Mais d'un côté ma femme s'y oppose; de l'autre, je crains d'être vexé pour mon emprunt forcé. Ils ont eu l'impudeur de me taxer 6000 £ (*livres*) et faute d'autre prétexte, ils pourroient bien me saisir au corps, ce dont je ne me soucie nullement.' D'André was on

'As soon as the answer was received (*from the King*) Mr D'André wrote to his wife, who had remained constantly at Paris, to come to him in Switzerland, together with a person of confidence that had been employed by the last ministers of the unfortunate Louis XVI, with whom he had been in close correspondence ever since the Revolution, and who was connected with many of the leading members in both Assemblies.' [1] D'André wrote for Wickham a memorandum stating in outline, and in understandably cryptic terms, what it was that the 'person of confidence' was to do on his return to Paris:

M. d'André fera partir pour Paris la personne aussitot que son passeport aura été visé. Il lui remettra des instructions conformes à ce qui a été arrêté dans son dernier voyage à Berne. Il l'adressera aux députés ...et autres de sa connoissance et son intimité. Il sera de plus porteur d'une copie certifiée de la lettre que M. d'André a reçu, afin de convaincre, soit les députés, soit autres, de la sûreté qu'il y a à traiter lorsque la Loyauté et la Franchise servent de guides. La personne est chargée aussi de voir les principaux membres du comité Constitutionnel, de les sonder, et de leur communiquer la lettre reçue...[2]

---

the list of émigrés, as we should expect, and as appears from later letters, e.g. his letter to Leclerc of 23 August 1796, where he refers to his *radiation* as a future possibility. His meaning here appears to be that he regarded the risk of his arrest *as an émigré*, at this date, lightly; but his arrest for default on the payment of his forced loan assessment was much more probable, and would remove him from freedom and safety just as effectively.

[1] Wickham, no. 66 of 1796, referred to above. The passage quoted in the text was deleted and replaced by a much briefer passage before the despatch was sent to London. References in D'André's letters of 16 April and 14 May 1796, show that the 'person of confidence' who accompanied Mme D'André on this mission was called Ramel.

[2] Wickham Papers, bundle 67, paper undated but filed between pieces dated 16 and 26 April 1796; headed, *Note sur la Mission qui va être faite à Paris*. This memorandum has a further paragraph, of which no use has been made in the text. It is of some interest, in showing, what other letters in this correspondence show also, that D'André was deeply concerned about the reputed Orleanist designs of some of the Directorials. 'Elle (= *la personne*) a aussi commission de voir une personne fortement initiée dans les menées Orléaniques, et de rendre compte courier par courier de ce qu'il aura découvert sur leurs menées, et doit s'attacher particulièrement à éclairer la conduite de Merlin de Douay, qui est l'âme de ce parti . . .' It appears from D'André's letter of 14 May in this correspondence that his emissary's return journey to Paris suffered some unspecified delays, and that it was only about this date (mid-May) that he re-entered the capital.

It will be observed that the messenger was to approach, in particular, two distinct groups—the deputies 'and others' of D'André's acquaintance (who needed, it was supposed, only to be satisfied that submission to the Pretender was a painless and safe experience) and, on the other hand, the leading members of the 'comité constitutionnel' (who were reputedly further from the right path, since they needed to be 'sounded'). From other evidence in Wickham's papers, it appears that D'André's friends consisted of—or at least included—the 'committee' which was at the same period entering into parallel negotiations with the Paris Agents.[1] This committee had five members, one of whom was not a deputy.[2] Wickham finally identified them to Lord Grenville as 'Messieurs Lemerer, Durand Maillane, Henri-Larivière, Thibeaudeau [sic] and a Mr Ribufet who has the direction of all the army contracts. Mr Durand Maillane carrys on their correspondence with Mr D'André, and Mr Lemerer with the King's Agents.'[3] The one name which gives rise to obvious doubt among these identifications is that of Thibaudeau.[4] As for the 'comité

---

[1] Wickham to Duc de la Vauguyon, 16 January 1797 (Wickham Papers): 'M. D'André's committee is the same as that which approached M. Brottier, etc.' Cf. Wickham to Grenville, no. 102 of 1796, 11 December, in Wickham, *Corresp.*, vol. I, pp. 484–6.

[2] Wickham's no. 66 of 1796: Wickham, *Corresp.*, vol. I, p. 403, 'the persons to whom Mr D'André had written' 'reconsidered' (*the matter*) in 'a small committee of only five Persons'—D'André to Leclerc, 24 June 1796, enclosing copy of the response to his approach at Paris: 'Je copie littéralement le résultat de leur comité composé de 5 personnes dont 4 seulement membres des conseils.'

[3] When Wickham wrote despatch no. 66, he thought it to be the case that these five men were Dumas and some of his associates. See Wickham, *Corresp.*, vol. I, p. 404. Wickham did not claim positive knowledge, for D'André had been adjured not to reveal their names to anyone until they judged the time ripe. Only a week later (Private no. 30 of 1796, not publ. in Wickham's *Corresp.*) he announced that he had been mistaken. 'The five whom I named to your Lordship form what is called, in one of Mr D'André's propositions, the *Comité Directorial* i.e. determined to support the Directory in every point.' He now supposed that Siméon was the 'chief' of D'André's committee; he did not attempt again to name the others. Only in his despatch no. 102 of 1796, 11 December (Wickham, *Corresp.*, vol. I, pp. 485–6) did he finally identify them in the terms set out in the text.

[4] There are glimpses of Thibaudeau in later parts of Wickham's correspondence, including a statement by D'André (from Paris, 27 July 1797) that 'Thibeaudeau (sic) nous a échappé'. There is nothing which tends to confirm

constitutionnel', it is fairly evident that this must have been the group of Mathieu-Dumas. Of course D'André had known some of the members of this group, at least as well as he knew those now described as his 'friends'; but he also knew that the Dumas party was at present passing through its period of rapprochement with the Directory, proclaiming meanwhile its attachment to the Constitution of the year III scrupulously interpreted.[1] Dumas and his associates thus had to be treated as possible, but by no means certain, converts.

It seems that both groups, when first consulted by D'André's emissary, united to give him a rather unencouraging reply ('. . . nothing was to be done for the present; the Directory was . . . so powerful that it could not possibly be attacked . . . nothing remained . . . for all well meaning people but to rally themselves round the new government, which was alone capable of saving

---

Wickham's statement that Thibaudeau was ever so closely identified with the right wing as to have been a member of this committee of pro-legitimists, and it seems needless to emphasize how improbable it is that he should have been such. On the other hand, there is a letter of D'André (14 December 1796) which confirms Wickham's identification of Durand-Maillane; there is no difficulty about Lemerer, and there need be none about Henry-Larivière.

There appears to be some doubt about the exact form of the name which is shown as Ribufet; and we may perhaps venture to express a little surprise that the name of the fifth member, not a member of the legislature, did not turn out to be Mersan, the unseated deputy who was, as has been seen, associated with Lemerer in the dealings of this group with the Agence.

[1] D'André appears to have referred to Dumas and his friends sometimes (as here) by the term 'comité constitutionnel' and sometimes as the 'comité directorial'. His usage of the latter term is referred to by Wickham in his Private despatch no. 30 of 1796, see p. 130, n. 3. In a letter to Wickham, 19 March 1797, D'André speaks of these politicians in terms which show fairly clearly that he used the two expressions in an identical sense: 'l'affaire des Constitutionnels que je vous ai designé dans le tems par Comité Directorial'. D'André probably used the adjective 'constitutionnel' in this connection to refer, both to their former identification with the constitution of 1791, and to their present attitude of support for that of 1795.

In a letter of 15 November 1796, D'André identifies the membership of Dumas's 'committee', on the authority of Valentin-Duplantier with whom he had just been conversing, and who himself belonged to it, in these terms: 'Le comité qui se tient ches Gilbert (sic) Desmoliéres composé de Dumas, Pastoret, Portalis, Simeon, Duplantier, Dumolard et Cadroi avoit cru d'abord ... se rallier au Directoire dans l'espoir d'abattre les Jacobins.'

them from . . . the Jacobins').[1] But D'André's 'friends', behind the backs of Dumas and his henchmen, were in fact prepared to go a little further. The 'small committee of only five Persons' later 'reconsidered' the matter and drew up a more favourable reply.[2] Towards the end of June, D'André was able to forward a copy of their written response to Wickham.[3]

The *résultat de leur comité*, as D'André calls it, is a document of great importance and interest to us.[4] In the first place, its authors

[1] Wickham, no. 66 of 1796, 3 July; see the passage in Wickham, *Corresp.*, vol. I, p. 402.

[2] The account of these two successive responses to D'André's overtures which is given in Wickham's no. 66 of 1796 must be read in conjunction with Wickham's own subsequent corrections of the identities of the persons concerned: see preceding footnotes.

[3] In his letter of 24 June 1796, addressed to Leclerc, in the temporary absence, as it would appear, of Wickham.

[4] The following passage of D'André's letter of 24 June conveys the 'résultat de leur comité composé de 5 personnes dont 4 seulement membres des conseils... On peut compter sur la prudence et la capacité de 3 des 5 qui composaient ce comité.'

'1. Que tot ou tard il faudra en revenir à la royauté.

2. Qu'il faut s'en tenir au Roy légitime (un seull a été d'avis qu'il n'y avoit pas moyen de rétablir Louis XVIII et qu'il falloit penser au duc d'Angouléme *Va. (? voilà) vous voyés que je ne vous cache rien.*

3. Que la paix étoit à désirer, parce que la guerre fournit des moyens aux rèpublicains.

4. Que la Masse de la Nation ne soupirant qu'après le repos, un mouvement général pour la Royauté, quoiqu'elle fut dans le coeur des trois quarts des Français, étoit impossible; qu'on ne pouvoit rien attendre que des autorités; qu'elles étoient mauvaises et interessées au maintien de la république et que par conséquant toutes les tentatives directes et immédiates seroient infructueuses et ne serviroient qu'à compromettre les amis du Roy, et à donner de la force aux républicains.

5. Que dans ce moment il n'y a rien à faire que de se réunir à la constitution de 95 pour anéantir ou du moins comprimer les terroristes qui sont les ennemis de tout gouvernement.

6. Que suivant les apparences il n'y aura rien d'efficace à exécuter jusqu'au premier renouvellement du tiers, que si les elections sont bonnes comme il y a tant à espérer, quand même on ne rèussiroit pas à cette epoque à tirer la Nation de son apathie, on pourroit agir par les autorités constituées, et surtout par les conseils dont les deux tiers seroient à peu près bons.

7. Que tous les moyens violens doivent être écartés comme inutiles et dangereux.

8. Que cependant il ne faut rien negliger pour se défaire des Jacobins, qu'il faut tacher d'attaquer Barras leur principal soutien ainsi que les thermidoriens.

9. Qu'il seroit à propos, si on avoit des fonds, de s'assurer d'un ou deux

expressed clearly their acceptance of the principle of legitimate monarchy (though one of them indicated his inability to believe in the possibility of Louis XVIII's wearing the Crown, and felt it would be better if his claims were transferred in advance to the Duc d'Angoulême). Secondly, these men—the men who, in their negotiations with the Paris Agents, insisted so stiffly on the King's acceptance of a constitutional basis—did not, on this occasion, stipulate for any constitutional conditions. Yet we cannot say that they wrote as men prepared to adopt explicitly the line of pure Royalism held out to them by D'André's example. What they asked of the King was expressed in terms which appear deliberately ambiguous. The King, they said, should make it more clear that he repudiated all thoughts of proscription, that he welcomed adherents from all quarters, and that he was 'not committed to the old order in its full extent'. Such phrases, when read in the light of the demands which they made of the Agents, seem to show that they were not prepared to go as far as D'André had gone, but were willing enough, under his influence, to go somewhat further than they admitted to the Agents. They were willing to offer Louis and his strict adherents their immediate alliance, on terms which the latter could interpret as being fully in accordance with the King's own position, but which they themselves and

---

journaux pour repandre insensiblement des idées favorables au retour du roy.

10. Que l'on travaillera sans relache à s'assurer d'une majorité ou du moins d'une forte opposition, soit en se liant au comité *Directorial*... soit en insinuant aux membres du directoire et des conseils qu'ils pourroient faire un traité avantageux avec le Roy; et á se renforcer de gens actifs, soit en faisant rapporter ou modifier quand les circonstances sont favorables la loi du 3 brumaire et autres, soit en favorisant par l'influence dans les tribunaux et administrations, la rentrée des emigrés les moins marquans et les plus en règle.

11. (*a minor point*).

12. Qu'une correspondance est dangereuse, que quand il en sera tems on la sollicitera, et qu'alors on se nommera.

13. (*a minor point*).

14. Qu'il seroit à désirer que le Roy put se prononcer de maniére à faire connoitre qu'il est disposé à ne persécuter personne, à acceuillir (*sic*) ceux qui se rapprocherent (*sic*) de lui, et qu'il ne tient pas à l'ancien régime dans toute son étendue.

15. Qu'il seroit très facheux que le roy se retirat en Angleterre.'

In introducing the contents of the *résultat*, D'André observed: 'Je ne vous envoie pas l'original, parce qu'elle contient plusieurs détails qui me sont personnels, et que d'ailleurs on me demande un secret absolu sur le nom des signataires.'

others of the interior could equally interpret in favour of a constitutional monarchy of some kind.[1]

Such an offer was not likely to be despised by Wickham, whatever the exiled Court might think of it. The authors of the *résultat* passed on to discuss ways and means of promoting the Restoration. Their proposals in this respect bear all the marks of good sense and realism, and incidentally they give straightforward expression to the policy towards which, at this date, the British Minister was slowly being driven, as the only policy which still offered any fair prospects of encompassing the overthrow of

[1] That the writers of the *résultat* did not mean to commit themselves purely and simply to the principles of pure Royalism is further confirmed by the fact that Wickham did not regard them as having done so. In his despatch no. 11, 20 May 1797, the envoy gave Grenville an account of the conduct of 'Mr Berger's committee' ('Berger' was one of the code names then being used in Wickham's correspondence for D'André) at the time of the all-important elections in year V. In this, he clearly distinguishes between 'Mr Berger's committee' and 'the Royalists'. By 'the Royalists' he means, as the context makes clear, the pure Royalists of Paris, then led by Des Pomelles. The distinction he makes is not simply a distinction between different groups pledged to the same principles, for he writes that in the 'more direct and intimate union' which took place for the purposes of the election campaign between 'Mr Berger's committee' and the 'Royalists', 'Mr Berger's committee acted with perfect good faith and without intriguing at all for themselves suffered the torrent of the public opinion . . . in favour of persons . . . attached to the antient government, but desirous of reforming its abuses'. There would be no point in acknowledging the disinterest of 'Mr Berger's committee' in face of pure Royalist successes in the elections, if the committee had itself, in Wickham's mind, been identified with pure Royalism.

Further still, there is evidence that D'André himself did not understand his friends to have adopted the principles of the Pretender unconditionally. In his despatch no. 12 of 1797, 24 May, Wickham recounted an interview which took place (as appears from collateral evidence) about the beginning of 1797 between D'André and a special emissary sent by the exiled Court to find out what D'André and his 'committee' were engaged upon. In his reply to the emissary's questions, D'André used (as Wickham reports it) understandably vague language. (There would have been no wisdom in blurting out, for the ears of Louis XVIII, that they meant to restore him only within the framework of a new-fangled constitution.) But, if they had really been pure Royalists, there would have been, evidently, no need for such vagueness and caution. What D'André said, according to Wickham's version, was that their 'endeavours would be constantly directed to the one point of restoring him to the Throne of his Ancestors as soon and with as much power and splendour as times and circumstances would . . . permit'. (The drafts of neither of these despatches were included in Wickham's *Corresp.*)

the Republic. The writers emphasized their conviction that it was useless to attempt any immediate 'general movement' in favour of Royalty, and worse than useless to expect public adhesion to any course of violent action. The public spirit was indeed Royalist fundamentally, but its exhaustion and apathy were now such as to rule out all undertakings of that kind. Moreover, for fear of providing an opportunity for the recovery of the Jacobins, it was not possible as yet to make any overt attack on the established order even by political action within the existing constitution. They pointed, therefore, to the next elections, for which they proposed to work, and which they hoped would be 'good' enough to result in the creation of a two-thirds majority of anti-Republicans in the legislative body. Meantime, they were anxious to build up the opposition in the existing Councils; to work for the annulment of the laws of 3 brumaire; to attack Barras and other Thermidorians who could be accused of undue partiality for the Jacobins; to proselytize other members of the Councils, and even perhaps members of the Directory, by showing them that it was possible to make 'un traité avantageux avec le Roi'; and to employ a few newspapers 'pour repandre insensiblement des idées favorables au retour du roy'.

The committee thought that after the elections it would be possible to proceed more directly along the road to the Restoration. The writers did not dwell upon the methods of action which would then be appropriate. They contented themselves with inferring that, at every stage, the King's interests could be promoted only by the interior. They could not be promoted by *chouans*, or by foreign armies.

The writers displayed marked caution in their response to the suggestion that they should enter into regular connection with the other quarters with which D'André was in touch. They gave D'André to understand that a 'correspondence' should not yet be entered into, and that their names, though appended to the *résultat*, must be kept a close secret to everyone except D'André. 'Quand il en sera tems, on... sollicitera une correspondance, et... alors on se nommera.' We have already seen that these men, who also placed themselves in touch with the King's Agents at Paris, at a later stage were shown to have repented of their dealings with them. The implication raised by these cautious touches in their *résultat* to D'André is that their disillusionment with the Agents had begun very early, and had already influenced their attitude towards every connection which extended back to the Royal Court.

So much for the response of D'André's acquaintances in the Councils. The general line taken by the writers, regarding conditions in the interior and the best ways in which to promote a return to a more conservative form of government, can have contained nothing to surprise the ex-Constituent. He had himself expressed in a letter to Wickham in mid-April[1] his own views on the situation in France, as brought up to date for him at that point by the impressions of his wife and his other intended emissary, who had just obeyed his summons to meet him in Switzerland. In their general drift, his observations correspond very closely with those set out in the *résultat*, though D'André's treatment is, naturally, less elaborate, and it also displays a more specifically pure Royalist sympathy:

Il n'y a pas un Républicain sur cent en France. Dans l'assemblée même il y a encore plus de Royalistes qu'on ne peut le croire; mais *tot capita, tot sensus*. Le parti d'Orléans est fort; et ce qui constitue surtout sa force, c'est qu'il est organisé. Il a des ramifications dans les administrations, les armées, et les tribunaux. Heureusement, ses chefs sont méprisés et détestés. La crainte des vengeances, la peur de la guerre civile, l'incertitude, l'apathie, l'egoisme arrétent bien des gens. Vous jugerés, sans que j'entre dans le détail, quelles sont les classes que ces divers sentimens affectent. Si on peut trouver un moyen de convaincre et de persuader, qu'il n'y aura point de persecution, si on peut tranquiliser sur les suites, la moitié, les trois quarts de la besogne sont faits. Il ne faut pas dissimuler, cependant, que les avis sont bien partagés; que quoique la Royauté soit généralement desirée, on est peu d'accord sur la forme du gouvernement Monarchique, et même sur la personne du Roi. Aussi faut-il se borner maintenant à attaquer la forme actuelle, en réunissant contre elle ses nombreux ennemis, sauf à s'arranger ensuite, en tachant de préparer d'avance les esprits.

It will be seen from this that D'André, though he had now adopted, and hoped for the final success of, the cause of the Pretender, was by no means under the illusion that France was capable of speedy mass conversion to pure Royalist principles, and that he, like the writers of the *résultat*, though expressing himself more specifically on this point than they, favoured a 'coalition of par-

[1] D'André's letter of 16 April 1796.

ties'. It will also be seen that D'André by clear implication rules out as firmly as the writers of the *résultat* all methods involving appeals to force, which the interior was simply not in a position to heed. And though D'André did not, in this letter, raise any suggestion of proceeding against the Republic in future only by electoral and parliamentary means, this is, again, logically involved in his remarks.

In one personal respect, however, the *résultat* left D'André at something of a loss. Wickham had suggested to him that he should make this approach at Paris and that thereafter he should act as intermediary between these legislators and their supporters, on the one side, and other elements which Wickham wanted to enlist for the 'coalition', on the other. The ex-Constituent had pointed out to Wickham that he could not afford to devote himself to 'full-time political duties' unless he were paid a salary. (He had four children to maintain, and he could not earn a living in Switzerland. He had been on the point of leaving for London to seek his fortune there, when Wickham had opened these political prospects to him.) His request for a salary had been admitted, and he thus became, at least in prospect, a servant, in a sense, of the British Government.[1] At last the response to his approach at Paris arrived; and though, as is clear from his covering letter, he approved of its general sense, he found that his 'committee' desired no 'correspondence' with him or with anyone else for the time being. D'André seems to have thought that Wickham would turn the dispositions of the writers of the *résultat*, sooner or later, to good purpose; but that his own new political activities had finished before they had well begun.

D'André accepted this verdict with apparent calm. 'Ce résultat m'annonce que je deviens inutile' he commented to Leclerc, 'car puisqu'il n'y a pas de correspondance à avoir avec ce comité, à quoi suis-je bon?'[2] It was as well that he did not distress himself, for in fact his new political activities were to have a future far larger than he then imagined.

Meantime, the *résultat* of D'André's committee lay before Wickham. Enough has already been said about the envoy's view of French affairs at the time when the *résultat* reached Switzerland

---

[1] See D'André's letter to Wickham, 14 May 1796.

[2] D'André's letter of 24 June 1796 (including the text of the *résultat*) to Leclerc.

to indicate that its general line coincided with and completed the movement of his own thought. To abandon, at least until a much later stage, any further pursuit of the goal by methods of a military or insurgent character; to build up the projected coalition of parties, and to direct it essentially to the task of eliminating the Republican majority in the French Councils; to secure from the Pretender such statements as would permit anti-Republicans of various shades to collaborate on this line without affront to their respective opinions as to the proper character of the future government of France—this was the policy towards which Wickham was impelled by all his recent experience of the French problem, and this was the only policy to which he could now attach serious hopes of success. We have already cited, in the text, words from a letter which he wrote to Drake late in July, which show all this very clearly.[1] There is, however, rather more to be said about the envoy's reaction to the *résultat* than has yet been pointed to here. Though it is true, and deserving of emphasis in its proper place, that Wickham now regarded a policy conceived in the general style displayed in the *résultat* as absolutely necessary to any further hopes of success, it is also true and important that Wickham was by no means fully confident of the final success even of this policy. We recall that in his letter to Drake, referred to again just now, there was an expression of uneasiness over the long interval which must elapse between the adoption of the electoral policy, and its critical moment. Wickham had good grounds for such a sense of impatience. The ruling party of the Republic had already developed a formidable reputation for its ability to produce most unpleasant surprises in rapid and endless succession. By the time that the elections occurred, would not Italy and Germany alike have sunk beneath the Republican tide? And Wickham's anxious eyes were already turning towards the further and even more unwelcome prospect of a Republican attempt to invade the British Isles.[2] Moreover, to look at French internal affairs alone, was it not a serious possibility that the Directorials would inaugurate

[1] Ch. IV above.

[2] In his no. 77 of 1796, 23 July, Wickham stated his belief that the Directory would try 'predatory' descents on the British Isles during the summer, and that a more serious expedition, which would have been launched already but for the very large current commitments of the Republic on the continent, might eventually be expected if the Republic should finally 'decide the business' on those fronts.

their reputed design of a non-legitimate monarchy before the electors had any opportunity to record their detestation of the ruling party in its present guise?

Even if the elections became due while there was still something left to save, however, Wickham foresaw other reasons for misgiving. The French opposition would have to behave with great discretion at every stage,[1] and Wickham felt doubtful if the Directory would even so 'be the dupe of this Manœuvre to the extent that was expected'.[2] If the Directory could not, in the event, be so completely duped, it was easy to foresee that at some point, and in some form, there would be a fresh appeal to force, and a new decision in favour of the ruling party imposed at the point of the sword.

It was, therefore, in no mood of shallow and rash optimism that Wickham identified himself with the general suggestions of the *résultat*, but rather in the knowledge that this policy must be attempted with a clear view, both of its quality as a last resource, and of its highly doubtful final prospects. And it was in this strenuously realistic frame of mind that he advised Lord Grenville that 'it would be wise to encourage and support' the committee of five in their propositions.[3]

[1] In his Private despatch no. 28, 4 July 1796, on the subject of 'Mr D'André's propositions', Wickham remarked: 'I think that the period we have all to look to now is the renewal of the third portion of the legislature. The part the Directory has to play is so extremely difficult that I cannot well foresee how it can possibly keep a majority in the two Assemblies. . . . It certainly *cannot* without having (? *recourse*) to some violent measures like those of Vendemiaire. If the opposite party be prudent, quiet and above all silent, it is possible that they may succeed, but not otherwise.'

[2] No. 66 of 1796.

[3] In no. 66 of 1796, Wickham speaks of the 'propositions' of D'André's committee in a tone of some slight disparagement, not, apparently, because of the risk that they might, after all, fail in the end of their purpose—this seems to be a separate line of thought in Wickham's mind—but because he doubted the resources of these men to attempt all that they proposed. His view seems to be that the policy is the only policy which now offered any hopes of success, and that its authors should accordingly be 'encouraged', but that there were grounds for scepticism about their power (even given good management) to take the policy very far.

What must have added further to Wickham's doubts as to the final success of the policy recommended by d'André's committee was the possibility, which cannot have been absent from his mind at any point during these disastrous months in the spring and summer of 1796, that his government would

This implied that communications must be kept open with them, and that there would have to be some degree of 'correspondence' with them, even though they wished as yet to avoid such contacts with the outside world. If there were to be such communication, D'André was the obvious person to manage it. And, accordingly, from a point early in August, we find a series of letters from D'André, still residing at Morges, to Leclerc at Berne, reporting further observations by his friends in the interior, together with reflections of his own. How the communication was resumed does not appear in Wickham's papers, but we can feel safe in stating that its resumption fulfilled the envoy's wishes, even if it did not arise from his own direct initiative.

The letters of D'André which we now have to study begin with accounts, delivered to him verbally, of the progress of his friends at Paris, and of the general state of affairs in France.[1] In the first of these letters D'André gave a more specific view of the progress which his friends hoped to promote in the existing Councils, before the decisive elections were reached. Their interim programme was ambitious enough:

1° faire revenir Vaublanc au sein de l'assemblée 2⁰ faire révoquer la loi du 3 brumaire. 3° faire casser les mauvaises élections du Directoire. 4° faire rentrer ceux qui n'ont pas porté les armes.[2]

---

reopen negotiations with the Directory, already once attempted by Pitt, and make peace with the Republic. Such a negotiation was indeed to be attempted by Lord Malmesbury in his visit to Paris during the autumn of this year.

[1] In the first of these letters (to Leclerc, 9 August) D'André begins: 'Je ne vous ai pas écrit le jour de l'arrivée de la personne que j'attendois, parce que ne m'apportant rien par écrit, il m'a fallu quelque tems pour receuillir (*sic*) le résultat de ses conversations.' This and his next letter (10 August) are concerned with the content of these conversations and with D'André's reflections on them. In another letter, dated 17 August, he reports the observations given to him by 'un Français qui vient de faire une très grande tournée en France'.

[2] The first article of this programme refers to the former deputy of the Legislative Assembly, and Fayettist, Vincent-Marie Vienot-Vaublanc, who had been elected as one of the first new *tiers* by the department of Seine et Marne. Unfortunately for him, he had also been condemned to death for his part in the insurrection of Vendémiaire by one of the military courts established by the victorious Convention. Not surprisingly, he did not appear to take his seat when the new Councils were inaugurated in brumaire year IV. However, no measures were taken to declare his seat vacant; and it is a sign of the increased activity and ambition of the opposition during the summer of

But the five were realistic enough to admit that this programme might prove very difficult to achieve. There was friction between leading members of the right wing, and jealousy between those of them who had sat in the Convention and those of the new *tiers*.[1] Far too many members of the Councils, though not at all sympathetic to the Directorial party, were, said D'André, too much afraid of fresh disturbances to desire the overthrow of the Republic, however much they might at heart prefer a monarchy. These made up the *Ventre*; and it would be difficult to win them over. In another letter of this time, D'André summarized the impressions about the state of French opinion generally, given to him by 'un francais qui vient de faire une très grande tournée en France'.

Il n'y a rien à attendre que du temps. L'opinion est bonne en gènéral, cest (*sic*) à dire que l'assemblée et le directoire sont mèprisès, que les jacobins sont dètestés, less émigrès plaints les riches nouveaux enviés mais que chacun songe á soi, qu'il n'y a ni énergie, ni ensemble, ni désir de sortir de l'état actuel par des mouvemens violens. C'est donc au temps seul à amener des circonstances plus favorables, cependant on peut les préparer et les faire naitre.[2]

With this passage we may compare D'André's remark in the first of these letters, that the views of the *Ventre* in the Councils were shared

par un nombre infini de français, qui quoiqu'ils prèfèrassent un roy, craignent tellement les convulsions qu'amèneroit un changement, desirent tellement le repos, qu'ils font des voeux pour l'affermissement de la rèpublique.[3]

1796, that D'André's friends should propose his admission to the Council, despite the verdict standing against him (Kuscinski, op. cit., p. 391, p. 84; Buchez & Roux *Hist. parl.*, tome 37, p. 146.)

The third of the points refers to the 'elections' to administrative offices, which had not been completed by the electors, and which the Directory had been empowered by the Councils to supplement by nominations of its own; see ch. II above.

In the fourth point, the reference is of course to émigrés who had not borne arms against their fatherland, i.e. against the Revolutionary regimes which had, at successive times, held sway over the fatherland.

[1] D'André mentions in the letter (9 August 1796) Boissy d'Anglas, Lanjuinais and Larivière as ex-Conventionals who found it difficult to enjoy good relations with the men of the new *tiers*. He also understood that these jealousies and frictions were deliberately fomented by 'le parti Syeies'.

[2] D'André to Leclerc, 17 August 1796.

[3] Letter of 9 August, already referred to.

In presenting this evidence of conditions and tendencies in France, which he derived at second hand, D'André no doubt shaped it to his own cast of mind, as well as putting it in his own words. The quotations just offered suggest that it was a vigorous and realistic mind, little subject to the rose-coloured delusions which had so often marked the reports of other Royalists. But meantime, D'André was already beginning to offer his own reflections to Wickham, throwing himself into the system proposed in outline by the writers of the *résultat*, elaborating it with arguments of his own, and seeking by every means to draw Wickham and his government into the fullest commitment to the plan of electoral warfare against the Directory. As we read his letters, we become clear that D'André had not merely a sound judgement of conditions existing in France, but also the talents of a political strategist and a political spokesman; though he had not invented the policy expressed in the *résultat*, (for it was a policy so obviously suggested by experience and by the existing situation that it needed no inventor) he was taking it up with such powers of exposition and apologetic that he was becoming something of potentially far greater importance for the whole design than a simple intermediary in a correspondence. We are prepared in advance to learn that in due course D'André was called on, by his associates in the interior, with the warm approval of Wickham, to assume the lead of the activities which he so ably commended.

It is worth while to display at some length the forceful and cynical reasoning which D'André uses to justify his friends' proposed policy. Briefly, his reasoning comes to this: much as the country detests its present rulers and little as it cares for their system, it will not, as yet, act for itself, or back any direct assault on the regime. But this does not matter; the nation, which offers no resistance to the coercion of the Directory, can in the same kind of way be manipulated by other agencies in an opposite direction. If the constituted authorities can be captured by the enemies of the Republic, then, whether the nation actually wills this result or not, the constituted authorities can be used to undermine and finally destroy the Republic, just as the constitutional machinery of 1791 had once been used to undermine and destroy the constitutional order in which it was embodied.

Je suis loin de regarder la constitution de 1795 comme solidement établie... mais si on veut la (*culbuter?*) tout à coup, elle servira de point de railliement à tous ceux qu'une contre rèvolution effraie. Ceux qui l'attaquent seront dénoncés et perdus. Voyés comme les girondins s'y sont pris. ils ont d'abord eux mêmes juré la constitution de 1791. Ils n'en ont attaqué que les agens. Ils ont cherché á se rendre maîtres des èlections, a se former une majorité dans l'assemblée, dans les autorités constituées, dans les états majors de l'armée et des gardes nationales. Ils ont ensuite profité des fautes du gouvernement et enfin ont tout bouleversé...

Que faudroit il donc faire à prèsent... (?) Puisque l'opinion fait tout il faut . . . la former, puisque la nation n'est rien il faut la nègliger et s'attacher à ceux qui la gouvernent. Si les gouvernans sont inaccessibles par principes oú par interét, examiner quelles sont les personnes qu' on peut faire agir, soit pour les gagner, soit pour les perdre. Je ne vois aucune folie à se flatter qu'on pourroit diriger les prochaines èlections de manière a avoir une grande majorité dans le corps lègislatif et les principales autorités constituées. Alors on verroit si on peut frapper un grand coup ou s'il faut miner l'edifice au lieu de le faire sauter tout à la fois... Je ne puis rèpondre du succés, car quel est l'insensè qui voudroit apres ce que nous voions depuis six ans, se mèler de prophétiser... (?) [1]

We will also reproduce a portion of another letter, of similar purport, but expressed with such detailed consideration, such formality and such studied eloquence that the suggestion inevitably arises that this was a statement intended for onward transmission to the exiled Court or to the government at London, and requested by Wickham for that purpose.

Je regarde d'abord comme prouvé 1° *qu' on ne doit plus rien attendre de la guerre extérieure* 2° *Que l'on ne doit pas d'avantage espérer un mouvement général de l'intérieur*. Quant à des mouvement partiels, il est convenu qu' ils n'ont rien que de dangereux.

Ces deux bases supposées, vous me dirés sans doute qu'il n'y a donc plus qu'à laisser marcher la République.

Si je croyais que le Gouvernement Républicain put convenir à la France, malgré mon attachement à la Monarchie je repondrois qu'il faut le soutenir, car le bonheur de mon pays passera avant tout. Mais je ne le pense pas. Sans les moyens extraordinaires qu'on a donné au Directoire, sans l'espèce de Gouvernement Révolutionnaire qui règne encore en France, vous verries cette charpente mal assemblée crier et s'affaisser de tous côtés. Or, un jour il faudra bien que tous ces pouvoirs extra constitutionnels cessent, et alors arrivera la dissolution du

[1] D'André to Leclerc, 17 August 1796.

Gouvernement... Ainsi donc, rendre à la France un Gouvernement sage, voilà le but.

Les moyens n'étant plus, ni dans l'étranger, ni dans le mouvement intérieur, il faut les chercher ailleurs.

Supposons que le Corps législatif qui a le droit général de surveillance et d'inspection, qui vote les subsides et s'en fait rendre compte, et qui joint à tout cela l'exercice terrible de l'accusation, fut bien composé. Ne seroit-il pas aisé d'y faire dénoncer les membres du Directoire, et pour dilapidation des finances, et pour malversation, et pour ses mauvais choix, et pour sa négligence à prévenir les Troubles du Midi, pour sa connivence même avec leurs auteurs? Ne seroit-il pas aisé de faire poursuivre les trois quarts de la Convention pour avoir souffert Robespierre ... et pour avoir même après le 9 Thermidor, rendu une foule de loix attentatoires aux droits de la Nation? Ne seroit-il pas aisé de faire rentrer les Emigrés? Et si a une bonne composition du Corps législatif on joignoit de bonnes élections pour les administrations Départementales, après avoir comprimé tous les anarchistes, ne seroit-il pas possible, en présentant à la Nation le tableau de tout ce qu'elle a souffert, de tout ce qu'elle souffre encore, de la ramener à ses anciens sentimens? Un mouvement communiqué par les autorités constituées, soutenu par des hommes forts, par les Prêtres et les Emigrés qui seroient rentrés, ne présenteroit-il pas l'espoir du succès?

Je ne sais si je m'abuse, mais la supposition des bonnes Elections une fois admise, l'evenement ne me paroit pas douteux.

Déja un Comité dans l'assemblée s'occupe sérieusement de préparer les voies, de se former une majorité, de chercher les moyens d'influencer les élections, de faire rentrer ceux que des loix injustes ont exclu. Il espère. Mais il ne faut pas se dissimuler que les deux tiers anciens lui opposent un grand obstacle. Il ne s'agiroit donc que de l'aider, de marcher dans le même sens, et surtout de reunir tous les efforts pour les prochaines élections.[1]

In this same letter, D'André moved beyond the discussion of the basis of his friends' policy, and proceeded to consider the resources which would be available for the organizing of such an election campaign. While, again, there is no need to credit D'André with any special originality in prescribing the use of such resources, his statement of the chief immediate end which all electoral arrangements should serve is very striking and proclaims a political strategist and organizer of very high quality. There is no doubt, says D'André, that, so far as its feelings are concerned, *la nation en masse* is deeply hostile to its present rulers. The only

[1] D'André's letter, or perhaps rather memorandum, 22 August 1796.

immediate aim at the elections is then very simple—to induce this 'mass' to go to the primary assemblies. If it can only be led to the polls, there need be no misgivings about the way in which it will use its votes. 'Il ne faut obtenir qu'un point, c'est que cette masse se rende dans les assemblées Primaires.' D'André was pointing directly to a state of things which had characterized French elections, at every level, since 1790: the polls had always been monopolized by a small, sometimes tiny minority, adherents of one or another phase of the Revolutionary movement. He was drawing a conclusion which seemed obvious once this fact had been observed, that the more genuinely popular was the response to the opportunity to vote, the more conservative would be the reflection of opinion that emerged from the process.

In his account of the particular methods which might be used to bring about this result, D'André revealed his own aspiration (which, perhaps, he had cherished from the beginning, but of which there is no earlier evidence) to organize and direct the whole plan:

On peut employer... différens moyens, 1. Quelques bons écrits jettés dans le public à l'approche des Elections. 2. Des Voyageurs capables, courageux et instruits 3. Les Prêtres surtout; c'est un des plus grands ressorts que l'on puisse mettre en action. Si on peut leur persuader de ne diriger leurs efforts qu'a faire aller le Peuple aux Elections et a lui faire faire de bons choix, quelques prêtres répandus en France pourroient produire un grand effet. Enfin quelque tems avant les élections on feroit des listes convenues qui seroient envoyées dans les Départemens dont on se croiroit assuré...

...Comme sans unité il n'y a point de force, je voudrois que le Comité établi à Paris fut le centre commun, qu'il connût tous les Voyageurs, lesquels correspondroient avec lui, et auxquels il donneroit des directions... et lui-même correspondroit par le moyen donné avec le moteur extérieur.[1]

This passage shows in outline the methods which were in due time actually used by D'André and his collaborators in their election campaign. By the time it was written, D'André and Wickham had already agreed that the ex-Constituent should himself re-enter France in order to take personal part in all that was now to be attempted.[2] D'André had engaged some of his friends in the

[1] Ibid.

[2] This seems to be clearly implied in D'André's letters of 17 and 23 August,

interior to try to procure the removal of his name from the list of émigrés;[1] but on 23 August he informed Leclerc that he would not wait for the outcome of these efforts, if it was still felt that his return to France was the best course. He intended, he said, to leave for France within a month, at the longest. He would seek for a passport from a 'safe' quarter, and had a plan to re-enter his native land in the character of a driver, working for and carrying the certificate of a haulage contractor of the Swiss town of Nyon. He accepted an offer by Wickham of an 'advance' to cover the cost of his journey, which included, necessarily, the purchase of a carriage and two horses with which to uphold the character which he was to assume.

In fact, D'André was not yet at all so near to his re-entry to his native land as he believed; successive difficulties were to delay his departure till February of the following year. In the meantime, the plans with which he had associated himself were to undergo changes of fortune also. They met with obstacles; they also received important new developments. By the time that all the difficulties, personal and political, had been removed, and D'André was able to proceed on his journey, the elections of year V, which had once seemed to Wickham to be so far distant, lay in the immediate future. But D'André returned to France not too late to take personal part in the great attempt to manage the elections; and the new developments, which his plans had meantime undergone, had transformed them from a mere paper project into a great and complex series of operations, already partly in process of achievement. All this evidently requires treatment in a chapter to itself. Enough has been done in this chapter, if we have brought

---

where he writes as though Leclerc is well aware of and approves his efforts to have his name cleared and to re-enter the country.

[1] It appears from his letter of 17 August that there were complications in D'André's case with the Republican authorities: his suit was being opposed, and new charges were (perhaps we should understand) being brought against him. D'André speaks of his *procès* and says it is going none too well for him, his friends being fortunate to have obtained a temporary stay of an *arrêté* of condemnation.

He also passed on information from his friends, that bribery would be his best resource: 'moyennant 200 louis, mon procés changeroit de face.' He commented that he could not raise such a sum. From his letter of 23 August, it appears that Wickham had thereupon offered him financial assistance—which he accepted gratefully, while insisting that he would treat it as a loan.

out a clear account of how D'André became associated with the contemporary efforts to design afresh the policy of the French Royalists, and some impression of the sentiments, the talents, and the *élan* which he brought with him.

VI

The ripening of the 'Great Design'

SEPTEMBER 1796 TO MARCH 1797

IT has already appeared, in the closing pages of the previous chapter, that during the time, in August 1796, when D'André was receiving further observations from his committee at Paris and was himself elaborating upon their suggestions, Wickham left the handling of D'André's business to Captain Leclerc. The envoy does not appear to have resumed his personal connections with D'André until the middle of September, when he drafted a letter to him which D'André can hardly have regarded as promising well for the future development of the plans he had been recommending.[1]

The letter began by commending—though in rather cool and cautious terms—the efforts which D'André's 'friends' had meantime been making in the Councils. At the same time Wickham expressed some disappointment that these legislators had not thought fit to carry on their interim programme rather more briskly, and his fear that they listened too willingly to the promptings of timidity:

> Having no good excuse to make for my long silence I shall not attempt to make *any*, but shall proceed immediately to the subject of your late letters. . . . The plan of operations adopted by your friends seemed to me at the moment perfectly prudent and judicious so far as it went and I observe with great pleasure that hitherto at least it has gone on successfully. I saw at the same time with pain that those gentlemen were persuaded that more could not be done; I was however by no means prepared to say that they were mistaken in that persuasion and therefore I could not but exhort you to encourage them to persevere in their present measures. I was only afraid lest they should grow too fat and sleeky for conspirators and that they should begin to sleep by days as well as by nights to which the large myriogrammes of corn allotted them either by the constitution by the Directory or by themselves no matter which will greatly contribute
> . . . They will certainly need the spur from time to time and I trust entirely to your discretion for the means and moment of applying it . . .

---

[1] Wickham to D'André, 15 September 1796, Wickham Papers.

It is very significant in connection with all this that Wickham made no reference to the ulterior parts of the plan, and particularly to the design to influence the elections. Nor does he comment on the general arguments in support of the plan, which D'André had so carefully constructed for his perusal.

It would appear that part of Wickham's motive in adopting this rather chilly attitude was to place, not D'André himself, but D'André's collaborators, in what Wickham's principal would no doubt have called 'a state of probation'. No doubt Wickham did feel some misgivings about their resolution and courage, as well as about their ability to sway the existing Councils in favour of their whole interim programme; and the whole previous history of the opposition might be invoked to show that such misgivings were by no means unreasonable. Yet it was also true, as Wickham certainly realized, that even the most resolute leadership of the French opposition had a difficult task in hand, that any degree of progress was encouraging, and that caution, even if carried to a fault, was better than overboldness if the Directory was indeed in the end to be successfully 'duped'. In fact, Wickham did not really look so doubtfully on the current efforts of the opposition as he gave D'André to understand. In a despatch home, about a week earlier, Wickham had expressed lively satisfaction over the two important points which the opposition had already gained—'the replacing Vaublanc in the Assembly, and the obtaining a resolution tending to facilitate the election of the new third part of the legislature'. He had also given his approval to the caution shown by D'André's allies in face of the 'still more important questions' which called for attention before the elections came on.[1]

There were, however, other considerations also which influenced Wickham's attitude towards the plans of D'André in mid-September, and which certainly were to some extent distracting his interest from them. The envoy's conviction that the methods of D'André and his friends represented the only feasible approach to the overthrow of the Republic had been temporarily, not indeed destroyed, but disturbed, by the dramatic counter-offensive of the Archduke Charles against Jourdan in South Germany. This had begun in August. By mid-September, under a rain of Austrian hammer-blows, the Army of the Sambre et Meuse was falling

[1] Wickham to Grenville, no. 85 of 1796, 7 September, Wickham, *Corresp.*, vol. I, p. 450.

back towards the Rhine. Wickham, who in mid-July had mourn-
fully predicted that Germany would be 'entirely lost,' now for a
moment half-recovered his faith in a military solution. In the same
letter to D'André, he wrote:

> The success of the Austrians which I am entirely persuaded will be
> continued at least to the Banks of the Rhine before a few more days
> have passed over our heads seem to open a new field for the attention
> as well as the exertions of all well-thinking and well-meaning people in
> France. *That* however is a subject upon which it is absolutely necessary
> that I should see and concert with you before your departure, as it will
> most obviously materially alter a great number of the arguments that
> have hitherto been the most proper to be used perhaps also the whole
> nature of our plans and operations may be entirely changed according
> to the new circumstances that this event may possibly produce.

The hopes which Wickham was thus disposed to build on the
progress of the Archduke beyond the frontiers of the Republic
were to be doomed to early disappointment.[1] By 20 September,
Charles had indeed completed the task of driving Jourdan back to
the West bank of the Rhine. He then turned against Moreau's
Army of the Rhine and Moselle, whose junction with Jourdan he
had so brilliantly averted, and disposed of this enemy also, forcing
Moreau to retire by way of the Black Forest and Huningen into
Alsace. Moreau reached Huningen on 26 October, by which date
the French invasion of Germany may be said to have come back
precisely to the lines from which it started. But, as Wickham had
already foreseen, the outcome of this part of the campaign was
such as to disallow any hopes that the Austrians would be able to
press forward in an immediate counter-invasion of France. The
envoy wrote on 16 October to Sir Morton Eden:[2]

> Could Moreau's army have been *intirely* cut off or destroyed, I should
> have had strong hopes even respecting Alsace, but that not being the
> case, I cannot look upon the fortifications of Strasburg, Landau,
> Bitche, Brisac, Huningue, at this late season of the year, without fear

---

[1] It is fair to say that even at the height of this period of Austrian successes,
Wickham's hopes of their being followed by a successful counter-invasion of
France and by any drastic change in the situation within the country were
tempered by a good deal of caution. In a letter to La Vauguyon, 10 October
(Wickham Papers, bundle 94) he did his utmost to moderate the extravagant
expectations of the exiled Court.

[2] Wickham, *Corresp.*, vol. I., pp. 467–8

and trembling ... I am by no means so sanguine about the result of this campaign as most persons on this side of the country appear to me to be ...

The event showed that Wickham's caution, though belated, was justified. Moreau completed his withdrawal in good order. This fact, together with the lateness of the season, 'left the Directory' (as Wickham put it to Lord Grenville in a despatch of 28 October) 'without any sort of fear of the Austrians being able to effect ... anything serious this campaign.'[1]

The end of the Austrian counter-offensive left Wickham not only sadder but wiser, for he emerged from this period with the conviction that, even if the Archduke had been able to invade France, the interior, even many of its 'best thinking' classes, would have rallied behind the Republican authorities, and not behind the foreigner or the mad émigrés whose premature jubilations had completely spoiled in advance whatever chance there might have been that things would take a different course.[2] Henceforward, Wickham would cleave with steadier resolution to plans for the solution of the French problem which excluded any reliance, whole or partial, on foreign armies and domestic upheavals in support of them.

But of course, while the Archduke's advance held out delusive prospects of a solid Allied footing on French soil, Wickham could not give his whole attention, or even most of it, to the proposals which D'André and his collaborators had been urging. And then, scarcely had Wickham abandoned his hopes in that quarter, than another conjuncture was reached, of a very different sort, which again compelled Wickham to regard with uncertainty the future development of D'André's policy. On 14 October Lord Grenville informed his envoy of the impending departure of Lord Malmesbury for Paris 'to treat for a general peace' with the Regicide Republic. While advising the envoy to 'keep himself prepared' for the very possible failure of this negotiation, Lord Grenville also naturally pointed out that in the meantime 'it might be prudent to suspend all operations'.[3]

While these successive uncertainties gathered over the future

[1] Wickham to Grenville, Private no. 93 of 1796, not publ. in Wickham's *Corresp.*

[2] See Wickham to Sir Morton Eden, 16 October 1796, already cited.

[3] Grenville to Wickham, no. 23 of 1796.

of his projects, D'André made few observations to his British patron—at least on paper; though he wrote enough to show us that he was not prepared lightly to give up his belief that electoral methods offered the only real promise of solving the French problem.[1] He also had occasion to write apologetically of the current fortunes of the opposition at Paris in their pursuit of the interim programme. On 17 September, he feared that the attack on the laws of 3 brumaire (which had been opened by Couchery three days before) had been made prematurely and would end badly.[2] On 4 and 11 October he admitted that the opposition was revealing its deficiencies, both of 'tact' and of 'tactics'; but he expressed his confidence that they would rapidly improve.

Not until mid-November did any fresh wind reach the more or less completely becalmed sails of D'André, who was meantime still as yet vainly trying to hasten forward the moment of his re-entry into France.[3] The new development came, not from the side of Wickham, but from Paris.

[1] On 17 September, D'André wrote that 'le changement survenu a l'extérieur, s'il se soutient, doit produire un grand changement dans l'intérieur', but added that he was not in a position to say what effect the flight of Jourdan had produced on his friends at Paris. This suggests that he was polite, but by no means enthusiastic.

On 4 October, D'André developed an elaborate argument against a project, which had latterly been interesting Wickham, (perhaps as a means of exploiting the situation which might arise if the Austrians effected a deep thrust into France) for the recruitment of a small secret force to act, in a sudden emergency, in the interior. (This is, presumably, the project latterly put forward by the Paris Agents, and discussed by Wickham in his Private despatch no. 40, 2 September.) In this letter of 4 October, D'André traces the history of several previous attempts, at earlier stages of the Revolution, to organize these secret armies for use in the interests of the good cause in some expected emergency. He seeks to show that such efforts were mere waste of time and money, and that their almost inevitable discovery and denunciation always resulted in fresh harm to the cause they were meant to assist.

[2] Buchez & Roux, op. cit., tome 37, p. 171. D'André's misgivings were to be by no means completely vindicated by the event, as will be noted later.

Jean-Baptiste Couchery, one of the new *tiers* of year IV, was deputy (Cinq-Cents) for the Doubs (Kuscinski, op. cit., p. 356). He is mentioned by Wickham in his Private despatch no. 12 of 1797 (27 June) as one of a number of deputies who, in the session of the summer following the election, worked regularly with D'André.

[3] On 20 September D'André wrote in terms which suggest that he was no longer so happy about taking the risks of returning to France while still on the government's list of émigrés. He said that he had recently had advice from

Je me hâte de vous informer [wrote D'André to Wickham on 15th November] d'une aventure assès singuliére. Dimanche j'ai eu la visite d'un individu porteur d'un billet de *Dumas* et d'une recommendation de *Duport*. Cet homme, qui parle bien, m'a dit s'appeller *Duplantier* reprèsentant du peuple, chargè expressément par Dumas et ses amis de me voir, ainsi que *Lameth* et de nous engager tous deux à rentrer en France. Il parait que *Lameth* est déja parti où (*sic*) va partir. Voici le rèsultat de ce que m'a dit *Duplantier*.

Le comité qui se tient ches *Gilbert Desmoliéres* composé de *Dumas Pastoret Portalis Simeon Duplantier Dumolard* et *Cadroi* avoit cru d'abord devoir se rallier au *Directoire* dans l'espoir d'abattre les Jacobins. Le Directoire les a trompés. Ils sont furieux et se rèuniront à tous ceux qui voudront les attaquer. Ils se doutent qu'il y a un autre comité parmi les *clichiens*, et que j'ai quelques relations avec ce comité, c'est pour cela que *Duplantier* vouloit me voir, m'engager où à rentrer, où à lui indiquer quels ètoient les moiens que je pouvois avoir, et à le faire aboucher à Paris avec les personnes avec lesquelles j'ètois en relation.

Here, then, was the offer of an important advance towards the consolidation of the 'coalition' against the Republic, the proffered adhesion of those members of the legislature who had hitherto, for a few months, maintained a doubtful alliance with the Directory and lent a delusive appearance of success to Carnot's *ralliement*. And it was to D'André, whom several of them had known well, that the Dumas group appealed, sending to the shores of lake Geneva to discover the identity of the politicians whose ally they supposed him to be, and over whom, it would be natural to suppose, they thought this elder statesman still short of forty years old had great influence.

D'André subsequently explained to Wickham more fully the background and nature of Duplantier's overture, and the envoy transmitted the impressions he had received of the matter in a long despatch home dated 11 December:

The Directory, . . . has been in direct treaty with . . . Mr Dumas's committee *as a Body*, for its support and assistance when matters of importance to Government were to be carried . . . This committee discovered about two months since, what nothing but the personal vanity and presumption of Mr Dumas could have prevented them from learning long before, that they had been in every point the dupes of

---

Paris to the effect that his return in these circumstances would be very dangerous.

the government, and that they had been aiding it in all its plans of finance, in all its military and political speculations, to no other end than the fixing more firmly the Directory in its usurpation, and destroying all the future hopes, power and means of themselves, and their own friends and party . . .

They alledge . . . *First* that the Directory refused, contrary to *their own express engagement*, to dismiss Mr Merlin of Douai and put Mr Demousseau in his place.[1] *Secondly* that they refused in like manner . . . to dismiss a number of their commissaries in the different Departments . . . who were proved to be in direct communication with . . . Jacobin societies. . . . *Fourthly* that the Directory instead of leaving the approaching elections free, *as they had promised to do* were secretly endeavouring . . . to secure a majority of their own creatures; and that finding it neither possible nor indeed safe to *bring in* a sufficient number of Jacobins, they were endeavouring to form a coalition among the purchasers of national property, upon whose support they thought they could entirely rely *from the motive of common interest*.

The Committee particularly complains that the Directory . . . had hastened the sale of the confiscated estates, and brought such an immense quantity of that property into the market at once, as had reduced its value to a mere trifle (*and*) made it accessible to all their own creatures and dependants . . .

Mr Duplantier . . . was charged to go into Switzerland and endeavour to engage all the members of the Constitutional party resident there to enter immediately each into their respective Departments, to endeavour to procure themselves, if possible, if not their friends, to be chosen at the approaching elections, and then to form a common cause with their Committee, the primary object of which should be an attack on the Directory, the ultimate one the restoration of a monarchy in the person of the present sovereign. Mr Duplantier first saw Mr Duport and Mr Theodore Lameth, both of whom he engaged to follow his advice without any difficulty . . . He next waited on Mr D'André, for whom he had a special commission, tending to persuade that gentleman to engage the friends, with whom they supposed him to be in correspondence at Paris, to unite with *their* Committee and to put himself at their head.[2]

---

[1] Merlin of Douai was, of course, the Directory's Minister of Justice; it is easily understandable that men who wished to make sure of the complete annihilation of the Jacobin party would be anxious that such a man as Merlin should no longer fill that position.

[2] Wickham to Grenville, no. 102 of 1796, 11 December: Wickham, *Corresp.*, vol. I, pp. 486–9. Wickham's papers show that when the Dumas group approached D'André, they also made an (originally separate) approach to

There are perhaps three points of special interest for us in all this. Firstly, it is clear, even from Wickham's own account, that the conduct of Dumas had been ruled by other motives in addition to vanity. His vanity may have been real enough; but it was not vanity which led him to press his Directorial allies for concessions intended, precisely, in his mind, to ensure that the ruling party would lose the next elections. Nor was it the case, even if Wickham thought so, that he had, until about October, served the turn of the Government without rewards of this very kind. Nor, when he finally decided to finish with the Directory, was Dumas yielding to irritation simply on the score that the government had behaved towards him and his friends in a manner which was not that of gentlemen. The real cause of the rupture of this strange marriage of convenience, as, again, appears clearly enough in Wickham's own account, was that the Directory—whether in breach of promises made, or not—would not and could not make the still further concessions which Dumas blandly asked it to make. It had dismissed many of its appointees, to the benefit of the *honnêtes gens*. It could hardly be expected to dismiss them all. It had, in this and other ways, facilitated the plans of the opposition for the next elections. It could hardly be expected to deny itself the luxury even

---

Wickham. Wickham's agent Bayard arrived at Berne from Paris on or immediately before 17 November; he left a note for Wickham at the legation, in the envoy's temporary absence, which bears that date and contains in the form of an enclosure a number of written questions, addressed to Wickham by certain (unidentified) persons at Paris. (The note and its enclosure are in Wickham Papers.) Together with these papers lies another sheet containing Wickham's draft replies. The grounds for thinking these questions originated with Dumas and his friends are provided chiefly by Wickham's letter of 17 November to D'André, in which the envoy responded to D'André's announcement of the approach which this group had just made to him, through Valentin-Duplantier. In this letter, Wickham refers to certain fears expressed by the Dumas group regarding the supposed disposition of the British Government to favour the designs of the Orleanists or those of the Jacobins, and informs D'André of the line which he invariably took in disposing of such fears. Now D'André, in his report to Wickham of the visit of Duplantier, had not adverted to this subject; therefore Wickham must have had it from another source that Dumas and his friends were concerned over this supposed sinister affection of English policy for Orleanism or Jacobinism. And, in fact, this matter is the subject of one of the questions carried to Wickham at this time by Bayard, while Wickham's drafted answer to that question is couched in terms closely similar to those in which he informed D'André of the line he took when these fears were mentioned. In other respects, moreover, the

of having an election campaign, even of trying to rally any support to its own side; it could not be expected to hand itself over utterly without defence to the tender mercies of men who, whatever their views about monarchy, certainly had no love for the Republic. To the Directory, the conduct of Dumas and his party must have seemed suggestive, not so much of vanity as of boundless ambition and an utter inability to see any point of view but their own.

The second feature of interest is the impression, given by

---

questions carried by Bayard are certainly consistent with their ascription to the Dumas group in its dispositions at that moment.

The more important of these questions are reproduced below, with Wickham's drafted replies:

1. 'Si on soumet un Plan *possible* pour renverser le système actuel de Gouvernement en France et y retablir la Royauté dans la ligne directe..., voudrait-on l'appuyer efficacement?

'Si un tel Plan fut réellement *conçu* et *soumis*, on l'appuyerait très surement de toutes les forces disponibles, à condition toujours que la paix ne se faisait point avec la Republique. Si la paix se faisait, on la conserverait avec la République de la même bonne foi qu'avec toute autre Puissance.

2. ...

...

3. Peut-on être assuré que le Gouvernement Anglais ne donnera, ni ne fera donner, aucun secours, d'aucune espèce, ni direct, ni indirect, à aucun des partis dont le but ne serait pas le même que celui-ci énoncé dans l'article premier?

Cette question... ne peut avoir en vue que les méfiances éternelles des bons Francais des Orleanistes et des Jacobins... Je ne peux trop répéter... qu'on... aura toujours en horreur les auteurs et fauteurs de pareils projets. On ne les protegera, on ne les favorisera jamais, on ne les aidera d'aucune manière.

4. *Article secret.*
Comme le Gouvernement Anglais peut, plus que tout autre, soutenir l'exécution de ce plan, s'il était possible que le Roi, influencé par ses entours, en contrariât en tout ou en partie les dispositions, et que le Plan fut de nature à être executé malgré ces obstacles, doit-on espérer d'être soutenu néanmoins *efficacement*, pour arriver au but?'

Mon respect pour l'illustre personnage en question, la connaissance intime et personnelle que j'ai de ses Talens comme de ses Principes, me seront le garant le plus sûr qu'il ne mettra jamais le Gouvernement Anglais dans le cas de discuter une pareille question.'

It will be agreed that the Dumas group, in taking the new departure which

Wickham's account, of the ambitious energy which the Dumas party displayed in planning their future steps. They had in mind nothing less than the rehabilitation of the old Feuillant leadership; the great figures of five years ago were to be summoned back to take an active share in the struggle; and, if the Pretender were indeed to recover his throne as a consequence of all the activities which they now planned, it would of course be on terms which provided for the Feuillants. 'The restoration of *a* monarchy in the person of the present sovereign' is the phrase in which Wickham significantly describes their intention, and we have already shown (in one of the notes to this chapter) how careful they were to seek precautions against the expected recalcitrance of the Pretender.

The third point, perhaps of the greatest interest for us, is the special importance which these men attached to D'André: not simply because he had now a group of his own in the legislature with which they might combine, but because they envisaged him as the acceptable leader of the coalition which was now to be built up. Thereby they acknowledged, not only his political talents, but, it is to be presumed, also his importance as providing them with an influential connection with the pure Royalists and with England.

We can now return to D'André. The ex-Constituent took immediate advantage of this development to begin to press Wickham for a rather more active support than the envoy had lately encouraged him to think he enjoyed. Of course D'André knew that a peace between Britain and the Republic would sever his

---

we are discussing, would very naturally make an approach to the British envoy. To work effectively against the established regime of their own country, they would need independent support and probably financial aid; the British Government was the most likely to supply these, for Britain—always assuming that she could be cleared of suspicions of deliberately keeping up disorder in France by such devices as encouraging Orleanists and Jacobins—had everything to gain by a legitimist Restoration on lines which the French public could sincerely accept, and had no observable motive for insisting on the restoration of the old regime in all its unpopular features. It will also be agreed that the fourth question, especially, is exactly what we should expect the constitutionalist politicians of the Dumas group to raise: could they be assured of British support in case they reached the goal of their present efforts in every respect, except the consent of the legitimate claimant himself to reign on the terms which they had arranged for him? Their subsequent conduct was to show how extremely nervous they were, that in working for a legitimist solution they should betray themselves into the hands of the pure Royalists of the emigration.

M

connection with Wickham completely, and that this issue was not in Wickham's hands. But D'André no doubt also felt that, pending the conclusion of Malmesbury's mission, his plans might provisionally have, and certainly needed, British support in a more substantial sense than Wickham's personal blessing and the payment of D'André's expenses, which was the utmost that was as yet forthcoming. D'André may well have felt, in view of Wickham's absorption with the prospects of the recent Austrian offensive, and of the rather cool commendation which he had given to the efforts of the opposition in mid-September, that even Wickham's personal blessing was something of a wasted asset, however much he might feel assured of the envoy's continuing good will towards him as an individual. However that may have been, D'André certainly threw into his letter of 15 November the following lines, in which the intention to urge Wickham to a fuller and speedy commitment to the plan is obvious:

Le Directoire cherche dèja à préparer les elections. Quoiqu'il ne le veuille pas tout à fait jacobites, il ne les veut pas non plus, et encore moins, Modèrées. Il veut des gens absolument à lui. Dèja il cherche à coaliser les acquèreurs de biens nationaux en les allarmant sur leurs propriétés, et on leur fait entendre qu' il ne faut nommer que des acquéreurs de cette sorte de biens. Cette coalition si naturelle peut produire beaucoup d'effet.

Si la paix ne se fait pas, il seroit sans doute essentiel de suivre le projet d'*influencer les elections*, afin de s'assurer la majorité dans le prochain corps lègislatif. Dans ce cas, il n'y auroit pas de temps à perdre, soit pour *rassembler les moiens nècessaires, soit pour les mettre en activité*... avant que les voyageurs ... aient fait leurs courses, ètabli leurs bases, formé leurs correspondances, leurs liaisons, et rendu compte de leurs opèrations, le mois de mars s'approchera ...

And to Leclerc, on the same date, D'André wrote in terms of frankly impatient entreaty for a clear decision, would the British Minister commit himself and, within his power, his country to aiding the opposition's election campaign?

Je voudrois qu'on décidat si on veut travailler les èlections, qu'on vit quels moiens on a à me donner, pour les ajouter à ceux de nos amis; qu'on se fixat sur l'emploi tres utile des prêtres qui peuvent nous aider infiniment. Cette machine, quelque simple qu'on la suppose, sera longue à monter. Il faut d'abord dècider ce point, veut on travailler pour les élections?

As for the overture made to him by Duplantier, D'André explained to Wickham that he had handled this with optimism strongly mixed with caution. Not knowing Duplantier or his real intentions, and not being at liberty to disclose the identity of his already established allies, he had not satisfied the deputy's curiosity. He had told Duplantier that he himself would be delighted to return as soon as he could do so with safety. But he had also sent off urgent messages to his other 'friends' at Paris, asking if they agreed to his proceeding further with Duplantier.[1]

Two days later, Wickham drafted a letter to D'André which must have disposed entirely of the doubts which had been suggested to his mind by recent conduct of Wickham. Though Lord Malmesbury was still at Paris and the possibility must, therefore, still have been presumed to exist, that England would reach terms with the Republic, the ex-Constituent was now assured completely that all his plans would have the full support of Wickham, (and not support only in a moral sense) until or unless peace was made. D'André also had Wickham's cordial support for any attempt, which he might think proper, to conclude an understanding with Dumas's group and with any other political elements in France which might be prepared to join in a wide coalition of conservative forces, prepared to join hands against the present regime, and to be tolerant of different ulterior objectives among themselves. Finally, the letter included the most flattering proofs of the high esteem which the envoy felt for D'André, and of his recognition of D'André's rightful place as the active director of the whole intended operation in the interior.[2]

[1] The reference here is again to D'André's letter to Wickham, 15 November.

[2] From Wickham's 'Draft to Mr D'A——', 17 November 1796: 'Your letter of yesterday and the communication made to you by Mr D—— has by no means surprised me. You know what has long been my opinion as to the conduct of that Gentleman's friends at Paris and how entirely I have been persuaded that they would at last discover that they have been the Dupes of abler persons than themselves.

I cannot too strongly approve of the reserve you made use of towards them in your communication with D—— . . . However I am decidedly of opinion that this is an opportunity of *bringing those Gentlemen to reason and of applying their Talents and Services to a better purpose* that ought by no means to be neglected, and I am at the same time fully persuaded that such a Task cannot be placed in better hands than yours.

As to the means of bringing it about, I can add little to what I said to you

It need not be thought difficult to account for this new and warm reassertion by Wickham of his support for the plans of D'André. The considerations which had, for a time, appeared to cloud his attitude towards them were being removed. The Austrian offensive was now at an end. Pitt had come round to the view, which Grenville had privately cherished throughout, that it was a mistake to attempt peace with the Republic at this stage;[1] and it seems probable that Wickham must, by this date, have become aware that Malmesbury's mission was destined to fail. On the side of the interior, Wickham, though he was disappointed by the

---

here when I *last* had the pleasure of seeing you. The *general* nature of our conversation applied as fully *to this case* as to any other of the same kind, and all matters of *detail* in what regards *its execution* must of course be left very much to the direction of the principal persons who shall be charged with it. I can only repeat to you what I have so often taken occasion to say already, that *provided you have a share in the general direction of the business* either by yourself or your friends I will immediately furnish you with *such means* as may be thought necessary to accomplish your great object . . .

. . . I have the best reason for believing that your information is correct respecting the intentions of the Directory—gaining the members of what you call the *Ventre*, and securing the Elections in the way and by the means you mention is certainly at this moment one of their principal objects. I have also good reason for believing that unless they should be perfectly sure of a *favourable return* means will be found of putting off the election to another year, . . .

As to the means of influencing the choice of the new elections, they must be all left to you and your friends . . . I most entirely approve of their present plan of their principal efforts being directed to that capital object, and I am also persuaded that it cannot be undertaken too speedily. As I have said before, you may address yourself to me with confidence, should pecuniary means be thought necessary and found wanting . . .

If you can *go in* with safety, I am most decidedly of opinion that you ought to do it, but if that measure cannot be undertaken without *personal* danger, my personal friendship for you as well as my persuasion that your services may be of infinite value to your country, impose a duty upon me to exhort you . . . not to think a moment of venturing yourself beyond the Frontiers'.

Cf. the terms in which Wickham subsequently reported his response to Grenville, in Wickham's no. 102 of 1796, 11 December: Wickham, *Corresp.*, vol. I, p. 489.

[1] See E. D. Adams, *The Influence of Grenville on Pitt's Foreign Policy*, 1904, pp. 48–51 and footnotes. On 10 November Malmesbury received new instructions, representing the new accordance of view between Pitt and Grenville. These, in his view, made the failure of his mission certain. He was correct, though the Directors severed negotiations only in mid-December.

results of the opposition's interim campaign, saw no reason to doubt that the opposition could win the elections;[1] the approaches made by the Dumas group indeed offered him a welcome assurance that the policy of D'André's other 'friends' had important potential

[1] D'André had told Wickham, in his letter of 15 November, that it was now clearly out of the question to 'attendre grand chose du corps lègislatif actuel'. 'Duplantier, auquel j'ai demandé la cause de la faiblesse en nombre des honnêtes gens de l'assemblée, a tout rejetté sur le *ventre* que le Directoire a su gagner par des places et des soumissions de biens nationaux.' Wickham, in his reply on 17 November, had echoed D'André's conclusion: 'I see, as your friends do, that nothing effective can be done till . . . the new elections.'

A good deal of discussion had been going on between the various parties to Wickham's correspondence regarding the doings and prospects of the opposition in the existing chambers. We have noted that Wickham was pleased by their early successes, but had also urged D'André to apply the 'spur' to his friends. From about mid-September, the envoy's hopes of any significant advantage from the opposition's interim programme declined; he concluded they were 'timid and irresolute'. (No. 86 of 1796, 21 September.)

Wickham urged D'André, through Leclerc, to apply pressure on his friends at Paris to conduct their immediate business more strenuously. D'André in reply informed Leclerc (15 November) that he was sending a sharp memorandum. He admitted that they had given cause for complaint; but he did not mean to accept the possible inference that their recent efforts had been simply worthless, if only because this would lead to the further inference that their future conduct would be worth no more. He pointed out to Leclerc that, though they had mishandled the campaign for repeal, it was not a negligible achievement to have attacked the government directly on a subject which, six months before, could hardly have been mentioned in the Councils; nor was it nothing to have mustered 120 or 130 deputies to oppose the directory on this issue. His remark to Wickham, above, that no 'grand chose' could be expected of the Councils before the elections must be read in the light of these observations. D'André meant to argue that, though the opposition's efforts had been disappointing, they had achieved enough to justify higher hopes if the elections could be won. Wickham, on 17 November, accepted D'André's admissions in this sense.

D'André was entirely justified in claiming that the opposition had not been working entirely in vain. Though they had failed to win the repeal they were at this very time working with some skill to win similar results by more oblique methods. On 16 brumaire year V (6 November 1796) they carried resolutions in the Five Hundred which proposed to repeal several sections of the law of 3 brumaire, particularly that relating to the non-juring clergy, and to redefine the Convention's final amnesty so as to extend it to the *vendémiaristes* while withdrawing from its full effect some of the persons on whose services the Directory wished still to rely. On 14 frimaire year V (4 December 1796) the Anciens accepted these resolutions. What was even more significant than these partial victories for the opposition was the fact that the government party had throughout behaved as though doubtful of the outcome of the

support, wider than they had yet been able to mobilize, and he also had D'André's seasonable warnings that, if the plan for influencing the elections were to be proceeded with, steps must now at once be taken.

Whatever the precise form of the calculations which now determined Wickham to act as he did, this at least is clear, that he had now given to D'André the decisive signal. From the moment of Duplantier's visit, and of Wickham's letter of the same week, the fortunes of D'André underwent an abrupt change. The slow waters, upon which they had seemed, for some weeks, to lie almost becalmed, now gave place to a bewildering and perilous course at headlong speed. We can trace the progress of the ex-Constituent through most of the stages of the daring voyage upon which he now set forth, and which was to end at length only upon the fatal reefs of Fructidor. It is very clear that throughout this hectic episode of his broken public career, D'André took upon himself without hesitation and without thought of rest the leading role in shaping, co-ordinating and executing the various parts and details of a great and complex design.

D'André's very next letters show both his friends at Paris, and himself (still in Switzerland) already deep in election plans and activities. D'André reports that his friends are now in correspondence with the departments, and are anxious to hear of complementary activity on his part. So far from desponding over the badly launched (but not yet concluded) campaign against the law of 3 brumaire, they are now meditating a resolution to unseat the one hundred and four deputies of the existing chambers who owed their mandates, not to the people, but to the *Assemblée électorale de France*.[1] On his own side, D'André, with the aid of a

---

struggle. In the light of these developments it became quite inappropriate to regard the revival of the opposition since September as having been a failure. (For these developments, see Buchez & Roux, op. cit., tome 37, pp. 171–7.)

[1] D'André to Leclerc, 23 November. In the same letter, D'André says that he had persuaded his friends in the opposition to put off until the last month of the session any further attempts to gain large advantages. 'C'est le meilleur moment parce que le tiers qui s'en ira n'aura plus de force et n'osera rien dire, de peur de se faire mal vouloir dans les dèpartemens, et que l'autre tiers des *anciens* restans sera en panne dans l'attente de l'opinion du tiers venant.' This reflects the mind of a skilful political tactician. But the bold proposal to unseat the deputies chosen in the *assemblée électorale de France* was, of course, not destined to be successful, whether in the last month of session or at any time.

new collaborator who was, apparently, Wickham's young agent Bayard,[1] was fast completing arrangements for the management of the elections in a more comprehensive sense than his friends the deputies. He was preparing the almost immediate despatch of four clerics, armed with powers from some of the exiled Bishops, on a fast tour of the whole country. They were to engage the local clergy of France to ensure that 'all the men they could dispose of' should duly attend the primary polls; they were also to distribute lists of reliable potential candidates—lists which were to be drawn up between D'André and his allies at Paris.[2] The subsequent correspondence shows that this clerical 'visitation' was indeed, and very rapidly, proceeded with, and that D'André himself meantime rapidly proceeded to work out further detailed plans, not only for the conduct of the election campaign, but for the management of the public mind after the elections had been held. These he clearly intended to implement and direct himself on his arrival at Paris.[3]

Also in this letter, D'André reports that his friends were already preparing the candidacy of Barthélemy for a place on the Directory.

[1] On 17 November Wickham had promised to send to D'André 'a person capable of talking with openness and ability' about certain matters 'which neither you nor I have thought proper to trust to paper'. 'You may expect him on Monday or Tuesday.' D'André, in letters to both Wickham and Leclerc on 23 November, acknowledges in appreciative terms the assistance of this mysterious visitor. He refers to him as 'B' and as 'Vincent' and comments that he displays 'le feu de son age'. These remarks identify the visitor as Wickham's young agent Bayard, 'Vincent' being one of the large number of codenames which Bayard uses for himself in his correspondence with Wickham: Wickham Papers, bundle 64.

[2] D'André to Leclerc, 23 November. D'André says that one of the four clerical emissaries was to be his old fellow-Constituent Lacombe. In his letter of the same date to Wickham, D'André shows that for all his anxiety to use clerical help in the elections, he had no very friendly feelings towards the clergy generally: 'les 4 ecclésiastiques que je vais envoyer . . . ne seront instruits de rien que de l'objet de leur voiage et n'auront aucune connoissance de la totalité des rouages mis en jeu. Il faut les tenir sous main, je connois l'égoisme de cette caste.'

[3] In a letter of 29 November, D'André announced that his old fellow-Constituent Lacombe (of whom he had already spoken on 23 November as one of the four clerical 'voyageurs') had obtained powers from some of the Bishops in exile at Fribourg to authorize their approach to the clergy of the French dioceses. In a letter of the following day, we read of Lacombe choosing one of his three collaborators (the abbé Bouillé). In a letter of 9 December,

One particular feature of his further plans, devised in the closing days of November, deserves exposition here as evidence of D'André's fertility in expedients. It is a very ingenious scheme, intended to ensure safe communications throughout France for all those who were to be involved in the future undertakings of the movement. It is quite breathtaking in its audacity: it involves the taking over of the Republic's postal services!

[Speaking of his discussions with Bayard, D'André describes the inception of this scheme as follows:] Nous nous sommes rencontrés sur plusieurs moyens d'exècution, par example sur celui d'avoir des moyens surs et prompts de communication par des voitures publiques dont les conducteurs seroient des gens à nous. J'avois déja proposè... à un excellent homme, voiturier à Nyon, d'établir une voiture de Lausanne à Paris, il doit venir me voir un de ces jours... Il m'est même venu en causant avec B— de ce moyen, une idée plus étendue et dont vous saisirés d'un coup d'œuil (*sic*) les avantages immenses. Ce seroit si l'on afferme les *postes*, de prendre cette ferme. Je lui ai dit de prendre à ce sujet des informations dès son arrivée à Paris et je l'ai adressè pour cela au dèputé *Lebrun*, homme *trés sur*, et qui par ses relations dans la finance trouveroit facilement les moyens de former la *Compagnie fermière*.[1]

---

we gather that Lacombe set out on his tour of forty or fifty French departments on the 7th of that month, and that he had received from D'André a payment of 230 louis to cover the expenses of the clerical tour in that 'arrondissement', the funds arising from a sum of 1,000 louis which Wickham had already made available to D'André.

In the letter of 30 November, mentioned above, D'André explained plans which he was making to follow up the clerical 'visitation': 'Outre les prêtres que je vais employer, je compte aussitôt que je serai à Paris, faire partir de conçert avec mes amis plusieurs personnes pour aller dans les dèpartemens, et concerter leurs moiens avec ceux des ecclèsiastiques avec lesquels je les aboucherai. Vers le mois de fevrier j'enverrai une note des départemens dont nous croirons être surs, et une liste des personnes que nous voulons porter. Sur la reponse que vous me ferés, j'enverrai encore mes gens dans nos dèpartemens pour l'èlection.'—There was, then, to be a *lay* visitation, to follow up the clerical, and to work in conjunction with the parochial clergy; but only, it would appear, in a selected number of departments ('nos dèpartemens').

D'André had referred to plans for activities after the elections were over in his letter of 23 November to Wickham.

[1] D'André to Wickham, 23 November. It will be remembered that D'André planned to re-enter France in the character of a driver working for a *voiturier* of Nyon; no doubt this is another reference to the same *voiturier*. The deputy referred to here must be Charles-François Lebrun, member (Anciens) for the

Nothing was to come of this daring proposal in the form suggested in this passage; but we shall see that when D'André resumed his discussions with Bayard on French soil in February 1797, the two collaborators brought forward an alternative project, to the effect that their movement should provide for its communications by operating a system of 'diligences' of its own; in this form, the plan was destined to be brought to realization.[1]

Amid all these designs for what may be called the mechanisms of the movement, D'André did not overlook the need to expand, with comparable urgency and energy, the basis of the operations upon which he was now embarked. Before November was over, he had determined, with or without the known approval of his own committee, to take up the offer of alliance made by Dumas's group. He charged Bayard, on the latter's return to Paris, to open discreet exchanges with Duplantier and Dumas. He also asked his own committee to receive Bayard, and, through Bayard, to come into direct collaboration with the Agence de Paris for the purposes of the election campaign. Thus, as he puts it, 'B— et ses amis, Duplantier et les siens, et notre comité secret' should work 'de tout côté dans le même sens'.[2] Meantime, D'André felt that he ought to take without hesitation the one further step towards the enlargement of the 'coalition' which he could himself personally and immediately take. Théodore de Lameth was still in Switzerland, though preparing to re-enter France for the elections; D'André seized the chance to bring this statesman into direct relations with himself, 'pour ne nègliger aucun des moiens qui peuvent aider une opèration entremise en grand'.[3] On 29 November, D'André was able to report to Wickham the outcome of a meeting which he had just had with Lameth, and with the latter's friend 'D—' who was, no doubt, Duplantier. The meeting impressed him quite favourably.

They gave D'André to understand that they, like the Dumas group generally, had hoped to enjoy the position of 'directing the

---

Seine et Oise from year IV to year VII (Kuscinski, op. cit., p. 373). Though described by D'André as 'homme *trés sur*', it will be noticed that he was not one of the victims of Fructidor. (He later became Third Consul.)

[1] See below, ch. VII.
[2] D'André to Wickham, 23 November.
[3] Ibid.

Directory', but, realizing at last that the Directory would not be imposed upon to the lengths they had intended, they were now 'bien dècidés a réunir tous leurs efforts aux nôtres pour renverser, non seulement les gouvernans mais le gouvernement actuel'. They were looking (of course) to the elections as the obvious means of achieving this end (though they had sadly few candidates of their own to offer).[1] They offered if need were to find D'André a safe secret residence at Melun from which to conduct his activities inside France, and discussed with him very earnestly the implications of his relations with the British Minister. D'André on his side exerted himself to dispel their very strong suspicions against English policy in the affairs of France, urged them to apply to Wickham for funds if their election activities required any,[2] and undertook to maintain connection with Théodore. D'André concluded his account with these hopeful expressions:

Enfin je n'ai rien négligé de ce qui pouvoit les ramener, et je dois convenir que j'ai trouvé en eux plus de confiance et de bonne foi que je ne m'y attendai... je ne suis pas sans espoir de tirer quelque parti d'eux et de leurs amis. Si nous nous combattions, l'ennemi commun (*le Directoire*) profiteroit de nos divisions, mais nous pouvons faire une masse assès forte pour produire quelque effet.

As for his responses to the overtures of Dumas's group, D'André was able, before the end of the year 1796 and while he was still, much against his own wishes, impatiently lingering in Switzerland, to report that these had turned out entirely well. Dumas and his friends duly received the messenger (Bayard) whom D'André

---

[1] D'André says in this letter (29 November): 'ils n'ont que trois personnes à placer qui sont T. dans le Jura, Giraud dans l'Ain, et Garnier à Paris'. None of the three men mentioned here was destined to join the legislature in year V.

[2] D'André's report of his interview with Lameth and his companion shows that the two old constitutionalists shared the fears of their friends of the Dumas group, that England wanted to prolong the disorders of France rather than to restore peace to the country, and kept up 'grands moyens... surtout parmi les *Jacobins*' with this aim in mind. D'André reported: 'Sans leur dire jusqu'à quel point nous ètions liés, je leur ai assurè le contraire. Je leur ai dit que j'avois vû de vos lettres, que vous ètiès de trés bonne foi dans tout ceçi... j'ai été jusqu'à leur faire entendre que s'ils avoient besoin de *quelques fonds*, vous ètiès tellement disposé a servir ceux qui vouloient franchement rétablir l'ordre en France que j'avois lieu de croire que vous pourriés leur en faire passer...'

had sent to them; and they then sent Duplantier a second time into Switzerland to assure D'André that they were quite satisfied with all that he had observed and proposed. They claimed that they had always desired the restoration of the throne, and that their temporary alliance with the Directory had never had any other object than to secure the final elimination of the Jacobins as a necessary step on the road to the Restoration. D'André observed that, whatever might be the degree of truth in these protestations regarding the past activities of the group, he did not doubt their good faith at the stage which had now been reached.[1]

During the months of December 1796 and January 1797, D'André continued, on the one hand, to elaborate plans for the great operation in the interior, and on the other to pursue, through a series of difficulties, about which we have as yet avoided all details, the opportunity to make his own re-entry into France. His letters during this time are largely concerned with the latter consideration; we still defer any account of this matter, so that we can mention here some further points in his letters which attach themselves naturally to our previous discussion of the development of the 'great design'.

We have already observed Wickham's offer of financial support for the operations of D'André and his allies. We are, consequently, not surprised to find that D'André, in the midst of preparations for (what he then believed to be his imminent) departure, wrote hastily and without details to request such support, both immediately and in the future. So far as concerned the future, he requested the arrangement of 'un crédit à Paris sous le nom et la signature de Kilien, afin de pouvoir me procurer des fonds en cas qu'il y eut quelque occasion majeure de les emploier'.[2]

We shall see later, with some detail, how these demands were met by the British Minister. It is of more immediate moment to notice that the request for a large sum in credit, to meet a 'major occasion', refers not to anything directly concerning the elections, but to a possible contingency which D'André had long since

[1] See D'André's letters to Wickham, 21 and 24 December 1796.

[2] D'André to Leclerc, 30 November 1796. 'Kilien' is one of the code-names of D'André in Wickham's correspondence; the other, which we have already met, is 'Berger'. In the same letter, D'André asked for 'des moyens de connoître et de m'aboucher avec les chargés de pouvoirs du roy'. This detail is part of the evidence that D'André was, to this date, a complete stranger to the King's Agents at Paris.

envisaged on the morrow of the elections. We recollect that D'André had spoken of the situation immediately after the elections in terms of an alternative: it would then have to be decided, he had said, whether to 'frapper un grand coup' or whether it would be wiser to 'miner l'edifice'.[1] The 'grand coup' which he envisaged as one possibility would not arise from a direct appeal to popular insurrection against the regime (he had already ruled out any calculation of a *mouvement général*) but would begin with proceedings, by the new legislative majority, against the existing Directors and others of the old ruling party.[2] In that case, the old ruling party could be expected to appeal to force; but the opposition (D'André seems to have meant) would never attempt such a 'grand coup' unless it was well assured in advance that there would be active public support available to meet force with force. Then, indeed, the partisans of 'l'action légale' would turn from the tribune to the sword; and there would be a *dix août* in reverse.[3] Now it seems clear from later references in Wickham's papers that it was with a view to the needs which might arise at the moment of this 'grand coup' that D'André was now asking for a large credit; and the reasoning behind the request is easy enough to discern: when that moment arrived, liberal supplies might be all important to purchase arms, to publish suitable literature, and even to buy the complacency of important officials.

There is, moreover, evidence that in the closing weeks of 1796 both D'André and his friends at Paris were cherishing rising hopes that the morrow of the elections would indeed bring this alternative course of procedure within the range of possibility; in one of his letters towards the end of November, D'André had already reported that his committee were even then at work preparing an impeachment against the existing Directors, for submission to the renewed Councils, and that he himself, with Bayard, was studying

[1] D'André to Leclerc, 17 August 1796: quoted in ch. V above.

[2] D'André's memorandum of 22 August 1796: quoted above, ch. V.

[3] In his letter to Leclerc of 17 August, D'André had sketched an interesting parallel between the tactics of the 'Girondins' in gaining control of, and then overthrowing, the constitution of 1791, and the tactics which he was now recommending for use against the Republic. The parallel seems to include, by implication, a Royalist version of 10 August. But, as D'André had ruled out any initiative in the use of force by his own party, it seems to follow that the Royalist version of 10 August was expected to come as the response to a Republican attempt to appeal to force.

means to ensure that public support should be rallied behind such an initiative by the opposition.[1]

It is a matter of further interest that D'André's appeal for British funds on this occasion illustrates very strikingly the capital role which the ex-Constituent was now arrogating to himself in the whole conduct of the enterprise against the Republic. The large credit is to be lodged in D'André's own (concealed) name. It will, D'André writes, enable *him* to procure funds in case a great opportunity arises. The 'grand coup' is to be a decision dependent in the last resort on his willingness to use these resources. But in taking such a situation upon himself D'André was only accepting the clear implications of the attitude which Wickham had now firmly adopted towards him. Wickham, in his letter of mid-November, referred to above,[2] had offered financial support, whether for the costs of the election campaign or for any other aspect of the new attempt to destroy the Republic, not to any professed adherent of that policy, but to D'André himself and for those particular developments of that policy in which D'André might repose confidence. It was the envoy himself who had decreed that D'André should be, next to himself, the paymaster of the whole operation.

The second point which arises here concerns D'André's decision to seek election for himself at the expected polls. He had formed, naturally enough, the ambition to lead the attack on the regime after the elections from the floor of the Council of the Five Hundred. He discussed this intention in a letter of mid-December, where he uses the following interesting expressions:

Si vous pensés, comme je le crois, qu'il seroit utile que je fusse èlu à la prochaine assemblée; vous devriés écrire au *Roi* pour qu'il ordonnat à ses agens à Paris et en Provence de me porter. C'est à ce qu'il me semble

---

[1] D'André to Wickham, 23 November. D'André speaks of himself and Bayard as having agreed 'de mener en même tems deux opèrations, le but de l'une sera d'influencer les èlections, celui de l'autre de tout prèparer (dans les parties de France ou cela sera possible) de maniére qu'après le renouvellement de l'assemblée, l'opinion publique et des agens surs soient à portee de soutenir une attaque qui sera faite au Directoire dès les premiers jours si on le peut. L'acte d'accusation sera prèt, mes amis recueillent les faits et les piéces et pour peu que le nouveau tiers soit bon, un mois ne se passera pas avant que les Directeurs ne soient culbutés.'

[2] Above, p. 159 and note 2.

surtout dans l'assemblée que je pourrois agir efficacément. Mon age me laissant dans les 500, j'aurois des moyens de pousser avec activité aux mesures qui améneroient au plûtôt la destruction de l'ordre anti-social qui règne en France. Quoique je ne croie pas que les *agens* aient une grande influence, cependant leur parti joint au mien pourra quelque chose.[1]

This passage evidently raises more than one point of interest, in addition to its indication of D'André's ambition to play a great part in the movement after, as well as on the occasion of, the elections of year V. It provides one of the several indications contained in this correspondence, that D'André had hitherto enjoyed no connections with the King's Agents in France. It also shows that he had, to this date, no direct means of communication with, and no direct influence with, the exiled Court.

This last observation brings us to another topic of main importance in the present chapter, which we shall do well to pursue here before we pass on to deal finally with the story of D'André's continued difficulties, and eventual belated success, in his efforts to return to France. It is obvious that the great operation in the interior, which D'André was now working so hard to promote, could not even be attempted without the compliance of the exiled Court. The legitimate King might never consent to do as his Agents and Pichegru had advised—to tear up the Verona Declaration and profess conversion to the principles of the 'monarchiens'. But he must clearly encourage his own strict adherents to join in a 'coalition of parties' against the Directory; he must use such language as would appear, in the eyes of all those who clung to constitutionalist principles, to be at least patient of an interpretation which did not disallow all their hopes; and he must authorize the efforts of the coalition to work for their ends through the processes of the existing Republican constitution. It was not, however, by the personal intervention of D'André that this degree of co-operation was finally secured for his cause from the exiled Court; this further and indispensable element in his combinations was indeed gained by the time that D'André was finally able to enter France and to throw his energies into the conduct of the elections, but it had been gained entirely by others. We have to explain how it was that D'André had no direct connection with the Court during the period covered by this chapter, and also how the Court finally

[1] D'André to Wickham, 14 December 1796.

accorded some measure of support to the projects which D'André was doing so much, in other respects, to promote.

We have already seen that when D'André made his overtures to certain deputies at Paris in the spring of 1796, he was acting without authority from the Court, and with the support only of the British Minister. It seems clear, from an account later given to Lord Grenville by Wickham, that the ex-Constituent deliberately placed himself in this situation, and deliberately persevered in it down to the moment of his re-entry into France. His reason was that he distrusted, not of course Louis XVIII, but the Ministers of the exiled Court; and he distrusted them because he believed them to be both ambitious for complete control in everything concerning the cause, and at the same time so dangerously indiscreet that they jeopardized everything which they did control. In view of the subsequent history of the Prince de Carency, the Royalist Prime Minister's son, it cannot be said that D'André's beliefs lacked justification.

From the date of Mr Berger's letter to his Majesty Louis 18 [wrote Wickham to Lord Grenville in May 1797] ... that gentleman constantly refused to have any communication with the King's Ministers. ... A few days before Mr Berger left this country (*he told an emissary of the King who had come to tax him with this conduct*) ... that he would on no account ... enter into any correspondence with Blankenbourg. ... The King's ministers had confidence in no-one and ... wished on that account to have the whole correspondence with the Interiour in the minutest detail pass through their own hands; and that till that system was abandoned they never would enjoy the confidence of the Interiour because there could be no safety for the persons who should endeavour to serve them ... that he should for the present continue his correspondence as he had begun it with Mr Wickham whose court was alone able to render any influential service to the cause, and that as soon as he had anything of real and immediate importance to communicate he would then address himself directly to Blankenbourgh. ...[1]

---

[1] Wickham to Grenville, no. 12 of 1797, 24 May. It is a fact that communications in the late summer of 1796 were passing between La Vauguyon and certain Republican, even Jacobin, circles. It soon became clear to those in a position to observe it, that the Royalist Premier had embarked on a course which was not only politically foolish, but also extremely slippery. The Duke's own son, the Prince de Carency, became involved in confidences with the Republicans which in effect, and perhaps at last even in intention, involved the betrayal of Royalist secrets to the enemy. The correspondence of the Paris Agents with Wickham shows that in the later months of 1796 the Agents

Taking this view of the Royalist Ministers, D'André necessarily from the beginning also eschewed any connection with the Court by the less immediate approach through the King's Agents at Paris; for the reports of these Agents necessarily passed through the hands of the same Ministers. His 'committee' at Paris, who had independently ventured into negotiations with the Agents, soon assured him that the latter had faults of their own, as well as connections with indiscreet superiors, and thus strengthened his resolution to have nothing to do with them.

As to the agents at Paris [Wickham quoted D'André as telling the Royal emissary] his friends there had so poor an opinion of their talents their means and above all of their discretion that they were ashamed of the connexion . . . and . . . for the good of the cause they had avoided introducing them to any more members of the two Councils . . .

Mr Berger having thus declined all connexion with the King's Agents he had no other means of communicating with the Royalists at Paris but thro' the medium of Mr Bayard untill the epoch of the Elections. . . .[1]

Yet of course it was obvious throughout that the projects upon which D'André and his allies were working would have to be submitted, in some form, and at some point, to the exiled Court, and its blessing obtained for them. And *some* details of the persons involved in these plans would also have to be revealed, for it could not be expected that the exiled Court would grant approval to plans of whose authors and chief agents it was in utter ignorance. And, whatever was divulged to the Court, however little and however late, would be subject to the risks of compromise which

---

were terrified and bewildered by the conduct of the La Vauguyons. They had good reason, for Carency was betraying their designs to the Directory and his information helped to bring about their arrest on 30 January 1797. It was not only their ill-judged designs for winning over Republican officers which the Prince revealed; he revealed also their relations with members of the legislative opposition and also the connection between the Court and D'André (Wickham's no. 10 of 1797, 13 April—portions not publ. in Wickham's *Corresp.*). As will be remarked in the text of the chapter, D'André could not, for all his distrust of the indiscretions of the Court, carry forward his designs without eventually submitting at least their main purport to Blankenburg, and without his own part in the business being known there; and long before his arrival in Paris this dangerous information had unavoidably been given to the King's Council.

[1] Wickham, no. 12 of 1797, 24 May.

D'André took so seriously. All that D'André could do was to reduce this risk, by withdrawing himself and his activities from
close inspection by the Court, and leaving it to Wickham, who
had not only the gifts of discretion but also an independence
which no-one at the exiled Court could contest, to convey to the
Court as little (and that as late) as would serve the needs of the
situation.

Wickham communicated the 'propositions' of D'André's 'committee' (embodied in the *résultat* of June 1796, which has been examined above) to the exiled Court (then at Riegel) as soon as he
received them.[1] He could not, of course, reveal the names of the
legislators who had made those propositions, if only because he
did not himself yet know them. It is a point of some interest that
D'André himself, at that stage, was willing to supply the Court
with the names of two members of his 'committee' if the legislators in question would consent.[2] But, whether because they
firmly declined this suggestion, or because D'André's own distrust
of the King's entourage meantime became even stronger, at all
events he never did this, down to the time of his re-entry; and he
told the Royal messenger who visited him immediately before his
departure 'that he would on no account . . . name any of his
friends without their consent'.[3]

Wickham, at some intermediate stage which it does not seem
possible to determine, revealed to the Court the connection of
D'André himself with the 'propositions', and expressed his own
very high opinion of the ex-Constituent, while still concealing
many details of the plan and its other executants.[4] Not till mid-
January 1797 did the diplomat explain to La Vauguyon that

[1] Wickham's no. 66 of 1796, 3 July: Wickham, *Corresp.*, vol. I, at p. 404.

[2] In his letter of 24 June, 1796, enclosing the *résultat* of his committee's
discussions, D'André had written to Leclerc: '... On me demande un secret
absolu sur le nom des signataires. J'ai répondu hier pour avoir la permission
d'en nommer au moins deux... quand j'aurai réponse je le (*sic*) nommerai soit
au Roi, soit au patron (*Wickham*) a leur choix.'

[3] Wickham's no. 12 of 1797, 24 May.

[4] These points appear from a letter drafted by Wickham to La Vauguyon
on 16 January 1797. The Royalist Minister had been informed, to a certain
point, about D'André and his undertakings by Leclerc. 'J'ai tout lieu', writes
Wickham, 'd'être foncièrement content de M. d'André. Il m'a communiqué
avec la dernière franchise toutes ses demarches... M. le Clerc vous en a deja
beaucoup dit. Je dois y ajouter, ce que ce dernier ignore, que le comité de
M. d'André est le meme qui s'etait adressé a M. Brottier, etc'.

N

D'André's committee was the same as had approached the Paris Agents;[1] it seems probable that D'André would not have given the Royalist Premier even thus much information about his associates, but it ought in fairness to Wickham to be said that in making this admission he was telling the exiled Court very little that it did not know already. And La Vauguyon acquired by this means the name of only one of D'André's close associates, Lemerer; neither the Agents nor the Court had ever known the names of the other deputies who had approached the Agence.[2]

It is clear that once the Court knew of D'André's connection with the design to promote the Royal cause by electoral and parliamentary methods, it developed considerable curiosity about the many points on which, it appeared, he alone could give it full information. According to Wickham, from whose account of D'André's dealings with these matters we have already offered some extracts, 'the Duke de la Vauguyon' first made 'a fruitless attempt through the Prince of Carency to engage . . . Mr Berger . . . in a separate correspondence'. When this approach failed in face of D'André's steadfast refusal to enter on any discussion, the Court had recourse to the services of a more official intermediary and thus brought about the incident which occurred shortly before D'André left Switzerland for France. Wickham described this development as follows:

The abbé de la Marre the King's confidential agent at Lausanne was at last sent for to Blankenburg and . . . received a special commission to return . . . and wait on M. Berger and to say to him that the King was well informed that there existed a commēē in the two Assemblies whose operations were directed by Mr. Berger, that his Majesty was disposed to believe that the commēē had at heart the restoration of Royalty and that its members were really labouring with that view but that he was much surprized that Mr Berger had never communicated . . . the nature and extent of the plan . . . the names of the persons engaged in it . . .

Wickham repeated to Lord Grenville the account which had been given him by La Marre himself of the reply which D'André gave. We have already glanced at some of the points which D'André made. When we consider his reply *in extenso*, we are

---

[1] As appears on p. 173, n. 4.

[2] The Agents had of course had dealings also with Mersan, but Mersan was an unseated deputy at that time.

struck by the skill, firmness and dignity with which D'André still refused, even in speaking to an official of the exiled government, charged with enquiries directly from the King, to enter into the details required:

Mr Berger answered in terms of the highest respect and gratitude . . . that H.M. might be assured that (*their*) endeavours would be constantly directed to the one point of restoring him to the Throne of his Ancestors as soon and with as much power and splendour as times and circumstances would . . . permit but that they ever would and must be guided by those times and circumstances only; that he himself had given a gage of his good intentions by putting his life in the hands of the King and his Ministers as well as of the British Government, as they would become the masters of it from the moment that he should enter into France; that *in prudence* he could and ought to do no more and that *in Justice* no more ought to be demanded of him—that he would on no account . . . name any of his friends without their . . . consent nor could he . . . enter into any correspondence with Blankenbourg or with the King's agents at Paris . . . (*we have already cited D'André's reasons for refusing to take either of these two courses*) he should for the present continue his correspondence as he had begun it with Mr Wickham . . . and . . . as soon as he had anything of real and immediate importance to communicate he would then address himself directly to Blankenbourgh. . . .[1]

Since he adopted this attitude towards the exiled Court, D'André could obviously do nothing in the meantime to win its consent to the plans which he so closely guarded. But, while these plans ripened during the closing weeks of 1796, the Court was in fact coming round to support the general line which D'André and his friends were trying to establish. No doubt the counsels of Wickham played an important part in producing the necessary change of attitude. But the British Minister was able to speak from a very strong brief, supplied by the notorious facts and circumstances of the time, and reinforced by the testimonies of others who were themselves high in the confidence of the Court. The Pretender and his ministers could hardly deny that all forcible methods had

[1] This passage, and the two quotations immediately preceding this, are taken from Wickham's no. 12 of 1797, 24 May.—It seems, from a hasty note of D'André to Leclerc, asking for information about 'un Abbé André, autrement de la Marre', that it was early in January that this emissary visited D'André. Wickham has endorsed this note '11th January 1797'.

as yet failed, that the country had been unimpressed by the previous gestures of the Pretender, that it shrank from further involvement in violence and disturbance, and that there appeared to be a considerable risk that unless the legitimist cause could find some different means of rapid progress, it would be placed in the presence of a successful Orleanist *fait accompli*. Nor could they deny that, the ruling Republican party being so profoundly unpopular, it would be a natural course for the legitimists at the point which had now been reached to try to exploit the contingency offered by the Republican constitution by promoting a union of all conservative elements in France in view of the elections. Such a policy could hardly be less successful than the methods which had been tried before. If these points were once admitted, it would follow easily enough that the Pretender must authorize this new policy, bless the union of parties in terms as widely encouraging as possible, and prohibit all further recourse to the *manière forte* pending the outcome of the new experiment. The Pretender might indeed have concluded that it was desirable to go somewhat further, and to meet the wishes of the very numerous section in the interior which favoured monarchy but still adhered in some degree to the constitutional principles of 1789. But at least he could hardly fail to see the expediency of going as far as has been outlined immediately above.

The Court indeed found the need for some change, not of heart, but of tactics, in the end irresistible.[1] Its efforts to secure more

---

[1] The exiled Court would certainly still have preferred to avoid any alliance with the moderates of the interior, if only it could have found any other source of new hope. Hence the efforts of La Vauguyon, about August 1796, to achieve the impossible and bring about a Restoration with Republican, even Jacobin, aid. The comments of Wickham on the folly and stupidity which lay behind these efforts, though bitter, are probably quite just. Wickham declares that he had warned the Duke in the strongest terms 'that a connexion of that kind would . . . bring a well merited odium and disgrace upon the King, and make the breach between him and his people eternal and irreparable . . . But it was all in vain, . . . though I declined taking any part in the Business.

'I have ever observed that the Royalists in general, and particularly those about the King, are far more disposed to a compromise with the Jacobins than with any other faction. . . .

It is indeed but too evident, that all views of humanity, of policy, of Justice, even of Interest are but light in the scale when opposed to the desire of humbling and punishing the first authors of the Revolution.

ample information about the plans of D'André and his associates are one indication of its growing interest in the policy of electoral and parliamentary action. The Court gave more formal expression of such interest in Instructions issued to the Paris Agents on 24 November 1796.[1] These may not have been drawn with a view to promoting the plans of D'André in particular, for the Court was at this time still trying to sound those plans more completely; the Instructions may have corresponded more directly, rather, with the new interest of the Agents themselves in this type of policy. But they certainly authorized inclusively, if not exclusively, the general drift of the proposals of D'André and his friends, for they announced that the best means of strengthening the Royalist interest in France at this juncture was to 'travailler à assurer le succès des nouvelles élections' and also to continue the efforts, already begun, to win over the members of the two Councils, with especial attention to 'les membres du parti connu sous la dénomination du *Ventre*'. The new year was to bring further manifestations of the Court's acceptance of this policy in general, and of its growing interest in the activities of D'André in particular.

On 3 January 1797, La Vauguyon, acting perhaps at Wickham's behest, addressed an official letter to two of the exiled Bishops residing at Fribourg. The effect of this must have been to reinforce the efforts which D'André was already making, to secure the services of the refractory clergy throughout the country in the elections. The two Bishops were invited to communicate the letter to their brethren in the same place, and it was intended to invoke their action as well as that of its immediate recipients. The Premier asked the Bishops to engage all the clergy of their dioceses who had remained 'faithful to their God and their King' to send to the primary polls all those persons 'dans qui ils reconnoitront le désir sincère du rétablissement de la Religion, de la Monarchie, et du Monarque légitime' so that they might 'y concourir à des choix

---

This new project, for instance, was caught at with eagerness, whilst the more wise and reasonable ones, concerning which I have of late frequently written to your Lordship, were either wholly rejected or received with coldness and indifference.' (No. 85 of 1796, 7 September: Wickham, *Corresp.*, vol. I, pp. 450–51.)—Only when it finally despaired of this unsound scheme did the Court at last condescend to the 'union of parties' and electoral warfare.

[1] Printed in Buchez & Roux, op. cit., tome 37, pp. 188–9.

conformes à leurs principes'.[1] On 16 January, Wickham drafted a
letter to La Vauguyon, the purpose of which (so far as concerns us
here) was apparently to reply in very reassuring terms to enquiries
which the Premier had been making about D'André, and in particular about D'André's personal sincerity and trustworthiness.
D'André's steadfast refusal to reveal the details of his plans to the
Court does not appear to have injured either him or his projects
in the judgement of the Pretender and his Minister; for on 14
February, La Vauguyon in a note to Leclerc referred to the 'hopes'
which he had been encouraged to form by the 'wisdom' which
characterized the views and observations of D'André, and requested to be kept informed of the ex-Constituent's further progress.[2]

When this letter was written, D'André must have been at last on
his way to Paris. He did not know, at the moment of his departure,
that the exiled Court was then about to give what Wickham called
its 'full and intire approbation' to the designs which he had adopted; but he must have known, from Wickham and Leclerc, that
this 'full approbation' was likely to be granted, and he no doubt
trusted to Wickham to do whatever might still be necessary to
secure it. Shortly after his arrival at Paris, the envoy was able to
send him this welcome intelligence.[3]

The Pretender's adoption of the general line of policy which
Wickham and D'André had worked to prepare was published to
the world, and more particularly to those in France who might be

---

[1] A copy of this ('Lettre écrite par M. le Duc de la Vauguyon le 3 janvier
1797 à m$\overline{grs}$. l'archevêque de Paris et l'évêque de Clermont') is included in
Wickham's correspondence with La Vauguyon: Wickham Papers, bundle 94.
The text begins: 'L'Epôque prochaine des assemblées primaires en France
paroissant au Roi pouvoir déterminer des résultats importants...'

[2] Wickham Papers.

[3] On 8 March 1797, Wickham enclosed to Lord Grenville copies of two of
D'André's letters of the previous summer 'containing a succinct develope-
ment of his views and of the means he meant to employ . . .' He added: 'They
are worth more attention as they have been communicated to the Duke de la
Vauguyon and have lately received full and intire approbation at Blankenbourg.' On 10 March, Wickham drafted a letter to D'André, now in France,
in which he communicated this welcome news: 'Pour vous encourager davantage je vous dirai que depuis votre depart le Marchand de sucre——(?) et pain
a entièrement approuvé le plan de travail que vous m'avez donné cet été
Vous voyez donc qu'on se radoucit de nôtre coté . . .' (*Le Marchand*, etc.
seems to be a code-name for Louis XVIII).

able to join in its execution, in the Royal Declaration dated 10 March 1797.[1] This document is framed with the elegant ingenuity of language which appears never to have been wanting in the published statements of Louis XVIII. On the face of it, it does not purport to notify any change of policy on the part of the King, even of the most merely circumstantial kind. On the contrary, it claims to clarify both the principles and the methods which the King had always followed, and to obviate the danger that the Directory, in its proceedings against his recently arrested Agents, would find new means of misrepresenting to the public what his intentions had always been, and still were. The Declaration accordingly sets out to restate the drift of the instructions which had uniformly been given to all the King's Agents, and to instruct thereby, not only those of his Agents who still remained in functions, but all well-intentioned Frenchmen, as to their duties in the immediate future. The document then goes on, not indeed to repudiate, even tacitly, the Declaration of Verona, but nevertheless to reinterpret this and the King's other better known utterances, under the pretext of explaining what the King had always maintained. In the process of reinterpretation, the King's well known general ideas are maintained, but with certain unacknowledged variations of emphasis, which were clearly intended to represent the largest olive branch which the King could offer to those of his subjects who had hitherto clung in some degree to the ideals of 1789. The Declaration sounds the praises of the old traditional 'constitution' of the realm, and insists, not only that this was 'également opposée à l'anarchie et au despotisme', but also that it was something very different from 'le régime qui s'était introduit depuis trop longtemps'—thus repudiating, with a skilful avoidance of detail, the more unpopular features of what living Frenchmen had known as the government of the Monarchy. Further, the Declaration admits that the old constitution, which the King wished to revive in its purity, might itself be 'susceptible de nouveaux degrès de perfection'—another masterly touch, calculated to attract many who thought a 'constitution' (in the more modern sense) necessary, but who might care little upon what particular theoretical basis it was made to rest.

So far as concerned the issues of moment in ordinary life, which in the opinion of some contemporary observers mattered far more

[1] Text in Buchez & Roux, op. cit., tome 37, pp. 242–4.

to the French people than the question (considered in itself) of constitutional forms, the Declaration again attempted to alter the emphases of the King's former pronouncements. The vexed points regarding the 'orders' of French society, the Parlements, etc., were pushed into the background. Heavy stress was laid on the King's determination to correct the old abuses. He promised to listen to 'le vœu public' on all that concerned this subject. He again guaranteed oblivion for all the 'errors' and even all the crimes of recent years, and pronounced an absolute ban on all private acts of vengeance.

The Declaration finally adverted to the immediate political issues before the country in a genuinely moderate and winning way. Referring to the forthcoming elections, the King urged all Royalists to make it their first concern to avert any return to Jacobin domination; and he suggested, in a number of phrases, his desire for a final settlement by peaceful means, to which all adherents of peace and good order might usefully contribute.

Though there was nothing in this Declaration which conveyed any clear and firm intention on the part of the Pretender to satisfy the constitutional aspirations of the country, to give up the empty dream of restoring the orders, the Parlements and the state of property existing before the Revolution, or to meet the natural wishes of those whose careers and professional ambitions had been given an entirely different turn since the Revolution began—it is nevertheless clear that it went far enough to offer a foundation of some kind upon which different elements *might* agree to rally, and that it distinctly authorized action against the Republic by the peaceful use of its own political machinery. If there was any promise at all in the idea of a coalition of parties, agreed to work together, by commonly accepted methods, against the existing regime, and resigned to tolerate for the time being different views of the character which should distinguish the final settlement, this document may be said to have provided—so far as such a document could— a *possible* basis for the carrying out of that idea. Its reticences and ambiguities left the moderate monarchists free to hope that the Pretender would make concessions wide enough to give them substantial satisfaction, and the pure Royalists equally free to believe that he would concede nothing which their own hearts were set on retaining. Its clear and unmistakable passages expressed plainly

enough the Pretender's determination to quieten many of the misgivings which the nation had formed about him, and to provide
for monarchists of every kind, even perhaps for moderates with
no clear preference for monarchy, common ground for immediate
action against a common danger.

Yet the document did not satisfy everyone, even of those whom
its author must have hoped with some confidence to satisfy. It did
not satisfy Wickham, and the reactions expressed by this former
rather uncritical admirer of pure Royalism are of obvious interest
in this context. Wickham had long since reached the conclusion
that the Pretender must resign himself to 'passing through' a form
of constitutional monarchy in the modern sense of the term, and
to offering the moderates of the interior such proposals for the
future government of France as would lead them to hope that he
indeed intended to meet their constitutional principles. He was
disappointed that the new declaration did not go by any means as
far to meet this need as his own judgement would have dictated.
No doubt Wickham would not have wished the Pretender to
court the moderates so exclusively that he risked the alienation of
his own thoroughgoing adherents, and no doubt, therefore, his
own choice of language for the declaration would also have been
marked by ambiguities and reticences. But his emphases would
have been thrown more heavily in favour of the moderate and
limited monarchists of the interior. He attributed the failure, as he
regarded it, of the new declaration in this respect to the utter
inability of the exiled Court to appreciate the true state of affairs
in France, an inability which (we must reflect) he had once shared.

It is a great publick calamity [he observed to Lord Grenville] . . . that
there should be no one person about the French King at all acquainted
with the real state of the interior and of the publick opinion in France,
or with the secret springs and causes by which the revolution has been
brought about, or who has any clear notion of the nature of a popular
assembly or of a mixed government. It is in vain talking with any of
those persons upon any of those subjects; they really *do not and cannot
comprehend them.*

It was not only on these grounds that Wickham questioned the
wisdom of the Declaration. Leaving aside entirely the question of
the proposals to be made about the future settlement, he felt that
it contained a major tactical error on a matter of more immediate
import: it avowed

the existence of different agents in the interior of the Republick, and direct(*ed*) the particular attention of those agents to the approaching elections. . . . There is nothing that the well disposed inhabitants, who have the restoration of royalty most sincerely at heart, dread so much, and with so much reason, as any interference on the part of the King and his agents, or any appearance whatever of concert or co-operation with the *avowed* Royalists either within or without the Kingdom. This is a point which, though obvious in its very nature, has never been at all understood at Blankenburg . . .

Wickham went on to explain to Lord Grenville that he had urged this point on the Duc de la Vauguyon, with every appearance of winning his agreement, but that the Royalist Minister had only been feigning assent, and had subsequently treated this advice on Wickham's part as another reason for regarding with suspicion the attitude of the British Government.[1]

It has to be admitted, however, that Wickham's attitude on this point, if the language quoted above represents his meaning accurately, was rather difficult to grasp. Granted that it was unwise to dwell on the activities of the Royal Agents who still remained in functions in France, it is not easy to follow Wickham in his apparent suggestion that there should have been no Royal 'interference' whatever in the immediate political conjuncture of France. Unless the King advised the pure Royalist element in the interior to take the opportunity offered by the elections, how were they to know that he wanted them to adopt this means of combating the Republic? Unless he gave the moderate monarchists of the interior some fresh incentive to join their efforts with his own party at those elections, how was the coalition of parties to be realized at all? And how could the King give this advice, and offer these incentives, but in a new public proclamation, which would inevitably suggest that there was, or at least was to be, 'concert' between 'the well disposed inhabitants' and 'the *avowed* Royalists'?

But whatever may be said in justification of the new manifesto, it is an unfortunate fact that the public utterance of the Pretender was once more destined to prove a misleading indication of the *whole* current policy of his Court. As has been noted above, the plan of action by electoral and parliamentary means involved the implication that the Court should meantime abandon all attempts

---

[1] The document quoted, or summarized, here is Wickham's no. 10 of 1797, 13 April :Wickham, *Corresp.*, vol. II, pp. 37–8.

to promote its cause by forcible methods. These had no fair prospects of success, and could only serve to irritate and alarm the interior, which had no taste for such adventures and which justifiably dreaded the ulterior intentions of those who had. But the exiled Court, in lending its support at last to the policy advocated by D'André and his allies, failed to grasp the necessity of that implication. It regarded the electoral and parliamentary policy as involving a 'long way round'; it persisted in thinking it legitimate to cultivate any opportunity which was offered in the meantime, to secure the 'short cut' of a sudden *coup* which would lay the Kingdom, willy nilly, at the absolute disposal of the lawful ruler.

This dangerous confusion which dwelt in the minds of the exiled Court was obvious enough to those who had close contact with it. At the time when the Paris Agents were arrested (30 January 1797) they were involved in an attempt to win over two Republican commanders and with their aid to carry through an immediate military *coup d'état* at Paris. They pursued this vain and fatally dangerous plan quite regardless of their own recent interest in the influencing of the elections, and of their recently received instructions to persevere with that undertaking. In so acting, they had the enthusiastic support of the Pretender and his entourage, who displayed an optimism quite as absurd as their want of logic.

The King himself and all his Ministers [reported Wickham] were entirely persuaded that the blow meditated at Paris would succeed and . . . in consequence of that opinion they had sent for their Royal Highnesses the Dukes of Angouleme and Berry to Blankenburg, that neither they nor the King might be found at the moment of the explosion in the hands of the Allies.[1]

The Court did not receive the deflating news of the arrest of its Agents, and the exposure of their design, for a considerable time; in the interval, the Royal entourage continued to cherish, and even to develop, its absurd hopes, and it is rather curious to find La Vauguyon writing to the British envoy in mid-February—the very day when he also expressed his admiration for the 'wisdom' of D'André's plans and his hopes of being kept informed of D'André's further news—a letter in which he earnestly requested substantial assistance for a revival of the old project of uniting the troops of a

---

[1] No. 5 of 1797, 8 March: Wickham, *Corresp.*, vol. II, p. 26.

converted Republican commander with the army of Condé, to act in support of the blow which was daily expected at Paris.[1]

By the time that the Pretender published his Declaration of 10 March, all these hopes were known to have been discountenanced by events, and the Pretender had a fresh opportunity to pursue the electoral policy without compromising it further by rash adventures in the medium of force. But, though in the Declaration itself he spoke warmly for a settlement by consent, and discountenanced recourse to methods of violence, in terms which the interior might be expected to appreciate,[2] it seems that at heart the exiled Court continued to cherish projects of the bad old kind. In a despatch two days before the Declaration, the British envoy lamented the fact that the Royalists and 'their unfortunate monarch' were still thinking of partial insurrections; and he expressed the strong wish that the French King might be 'brought to sanction . . . instructions' ordering his adherents to 'conform their conduct for a time to the laws and customs of the Republick, which will furnish them with far better and safer means of attacking the government . . .'[3] The Declaration went far to gratify Wickham's desire for such 'instructions', but what security was there that the Court, in adopting this language, had thoroughly embraced its meaning?[4] It was a precarious and doubtful support which was thus given to the policy advocated by D'André.

Nor was it only in this respect that the Royal Court was to prove

---

[1] La Vauguyon to Wickham, 14 February 1797, in Wickham Papers, bundle 94. Cf. Condé's report to Wickham of a letter from Louis XVIII to himself, also dated 14 February (publ. in Wickham, *Corresp.*, vol. II, p. 12). The Republican general in question was Moreau.

[2] To speak more strictly, the language of the Declaration on the subject of violent means is as follows: '... Gardez-vous [says the King, speaking primarily to his Agents] d'employer pour rétablir ...la religion, les lois, et l'autorité légitime... les moyens atroces qui ont été mis en usage pour les renverser: attendez de l'opinion publique un succès qu'elle seule peut rendre solide et durable; ou, s'il fallait recourir à la force des armes, ne vous servez du moins de cette cruelle ressource qu'à la dernière extrémité, et pour lui donner un appui juste et nécessaire.' This, so far as the words went, was quite in accordance with the policy of D'André.

[3] Wickham to Grenville, 8 March 1797: Wickham, *Corresp.*, vol. II, pp. 17–18.

[4] Much might evidently turn on the manner in which the Court, and still more its adventurous adherents in the interior, interpreted the phrases 'à la dernière extrémité' and 'un appui juste et nécessaire'.

itself an inadequate sponsor of the great design. We need not pursue the details here, since they will fall more appropriately into
later sections of this work; but we may properly say at once that
the bad habits of the Court, which D'André had so roundly denounced to La Marre—its itch to control everything in detail, and
its very doubtful ability to take good care of whatever valuable
information it possessed—militated against the good progress of
his plans from the time that he returned to France.[1]

In saying, therefore, that when his return to France occurred,
D'André's plans were assured of the support of the exiled Court,
it is as well to add suitable qualifying expressions. It should be said
that the plans had the approval of the Court, *so far as* the Court
was capable of understanding what those plans really involved;
and that the Court's approval, though necessary, was also (as a
result of its own meddling incompetence) an embarrassment in at
least the same degree as it was indispensable.[2]

In leaving the matters discussed in the immediately preceding
pages, one can hardly avoid expressing astonishment over the
shortcomings displayed at this juncture by Louis XVIII. For all
his many high qualities—dignity, mildness of temper, literary
skill, firmness of purpose—he seems to have been unable, even at
this stage, really to grasp the fundamental inconsistency between
the policy advocated by D'André (which he had at last resolved to
sanction) and the use of force (which nevertheless still had, for him
and for his entourage, a kind of fatal allure). It also seems remarkable
that a prince who was in many ways so intelligent should have been
unable to find Ministers and Agents who could unite fair competence
in office with reasonable freedom from professional jealousy, and
reasonable ability to safeguard the secrets of their own side.

It only remains, for the present, to say a little about the topic
which we have so long deferred, the protracted difficulties which
D'André encountered in his efforts to return to France. In late
August 1796, D'André had expressed his intention of going in
within a month of that date, even if he could not, in the meantime,

[1] See below, ch. IX.

[2] The disgrace of La Vauguyon, who was in fact tottering to his fall at the
time of D'André's return to France, and his replacement in the King's counsels by the Maréchal de Castries and M. de Saint-Priest, undoubtedly resulted
in some improvement in the conduct of the exiled regime; though, as will
appear later, we must not exaggerate the importance of this improvement so
far as the matters under discussion here are concerned.

clear himself with the Republican authorities.[1] By mid-September, he had become impressed by reports of the great danger he would run, if he re-entered while still an unerased émigré; he was also discouraged, it is to be supposed, by doubts as to whether Wickham would after all be willing, or even able, to support him in the designs which he and his allies at Paris were working out.[2] In mid-November, the latter obstacle was removed. Duplantier came and invited D'André, in the name of Dumas and his group, to return; Wickham emerged from his recent reserve, reasserted his warm interest in the plans, and expressed high approval, moreover, of D'André's intention to return, even though he were not officially in a state of peace with the Republic, provided that D'André was sure that he could return without incurring harm to himself. By that date, however, the former difficulty had only intensified itself. D'André had been informed that the expedient of using bribery to obtain his *radiation*, which he had earlier considered, would be useless, since the Directory would not dream of striking off his name before the elections had been held. He had the flattering, but not very helpful, impression, that the Republicans regarded him as far too dangerous a person to let him return easily.[3]

In fact, once D'André had the assurance of Wickham's full support, and the encouragement of the Dumas group and of Théodore de Lameth, he resolutely put behind him from that point onwards both hopes and fears of the Republican authorities, and worked consistently to effect his re-entry in defiance of the repeated warnings of danger which he continued to receive. When he finally crossed the frontier, he had to do so in the knowledge that the Republican authorities expected him and were looking out in the hope of arresting him. If his projected journey was still destined to suffer long delays, these did not arise out of any wavering in his plan, but from difficulties in arranging, with fair prospects of success, what perforce had to be a clandestine re-entrance.

On 29 November, D'André believed his journey to be imminent. He was expecting, every day, a letter which would, he hoped, give him the signal to start.[4] When the letter arrived, it

---

[1] D'André to Leclerc, 23 August 1796.
[2] Idem., 20 September 1796.   [3] Idem., 23 November 1796.
[4] D'André to Wickham on that date: 'Je crois trés necèssaire que j'ai une entrevue avec vous avant mon dèpart pour la France, qui peut être trés prochain, car j'attends tous les jours la lettre qui doit la déterminer.'

brought him, not a green signal but a red one. It seems that D'André had, at some rather earlier date, sent forward a (false) passport for inspection by the French authorities. Early in December it was returned to him accompanied by a letter of friendly warning that it would not do:

une lettre fort honnête, dans laquelle on me dit que, la surveillance étant trés sèvére sur la frontiére, il y a *telle et telle chose* qui pourroit me nuire. On m'indique comment le passeport doit être rèdigé... je vais donc en faire partir un autre.[1]

This difficulty was overcome with some skill. By the new year, D'André had a passport authorized by no less a personage than Barthélemy, the Republic's Ambassador in Switzerland (but at heart no fervent admirer of the regime which he served) to cover his journey over the frontier, and was proposing to obtain another, through Wickham, to be used when he was inside France; this second passport would purport to show that his journey had started from some point on French soil[2] and would clear him of any suspicion of being an émigré. But in the meantime, a new difficulty arose. A letter which he had written to one of his associates in France had been seized at the frontier; it contained details of his intended method and route of entry.[3] Consequently he had to rearrange his plans. Finally, in the latter part of January, D'André was at last on the point of departure, when he had information that the French frontier police, as a result of the

[1] D'André to Leclerc, 9 December. In this same letter, D'André remarks that he had by this time received repeated warnings against going back: 'on ne me dit rien autre sinon que je fais une imprudence, mais je m'en moque. Le dez est jetté, il faut subir son sort.'

[2] Note from D'André to Wickham, inscribed by Wickham '7th January 1797'.

[3] D'André to Leclerc, 13 December 1796. On 17 December, D'André informed Leclerc of yet another embarrassment, which we do not mention in the text: having sent for his own available financial resources (£500 deposited with a friend at London) to increase his means at Paris, he had now discovered that the friend had been disloyal and had embezzled the money. To Wickham, on 14 December, D'André recurs again to 'les lettres rèiterées que je reçois pour me... détourner' (*de partir*). The main reason given by the latest dissuasives against D'André's return to France was that this would make against his being elected to the legislature. (A fresh proclamation of his name by the government was likely if it was known that he had re-entered the country.) D'André's comment on these warnings was: *a vaincre sans peril, on triomphe sans gloire.*

compromise of his original arrangements, were specially looking out
for him. This forced him to take elaborate new precautions. He
changed his vehicle and horses, and arranged to send one of his
children who was to have travelled with him by another route.[1]
Luck now at length turned in his favour. We learn from a note by
Bayard, dated Paris, 21 February, that the young agent met the
distinguished traveller whom he had long been impatiently await-
ing in the Republican capital on the preceding day.[2] The director
of the 'great design' had arrived to take personal charge of its fortunes.

[1] Note to Leclerc, inscribed by Wickham 'Nyon 21st January 1797'. It is
presumably a second change of vehicle and horses which is referred to here.

[2] Wickham Papers. In a somewhat earlier letter, Bayard had complained
bitterly of the effects of the long delay in D'André's arrival, which was spoiling electioneering opportunities.

VII

The Illusion of Succe

THE ELECTIONS OF YEAR V AND THE F
MARCH TO JULY 179

D'ANDRÉ'S first concern after his arri
to extend as widely as possible, the net of political connections at the centre of which he stood. This involved firstly a
double series of discussions: between his established allies in the
legislature and the pure Royalists of the metropolitan area, supposedly under the direction of the Agence; and, again, between
his established allies and the party of Mathieu-Dumas. In both
directions, it was necessary to confirm the alliance and to secure
agreement on everything concerning the conduct of the elections.

The Agence had now undergone great changes. Brottier,
Duverne and La Villeheurnois were not available for these discussions. The end of their careers as Agents had been as unfortunate for their cause as most of their previous activities. Election
preparations, made under their auspices by Royalists in various
parts of the country, had been compromised in the seizure of
their papers. Their plans for a military *coup* gave the Government
a chance to make the flesh of the public creep and to strengthen
the attractions of the existing regime in the eyes of the nation.[1]
Wickham feared, not without apparent reason, that these would
not be the worst consequences of the Agents' folly. He told

---

[1] For efforts by the government to make political capital out of the conspiracy of the Agents, see the summary of the report promptly given by the
Police Minister Cochon to the Five Hundred, and the long report subsequently read to the Council by Debry on behalf of the commission of enquiry that the Council set up, in Buchez & Roux, op. cit., tome 37, pp. 182–3,
pp. 212–41. The government seems, in the end, to have gained little advantage by all this, for the conspirators were generally regarded as pitiable rather
than as dangerous, and it was widely suspected that the plot was at least as
much a police arrangement as a real Royalist undertaking. For the compromise of Royalist election arrangements, see Wickham, no. 5 of 1797, 8
March, in Wickham, *Corresp.*, vol. II, p. 25 f. See the blistering comments of
Mallet du Pan on the Agents and their ill fated design in Michel, op. cit., tome
II, pp. 227–30.

...y, whose rival La Vauguyon quitted the scene not long ... the Agents, that it was now only to be expected that the ...ectory would use the plot as an excuse to 'justify . . . violent ...easures to influence the freedom of the elections'.[1] Meantime, however, there was no lack at Paris of Royalists with pretensions to leadership, hoping for the succession of Brottier and Duverne. There was, in particular, Des Pomelles, who had not only escaped the government's blow, but also was, apparently, little if at all known to the Republican authorities.[2] D'André was, accordingly, 'introduced by Mr Bayard to Mr Des Pommelles, and concerted all his measures with that gentleman until the Electoral Assembly had separated'.[3] D'André was so far satisfied with his new acquaintance that he instructed Bayard to advise the Court that he would in future willingly keep up communications with Des Pomelles—provided it were with him *alone*, and not (for reasons of security) with a plurality of Agents.[4] The next step was to introduce Des Pomelles, as representative of the pure Royalists, to D'André's 'committee' and to secure a 'direct and intimate correspondence and union' between them.[5] This was attempted 'a few days previous to the meeting of the Primary Assemblies'. The results, according to Wickham, were perfectly satisfactory so far as concerned the needs of the election campaign: 'the Royalists themselves' 'transmitted to Blankenburg' the report that 'Mr Berger's committee . . . throughout the whole of that trans-action . . . acted with perfect good faith'.

Meantime, D'André had been having 'repeated conferences with Mr Dumas . . . as with all the leading members of his committee'. His friends of the Lemerer group empowered him to speak to the Dumas group, not only for themselves but for 'the great majority' of the existing opposition. They gave themselves the pleasure of treating Dumas and his adherents as eccentric and erring members of their own much larger body. This no doubt did not make the negotiation easier; but Dumas and his friends

[1] Letter publ. in Wickham, *Corresp.*, vol. II, pp. 28–9. Wickham continued to worry over this possibility until towards the end of the election period.

[2] Meynier, *Le 18 fructidor*, p. 188.

[3] Wickham's no. 12 of 1797, 24 May. The last words quoted refer to the (secondary) electoral assembly (of the department of the Seine): this phrase means 'until the elections were over'.

[4] Ibid.

[5] Wickham's no. 11 of 1797, 20 May.

had other and larger griefs than this. Their inclination towards the legitimate claimant had already been shaken by the publication of the Agents' conspiracy. Could they afford to join with pure Royalists in face of this fresh evidence of pure Royalist persistence in mad attempts to snatch—without need of coalitions or conditions—an unconditional mastery? D'André did his best; and, for the period of the elections, he succeeded.

Mr Berger, in answer to the doubts and fears by which he found many of them affected, took as the principal grounds of his discussion, first the letter that he had himself received from the King, secondly the facts that had passed last year previous to the quarrel between Mr Dumas's committee and the Directory, and the inferences that had been drawn from those facts by Mr Dumas himself at the time when Mr Duplantier was sent into Switzerland to negotiate with Mr Berger. Upon these grounds, Mr Berger pressed the utility of a closer and more confidential union, of a more regular and methodical attack on the government, and showed at the same time the necessity of extending their connections much more widely, *particularly among the Royalists*.

Thus pressed with the arguments that the King was not so terrifying as they feared, and that the Directory was, to say the least of it, no better, Dumas and his friends for the moment rallied again on D'André's line; and the effects upon the elections of their close alliance with both D'André's friends and the pure Royalists were, according to Wickham, very satisfactory. 'We certainly owe to it . . . the happy choice of Deputies, as well as of administrators and Judges, that to the astonishment of everyone has been made throughout allmost all France.'[1]

The long awaited elections were now at last imminent; the primary assemblies were convened for 1st germinal (21 March) and the electoral (secondary) assemblies for 20 germinal (9 April).[2]

[1] For all these points and quotations, see Wickham's no. 11 of 1797, 20 May.

[2] Pariset, op. cit., tome II, p. 335. The government, despite many fears to the contrary, made no direct effort to avert or frustrate the appeal to the country which it had so much reason to dread. What it did attempt was to debar those on the émigré lists from voting (120,000 persons in all, of whom about 60,000 were actually residing in France). The Councils, led by the opposition, insisted on passing a law permitting the *radiés provisoires* to vote; but there were only about 1500 of these. In practice, however, the Directory's efforts to exclude all the others cannot have been very successful.—Lefebvre, *Directoire*, p. 59; Buchez & Roux, op. cit., tome 37, pp. 244–5; *Pariset*, op. cit., tome II, pp. 331–2. The Directory also tried to insist that *électeurs* must

The inevitably scanty written correspondence of D'André and Bayard with Wickham at the election period affords perhaps just enough tantalizing but illuminating glimpses of the ex-Constituent's conduct in the campaign to make possible an outline picture of this capital feature of his career. This outline can be supplemented, though only a little, from points made by Wickham in his drafts to Lord Grenville.

What these sources have least to tell us about are the nature and extent of the arrangements made, with reference to the elections, by the various other politicians and Royalist leaders with whom D'André was now allied. But our sources certainly show that D'André brought within the scope of his own control, mediately or immediately, a very extensive series of operations. We see that before the primary assemblies were opened, seven 'voyageurs' (the 'lay' visitors who had been envisaged to follow up the tour of the four clerics, and who were to supervise the action of the local clergy) had set out on a systematic mission throughout the territory of France, while two more were being prepared for the visitation of the Belgian departments.[1] We have the claim that, in Belgium at least, the efforts of D'André's collaborators to rouse the *honnêtes gens* from their stupor and to bring them to the polls, were strikingly successful.[2] Not the least interesting glimpse into the crowded and hurrying scene over which D'André attempted to preside is that provided by a letter which shows that D'André himself joined in the work of itinerant electioneering, making exertions which were as exhausting as (he was sure) they were rewarding. It appears that he left Bayard to gather up, in the meantime, the many reports which the *voyageurs* were sending in.[3] After these canvasses for the primary stage of the elections, there followed another series of operations by the local agents of the plan,

---

adopt the oath of abjuration of Royalty and of the constitution of 1793; the Councils turned the oath into a promise. Lefebvre, loc. cit. supr. and Buchez & Roux, tome cit., pp. 245-6. There is some evidence that the government tried to exert administrative pressure in favour of its own candidates, see Buchez & Roux, tome cit., p. 246; D'André told Wickham (19 March) that it was also spending a good deal ('croupes dans les fournisseurs, la vente des bois, la caisse des comptes courans leur fournissent . . . beaucoup... d'argent).

[1] D'André to Wickham, 19 March.

[2] D'André to Wickham, undated letter delivered to Wickham by Bayard about the beginning of May.

[3] D'André to Wickham, 28 March.

the 'travail direct' upon the (secondary) electors whom the primary voters were to choose and who were then to proceed to the definitive choice of legislators and administrators.[1]

D'André and Bayard were not content with the services of *voyageurs* and of the local clergy to galvanize the voters into determined action against the ruling party. They had resumed their ambitious planning, both for the immediate and for the further future, as soon as they met again on French soil.[2] They arranged, in time for the elections, a system of diligences under their own control, and they employed this in the first instance to carry copies of the opposition press to the departments, as Wickham expressed it 'earlier than the Post'. Presumably they meant to ensure that this should be done, not only punctually, but also more copiously, than would have been the case without their intervention—certainly, both more promptly and more copiously than the Directory would have permitted, if it had been able to control the circulation of the opposition's papers. Wickham believed, indeed, that 'the Directory had in vain endeavoured to prevent' this device, 'a measure', he added, 'to which the success of the . . . Elections is greatly to be attributed'.[3] In this connection we must also notice that D'André and Bayard had in addition embarked upon a still larger measure to influence the direction of public opinion, the establishment, throughout the country, of 'societies', or cadres of reliable adherents in every department and in every Parisian section, part of the purpose of which was to be, to supply the central leadership with 'intelligence' and the accessible public with the instruction which the central leadership wished to impart.[4]

This project was very similar in general conception to the plan of Des Pomelles for the *Institut philanthropique*. It may, indeed, have been from its inception identical with that; and if it was not originally identical, then at least D'André at an early point adopted the plan of his new acquaintance Des Pomelles, which had long existed on paper, but which had hardly advanced further, in preference to his own ideas on this subject.[5] It seems that work was

[1] Referred to in D'André's letter of 19 March.
[2] Bayard to Wickham, 21 February 1797, in Wickham Papers.
[3] Wickham's no. 12 of 1797, 24 May.
[4] Bayard to Wickham, 21 February 1797.
[5] Meynier, *Le 18 fructidor*, pp. 188-9, states that D'André had had a plan for the establishment of 'societies' but when he learned of the project of Des Pomelles he preferred this to his own. But it seems, from the evidence of the

begun towards the formation of these societies in several departments during the election period, and D'André was confident that
within three months following they would be established everywhere.[1] It is, however, important to notice that there is no suggestion in Wickham's correspondence that the societies (or, as we
may henceforward say, the *Institut*) had been sufficiently developed
to exert, or even to be expected to exert, any influence in the elections of year V. The point is worth some emphasis, because a
strong contrary impression was formed, at that very time, by
Mallet du Pan,[2] and also because D'André himself, in a well
known account of his activities, written after the *débâcle* of Fructidor, wrote of the progress made by the *Institut*, even in the short
space of the six weeks following his return to France, in terms far
more ambitious than the contemporary references in Wickham's
correspondence justify, and distinctly claimed that the *Institut*
had, in some degree, influenced the outcome of the Germinal
elections. This later account was cited by Pariset,[3] and from the
same source Meynier took his statement that the *Institut* had
indeed had a real, though not sufficiently decisive, effect in those
elections. Relying at least in part upon this *ex post facto* evidence,
Meynier formed the conjecture that the members who were ex-
truded at Fructidor had actually for the most part been members
of the *Institut*, though not belonging to its inner, and more
strenuously legitimist, circles.[4] The evidence, so far as it goes

---

Wickham Papers, to be just as likely that D'André's original ideas for the
establishment of these 'societies' were suggested to him by his prior knowledge of the general sense, at least, of Des Pomelles's plan for the *Institut*.
D'André met Des Pomelles only in February 1797; but he had discussed
future developments with Bayard as early as November, 1796, and Bayard
certainly knew the personnel of the Agence, and may then have planted
in D'André's mind the plan for 'societies' which he (Bayard) might already
have gathered from Des Pomelles.

[1] D'André to Wickham, 19 March and undated letter delivered to Wickham
by Bayard early in May.

[2] Mallet du Pan to Ste Aldegonde, 16–19 April 1797, in Sayous, op. cit.,
tome II, pp. 298–9.

[3] Pariset, op. cit., tome II, p. 332. In the passage which Pariset cites,
D'André claims that the *administrative* elections in several departments had
been settled entirely in favour of members of the *Institut*. (It will be noted that
Pariset believed that D'André returned to France only in April; this error
must be mentally corrected in order to seize the full significance of what
D'André here asserted.)   [4] Meynier, *Le 18 fructidor*, p. 189.

(and, beyond this point, even the *lack* of evidence) in Wickham's papers suggests that D'André's later account of the early progress of the *Institut* was coloured by inaccuracy of memory and by a natural instinct to over-represent the success of his undertakings; it confirms the scepticism expressed by Pariset on this point,[1] and agrees with the impression of Lefebvre, that the *Institut* was so little developed at the time of the elections that it could have made no important contribution to their outcome.[2]

The sources which we are using offer a few details of candidatures which were supported by the coalition, and of the general progress of the battle. These details, scanty though they are, are sufficient to confirm the impression that D'André was indeed working on a grand scale. We see D'André sending his 'person of confidence', Ramel, to collect 'friends' of D'André in support of a promising candidate in the Pas de Calais, and to carry funds to ensure this candidate's nomination.[3] Wickham writes to express his approval of two of the coalition's candidates at Paris, the *vendémiariste* Bonnières and the defender of Louis XVI, de Sèze.[4] On another occasion, Wickham offers D'André help from his own side in the elections in the Saône et Loire.[5] There are traces of difficulties and disappointments in this work, as well as of hopeful prospects. Wickham complains that a collaborator (unnamed) of D'André has completely wrecked election arrangements already independently settled in the Jura.[6] Much more serious, as it was to prove, is the failure of D'André himself to secure election.[7] But the disappointments are chiefly on the enemy side: D'André rejoices over Jacobin reverses in the departments near Paris, as well as in his own native area, the Bouches du Rhône and Vaucluse;[8]

---

[1] Pariset, loc. cit., suggests that D'André's later accounts reflected 'quelque exagération meridionale'.

[2] Lefebvre, *Directoire*, p. 57.

[3] D'André to Wickham, 19 March.

[4] Wickham's draft to D'André, 27 March.

[5] Wickham's draft to D'André, 30 March.

[6] Wickham to D'André, 26 April.

[7] D'André to Wickham, undated letter delivered by Bayard early in May: 'Le porteur vous instruira des causes qui ont empêché Kilien d'être nommé.' No written explanation of the reasons for this very important failure appears in the correspondence.

[8] D'André to Wickham, 28 March. D'André had regarded the Jacobins with some apprehension in these elections: 'leur union, leur correspondance, le soutien du Directoire ne permettent pas de les mépriser' (letter of 19 March).

Wickham announces the rout of 'the Bishop of Autun, Mr de Montesquiou, Messrs Roederer and Garat and all who had entered into the service of the Republick on its first formation' in the elections for Paris.[1]

All this activity was not embarked on without considerable expense, and it is clear that Wickham provided D'André with funds so large as to draw handsome tributes of thanks from him and his associates. 'Mr Berger and his friends . . . acknowledge with thankfulness their great obligations to H.M. for the liberal assistance which they have already received, which, they say, tho' their expences were large and various, have been fully sufficient for the first moment . . .'[2] And it was not only to the donor of the funds that D'André offered these acknowledgements.

The Abbé de la Marre is returned from Paris. . . . The Abbé carries with him to Blankenburgh the most honourable testimonies of Mr Berger's conduct at the late elections and the most unequivocal assurance from Mr Berger himself that his success was entirely owing to the liberal supplies he had received from the British Government.[3]

---

[1] Wickham's no. 11, 20 May. It appears from D'André's letter of 23 November 1796 to Wickham that Talleyrand was one of the politicians whom D'André had tried to enlist. Talleyrand had called on D'André's wife, and had told her 'with many protestations' that there was little that he could do. D'André claimed that he had some hold over Talleyrand ('il est *impossible* qu'il agisse publiquement contre moi') but understood that Talleyrand nevertheless intended to pursue his own ambitions and was already hoping to become Foreign Secretary to the Republic.

[2] Wickham's no. 12 of 24 May 1797.

[3] Wickham's no. 19 of 1797, dated 30 June, 'dispatched Saturday 8 July 1797'. It does not seem possible to say exactly what amount of British funds was used in the election campaign, since all the correspondence on financial matters between D'André and Bayard, on one side, and Wickham on the other, after D'André's return to France, is concerned with projects of D'André and his collaborators for the development of their party *after* the elections, rather than with the costs of the election campaign itself. We have however, some evidence: it appears from a letter of D'André to Leclerc, 9 December 1796 (i.e. long before his departure for France) that D'André had already received from the legation 1,000 louis (? or Pounds) and had by that date paid out 230 to Lacombe for the expenses of the clerical *voyageurs*, and 110 for the purchase of horses, carriage, etc., for his own voyage to Paris. D'André was keeping 140 for the costs of his journey and sending 500 forward to Paris. From Wickham's letter to D'André of 10 March it appears that Wickham had also granted D'André a credit, at Paris, for an unspecified sum, and that he had at this date (10 March) decided to increase it, apparently in view of the demands made by Bayard (in his letter of 21 February, Wickham

The terms in which these acknowledgements were rendered form a natural introduction to the next topic with which we must deal. 'Success' was the keyword of everything which either D'André or Wickham wrote about the election campaign at the time when it took place. It is clear beyond all doubt that they both emerged from the great experiment in a jubilant condition of mind. We have to consider how far this jubilation was justified. There is no question but that the Directory lost these elections. Of the old Conventionals whose mandates had been ruled, according to the procedure fixed by the law of 20 nivôse, year V

Papers, bundle 64) for support for the *future* developments of the movement. Only in the light of two subsequent letters (D'André and Bayard to Wickham, 19 March, and Wickham to D'André and Bayard, 30 March—both in Wickham Papers, bundle 67) can it be discovered that the sum *to which the credit was thus increased* was 20,000 louis. In addition to this, Wickham had arranged to credit a further sum at Paris to be used in 'attempts to save the Prisoners (i.e. the arrested Agents) or bribe their Judges'. This is referred to in his letter of 30 March to D'André and Bayard, and more specifically in his Private despatch no. 8 (wrongly headed no. 10) of 1797, dated 1 April. From this despatch, it also appears that the amount of this credit to save the Agents was £6,000 (Pounds, not louis); and that Wickham was, by that date, quite prepared to let this sum be spent on the operations of D'André and his friends, together with the rest, rather than allow it to be wasted in efforts to 'save the Prisoners' which would only too probably turn out to be 'idle'. Hence it becomes clear why Wickham, in that same despatch, advises the Foreign Secretary that he has 'engaged to lodge immediately at Paris the sum of 30,000 Pounds' to 'support . . . the opposition' . . . 'it appears to me indispensable whether the general plan of Mr Dandré's friends be *peaceably* put in execution or whether the Directory should attempt to provoke the people to another insurrection like that of Vendémiaire.' Wickham was meantime assuring D'André and Bayard (who were rather anxious on this point) that the credit made available to them was 'pour le premier moment', and that they need not fear making further applications for British funds (Wickham's letter of 30 March). The language of the letters and despatch referred to in this note, carefully considered, will show that by this phrase 'le premier moment' the envoy was referring to three current undertakings: 1. the elections. 2. the primary undertakings of the plans for future developments (e.g. foundation of 'societies', etc.). 3. Provision in case there should arise an early emergency, in which the opposition might have the need, and the chance, to meet force with force, cf. D'André's proposals in his letter of 30 November 1796, discussed in ch. VI above, pp. 167-8. All this leaves us with the most imprecise ideas possible as to what was spent *on the elections*. No doubt details were given by Bayard when he made his visit to Berne after the elections were over. It would seem clear that the sum involved must have lain *within the region* of £10,000.

(8 January 1797) to expire at the end of floréal then following (19–20 May 1797) only eleven secured re-election on this occasion.[1] The grip of the old ruling party on the legislative chambers was completely broken. And, as was to become painfully obvious to the government during the summer which now lay ahead, the elections to the local administrations had by no means been more favourable to its interests. But granting that the old Conventional party had lost the elections, we find ourselves dealing with further and different questions when we ask who won them, and what was the significance of the victory.

D'André and Wickham believed, at the time of the elections and on their immediate morrow, that they had been won for, and in a real sense by the efforts of, the coalition of monarchists who were agreed at least in rejecting the Republic, in shunning an Orleanist compromise arranged by the old ruling party, and in accepting (with whatever conditions) the claims of Louis XVIII. D'André indeed recognized, on the very eve of the polling, that the public mind, though bitterly opposed to the powers that were, was still divided and perplexed:

L'opinion est toute contre le Directoire, Elle semble même royaliste dans la majorité. Mais les orateurs, les bourgeois, les avocats, les acquéreurs craignent. Ils voudroient essaïer la Constitution. Les Royalistes sont divisés.[2]

But even at the moment of making this sensible and cautious judgement, D'André was sure that the result of the appeal to this embarrassed public mind would not only be defeat for the Directorials, but also defeat for the numerous and influential middle class people who would have preferred to 'try the Constitution'—without its makers—and an overwhelming victory for the cause of the King; so overwhelming that it would leave the Republicans only the expedient of naked force with which to stave off the Restoration:

---

[1] Lefebvre, *Directoire*, p. 59. The text of the law of 20 nivôse, year V, which determined the procedure to be adopted to decide which of the old Conventionals should vacate their seats in year V, and which should remain for a further period of one year (a system of lots) is printed in Kuscinski, op. cit., pp. 118 f. Kuscinski then prints the documents drawn up by each Council in Ventôse, year V, showing how each of them actually applied this procedure, and publishing the names of their members falling into these two categories (pp. 127 f.)

[2] D'André to Wickham, Paris, 19 March 1797.

Voulés-vous que je finisse par une prophétie? Le Gouvernement militaire ou la Royauté, voilà ce que nous aurons dans un an.[1]

Nothing happened during the campaign to shake his confidence; quite the opposite, and he was equally sure that it was above all the efforts of himself and his collaborators that was bringing Royalist successes out of the confused processes of the national mind. Reporting to Wickham his own election tour, he commented: 'Vous dire que je suis content, et que je ne perds pas de ma peine, c'est assés, et autant qu'en comporte une lettre.' And in a letter which he entrusted to the hands of Bayard, who made a mission of report to Wickham when the elections were over, D'André claimed that the campaign had not only been successful, but even in a sense too successful, since the results favoured the stricter Royalists to an extent which threatened to disrupt the 'coalition', and had indeed already partially done so:

Quoique nous soyons arrivés tard, vous aurez vu combien le travail des élections a reussi. Je vous ai dit que même nous allions trop bien, puisque les nominations trop Royalistes nous font craindre avec raison que ces nominations n'operent une réunion entre tout ce qu'il y a, non seulement de constitutionnels, tant de 90 que de 95, et tous les partisans du Directoire, et meme les terroristes, deja même ceux que je vous ai appellés le comité *Directorial* ont fait une alliance offensive et defensive avec le Directoire, deja plusieurs de nos amis sont effraiés et craignent qu'on ne se precipite trop vivement dans un changement... deja bien des braves gens sont atteints de l'idée que les nouveaux venus voudront tout bouleverser...

D'André went on to say that in these circumstances it would be all important to 'rallier tant de monde la..., mettre de l'ensemble et de l'union... reunir les nouveaux aux anciens', but he felt sure that, if this could be secured, the effects of the elections would within a few months be striking: 'Quand à moi' he concluded, 'j'espere tout.'[2]

Wickham formed the same impression of the elections— largely, of course, though not solely, from the information which he received from D'André. We have already noted his reference to 'the happy choice of Deputies, as well as of administrators and

[1] Ibid.
[2] D'André to Wickham, undated letter delivered by Bayard early in May.

Judges . . . throughout almost all France', and his belief that the
cause of this happy choice lay in the coalition which had been
cemented between D'André's friends, the pure Royalists, and
the constitutionalists represented by the Dumas group. What
Wickham understood to have been the precise character of this
choice he made clear in the following passage, which he began
with words of praise for the conduct of the friends of D'André
in their collaboration with the pure Royalists:

Mr Berger's committee acted with perfect good faith and without intriguing at all for themselves suffered the torrent of the public opinion
to take its free course. That opinion was most distinctly pronounced
in favour of persons of moderate sentiments, attached to the antient
government but desirous of reforming its abuses . . . all the Deputies at
Paris were nominated upon that one principle. Not only the Bishop of
Autun Mr de Montesquiou Messrs Roederer and Garat and all who had
entered into the service of the Republick on its first formation were rejected with evident marks of contempt, but the framers of the constitution of 1791 *who had remained faithful to that Constitution* and the friends
of Mr de La Fayette . . . all shared the same fate.[1]

And again in this passage:

Your Lordship will learn . . . from the inclosed Gazettes . . . what a
serious progress the spirit of Royalty has made, even at Paris, and how
much all those who have taken any active part in the revolution begin
to be alarmed. I am sorry to see anything like a *system of exclusion* beginning to prevail, but the impulsion . . . once given to . . . public
opinion, . . . that impulsion will be found far above the management of
those who have given it . . . the people . . ., animated against the
Government by the leaders of different factions seeking only their own
personal aggrandisement, have allmost universally (wherever they
have been left to their own free choice) rejected those leaders, and
chosen either persons notoriously attached to the antient Government,
or people of property and character who, having taken no part whatever in any political dissensions, are supposed to be desirous of estab-
lishing a Government that may secure, as far as possible, permanent
tranquillity at home, and Peace abroad. . . . I have constantly holden . . .
at Blankenburgh that the Monarchy was entirely and exclusively in the
hands of the third Estate and that it was to that estate principally that
the King ought to address himself . . , as I am sure he might with
perfect safety . . . What is now passing verifys my opinion.[2]

---

[1] Wickham's no. 11 of 1797, 20 May.

[2] Wickham's no. 10 of 1797, 13 April (portion not publ. in Wickham's
Corresp.).

We now proceed to examine these impressions and claims of the moment by reference to other evidence about the character of the elections. Two issues, distinct in principle, but difficult to dissociate in practice, are involved here. The first is, are there independent means of assessing the claim made by D'André and Wickham that it was the electioneering efforts of D'André and his allies which made possible, and determined, the movement of the voting public on this occasion? The second is, how far was it the case that the newly elected personnel were, as D'André and Wickham believed, in a high degree pure but sensible Royalists —men who, after the heart of Louis XVIII, wanted 'the antient government' though not its 'abuses'—or else men who had had nothing to do with the Revolution and were, as Wickham clearly meant to claim, at least potential converts to the same kind of Royalism?

On the first issue, we must emphasize the fact that there is not, and was never, any doubt that the vast majority of the French people detested their existing rulers; and we may also reassert, what was remarked in the discussion offered above on the elections of year IV, that the majority of voters must have found it very difficult to distinguish between the Republic as an abstract principle and the party which, with whatever changes of leadership and personnel, had dominated the Republic almost from its foundation. Purchasers of nationalized properties and 'lawyers' no doubt wanted to preserve the Republic, if not to give a new mandate to its existing ruling party; but these were of course a not very large minority among the primary voters. All this need not be regarded here as coming within the discussion. The question is, how far was it the case that it was D'André and his collaborators who provided the voters with the impulsion, and the direction, which they needed to express what they undoubtedly felt in the way in which in fact they did express it?

It is difficult to bring D'André's and Wickham's assertions on this point under satisfactory control, largely because it is impossible to say with any accuracy how far D'André's connections among the various opponents of the Directory extended, and how his collaborators arranged and conducted their election activities. D'André's committee claimed to act on behalf of the main body of the existing legislative opposition. It is not in dispute that many opposition deputies attempted to make interest in their

respective constituencies in view of these elections.[1] But it does
not follow that in so doing they were acting for the most part on
agreed lines and accepting common direction. All that we know
of these deputies renders such a suggestion very doubtful. Again,
Mathieu-Dumas and his friends, Théodore de Lameth and his,
represented the Feuillant tradition. But this is not to say that all
the old constitutionalists who were active at the time of these
elections acted on lines agreed with the Dumas group, and still
less that they accepted collaboration with the 'friends' of D'André
and with his other allies on the pure Royalist wing. The strong
presumption arises that D'André and his 'coalition' were in fact
only part of a larger and, as a whole, *unplanned* 'coalition' of elements which jostled in an untidy rush to attack the outgoing *tiers*
and the other friends of the Government.

This is not to conclude that D'André and his coalition did
nothing; and it even leaves open the possibility that they, with
their agreed arrangements, their diligences, their newspapers,
their clergy, their *voyageurs*, and their British gold, made the
decisive contribution, so far as any contribution was decisive.
There are, however, a few available facts which are disconcerting
for anyone inclined to accept their claims. Not more than one of
the persons whose candidature for a deputyship on this occasion
is mentioned in D'André's correspondence with Wickham actually secured a seat. This was Bonnières, who was duly elected at
Paris.[2] It is quite true that only a handful of candidacies is mentioned in that correspondence, but the indication arising from the
fate of the few which are mentioned is not reassuring. Again, we
remember that it had been a very just and striking feature of
D'André's plans for the campaign, that he recognized the need to
convert the primary voters, not from Republican opinions, but
from apathy, and to bring them *en masse* to the polls. Hence, of
course, the device of using the anti-Republican clergy as election
agents. But it seems clear that this objective was only very im-
perfectly achieved, if we accept the judgement of Lefebvre on the
present state of that question.[3] And, in so far as a larger attendance

[1] See, e.g., Buchez & Roux, op. cit., tome 37, p. 246.

[2] Kuscinski, op. cit., p. 173.

[3] 'Le nombre des votants fut plus considérable qu'en l'an IV, sans l'être
beaucoup, au moins dans les campagnes' (Lefebvre, *Directoire*, p. 59). On the
other hand, Mallet du Pan in a note to the Austrian Court, 7 March 1797, observed that the number of primary voters *at Paris* who had registered their

at the polls did occur, it is another question again how far this resulted directly from the arrangements made by D'André.

When all this is said, however, the claims of D'André and Wickham in this matter are not completely disallowed. There remains a wide area of possibility, quite uncertain in extent, that they were, to that uncertain extent, justified.

Turning now to the other issue: this, it will be remembered, is raised by the claims of D'André and of Wickham that the elections produced a very heavy shift to the further Right: the deputies returned were in general men of a strongly Royalist character, or at least of a character likely to be very sympathetic to a strongly Royalist line. This was the reverse side of that other striking feature of the elections, the rout of the old constitutionalists. Such results, it was said, were even too good. The coalition had not, and in its whole general interests could not have, planned for anything so catastrophic; the moderates everywhere were alarmed, if not alienated, and the coalition was already weakened by the withdrawal of the 'comité Directorial', the group of Mathieu-Dumas. D'André and Wickham were not unwilling, however, to accept the overflowing fortune which they believed had been poured upon them. D'André felt that, provided the different elements of the swollen opposition could be brought back into harmony, and the fears and jealousies of the older opposition about the new appeased, all would be well indeed, and it would be Restoration—or military tyranny—within a year.[1] Wickham accepted this brilliantly coloured appraisal without misgivings (except that the sinister side of the prophecy might be fulfilled). How far was this appraisal an accurate one?

There is no doubt that the elections to the Councils produced results which many moderates, inside and outside their existing membership, found very disconcerting. The Dumas group was in fact lost to D'André's coalition and driven back into the arms of

---

names in view of these elections was double that which had done so for the previous elections: Michel, op. cit., tome II, pp. 238–9; and Wickham, in his no. 9 of 1797, 1 April, claimed that 'the Primary Assemblies in Franche Comté, Bourg Bresse, the Lyonnois, part of Champaigne and Alsace have been attended (with very few exceptions) by all the well disposed inhabitants in those Provinces'.

[1] D'André, in the letter which he sent to Wickham with Bayard, echoed the sense, but not the very words of his earlier prophecy when he wrote: '... vous serez surpris de l'effet dans quelques mois, quand à moi j'espere tout.'

the Directory.[1] In the minds of these people, disappointment over the electoral defeats suffered by such men as themselves, and mortification in feeling that the public had turned its back upon them and upon the tradition of moderately popular ideals for which they stood, undoubtedly played a large part. But it seems clear that fear, as well as wounded pride and jealousy of those who had been more successful, entered into their reaction also. They had been prepared to make common cause with the stricter legitimists, while they could cherish the hope that it was their own kind of monarchists who would take the lion's portion of popular favour, and could assume that the purer Royalists, and even the Pretender himself, would have to accept their own direction in the end. The results of the elections swept all these comforting suppositions from their minds. Reasonably or unreasonably—we have to try to decide which—they were seized with panic, and saw pure Royalism, arrogant and unrepentant, grown to a great and menacing height by standing on their own shoulders.[2]

[1] Wickham gives a circumstantial account of the conduct of the Dumas group at this time in his no. 11 of 1797, 20 May. He says that Dumas, with Portalis, Siméon, and others (but not all of his former committee) 'in spite of the strongest entreaties and remonstrances of Mr Berger's committee' made a new compact with the Directory. They 'most solemnly engaged', however, 'to abandon the Directory immediately' if the Directors failed to honour the terms of the new engagement. These terms had been arranged between Dumas and Carnot. Carnot had never broken contact with Dumas, and it was he who had taken the initiative to regain Dumas and his friends to the Republican side. Other members of the group, however, while breaking their alliance with the friends of D'André, had not gone so far as to join the new understanding with the Directory, but had adopted a position of temporary neutrality. Among these Wickham mentions Dumolard and Cadroi.

[2] Wickham's account of the motives of the Dumas party (in his despatch of 20 May) lays emphasis on considerations other than fear of the swing to the further Right. He says that these deputies were struck with 'infinite surprise ... disappointment and rage' at the turn taken by the elections, especially at Paris. Some, notably Dumas himself, were ruled by 'ambition and personal vanity'; what they chiefly disliked was 'the probability of a change in the government being brought about by other hands than their own'. Others, including Portalis and Siméon, followed Dumas for rather different reasons: they feared, not so much that a reaction of excessive extent would succeed, but that the Republicans would revive the system of the terror rather than let it succeed; and they felt that it was for this reason specially that the brakes must be applied to the swollen Royalist party. Others again, Dumolard and Cadroi, felt that it was largely a question of timing. The new majority was likely to travel, not so much too far as too fast.

Thus Dumas and his friends shared the belief of Wickham and of D'André, though with different accompanying emotions. And, as this coincidence itself suggests, there was indeed some evidence to support such an interpretation of the results. The deep Royalist colour of some of the newly elected deputies was too obvious to miss. This was most especially clear in the returns for Paris and for Lyon. At Paris, the six new deputies included Claret-Fleurieu, a former Minister for the Navy and sometime governor to the Dauphin; General Murinais, former Inspector-General of the Cavalry; Du Fresne, *premier commis* at the Treasury in Necker's time; Bonnières, who had connections with the Comte d'Artois before winning fame in the sectional movement of 1795; and Emmery, a former Fayettist who, however, was now reported by Mallet du Pan as having just made his submission to Louis XVIII, and as owing his election to the support of the genuine Royalists of the capital. Such men could properly be described by Wickham as 'attached to the antient government', whether or not they were all 'desirous of reforming its abuses'. At Lyon, where the feeling of the public was visibly and expectantly Royalist, only two deputies had to be returned. The choice fell upon Imbert-Colomès, a notorious Royalist partisan, and upon Camille Jordan who was soon to become celebrated as 'Jordan les Cloches'.[1]

It may well be the case that all these motives were operative; but we have already had occasion to argue, at an earlier stage, that it seems too simple to attribute the conduct of Dumas solely to vanity, and similar comments could now be made on the motives attributed to the others. The Portalis and the Siméons, the Dumolards and the Cadrois, may well have found it too humiliating to admit to the friends of D'André that they were *afraid* of the swing to the Right, in the proper sense of the word; but their action, and the whole circumstances of the moment, suggest that it was this essentially which swayed them.

[1] Kuscinski, op. cit., pp. 172–73; Mallet du Pan to the Court of Vienna in Michel, tome II, pp. 265–7. In a letter to Ste Aldegonde, 19 April 1797, Mallet said he understood that it was D'André who had gained Emmery for the cause of Louis XVIII. If this was so, it marked another important success for D'André's campaign. Mallet also makes comments on Imbert-Colomès: 'agent publiquement avoué du roi... un homme excellent... mais une tête médiocre et trop ardente' (Sayous, op. cit., tome II, pp. 299–300). Imbert-Colomès corresponded with Wickham.

The choice of Pichegru, in the Jura, and of Willot, the secessionist-Royalist commander of 1793 and more recently the protector of the White Terrorists in the South, for the Bouches-du-Rhône, appear in retrospect to be quite as significant as the instances referred to in the text. But neither of these

With such instances staring them in the face, it is not surprising that other contemporaries besides D'André, Wickham, and the Dumas group should have concluded that the new elections as a whole were characterized (no doubt with some variations) by the same kind of heavy shift to the further Right. Mallet du Pan commented on the results in very much the same terms as D'André and Wickham; and though it may be said that his sympathies were as heavily engaged as theirs, he was at all events spared the temptations which inevitably affected the men actively engaged in the attempt to influence the elections. Mallet believed that the returns over the much greater part of the country had favoured 'Royalistes avec plus ou moins de modifications'. By this phrase he did not mean to include old constitutionalists and their sympathizers, for he had also observed that the constitutionalists had done very badly in the primary stage of the elections, and that a view of the choices of (secondary) electors made in a representative number of primary assemblies showed that public favour was turning heavily towards such persons as noblemen, *chevaliers de St-Louis*, judges of the old regime and 'officiers publics qui restèrent fidèles à la Monarchie'. Mallet, indeed, did not hesitate to say that in these elections the country had repudiated, not only the Convention, not only the Republic, but *the Revolution*.[1] The 'Royalisme de 1789', to the all-importance of which Mallet had often pointed in the past, had apparently evaporated. Mallet did not think, any more than he had ever done, that the old regime could or should now be restored in detail; but he certainly thought that the interior was turning towards a purer (though intelligent) variety of Royalism.

Generals was then known to be so deeply committed to the reaction as later became notorious.

[1] Mallet's contemporary notes to the Austrian Court, in Michel, tome II, pp. 262, 265–6, 268. It will be noted that Mallet describes the choices for Paris in terms closely similar to those used by Wickham: the deputies elected there, he says, are neither 'sectateurs de l'ancien régime' nor old constitutionalists 'connus... pour avoir pris une part trop essentielle à la première révolution', but men who 'aspirent à la monarchie modifiée et non dénaturée' (tome cit., p. 265). In a postscript to one of these notes Mallet claims that the departmental choices are in general closely similar to those of Paris (tome cit., p. 267). In the same sense he told Ste Aldegonde that the returns in the South generally were analogous to those made at Lyon. Sayous, op. cit., tome II, p. 300.

We can agree, then, that D'André and Wickham committed no absurdity in their first appraisals of the outcome of the legislative elections. The fact is, however, certain, for all that, that their first appraisals were much too highly coloured. It was, of course, in the conditions of that time very difficult to appraise in advance the political opinions and character of a large body of legislators, for the most part unknown to the political life of the Revolutionary era, and for whom no public and defined party organization could vouch. After only a short experience of the new legislative session, which was opened on 1 prairial, year V (20 May 1797),[1] they were brought to restate their earlier estimates in terms decidedly more modest. On 27 June, Wickham reported home the first details which he had from D'André about the state of parties in the new Councils.[2] *The two Councils together*, said the envoy, now contained more than two hundred 'firm decided Royalists'; there were about two hundred steady Republicans, and a large balance (roughly three hundred on this computation) of independents, fully committed to neither of these blocs. There was, then, still nothing like an overall Royalist majority. D'André had earlier pointed out that it would be necessary to win, or recover, many moderates who felt that the elections had produced a swing dangerously far to the right. On this calculation he would need to secure at least about a hundred and fifty deputies from the middle section, and this all important achievement still lay in the future.

Wickham described the two hundred or more 'firm Royalists' in terms which show an even more striking declension from the high hopes expressed a few weeks before:

firm decided Royalists . . . resolutely bent on restoring the Crown to its rightful possessor, with as much power and splendour as the temper of the people, the ideas of liberty and independence that have possessed every class . . ., and the necessity of securing the Kingdom against future convulsions, will possibly permit.

In the next breath, Wickham says that of these 'firm' (but evidently far indeed from unconditional) Royalists, there were scarcely ten who were

attached to the person of the present King, and by far the greater number are either animated by strong prejudices against him, or entertain the most marked jealousy of his intentions and principles.

---

[1] Buchez & Roux .op. cit., tome 37, p. 269.　　　　[2] No. 17 of 1797.

Most of them, Wickham understood, thought that both the Royal brothers should cede their claims to the Duc d'Angoulême. Finally, these deputies had the most various ideas of the limitations which would have to be placed on the restored Crown.

We must next consider a written report of D'André to Wickham, dealing with the same subject and dated exactly a month later.[1] Whether Wickham had misunderstood the numerical estimates which D'André had sent to him earlier, or whether D'André had in the interval revised his own conclusions on that matter, is really indifferent for our present purpose. In either case, we are bound to pay greater attention to the later account; and this is quite incompatible, so far as numbers are concerned, with Wickham's report of 27 June. It represents the strength of the good cause in the renewed Councils in terms even more modest. D'André says that there were now about eighty 'francs Royalistes' *among the two new 'tiers' of the Five Hundred*. He plainly implies (what is indeed beyond dispute) that his cause was far weaker in the Anciens than in the junior Council.[2] Of the other elements *in the Five Hundred* he says that there were about eighty 'Jacobins' (under this description he presumably means to include the surviving regicides, whether strictly identifiable as Jacobins, or simply Directorials),[3]

le reste est constitutionnel, mais dans la majeure partie hait tellement les Jacobins qu'elle se tourne plutot vers les Royalistes.

'Constitutionnel' here must be supposed to cover, in accordance with D'André's usage elsewhere, both constitutional *royalists*, in the manner of 1789–91, and *also* those who accepted the constitution of the year III (though without enthusiasm for the existing Directors, and in some cases with an *ulterior* preference for a constitutional monarchy; the position represented by Mathieu-Dumas

[1] Inscribed by Wickham 'Paris 27 Juillet 1797. Berger'.

[2] Of the situation in the Anciens, D'André says in this letter: 'Aux Anciens, les Parleurs sont tous constitutionnels. Cela met les Royalistes en minorité... les Orléanistes ont un très fort parti dans les anciens'. Contemporaries agreed that the situation of parties in the Anciens was different from that which obtained in the Five Hundred, see, e.g., Buchez & Roux, op. cit., tome 37, p. 270.

[3] It seems that the anti-Directorial deputies of the Club de Clichy used 'Jacobin' as an acceptable slang term for supporters of the government as well as for the Jacobins proper. See Pariset, op. cit., tome II, p. 337.

and his friends).[1] The willingness of these men to *tourner... vers les Royalistes* was less encouraging, however, than it sounded; for elsewhere in the same report D'André observes:

Si on alloit directement au but, le Parti constitutionnel, qui est encore très nombreux, se réuniroit aux Jacobins; et nous retomberions dans la terreur.

There was, then, little hope of using the renewed Council of the Five Hundred to 'frapper un grand coup'; it would, at best, be a matter of inducing the 'constitutionnels', or independents, to join in a policy of sapping and mining.

The Royalists, moreover, needed several assets at least as important as numbers, if they were to pursue even a policy of sapping and mining to good advantage. They needed, if not complete agreement among themselves as to their eventual aims, at least sufficient agreement to foster mutual confidence; they needed speaking talent; accepted leadership and discipline; and skilful tactical direction to make the most of the only partially favourable attitude of the great middle bloc of the independents. It soon became clear that they lacked all of these, except, to some extent, the gift of oratory. A few were over adventurous, and attacked both the government and, by implication, the regime, with dangerous indiscretion. Many displayed a timidity which perhaps reflected their reluctance to engage themselves too far for the benefit of the prince they so much distrusted as well as their inexperience and their fear of the Directory. They acquired neither discipline nor effective tactical direction. No accepted leader emerged from their own ranks except Pichegru, and he had neither knowledge of, nor interest in, parliamentary management. There was, as D'André put it in a quaint attempt at English usage, no 'satisman' to direct their efforts on the spot. D'André himself had failed to win a seat, and though he tried to supply leadership from the background, this was at best a poor substitute for his presence in the *hémicycle*.[2]

[1] D'André's usage of 'constitutionnel' in the comprehensive sense of 'constitutionnels tant de 90 que de 95' has been illustrated above, pp. 131 n. 1, 199.

[2] D'André makes statements on most of these points, including the point that his party lacked a 'satisman' in the legislature, in the letter of 27 July. The details both from this and from his other letters which bear upon the subject will be taken up in ch. VIII below.

To go no further into the evidence for the moment, it is quite clear already that D'André and Wickham had hailed a false dawn. The defeat of the Directorials had been real enough. But there had been nothing like a decisive success for Royalism, in any sense of the word that matters. There was an enhancement of Royalist strength in the Councils. But not only was this of very moderate dimensions, it had been purchased at a very high price. The return *of a very few* thorough-paced pure Royalists, and men of the old regime—the defeats suffered at the polls by the old constitutionalists—had frightened away many deputies, both old and new, who would otherwise have collaborated without hesitation in attacking the old Conventionals in their last entrenchment—the Directory—and, in many cases, might have collaborated further in bringing the Republic to an end. These numerous deputies who were terrified by the illusion that the pure Royalists had emerged very strong could have worked happily enough, if only they had realized it, with the great majority of Wickham's 'firm decided Royalists', who were no more partizans of the old regime (even of the old regime amended) than themselves, and who differed from them chiefly, it would seem, only at this point: 'the firm decided Royalists' were not unduly scandalized by the election of a handful of pure Royalists, while the other deputies, now pushed into neutrality or something worse, were both scandalized and afraid.

The implications of all this are very important. The character of the new deputies, both 'Royalist' and independent, when tested by experience, showed that France as a whole had by no means reverted—even for the limited purpose of ridding herself of old Conventional rule—to reliance upon Royalists of deep colour. There was no attempt to repudiate the *Revolution*. Moreover, it appears clearly that the whole concept of the coalition of parties, agreed in working to overthrow the Republic, but not necessarily agreed upon the system of government which was to replace it, had been exploded. The moderate monarchists, like the other moderates who were opposed to the ruling party but not to the bourgeois Republic as such, still feared and distrusted those who came from the side of pure Royalism far too much to afford any chance of significant progress to such a coalition. The least sign that pure Royalism might become an important element in the coalition was sufficient to alienate some of its most important members, and to drive others into an attitude of suspicious reserve.

It is not suggested that this could have been certainly foreseen before trial had been made of the policy, or that the policy was, from the point of view of its authors, in any degree unworthy of trial. On the contrary, it offered, at the stage which had then been reached, the only hopeful means of progress towards a legitimist Restoration. But, in the circumstances and conditions in which it had actually to be attempted, there were causes at work which were only too likely to bring about the embarrassing situation which we have now tried to describe. Prominent among these ill-disposed causes was the attitude and conduct of the Pretender. If the Pretender had been willing, even on the brink of the election period, to do as Wickham would have preferred, and let it be known in some terms of frank self-commitment that he would leave the forms of the future Royal government largely in the hands of his subjects, it is at least arguable that he might have assuaged the fear and anger with which most of the French public had long regarded him. In this case, his firm adherents in the interior would have been committed by their King's word, would no longer have been, strictly speaking, pure Royalists at all, but only *former* pure Royalists, and might not have attracted the terror and resentment of the moderates even if they had won much more numerous successes than in fact they did. But Louis consistently refused to take this line. Instead, he adopted the far more ambiguous language of the March Declaration. This, for all the skill with which it was worded, apparently failed to satisfy any large number of the moderates that the King was at last prepared to be sufficiently reasonable. It is not possible to blame them, for in their sense he still did not mean to be reasonable.

We must not, however, place too much stress on this point about the Declaration. Even if the Declaration had made more concessions, it would still have proceeded from the same author, and the interior would have judged it, not only by what it said, but by all that it knew (or thought it knew, which was just as important) about him. In the eyes of the interior, Louis's past record was heavy against him; and, for all that we might fairly urge about his personal mildness, intelligence, dignity and grace, it cannot be said that the interior had no grounds for feeling this. If he had now torn up the Verona Declaration and done all that Wickham, or Pichegru, or his own Agents, had wished, might his actions not still have appeared only an insincere and deceptive gesture?

Nor, in any case, should we lay the whole responsibility at the door of Louis XVIII. Whatever he might now have offered his fellow-countrymen, much hung upon the behaviour of other pure Royalists at and after the time of the elections. Wickham might prescribe 'moderation', 'conciliation' and 'mutual sacri-fices' to all and sundry; D'André might try to practise Wickham's remedies and persuade others to adopt them.[1] But how many of the pure Royalists could be reached by this good advice? And how many of them now acted in accordance with it?[2]

We have said nothing as yet about the results of the other elections which took place in Germinal. These (for the recruitment of the local administrative and judicial authorities) proved in fact to be far more successful, in their manner, for the ulterior purposes of the great design, than the legislative elections in theirs. How far the newly elected local personnel consisted of serious Royalists matters little for our purpose; it is certain that during the summer of 1797 the local authorities did most of what the reaction expected of them, by allowing the legislation still in force against émigrés and refractory priests to lapse completely and by tolerating without apparent reluctance the often violent proceedings in which these elements and their supporters now openly indulged.[3]

At the end of the election period, as can now be seen, both D'André and Wickham were enjoying the illusion of successes far greater than their cause had actually won. Even the departure from the Royalist alliance of Dumas and his group seemed at the time to be providential in the eyes of the British envoy. He had feared, until this occurred, that the Directory would spoil the game without further delay, by laying violent hands on the opposition deputies in the existing Councils, and by inducing what remained

---

[1] Wickham urged D'André, in view of the election campaign, to practise 'conciliation' as comprehensively as possible: 'Mettez tous vos moyens de conciliation bien en avant—et n'oubliez rien pour faire les bases de votre travail aussi larges que possible', Draft to D'André, 10 March. D'André replied, 19 March, that 'conciliation' was '(ce) dont on s'occupe principalement.'

[2] Mallet du Pan gives a highly indignant account of the unbending and arrogant attitude of the pure Royalists before these elections in a note to Vienna, 15 March 1797, Michel, tome II, p. 245.

[3] See, e.g., Lefebvre, *Directoire*, pp. 63–4.

of the legislature to quash a large number of the new elections before the successful candidates could take their seats.[1] This would have been, if we may put it in such a way, the *coup d'état* of Fructidor in advance; and it is certain that such remedies were proposed in Republican circles, and discussed inside the Directory itself.[2] The Directorials were not only frightened by the very obvious sentence which the voters recorded against them; they were also, in everything but their lack of wide support at home, in a very powerful position. The French hustings might repudiate them, but their armies now more than ever gave the law to Europe. In January, Bonaparte had smashed the last Austrian attempts to retrieve the Habsburg positions in North Italy; he had gone on to invade, despoil and dismember the States of the Church; before the end of March he had embarked on the invasion of the Austrian Monarchy from its southern frontiers; on 7 April he met Thugut's emissaries at Leoben; on 18 April he was to sign the preliminaries of peace there, by which Austria surrendered both Belgium and Lombardy; at that same date, Hoche (commanding the Army of the Sambre et Meuse) and Moreau (commanding the Army of the Rhine and Moselle) were once more carrying the flag of the Republic beyond the Rhine. Why should the masters of Europe, before whom all princes trembled, themselves tremble before public displeasure which was obviously the artificial product of Royalist conspiracy?

The expected *coup d'état* did not, however, take place. Wickham correctly understood that it was Carnot who, in the Directory, had successfully set his face against a monstrous infringement of

---

[1] There are numerous references in Wickham's letters and despatches to the envoy's fears on this point. E.g. he urged 'Kilien' on 27 March to the greatest possible caution: 'Je n'ai garde de vous pousser. Je crains plutôt que le Directoire ne vous pousse à quelque imprudence: et j'ai constamment l'affaire de Vendémiaire devant mes yeux. Pour l'amour de Dieu soyés tous calmes et patients.' Wickham recounted his impressions of all that might have happened in this respect in the despatch of 20 May (no. 11) where he claims, by this date, that 'it was certain . . . that at one time the Directory was upon the point of having recourse to Revolutionary measures . . .' It appears from later passages in the same despatch that Wickham was now convinced that 'the arrival of the new deputies at Paris', as well as the safety of the existing opposition deputies, had been secured only by the latest volte-face of Dumas and his friends.

[2] Lefebvre, *Directoire*, pp. 59-60.

the due processes of the constitution.[1] Wickham also understood that it was the cheering signs that the Directory's opponents were beginning to fall out among themselves, and especially the signs that Dumas was willing once again to make a bargain with the government, which chiefly induced Carnot to argue that there could be no excuse for revolutionary measures.[2] Believing this, Wickham understandably felt that there was no need to regret the conduct now adopted by Dumas and his colleagues:

I believe myself that the arrival of the new Deputies at Paris could have been brought about by no other means . . . Had more favourable events taken place in Italy and Germany, I should perhaps have thought differently. And it is not only the return of the new members that has been secured by this union (*of Dumas with the Directory*) but also the election of the administration of the several Departments and municipalities, a circumstance perhaps of equal importance. . .[3]

The real significance of the situation produced by the elections to the constituted authorities was now to be tested by experience. But before offering any details of what took place during the new session, we must pause to consider the plans for the future development of the cause, which, in the hands of D'André, of Bayard, and of D'André's collaborators in the legislature, had meantime been worked out with great thought and skill, and which, in this elaborated shape, now claimed considerable financial support from Wickham. The envoy regarded these plans with enthusiasm, and, so far as it lay with him, he was quite prepared to concede the funds which their authors solicited for them.[4]

[1] Lefebvre, *Directoire*, p. 60. Mallet du Pan told the Austrian government that La Revellière also was opposed to revolutionary measures, while Barras and Reubell favoured them. Michel, op. cit., tome II, pp. 269–70.

[2] No. 11 of 1797, 20 May.

[3] Ibid.

[4] In his despatch no. 9 of 1797, 1 April, Wickham had already observed: 'The plan of operations which those Gentlemen are following is large and will be found expensive extending . . . to the whole of France. I have not, however, hesitated to encourage it in its fullest extent . . . it is the first time that I have as yet disposed of the public money with perfect satisfaction. . . .' The 'plan of operations' to which Wickham referred was not merely the plan for winning the elections, though he of course included this, but more particularly the arrangements for exploiting the success of the elections. In a despatch of even date (Private no. 8 of 1797) the envoy announced his decision to spend £30,000 in supporting the 'general plan of Mr Dandré's friends';

D'André had resumed with Bayard their discussions on means of exploiting the success which they hoped to gain in the elections as soon as he re-entered France. The results of these discussions had been communicated without delay both to D'André's allies in the legislature and to Wickham. We have already glanced at some features of the design which emerged, but we must now attempt to display it more fully and in the mature form in which it was finally laid before Wickham by Bayard when he travelled to Berne at the end of the election period.

We may preface this discussion by making one point of great general importance. In the sketches of these plans which D'André had attempted at an earlier stage, before he left Switzerland, he had put forward, as being much the most desirable course and as the line which his colleagues in the Councils also preferred, a plan for a motion of impeachment against the existing Directors at the very outset of the new session. But from the time of his return to France this proposal for an *early* 'grand coup' was dropped. Even under the impression that his cause had won brilliant success in the elections, D'André did not revive it. He seems to have realized that, even in the most favouring conditions inside the legislative body and the other constituted authorities, such an early appeal to final judgement would be impossible, because it would give no time adequately to prepare the public to support it, if need be by force. The whole time scale of the plans is henceforth more extensive, and preparations to secure public support at every one of a long succession of stages assume a much greater importance in the design.

The general shape of the earlier stages of the plan in its mature form can best be presented in the words with which the envoy finally summarized them for Lord Grenville at a rather later date (30 June 1797):

The abbé de la Marre is returned from Paris . . . to Blankenburg . . . He is accompanied by Mr Bayard, who is charged by Mr Berger to submit to the King's formal approbation the plan of operations which has

---

'measures tending to influence public opinion', and added: 'This appears above all others to be the case where I ought to use the powers reposed in me with a liberal hand . . . I shall now venture to advise that the opposition at Paris may be supported to the full extent of their demands and that . . . they may be fully satisfied that their operations shall not fail for want of pecuniary resources.'

lately been followed up with such success and which may be reduced to four leading points:

1st. the securing a decided majority in the legislative Body.

2nd. obtaining full possession of the public opinion and giving it a direction conformable to the conduct of the legislative Body.

3rd. preparing the means of force to support that opinion, by rearming the national guards, gaining the administrative Bodies in the departments, and giving them a uniform plan of conduct.

4th. forming associations of the well disposed Proprietors in every department, according to the plan known to your Lordship by the name of Philanthropic Institutes, whose principal object shall be to influence the choice of Administrators and to encourage and support them when in office.[1]

Some of the details can be filled in by reference to D'André's and Bayard's scanty correspondence with Wickham at and about the time of the elections, and also from comments by Wickham to Lord Grenville on the report given by the friends of D'André when the elections were over. The gaining of a decisive majority in the Councils would be pursued chiefly in efforts to 'rallier tant de monde la... mettre de l'ensemble et de l'union... empecher la trop grande effervescence et reunir les nouveaux aux anciens.' [2] The direction of public opinion would be secured, not only by the dissemination of existing opposition papers, but by the acquisition of new ones. All would be distributed in the provinces by the same system of diligences as was used in the election campaign. The societies were to be extended across the whole of France, and to each of the Paris sections, within three months.[3]

More important than any single point in the plan is the psychological appreciation of prevailing conditions in France which it revealed. Its authors and its British patron laid very great emphasis on the importance of pushing on the movement, rapidly

---

[1] No. 19 of 1797. The draft is noted by Wickham: 'dispatched Saturday 8 July 1797.'

[2] Phrases used by D'André in the undated letter delivered to Wickham by Bayard in May.

[3] 'L'opinion sera formée par les Journaux que nous allons avoir et par les sociétés qui seront etablies dans les Sections et les Départemens', D'André to Wickham, 19 March. (Cf. Bayard to Wickham, 21 February.) 'Le jeune homme vous fera part de tous les moyens de detail, journaux, voitures, etc. Les sociétés s'organisent dans plusieurs Departements. Avant trois mois elles seront etablies partout', D'André's undated latter referred to in previous note.

no doubt, but also evenly along the whole front of operations, and above all cautiously and gently. 'Combien etoit foible Brotier et Compagnie [*sic*]... Pour nous, nous ne ferons ni recrutemens ni provocations au Royalisme... Eviter tout evenement violent,... diriger l'opinion, la suivre, la dévancer peut être pour hâter son cours, forcer les résultats par les circonstances, suivre une marche graduelle et regulière...' [1] Or, as Wickham expressed it in more flowing terms:

The plan of operations which those Gentlemen are following is large and will be found expensive, extending ... to the whole of France. I have not, however, hesitated to encourage it in its fullest extent ... I am ... fully aware of all the difficulties that this Plan must ... meet with ... I only mean to say that this is the only one I have yet seen that had for its basis ... the real situation of public affairs ... and was perfectly conformable to the general spirit wishes and opinion of the people. It has also ... this singular advantage that at the same time that it is working out its own more immediate end it preserves its actors from personal danger, and tends in its very nature to the revival of the principles of order and good government in France ...

I agree entirely with M. D'André that it is more than probable that we shall see in the course of the year either Royalty or Military Tyranny fairly established. The plan therefore of that Gentleman has in this respect also a singular advantage ... it tends .. to unite the great body of the people in one mass ... to give them courage and the means of resistance. [2]

Cautious and reticent as the makers of the plan might intend to remain, during many stages of their design, it was of course agreed on all hands that sooner or later a critical moment must probably arrive. It was not very likely that the old ruling party would abandon the last citadel of its power, which was also the strongest, without a struggle. This would be the moment for 'resistance'. Whether it came early or late, whether it arose out of a 'grand coup' by the Councils against the old Directorials or not, at all events the makers of the plan envisaged that at this point they would 'determine', as Wickham expressed it, '*to put everything to the hazard*'. [3] D'André and his friends among the deputies agreed that to meet the special needs of this moment they would require not only a well indoctrinated public ready to support

[1] D'André's letter of 19 March; undated letter referred to in previous notes.
[2] No. 9 of 1797, 1 April.　　　　　[3] No. 12 of 1797, 24 May.

them in arms, but a large emergency treasury. They asked Wickham to supply a special reserve credit for this purpose, over and above all the other financial support they were asking of him, and they proposed that this sum should not be used unless three persons should concur in judging the occasion appropriate. The three persons were Wickham himself, D'André (of course) and Pichegru.[1] 'Baptiste' had just been elected deputy for the Jura. He enjoyed a vast popularity both in the streets and with his future colleagues of the opposition in the legislative body. This rested at once upon his repute as one of the heroes of the war, upon his known opposition to the ruling party, and (in certain quarters) upon the impression that he was also a moderate monarchist. He was an obvious choice for the role of man of action when the moment arrived *to put everything to the hazard*, and it was quite natural that D'André and his friends should propose to associate him with Wickham and with D'André himself in the decision to use the emergency credit. D'André did not yet know Pichegru personally, but Wickham had warmly commended Pichegru to him, even before his election occurred,[2] so that D'André had no need to doubt that the proposal would have Wickham's assent.

We have come quite naturally to the question of the finances of these plans. As early as 21 February, that is, immediately after his reunion with D'André, Bayard had sent Wickham a sketch of the various undertakings which we have now reviewed, and joined with it an estimate that the cost of implementing them would be at least 25 or 30,000 louis. This did not allow, apparently, for the cost of the critical moment, which does not seem to have been in Bayard's mind at this juncture. The estimate, not unnaturally, shook Wickham considerably. He had already granted a credit to D'André, presumably intended chiefly to meet the costs of the immediate matter in hand which was the election campaign.[3] It was certainly nothing like so large a sum as this.

---

[1] No. 12 of 1797, 24 May.

[2] Wickham forecast the election of Pichegru, in more than one department, in a letter to D'André, 27 March. In the same letter he urged D'André: 'Caressés bien ce brave cavalier à son arrivée. Il mérite toute votre confiance.' In his no. 12 of 1797, Wickham told the Foreign Secretary that 'Baptiste and Mr Berger' would henceforward be 'concerting all their operations together'. This was, apparently, one of the messages carried for 'Berger' by Bayard.

[3] For the provision made by Wickham for the election see p.196 n.3, above.

Wickham wavered a little. To Bayard, he sent a demurrer;[1] to D'André he sent a rather reluctant agreement to the general lines now suggested,[2] and announced that he had increased the credit already conceded, so that D'André and his collaborators might be 'à meme de profiter de toutes les circonstances.' [3] This increase raised the credit to a total of 20,000 louis.[4] 'Ménagez-le bien' he concluded, 'et souvenez-vous toujours que je me suis rendu responsable de toutes vos sottises, passées, présentes et à venir.' This was an illustration of Wickham's sense of humour.[5]

It was now the turn of D'André and Bayard to be dismayed. Since at most only a portion of this credit could be used for their plans of future developments, it was clear that it gave them nothing approaching what they asked for these. They sent Wickham a joint remonstrance and pointedly asked him to clarify his grant and to take a more realistic view of the case.[6] The envoy replied (it was now the end of March) in much more encouraging terms. His confidence in D'André and his associates was rising even higher than formerly; the apparent success of the election

[1] Wickham to Bayard, 10 March 1797 (Wickham Papers, bundle 64): 'Je trouve votre nouveau plan trop vaste et trop dispendieux. L'opinion, l'opinion, travaillez-la bien, et vous scaurez tout faire sans argent.' This, of course, could not possibly be literally true.

[2] Wickham to D'André, 10 March: 'Je trouve votre plan avec le jeune commis difficile dans l'execution et dispendieux, mais je vous donne carte blanche la dessus, n'étant pas moi-même en état de le juger'.

[3] Wickham to D'André, 10 March.

[4] See p. 196, note 3.

[5] Wickham to D'André, 10 March. D'André responded rather stiffly to this warning on 19 March: 'permettés moi de réclamer sur la phrase ou vous dites... (etc.) C'est bien dire, mais vous n'avés peut être voulu faire qu'une plaisanterie. Soyes assuré qu'on n'aura point de sottises de ma part à vous reprocher.' Wickham in due course rejoined again: 'On n'entend donc plus la plaisanterie à Paris; eh bien, soit!' (Wickham to D'André, 27 March).

[6] D'André and Bayard to Wickham, 19 March: 'Nous regrettons de ne pas savoir si le crédit de vingt mille louis est la chose demandée d'abord pour notre établissement, et pour se saisir de tous les moyens qu'offrent les circonstances, ce qui seroit asses vraisemblable par la lettre de Rustique (= *Wickham*); ou si les secours pour le (*blank*) nous étoient indiqués de la manière demandée, la lettre de Wickham ne nous dit que des choses vagues et indéterminées;... tout cela nuit à l'exactitude du travail et à son succès.

'On nous représente que ce travail est vaste dangereux et dispendieux... nous nous bornons à dire que ce qui sera vaste ne sera pas dangereux... Le travail est dispendieux, si on le regarde comme une affaire de particulier à particulier; ou peut-être si on en regarde les fonds comme sacrifiés au hasard...'

campaign made it easier to believe in their plans for the future. He pointed out that he had already given Kilien *carte blanche*, implicitly withdrew the note of reluctance he had sounded earlier, and accepted without demur the principle that they should be free to ask for more funds in the future.[1]

When Bayard came to Wickham on his mission of report at the beginning of May, we are not surprised to learn, he brought with him proposals for expenditure in the future far larger than the sum which had shocked Wickham in February. 'Mr Berger and his friends' not only acknowledged with grateful thanks the assistance they had already received from Wickham, but pleaded . . . that to give full effect to this plan a sum of £10,000 per month will be absolutely necessary, that they should earnestly wish, though they do not venture to ask, for a still larger sum . . . to do any real efficient good they declare that they have fixed their demands at the very lowest.

And, for use in the event of the critical moment, identified as such by Wickham, D'André and Pichegru, they made a further request for a sum of £50,000.[2]

Wickham had long since expressed to his principal his complete confidence, both in the persons who thus petitioned him, and in the plans which claimed these sums. But, especially in view of the capitulation of Austria and the consequent renewed possibility that Britain would again attempt to reach terms with the (now more than ever) victorious Republic, he felt compelled to leave with his superior the question whether he ought to agree to such arrangements.[3] And there we also can, for the moment, leave this part of the matter.

---

[1] Wickham to D'André and Bayard, 30 March. 'J'entre parfaitement dans vos raisonnements et je crois que vous êtes loin d'avoir tort. J'avais cependant cru prévenir toutes vos objections en donnant à Kilien *carte blanche*'. Wickham went on to explain in rather obscure terms that, of all the funds he had now credited at Paris, the greater part was 'pour les besoins de Kilien', the *rest* 'pour les personnes que vous connoissés'. (These are, evidently, the Agents.)

[2] No. 12 of 1797, 24 May.

[3] In the despatch of 24 May, Wickham took considerable pains to present the reasons why he thought that his Government should meet the new estimates of the cost of the plans, while admitting fully that the situation of affairs on the Continent might justifiably incline the authorities at home against such a commitment. His observations include certain features of particular interest in this study.

(1) 'Mr Berger and his friends . . . acknowledge with thankfulness their

It is more to our immediate purpose to point out that these plans, in all their parts and stages, laboured under the same radical weaknesses as characterized the central and original part of the whole design, namely the effort to secure a decisive majority in the legislature. The summer months of 1797 were to witness the progress of the plans in all their branches. But this progress was threatened by arrest at a critical stage. Journals might be distributed, societies founded, measures to weaken the government and to prepare for the arming of the public proposed and even carried in the Councils. But, even assuming that the Directory failed to arrest all this

great obligations to H.M. for the liberal assistance they have allready received . . . They acknowledge themselves bound on that consideration, independent of every other motive, to serve H.M. Interests in every point in which they shall not be in *direct opposition* with those of their own country . . . in particular they consider it as their duty to remove as far as possible those prejudices which exist so unhappily . . . against the English nation and Government, and to encourage such sentiments in the publick as well as in the two assemblies as may compell the Government to accept of reasonable terms of Peace . . .

'With respect to their own country . . . the success that attended their operations during the elections must convince H.M. Ministers that the Directory has a formidable enemy at home to contend with . . . they will however *engage* for nothing more than the keeping a strong party together composed of able and well meaning persons ready to take advantage of any favourable circumstances . . .

'That for the giving full effect to this plan a continuation of large pecuniary supplies are (*sic*) absolutely necessary . . . They earnestly entreat H.M. Ministers to . . . leave nothing uncertain . . . but to say . . . fairly whether this sum can be *regularly* allowed them or not . . . and particularly whether . . . all further payments must not necessarily be suspended at the peace; they protest at the same time . . . that . . . though they should have the certainty in that case of receiving no further assistance, yet that they would not cease to promote and hasten that event . . . provided, as appears to them most probable, it were thought a desirable point by the British Government . . .'

(2) 'With respect to the person principally concerned, I am bound in Justice to say that his conduct throughout from the moment I have known him has been judicious fair honourable and full of confidence. His talents for conducting a popular assembly are well known and no man has a more thorough knowledge of the different parties and factions by which France has been so long agitated and governed. He has made the most unequivocal and manly avowal of his former errors, and I firmly believe him to be penetrated with the deepest sense of the evils that the leaders of the Constitutional Assembly had brought (many of them unknowingly) upon their country, and animated by the most earnest desire of expiating them, if necessary by the sacrifice of his life and fortune in the service of his lawfull Sovereign . . .'

Q

before it grew ripe, the project was only too likely to arrest itself just when its maturity approached. Later, if not sooner, the drift of the whole design must become apparent to all; would the mass of the public, any more than the numerous deputies who were now taking up an attitude of suspicious independence towards the Right in the Councils, be prepared to take decisive steps to end the existing regime at the bidding of a movement which seemed only too likely to be working with and for the princes and the pure Royalists who had, so notoriously, abandoned none of their hopes of an 'absolute' counter-revolution? Here again we come across the fatal complications involved so deeply in the national problem by the acts and attitudes of the militant emigration and the princes over a period of years. D'André and Wickham might congratulate themselves with good reason upon the skill, the patience, and the psychological insight which their plans embodied. In circumstances only a little different the plans might have been as operable as they were skilful. D'André and his allies are fully entitled to the credit which he claimed from the contrast between their plans and those of the old Agence de Paris. But for all this their plans were unsound in the foundation which circumstances imposed upon them. D'André's prospects of future and final success were as illusory as the claims he made to have succeeded in the elections.

It is fair to say that D'André did not remain wholly unaware of these dangers which threatened his further and wider designs. He himself, having submitted to Louis XVIII, accepted and had worked to persuade others to accept the principles of the King. He had always known, however, that many of the elements with which he was trying to co-operate would not accept those principles and must not be pressed or frightened with them; and it appears that after the elections, if not before, he realized that the image of Louis in the eyes of the public required drastic reshaping, and the public a reassurance that it would at no stage be requested to leap blindfold into what it feared might prove to be an 'absolute' reaction. It seems, moreover, that D'André, having little hope that Louis would make the necessary gestures, proposed to make them for him, incorporating them into his plan, and contenting himself with urging the King to throw no contradiction in the way.

This is the evident meaning of the action which D'André

took when he sent Bayard to Blankenburg in June. Bayard was commissioned to explain and seek the King's approval for the plans of further action which had already won the warm support of Wickham. He was also instructed to

entreat of the King that he will . . . issue no new Declarations, form no fixed plan of government, nor bind himself to the adoption of any particular form of constitution . . . untill the *whole* Kingdom shall have been prepared (by the entire execution of the plan . . .) to discuss so important a question with calmness.[1]

The intention, then, was to assure the country, once all the existing obstacles were removed, that it was perfectly free to *discuss* and state what form and character of regime it desired for the future; and presumably D'André was prepared to accept the possible consequence that this might result in a clear preference for a regime quite different from that which Louis had in mind, however much D'André himself might wish to see Louis restored on his own terms. What the King must do in the meantime was to keep quiet and allow the directors of the great design to suggest that he would prove perfectly amenable to reason when the time came.

This interesting and instructive proposal had, however, one all important weakness, even if the King could be persuaded to agree to it. It assumed that the country would believe in the sincerity of these gestures which the King's champions proposed to make on his behalf. But how could this be taken for granted? Suspicion and dislike of Louis XVIII were too deeply rooted to be overcome by anyone except the Pretender himself; and it would have required actions, as well as words on his part to achieve it. Mallet du Pan had long ago pointed out what those actions should have been.[2] A mere abstention from further unfortunate gestures was certainly not enough. D'André's appeal to Blankenburg shows that he partly, at least, appreciated the fundamental difficulties which lay before his future plans; but it did not supply an adequate remedy. And it is, after all, very much open to question whether even Louis XVIII himself could now have done anything which would still have been adequate: unless, indeed, he could have resolved to renounce the Crown which he truly was, in some

[1] No. 19 of 1797, draft dated 30 June: unpublished portion.
[2] See ch. II above.

respects, well fitted to wear; to induce his brother to do the same; and to place one of his nephews in the hands of the nation. Such a policy would have demanded great sacrifices, and it would have involved great risk. It is hardly for us to blame him for not adopting it.

The problem thus remained unsolved. And while it remained unsolved, D'André and his allies, for this reason above all others, were building over a void.

VIII

The Struggle for Mastery in the Councils

D'ANDRÉ AND THE LEGISLATIVE OPPOSITION FROM THE
OPENING OF THE NEW SESSION (20 MAY 1797)
TO THE CRISIS OF JULY

IN this chapter an attempt will be made to examine the progress
of the efforts which were made during the first two months of
the new session to give effect to the first main feature of the further
plans now adopted by D'André and his associates—to exploit the
successes which had been gained in the legislative elections and to
dictate the action of the Councils. Though D'André devoted himself to every aspect of the plans, it was their parliamentary side that
throughout attracted his greatest attention.[1] It was also on this
side that he found his greatest disappointments. It was entirely
natural that he, who had been one of the stars (of second magnitude, at least) in the great Constituent Assembly should have pursued this part of the design with especial interest, even though
he had not secured a mandate for himself and had (rather like the
Feuillant 'Triumvirs' at the time of the Legislative Assembly) to
conduct the campaign in the Councils from some obscure point
in the wings of the theatre.

The campaign which he had to conduct was still that of an
opposition, even after the elections had destroyed the conciliar
majority of the old Conventionals. For the old Conventionals still
controlled the executive branch of the government; and even
when the anti-Directorial majority in the Five Hundred succeeded
in placing Barthélemy in a Directorial chair, even when Carnot

---

[1] 'Je ne m'occupe presque que de l'assemblée', D'André to Wickham, 4
June 1797. With some element of exaggeration, D'André could have said this
at any period during the following three months, as his letters to Wickham
show. He nevertheless found time, as will be seen, to give some real attention
to the other aspects of the plan. Moreover, though this is not a topic for detailed treatment in this study, the correspondence shows that D'André also
exerted himself to procure information for Wickham about the military and
naval designs of the Directory.

joined Barthélemy in favouring, to a certain point, the wishes of the Councils, and divided the Directory by two against three, it still remained true that the other three Directors, Barras, Reubell and La Revellière, while they remained united, constituted the effective governing power in France. Nor was it at all certain that even the Councils were now completely outside the influence of the government. The Directory no longer had a majority there, but they still had friends there, and, as soon became apparent, the much greater mass of non-Directorial deputies was deeply divided. None of these men had any love, or even much respect (as opposed to fear) for the Triumvirs.[1] This, however, was the only sense in which any commanding number of them was agreed. D'André and his allies now faced a very difficult and complex task; and at the same time, two other bodies of men embarked on other and contrary difficult and complex tasks, thus setting in motion a three sided battle for the control of the legislature.

D'André and his friends had to bring about a union between themselves and as many as possible of the non-Directorial deputies to embarrass and weaken the Directory; and (as they hoped) to go much further, by passing legislation to facilitate their own ulterior designs, by creating conditions in which the Directory could be attacked and impeached, and finally by repudiating the regime itself. D'André realized at the outset that it would be no light matter to bring a large body of the non-Directorials to accept all this. Far too many moderates had been scared and offended by what was supposed to have happened in the elections. He realized that it would be necessary to proceed very skilfully and to assuage many doubts and fears on the way. But, as has been seen, he tackled the business with expressions of high hope. It all proved far more difficult even than he had expected, partly because his own party emerged much smaller and much more wanting both in resolve and in patience than he first imagined; partly, again, because it was much less possible to cajole the suspicious moderates than he thought it would be.

It cannot be said that D'André and his friends had no successes. But it is fair to say that D'André emerged from the first serious brush between the Councils and the Directory which occurred in this short and stormy session (we have called it, in the title of this chapter, 'the crisis of July') in a state of mind bordering on

[1] 'Triumvirs' now meant the three Directors just mentioned.

despair of the legislature of year V, and especially of his own party in it.[1]

At the same time the Directorials were trying to rally their own remaining strength in the Councils,[2] and to govern by playing off different elements of the non-Directorial majority against each other. The recovery of Dumas by Carnot had already set the example for this.[3] To help them in the battle to regain, if not the support, at least the acquiescence of a majority, the Directorials tried to build up their strength outside the walls of the legislature and thereby proclaim more convincingly that the government had public support and might even win the next year's elections. This would not impress Royalist conspirators, but it might impress the independents.[4] The Directorials also tried to show that

---

[1] D'André wrote at length of his mature impressions about the legislature and his own party in a letter of 27 July, immediately after the 'crisis of July' had begun to pass over. His attitude at this time is examined in the text below, pp. 256–8.

[2] Mallet du Pan had observed at the time of the drawing of lots to decide which of the old Conventionals should vacate their seats (unless re-elected) on 30 floreal, that there would still be about 80 of the regicides in the Corps légis-latif, including Sieyes, Chénier, Tallien, Legendre and Bourdon de l'Oise (Michel, op. cit., tome II, p. 244). Many of the governmentalists, regicides or otherwise, put up a stout defence of their cause in the session before the coup d'état, as can be seen even from the summaries of some of the chief debates printed in Buchez & Roux, op. cit., tome 37.

[3] Dumas, indeed, according to Wickham (no. 11, 20 May 1797) had agreed with Carnot that besides giving the Directory (upon conditions) the support of himself and his friends, he and his friends would also try to win over as many as possible of their acquaintances among the second new tiers to take the same line.

[4] In June, the Cercle constitutionnel was founded by friends of the government as a club for Republicans (not for deputies only). Benjamin Constant claimed credit for the venture, which enjoyed the support of the circle of Mme de Staël, of Sieyes, of Talleyrand and of Barras. Within a month it numbered 600 members. About forty other Republican clubs sprang up, after this example, in the city and its neighbourhood. Old members of the comités révolutionnaires were said to be joining them, forgetting the quarrel between Directorials and Jacobins and anxious only to uphold the Republic against the new menace from the Right (Lefebvre, Directoire, p. 64; Pariset, op. cit., tome II, pp. 337–8; Buchez & Roux, op. cit., tome 37, pp. 272–3). Wickham, reporting advice from D'André on the subject in his no. 17 of 1797, 27 June, says that the club 'which assembles at the Hotel de Salm' (phrase subsequently deleted from the draft) (i.e. the Cercle constitutionnel mentioned above) aimed not only to concert support for the government in the two Houses, but at

the measures for which the government contended were absolutely necessary and that their denial would only play the game of
the counter-revolutionaries.[1] In the last resort, the Directorials
could always contemplate the use of force—not that of the streets
(this would play into the hands of the Jacobins) but that of the
armies. The soldiers could always be encouraged—even commanded—to rescue the true patriots in the seat of power from
the menace of a Royalist conspiracy.[2] They had the means to make
such an appeal very convincing. Not only were there at least a
handful of very suspicious returns at the recent elections, but
there were the confessions (as yet unpublished) of Brottier and
Duverne regarding their negotiations with Lemerer and a large
group of deputies seated in the Houses since long before these
elections. This possibility that the Directorial party would cut the
legislative knot with a military sword was just as obvious to every-

---

propagating Republican principles and action in the provinces as well as at
Paris, and to prepare the way for better success in the next elections.

All this Republican activity in clubs was destined to be interrupted by a law
carried in the Houses towards the end of July, which 'provisionally' prohib-
ited 'all private societies concerned with political questions'. The law was constitutionally of doubtful validity since the constitution of year III authorized
no such shackles on public discussion. The anti-Directorials were understandably anxious to put a stop to the new Republican activity nevertheless;
and their bill succeeded, partly because the issue was no longer a clear one
between good Republicans and suspected adherents of the counter-Revolution: all parties, including the Directory itself, had begun to fear that the new
clubs were falling into the hands of the Jacobins. Lefebvre, *Directoire*, 64, 86;
Pariset, op. cit., tome II, pp. 344. The clubs had, however, expressed plainly
enough the will of the Republican minority to survive and to fight back.

[1] This was one of the lines adopted by the Directory in its well known
Message to the Five Hundred on 10 August (23 thermidor), Buchez & Roux,
op. cit., tome 37, pp. 323–5.

[2] Even in June, there were reports of speeches and toasts at banquets arranged by the victorious generals, in which the soldiers' attitude towards the
reputed counter-revolutionaries of the Corps législatif was plainly expressed.
A month later there came, in addition, proclamations to the troops by the
Generals commanding and loyal addresses from the troops, many of them in
connection with the anniversary of 14 July 1789, which expressed the same
sentiments more copiously. It was suspected from the beginning that the
Directory encouraged, or even provoked, all this military interference in the
affairs of the civil government. Wickham wrote in his no. 17, 27 June: 'the
evident plan of the Directory is to make the two Councils odious to the army
as well as to all persons in public employment.'

one else concerned from the beginning of the session.[1] It greatly complicated the task of D'André; for it dictated ultra-caution to him and terrified many, both of his friends and of the neutrals.

In the midst of all this, many of the moderates who disliked the old ruling party and its methods, and in some instances had no love for the Republic, but who were much alive to the danger of an 'absolute' counter-revolution and very suspicious of some of their newly elected colleagues, tried to have a policy of their own. They were a real part of the opposition to the Directory; they willingly joined in efforts to force it to govern in strict accordance with the law, in criticism of its administrative blunders, and even in movements to repeal portions of the surviving revolutionary laws, which they opposed not, of course, because they wanted thereby to favour the 'absolute' counter-revolution, but because they thought them to be undesirable abnormalities, to some extent unjust and socially harmful. Many of these deputies had been opposed to the Directory in this sense during the previous session. But they were unwilling, more unwilling than some of them had been earlier, to carry opposition much further than this. They would not join in any initiative to go all lengths against the Directory—unless there were convincing proofs that the Directory was planning an illegal stroke against the Councils; but what convincing proof was there likely to be, except the event? Still less (had the opportunity ever offered) would they have joined in a proposal to bring the regime itself to an end, unless they could have felt sure, at least, about the character of what was to come in its place. They were now suspicious of being led, without knowing it, towards the regime of the princes. They were also, quite comprehensibly, afraid of what the Directory might do if too much pressure were exerted on it.

[1] On 29 April, Mallet du Pan gloomily predicted that, as a consequence of the Austrian peace, 'Hoche et ses Francs, Bonaparte et ses Vandales, vont être lâchés sur la France: ils auront bon marché, je vous en réponds, des journalistes, des orateurs, des legislateurs et des bourgeois mutins... le sabre des soldats fera taire l'artillerie des langues et des plumes; c'est une révolution nouvelle qui va commencer', Sayous, op. cit., tome II, p. 300. Wickham told Grenville on 20 May that the knowledge that the Directory had such power in Europe, and such military resources, behind it, had been a very important factor in deciding the *volte face* of some of the friends of Dumas. Though both Mallet and Wickham inclined to the conclusion that no *immediate* stroke was probable, its eventual occurrence still oppressed their calculations.

Thibaudeau offers a clear example of the reactions of these deputies to many of these issues. Dumas himself provides another; for Dumas, in breaking off relations with D'André and his friends, and entering again into an agreement with the Directors, had no more agreed to support them unconditionally than he had done the year before. His line was rather that the Directors were worth supporting as a bulwark against the new threat from the further Right, *provided* that they ruled strictly according to law, dismissed their more objectionable Ministers, and acquiesced in the repeal of the surviving revolutionary laws.[1] The last condition suggests that Dumas still regarded the Directors, and even their regime, as only a temporary makeshift for something better; what he thought the something better was to be is more doubtful.

It is clear from what has now been said that D'André's best chance of winning these deputies to join his own party in a 'grand coup' against the Directors would come, if at all, at some moment when it appeared very strongly indeed that the Directors were meditating force against the Councils, but before the blow was actually delivered. Then, possibly, the whole opposition would join in a vote of impeachment, even of outlawry. But it was both a dangerous and a difficult moment to wait for.[2]

It is time to leave this rather general and abstract view of the conditions governing the session, and to speak in more concrete (and chronological) terms.

D'André more than once complained of the difficult and unsatisfactory task which it was, to try to lead the opposition, not being himself a deputy.[3] He never gave up the attempt, however; and he certainly did not want for collaborators inside the Chambers.

---

[1] This, at least, is the account of the bargain between Dumas and Carnot given by Wickham in his no. 11 of 20 May. Speaking of the revolutionary laws, Wickham noted 'especially the famous one of 3rd Brumaire'. The Ministers whom Dumas desired to see removed were Merlin, Minister of Justice; Admiral Truguet, Minister for the Navy; and Charles Delacroix, Secretary for Foreign Affairs.

[2] The subsequent efforts actually made by D'André and by certain members of the Councils to identify and exploit such a moment are considered at a later stage of this chapter and in ch. X.

[3] D'André to Wickham, 1 July: 'Vous deves etre tres satisfait des 500. Il n'y manque qu'un chef. Il est facheux que Kilien n'y soit pas, car le mouvement se communique avec peine du dehors.' Same to same, 27 July: 'Quand on n'est pas dans le Corps législatif, on n'a pas de moyens de direction. Il y a une foule d'à propos qu'on ne peut saisir que sur les lieux.'

How far they were qualified to act for him in the debates is another question; and we cannot help wondering how seriously they listened to what he said. To take advice on the affairs of a deliberative assembly from one who is not a member of it would be a severe strain for the patience of most of us. On the other hand, we must remember that D'André was, to all intents and purposes, the paymaster of the movement, and this may have helped a great deal.

At some point, or points, which we cannot identify, D'André's original small committee of five broadened out into a much larger committee of nearly twenty. The greater number of the members of this bigger committee had been members of the Councils since the elections of year IV, and two of them were old Conventionals. It is reasonable to suppose that D'André's original small committee, and perhaps D'André himself, had been in close connection with such of these as were not themselves members of the small committee, since long before the new session began. In his private despatch no. 12 of 27 June, Wickham announced:

The names of the members on whom Mr Berger mostly relies and who now form the committee with which he concerts all the motions that are made by his party in either assembly are:
Jourdan des Bouches du Rhone—Couchery—Tarbé—Barbé Marbois —Desmolieres—Quatremere—Emery—Henri Lariviere—Lemerer—Gossuin—Muraire—Cadroi—Jordan of Lyons—André de la Logerie (= *André* (*de la Lozère*)) Job Aimé Polissard Bonaventure and occasionally my friend Imbert Colomes and his colleague of the same name.

These names can be classified in more than one interesting way. All but two of them (Gossuin and Bonaventure) were destined to be unseated, or sentenced to deportation, when the *coup d'état* occurred. Most of them, as already observed, had come into the legislature in year IV. Two of these, 'Job' Aymé and Polissard, had been formally or in effect deprived of their seats before the session of years IV–V was very old; but at the beginning of the new session the anti-Directorial majority made no difficulty over readmitting them, despite the past record of 'Job' Aymé in particular. Mersan also was readmitted, but he does not appear on this list of D'André's larger committee. The only deputies on this list whose mandates were then new were Tarbé, Quatremère de Quincy, Emmery, Jordan of Lyon, Bonaventure and the two Imberts.

The deputies can of course also be classified according to the branch of the legislature in which they sat. It is a striking fact that all but two of them sat in the junior Council. This shows both that, as a body, they were quite young, and that their party was deplorably weak in the upper house.[1]

The list has other memorable features. Only two of the four deputies included in D'André's original small committee figure in it: Lemerer and Henry-Larivière. The third deputy on the small committee, Durand-Maillane, was an old Conventional who was nevertheless elected by the Bouches du Rhône in year IV; he was, however, one of those chosen by lot to leave the Council (of the Elders) on I prairial, year V, and he was not re-elected.[2] The fourth deputy on the small committee was, of course, according to Wickham, Thibaudeau; if he was ever on any committee working with D'André, we should certainly not expect to find him there after the elections of year V. Of the two remaining members of the old committee, Lemerer eventually disappointed D'André.[3] On the other hand, one or two names on the larger committee are such as we should hardly expect: Gibert-Des-molières and Cadroi. These had been members of the Dumas group. They, like their colleagues in that group, had been apprehensive over the turn taken by the elections. The explanation is, however, that Cadroi (at least) had nevertheless declined to go back to alliance with the Directors;[4] and both he and Desmolières were soon won back by D'André and his friends.[5] From this fact alone it appears that D'André's hopes of winning back the offended moderates were not wholly vain.

It will be noticed that Pichegru is not mentioned in the list. D'André's friends shared in the admiration felt by the non-

[1] For all these points see Kuscinski, op. cit.

[2] Ibid., pp. 38, 132, 363.

[3] D'André to Wickham, 27 July: '*Lemerer*, dont on pourroit tirer un grand parti n'aime que l'argent et les plaisirs.'

[4] It will be remembered that, according to Wickham's no. 11 of 20 May, Cadroi, like Dumolard, had left the alliance of D'André and his friends to lapse into neutrality 'for a time'.

[5] In drafting his number 17 of 27 June, Wickham mentioned Desmolières and Cadroi as illustrating his statement that the Royalists had 'gained over some of the ablest members of the independents'. Wickham subsequently deleted the names, however, and wrote instead: 'whose names I am particularly requested not to commit to writing.'

Directorials generally for the famous soldier (who was promptly elected by the Five Hundred as their first President, with the handsome majority of 387 out of 444 deputies present.)[1] D'André and his friends indeed admired and trusted Pichegru in a very special degree, as has been shown in the previous chapter.[2] But Pichegru for several weeks disappointed all those who set store by him in his new surroundings. Not only did he show himself to be no politician and politically speaking no leader, but his apparent lack of interest and deep reserve disconcerted everyone.[3] Not till the crisis of July, when possibilities of force came to the fore, did he begin to amount to something in the politics of the opposition; and not till early August did he come into close relations with D'André, despite Wickham's obvious desire that the two men should work closely together in all that concerned the cause.[4]

[1] Buchez & Roux, op. cit., tome 37, p. 270.

[2] Wickham was anxious to lose no opportunity to promote the closest relations between Pichegru and D'André, who were as yet personally unknown to each other. On 24 May, as has already been noted, he informed Lord Grenville that 'Baptiste' and 'Mr Berger' would henceforward 'concert their operations'. Apparently Bayard had expressed D'André's willingness to join in this 'concert'. To make it all more certain, Wickham had just drafted a note to D'André (20 May) and another to Pichegru (18 May) introducing them to each other and exhorting each to 'concert everything' with the other. The drafts are both contained in Wickham Papers, bundle 67. As finally sent, the notes were both despatched in the first instance to D'André, who was requested to hand the second to Pichegru. The note to D'André indicated the code-name 'Avre' to be used for Pichegru in the future.

[3] In his no. 17, 27 June, Wickham reported home, as from D'André, what reads like a rather apologetic account of Pichegru's current behaviour. He said that 'Baptiste' was deliberately refusing any leading political role, as being incapable of playing the part, and preferred to wait quietly, ostensibly unconnected with any party, but seeking meantime to build up 'a solid influence in the army' (his appointment as head of the Military Committee of the House making it the easier for him to do this) until he should be 'called on by the voice of the people to put himself at their head'. Cf. Lefebvre, *Directoire*, p. 61. D'André himself seems to have been unimpressed by the General's early attitude, whatever he may have thought of his subsequent explanations of it. On 4 June he responded coldly and briefly to Wickham's letter introducing him to the General: 'J'ai été content d'Avre, mais sans exces.'

[4] Wickham, in his draft to D'André on 27 July, reiterated his desire for really close relations between the two men, and suggested that he felt some anxiety about the matter. 'Recommandés moi très spécialement à l'amitié du bon Avre. Dites-moi ce que vous pensez d'Avre et de sa conduite.' This was

D'André's (larger) committee was apparently designed to con-
stitute a suitable selection from within the 'francs Royalistes' who
now belonged to the Councils. It is quite credible that D'André,
and his colleagues on this committee also, at first believed the
number of legislators whom this committee in some sort 'represented' to be far greater than it really was. It is quite possible that
Wickham, in reporting on 27 June that there were not eighty but
two hundred or more 'firm Royalists', correctly understood what
D'André until then himself believed.

To explain this will involve a brief discussion of the two large
social-political groupings of opposition deputies which were
established during this session. Let us refer in the first place to a
grouping of about eighty deputies which met under the roof of
Desmolières and was understood to contain all the more 'exalted'
members of the opposition. It is natural to suppose that these
eighty correspond pretty closely to the eighty deputies whom
D'André *finally* categorized as 'francs Royalistes'. This seems the
more likely as Gibert-Desmolières, the host of the 'exalted'
eighty, was himself a member of D'André's committee.[1]

We next go on to observe that this 'exalted' eighty seems to have
filtered out of, and still kept up connections with, a much larger
opposition gathering which *also* met in the same place. It seems
reasonable to suppose that D'André, his committee, and the rest
of the eighty, at first thought that this larger gathering, out of
which the eighty more or less seceded, were kindred spirits of
their own; for the number of the larger gathering was about two
hundred at the opening of the session—very much the same number as Wickham in his report of 27 June ascribed to the 'firm
decided Royalists' in the two Councils.

This larger gathering, which the eighty came to regard as being
in general too lukewarm for their tastes, is famous in the history
of the period as the Club de Clichy. It took its name from the
street in which Desmolières had his *hôtel*. The Club de Clichy had
been growing ever since the first days of the Directory, when

---

written at a moment when it might be all important that D'André and Pichegru should be able to agree that the point had been reached for a 'grand coup'.

[1] The grouping of eighty of the 'more exalted' opposition deputies is
referred to by Meynier, *Le 18 fructidor*, pp. 16–17. D'André's eighty 'francs
Royalistes' were members of the two new *tiers in the Five Hundred*; but it seems
clear that his party had few firm friends in the upper Council.

Desmolières first began to welcome a few fellow-members of the opposition to his house. It had long since included deputies of rather different political tendencies, and it was in no sense a party or a 'club' such as the Jacobin Club became. But the invasion of new non-Directorial deputies, carried to the capital by the elections of year V, not only greatly increased its numbers, but also increased the heterogeneous character of its members (if such they can be called). It now included a very high proportion of the swollen opposition—those who were, in some sense of the word, Royalists; the Dumas group; others who, like them, were distracted between opposite evils; and others again who were fishing in troubled waters without much regard for principle.[1]

The eighty who came to form, in some degree, an inner, and higher, circle in the variegated world of Clichy politicians clearly did not intend to separate themselves wholly from it. They seem to have regarded the other *Clichiens*, after a little experience, as more or less deficient in political views or in conduct; but they were anxious to cultivate at least some of them, and to influence them. This was in obvious accordance with the policy which D'André and his allies had followed from the beginning nearly twelve months before. The line which divided the eighty from the remainder of the two hundred cannot ever, indeed, have been sharp or firm. We have already suggested that the differences between most of D'André's 'francs Royalistes' and many of the other non-Directorial members were not differences of substance.

The larger gathering was indeed too important for D'André and his friends to ignore. Important, if sometimes inconclusive, discussions occurred there over matters of policy and of appointments.[2] If the 'francs Royalistes' did not sway the fortunes of

[1] On the origins and development of the club de Clichy (the wider of the two circles discussed here) see, for instance, Pariset, op. cit., tome II, pp. 326–7, and Meynier, op. cit., pp. 16–17. Meynier brings out the point, from contemporary memoirs, that a number of important non-Directorial deputies, of various shades, did not frequent the Club.

[2] According to Barbé-Marbois, a number of 'propositions indiscrètes et violentes' were made there by certain deputies before the new session began, which however the majority of those present reprobated. (This is a first illustration of the 'ardeur' of which D'André was to complain, as characterizing some of his collaborators, during the opening weeks of the session.) The first elections to the 'bureau' of the Five Hundred, and the candidacy of Barthélemy for a seat on the Directory, were also settled at Clichy. See Meynier, loc. cit. supr.

'Clichy', or at least did not attempt to do so, it might become consolidated in other and undesirable hands. In fact, within the period covered by this chapter, D'André found the larger club an exasperating problem. It seems that it fell largely under the influence of men who were not close associates of his, but who made some show of Royalist sympathies and thus rivalled the influence of his own friends in a particularly dangerous way. D'André believed that these men were not in fact Royalists at all and declared that their influence was confusing and driving away men who might otherwise have been won (or kept) for the good cause:

Pastoret et *Dumolard* qui dominent les Clichiens se donnent pour Royalistes, mais ils ne sont qu'ambitieux . . . *Thibeaudeau* (*sic*) nous a échapé, ainsi que *Siméon*, et *Emmery*, par la maladresse des Clichiens qui n'ont pas voulu les porter aux places.[1]

How far these impressions of D'André were well founded is of course another question. They certainly give us a first illustration of the difficulty which surrounded the effort to recruit the party and gather into it sufficient numbers of the waverers and neutrals to achieve 'a decided majority.'

D'André soon found that the whole question of the independents was almost insuperably difficult. Desmolières and Cadroi might be won back; but how many could be induced to follow their example? He found that, in the legislative debates, the independents regarded the efforts of the Right with such jealousy that they often hacked at statements and proposals from that side, even when they by no means disagreed, in principle, with what was said. A good illustration of this was afforded in a debate, in the Five Hundred, at the beginning of June, on the state and administration of the colonies. Tarbé heavily attacked the government in a speech which made a sensation; he was himself counter-attacked not only by Merlin (de Thionville) from the side of the old Republican ruling party, but by Pastoret and Thibaudeau.[2] It is true that

[1] D'André to Wickham, 27 July.

[2] Wickham's no. 17 of 27 June: 'If your Lordship has paid attention to the debate of 3 June on M. Tarbé's report on the state of the colonies you will have seen in the attack made upon the reporter by Messrs. Thibaudeau and Pastoret a striking proof of the extreme personal jealousy entertained by the leaders of the Independents against any person whom they may consider as too closely connected with the Royalists. To make their own importance most

the independents sometimes accepted, or at least acquiesced in, proposals from the Right; at the very beginning, they allowed the Right to place some of its candidates in appointments within the Chamber (Pichegru in the speakership, Henry-Larivière and Siméon in the secretariat)[1] and, more important, endorsed the Right's suggestion of Barthélemy for the Directory;[2] and we shall

---

evident and to show the necessity of making due court to them it is now their established system to eject or alter some one article in each report made by the Royalists, on which their own opinion has not previously been taken, even when they really agree in every point, not excepting the article rejected.' (It will be observed that Wickham puts down the attitude of the independents on such occasions entirely to *personal* jealousy and self-importance. No doubt such sentiments came into the matter; but Wickham himself, in the same despatch, referred to Thibaudeau as one who had 'long expressed his apprehensions that the Royalists were carrying matters too far'.)

The speech of Merlin, on the governmental side, in this debate is referred to by Wickham in his letter of 13 June to D'André.

[1] The other secretaries appointed on this occasion were Vaublanc, the former Fayettist and *vendémiariste* (see pp. 140 n. 2, 149 above) and Parisot, who passed for an 'Orleanist', Buchez & Roux, op. cit., tome 37, p. 269; Meynier, *Le 18 fructidor*, p. 16. Jourdan, a loyal Republican officer whose military reputation was equal to that of Pichegru, was proposed for office inside the House, but was passed over by the majority.

[2] The replacement of one single Director at this time, according to the terms of the Constitution, was a more critical moment, relatively to the balance of parties in the central organs of the State, than may at first sight appear obvious. The choice of the outgoing Director was to be determined by lot. If the lot had fallen upon either Barras, Reubell or La Revellière, the control of the Directory by representatives of the old Conventional majority might have been broken; for the new Director was almost predetermined to be an opponent, whether secretly Royalist or otherwise, of the old ruling party, while Carnot still wished to pursue a policy of conciliation towards the *honnêtes gens*, which most of the Directorials thought (quite rightly) would have played, whether intentionally or otherwise, into the hands of the enemies of their party, and Letourneur, the fifth Director, had, at least latterly, been following the lead of Carnot. The Councils quite understandably suspected that the 'Triumvirs' might rig the drawing of lots, and to prevent this they enacted that the draw must take place in public. The lot fell on Letourneur, which meant that even when the Councils elected Barthélemy to take his place, the non-Directorials had not broken the grip of the old ruling party on the Directory. See Lefebvre, *Directoire*, p. 60.

We have seen that D'André's friends had been considering Barthélemy as their candidate for the vacancy on the Directory before the elections, and that he had given D'André a passport when the latter arranged his return to France. All testimonies agree that Barthélemy was ineffectual, even if sincere

R

see later that they even allowed certain important legislative proposals from the Right. But, without entering into further details
here, it is clear that long before June was over D'André was dissatisfied with the influence his party could exert over the independents,[1] and was being driven to strange expedients to increase
it:

... These men are easily gained by attention and flattery ... Mr Berger
(whose influence at Blankenburg seems now established) has sent to the
King to request that some specific offers (the nature of which he has
pointed out and which he has no doubt they will accept) may be made
to the leading men among them.[2]

But if hopes for the conversion of these men had come to
depend chiefly on gracious personal attentions from Louis XVIII,
they were surely slender indeed. We can only remark, if even the
'firm decided' Royalists for the most part regarded Louis with
strong aversion, what hopes were there that *private* favours,
which could in no way commit the Pretender to any change of
course in matters of national importance, could convert the even
more suspicious and hostile independents? Suppose that these
men were quite lacking in matters of moral principle, and were as
susceptible on the side of vanity as Wickham often suggested:
were they not amenable to fear, as well as to the promptings of
vanity?

in his abhorrence of much of the work of the Revolution and of the Directorials; it is interesting to find that D'André regarded his party's candidate without enthusiasm. D'André wrote on 8 May, 'Ce sera vraisemblablement Barthélemy qui sera porté au Directoire. Il n'y a personne autre qui réunisse les
voix, et à tout prendre c'est le moins mauvais.'

[1] It is quite clear, from D'André's own admissions, that during the first
month of the session the general movement of the independents was rather
away from than towards the state of mind to which D'André wished to bring
them. On 8 May, before the session opened, D'André reported that 'presque
tous les bons membres des Anciens se sont jettés dans (*la*) réunion du Gouvernement avec le comité Dumas, par la peur qu'on leur a fait des nouveaux
venants'. By mid-June this tendency had, to say the least of it, not been arrested, for on 27 June (in his despatch no. 17) Wickham reported, as from
D'André, that the 'committee Directorial', i.e. Dumas and his adherents, was
beginning 'to acquire both strength and consistency', had 'lately been strengthened by the addition of Thibaudeau', and was even raising pretensions to provide leadership for the whole of the middle bloc, regarding it as one single
party, the moderate or independent party.

[2] Wickham's no. 17 of 27 June.

Even if, by these and other methods, D'André succeeded in winning over a sufficient number of the independents to be able to force the Councils, or at least the Five Hundred, to follow a 'fixed determinate plan of operations',[1] he was now very doubtful whether these operations could include all that he had originally hoped to secure in the session. He intimated his doubts to Wickham as early as 4 June:

J'ai tout lieu d'espérer... qu'avant peu de mois nous aurons une majorité asses decidée, sinon pour remporter une victoire complette, du moins pour assurer le retour des François fugitifs, les propriétés de chacun, et pour préparer les voies d'une maniere certaine à ceux qui viendront l'année prochaine et qui doivent tout consommer.[2]

By the end of the month these doubts had confirmed themselves in his mind and he was beginning to accept the conclusion that what he could hope to achieve in the session of years V–VI was about the same as the opposition had earlier hoped to achieve (though their hopes had proved too high) in the session of years IV–V.

Ce sera asses pour cette année, si nous faisons révoquer toutes les Loix Révolutionnaires, et arrêtons toutes les dilapidations en finances.[3]

If so much as this could be achieved, it would assuredly not be nothing; but the contrast between this relatively modest programme and the prophecy of a couple of months before about Restoration or military tyranny within a year is too obvious to require emphasis.

It appears from this that D'André did not expect the other elements of the opposition to be brought round fully to the support of the Royalists, even if their 'leading men' were indeed treated to blandishments from Blankenburg. But the declension of his hopes did not depend only upon the attitude of the independents; in the meantime he was discovering that his own party

[1] Wickham's expression in his despatch no. 17 of 27 June.

[2] If 'les propriétés de chacun' means 'les propriétés de chacun des émigrés', this was in itself a formidable programme. D'André was himself one of the expropriated, and he had remarked to Leclerc in his letter of 23 August 1796, that 'ma radiation même me sera peu avantageuse puisque tous mes biens sont vendus'.

Those 'qui viendront l'année prochaine et qui doivent tout consommer' are of course the deputies of the third new tiers.

[3] D'André to Wickham, 29 June.

was far less numerous than he first thought it, and that its abilities, courage and discipline were alike in some degree defective. D'André was worried from the beginning by 'indiscreet ardour' on the part of some of his close associates.[1] This threatened to destroy the illusion which he was now, all the more so in view of the attitude of the independents, so anxious to maintain—that the Right cherished no ambitions against the basis of the State, and wished only to secure that the Republic was ruled in accordance with law and good policy.[2] But he soon had to worry, not only over the 'indiscreet ardour' of a few, but over the undue timidity or hesitation of other members of his party. The party appeared to suffer from a hot head and cold feet—a disturbing combination of symptoms, it must be admitted.

The leading illustration of 'indiscreet ardour' in the early days was provided by Tarbé's outburst on 3 June. It was indiscreet, because it attacked not only the management of the colonies but, by its implications, many features of French policy ever since the Revolution began. This was why the independents reacted so badly to it: perhaps they did not at all wholly disagree, but they suspected here the hand of the 'absolute' counter-revolution.[3]

L'influence de Tarbé a tout gâté. Ce mal n'est pas sans remede; mais une faute recule plus que huit jours de manoeuvres sages ne peuvent avancer.[4]

Wickham promptly pointed out, what D'André also no doubt felt but did not mention, that this had not been the only unfortunate feature of the debate of 3 June. The debate, said the envoy, sug-

[1] D'André uses this expression in the letter of 29 June: 'Fasse le Ciel que l'indiscrette ardeur de quelques uns ne nous recule plus que jamais.' The immediate reference was to the outburst of Tarbé against the colonial administration, and, by inference, against the whole record of the Republic, on 3 June.

[2] Most of the opposition deputies appear to have thought this the proper line to take, whether they were really looking, like D'André, to the ultimate overthrow of the Republic itself, or whether they were, as was the case with many of the independents, anxious enough to be rid of the existing governing personnel, but not necessarily opposed to the Republic as such, and very anxious indeed not to make a bed for the advanced counter-revolutionaries.

[3] Thibaudeau, in his indignant protest against Tarbé's speech, said that those whose secret aim was to destroy the Constitution would not succeed, except by passing over the dead bodies of himself and of all good Republicans (Buchez & Roux, op. cit., tome 37 p. 278).

[4] D'André to Wickham, 4 June.

gested that too many friends of the good cause were excessively timid:

Tout le monde ici trouve que... Tarbé... a été scandaleusement mal soutenu; et on en tire les augures les plus sinistres pour l'avenir. On trouve surtout honteux que le discours de Merlin ait passé sans re-plique... sans se compromettre on auroit bien pu tirer Tarbé d'affaire et appuyer efficacement la substance de son discours.[1]

D'André did his best to defend the party before the British Minister. He introduced another argument why matters should be taken forward gently and shocks like that administered by Tarbé should be avoided. There is no reason to doubt that this further argument was perfectly valid as against Tarbé; and it comes to us as an opportune reminder that the conduct of affairs in the Councils could not be conducted without attention to external factors, and shows that D'André constantly had this fact in mind. Public opinion, he urged, was as yet far from ready to support gestures like that of Tarbé; and that being so, there would have been no merit whatever in Tarbé's colleagues supporting him in the Chamber—not only because of the attitude of the independents there, but because of the effect on the public outside.

Voici en deux mots quelle est l'opinion publique, que nous ne pouvons pas devancer. Haine du Gouvernement mais peur effroyable des Jacobins... surtout crainte, terreur d'une secousse.. Pour peu qu' on aille en avant, un cri général s'eleve, *point de secousse, point de com-motion...*

Les attaques directes deviennent dangereuses, n'étant pas soutenues par la masse nationale... Ainsi ne soyes pas étonnés de notre marche. S'il y a quelque chose à lui reprocher, c'est *(de)* trop d'activité...[2]

C'est a arrêter les efforts inconsidérés que tous les notres doivent tendre. Les choses ne sont pas avancées au point d'attaquer brusque-ment... Marchons pas à pas, et nous arriverons surement au but... On suit la marche convenue, et vous devés être très satisfait des 500.[3]

These explanations, however, do not really come up to the point which Wickham had urged. He was not suggesting that other members of D'André's party should have echoed Tarbé's impru-dences, but that they should have stepped in to cover (so to speak) Tarbé's retreat, reinforcing his points on the question immediately at hand, and suggesting that Tarbé might easily

[1] Wickham to D'André, 13 June.   [2] D'André to Wickham, 29 June.
[3] D'André to Wickham, 1 July.

be as worthy a citizen of the Republic as Merlin. In this sense, D'André's defence of his party was irrelevant, and showed that he had no satisfactory answer to give.[1]

Moreover, what security had D'André that there would not be further outbreaks of indiscreet ardour from his intimate allies (to say no more about instances of timidity and hesitation on the part of the others)? None; there had been indiscretions before Tarbé,[2] and there were other indiscretions after Tarbé: particularly Camille Jordan's famous demand that the clergy should be released from either oath or promise of submission to the Republic, and Lemerer's eulogy on 'the religion of our fathers', pronounced in a context which left no doubt that the speaker stood far indeed from Republican orthodoxy.[3]

Meantime, it must be said, many measures were being brought forward, and sometimes carried, in the Five Hundred, which tended towards the eventual goal that D'André had in view, without involving, either in their terms or in the speeches by which they were directly recommended, any overt attack upon the regime or even any immediate challenge to the position of the reigning Directors. The measures in question were capable of being presented to the independents in a light which might win their acquiescence, or even their favour, even though they might harbour doubt about the intention of the Right wing in pressing them. It is natural to suppose that D'André took a personal part in the confection of these.

Among these measures were the readmission, on the very first day of the new session, of 'Job' Aymé and other deputies of the new *tiers* of year IV, whom the governing party had previously unseated, or suspended;[4] the proposal (30 prairial) launched by

---

[1] In fact, both Henry-Larivière and Vaublanc had come to the aid of Tarbé (Buchez & Roux, op. cit., tome 37, p. 278); presumably D'André did not feel very happy about the efforts which they had made, or felt that this degree of support was indeed inadequate.

[2] Several deputies who spoke on the colonial question before the session in which Tarbé presented his report had spoken in terms which clearly revealed their hostility to the Republic and all its works (Buchez & Roux, op. cit., tome 37, p. 271).

[3] 28 prairial (16 June); 20 messidor (8 July): Lefebvre, *Directoire*, pp. 62–3.

[4] Buchez & Roux, op. cit., tome 37, p. 269. Measures were also taken to confirm the election of two new deputies who were unerased émigrés and as such legally incapable of having been elected, Imbert-Colomès being one; Pariset, op. cit., tome II, p. 338.

Gibert-Desmolières (who was the *rapporteur* of the Council's finance committee and who searchingly criticized the Directory's financial management) to pass a law liberating the Treasury from its already only very partial dependence upon the Directory (the real intention of this, as Desmolières, at least in private, boasted, was to starve the government of supply);[1] the resolution carried on 21 prairial (9 June) to repeal the much fought-over law of 3 brumaire so far as concerned its penalties of exclusion from public functions, and to reinstate all functionaries who had been put out of office by virtue of this law;[2] and the resolution, following several weeks after Camille Jordan's famous report, to nullify the old laws against the non-juring clergy (though a narrow majority insisted on a 'declaration' of submission to the Republic by the clergy: 27–28 messidor.)[3]

All these matters were carried through the Five Hundred; and it is easy to see how the independents there were induced to put a good construction on each of them. The excluded deputies were, after all, and much more than some of the governmental deputies, the chosen of the people. The ostensible ground of their exclusion had been the provisions of the law of 3 brumaire, which the independents disliked in principle; and the repeal of that law would in any case have opened the way for the readmission of the excluded deputies. The independents also doubted the wisdom and rectitude of the persecution of the non-juring clergy; though the insistence of a sufficient number of the independents upon a declaration of submission has obvious significance. As for the financial issues, the independents, like all independents everywhere, regarded the government, in this respect especially, with dissatisfaction and distrust; they readily found fault with its management of them, and supported measures, such as giving all powers of spending to the tight-fisted reactionaries of the Treasury, which would prove their zeal for retrenchment.

D'André also had the satisfaction of seeing some of these measures carried through the Anciens, and so becoming law, whatever the Directory might wish in these respects. But it was another weakness in the position of his party, and a weakness of

---

[1] Lefebvre, *Directoire*, pp. 65–6; Buchez & Roux, op. cit., tome 37, pp. 271, 275, 281.

[2] Buchez & Roux, op. cit., tome 37, 278–9.

[3] Ibid., pp. 279–80; Lefebvre, op. cit., p. 63.

capital significance, that they had virtually no influence in the
House which had the sovereign prerogative of saying yes or no
in last resort. Such successes as these measures achieved in the
Upper House owed nothing, as D'André practically admitted, to
the influence of his party. If the Elders accepted the repeal of the
law of 3 brumaire[1] and, after a very long delay which was not to
be terminated until early August, the abolition of the old laws
against the non-jurors,[2] the Royalists had to count these as un-
covenanted mercies, springing from the wishes of the independents in the Upper House, and, perhaps, to some extent, from the
pressure of public opinion, which wanted no trouble with government but which did want, very vocally, to be rid of as many
relics of the Revolutionary laws as possible.[3]

Thus sapping and mining had its successes; but, even though
D'André was resigned to attempting nothing more than sapping
and mining during the session of years V–VI, and was willing to
leave the 'grand coup' and the rest of it until after the elections
of May 1798, he soon quite naturally found that sapping and
mining brought difficulties of its own. Each of these measures to
embarrass the Directory, and to strengthen, soon or later, the
position of the Royalists in the country, might be presented to
the world without any overt sign of hostility to the Republic, or
even, in principle, to the established government. Each could be
commended to the independents on ostensibly very respectable
grounds. But, like the clues discovered by a detective, the cumu-
lative effect of a whole series of such apparently legitimate steps
might place them in a light quite different from that which they
individually reflected. Both the independents and the Directorials
had been deeply suspicious from the time of the elections onwards
that a large party of advanced counter-revolutionaries had entered the legislature, to say nothing of the other constituted
authorities. Both would have been preternaturally stupid not to
suspect, at some point in the accumulation of measures put forward by the Right in the new session, if not from the outset, that

---

[1] Buchez & Roux, op. cit., tome 37, p. 279.
[2] Lefebvre, op. cit., p. 63.
[3] Wickham, in his no. 17 (27 June) asserted that, in what the new legislature had so far attempted, it had been 'only following the public opinion'.
Cf. the remark of Meynier, *Le 18 fructidor*, p. 192: 'L'opinion publique ap-
plaudit', etc.

the Right wing intended to encompass the destruction of the Republic, and probably of the Revolution too, by turning the Republic's own institutions against it.

D'André's game could not be played at all without accepting the risk that the Directory would not only realize the purpose of it, but act by force to put an end to it, before his whole plan had matured so far that his party could hope to rally public support in resisting force with force. But prudence clearly demanded, in the circumstances which actually confronted his party in the summer of 1797, that this risk should be carefully minimized, by proceeding, not only without open provocation, but also without haste. D'André saw that a 'grand coup' could not yet, for many months, be attempted; he saw that verbal manifestations of hostility to the regime could not be risked. But it was just as imperative to conduct the programme of sapping and mining, even without oratorical thunder, at slow pace, and with a good deal of camouflage. The attitude of the Directorials, if not that of the Directory itself, was menacing from the outset; they were forming, or encouraging the formation of numerous Republican clubs in the metropolitan area, imbued with the belief that the Republic was in deadly peril and anxious to contribute, by classic Revolutionary methods, to its rescue. There were signs, even in June, that the Directors were encouraging, not indeed the streets, but the army, against the reactionaries in the Councils.

This was enough to suggest that the policy of undermining the regime was being carried on much too obviously, and much too fast. At the same time there were parallel pointers coming from the direction of the independents. In mid-June, Thibaudeau and other independents in the Five Hundred joined the governmentalists in objections to the programme of (so called) retrenchment. On 9 messidor (27 June) the Anciens threw out the proposed plan to make the Treasury entirely independent of the Directory.[1]

One cannot but wonder whether these threatening reactions to the efforts of the Right would have been significantly less speedy than they were, even if there had been no such outbreaks of indiscreet ardour as D'André complained of. The measures of the Right, especially when viewed together, spoke already with a loud enough voice, even if there had been no rash oratory to

[1] Lefebvre, op. cit., pp. 65–6.

specify the real intentions of the party. Tarbé and others were shouting 'fire'; but the flames kindled by their own colleagues were already becoming obvious to the neighbours. It seems unlikely that D'André, in professing that everything was going well in the Five Hundred except for the rash words of a few hot-heads, can really have been as happy about it all as his words conveyed.

Other comments which D'André made, towards the beginning of July, indeed show that he was becoming uneasy about the substance and pace of the programme, as well as about the manner in which it was sometimes presented.[1]

If the programme incurred the general displeasure of the independents, its legislative progress would be arrested, and it might become impossible for many months to induce them to relax their vigilance on the side of the Right. This would mean that, while those conditions persisted, the independents would be the ascendant party in the battle for the control of the Councils. With support from the Right, the independents would have a stranglehold on the spending power of the Directors; and they would be able to claim the blessings of the Directorials in placing a barrier against any further measures which might not only embarrass the government, but endanger its survival. D'André and his friends had every motive to avoid such a stalemate. But this was by no means the greatest evil which threatened them. And this is almost too obvious to need statement. Supposing the Directors were not only as suspicious of the Right's intentions as the independents, but were not willing to acquiesce in a temporary stalemate dictated by the independents? They might well be not in the least

---

[1] Thus in a short note of 27 June, D'André says: 'Nous avons besoin ici d'arrêter plutot que de pousser. Le Directoire est trop fort pour vouloir le culbuter dans ce moment.' On 1 July he writes: 'Nous sommes dans une position un peu critique. La baisse extrême des rentes a effrayé l'immense classe des rentiers qui a cru en voir la cause dans les Résolutions des 500 et qui s'est mise à crier qu'on alloit trop vîte. Les partisans du Directoire ont habilement profité de ce mouvement, ont excité les peureux, les Constitutionnels, etc., et sont parvenus à former une masse considérable criant contre les Royalistes.' This passage comes in the very same letter in which D'André had exhorted Wickham that he ought to be 'très satisfait des 500'. The admissions which it contains are very significant; if the resolutions of the Five Hundred were thus disturbing the repose of *rentiers* and *constitutionnels* among the public, what reason could there be to think that they were having any lesser effects in the governing circle or among the independents of the Corps législatif?

satisfied to do so. Already they were confronted with a prospect of financial dependence which promised to be extremely embarrassing, even though its exploitation lay in the hands of the independents rather than of the Right. Already there were too many dangerous measures passing through the Five Hundred to allow the Triumvirs to feel complacent about leaving the eventual safety of the system to the mercy of the independents.[1] If the Triumvirs decided to act without further delay on the implications of these facts, and to call on the soldiers to intervene with weapons more substantial than words of abuse for the opposition, the manoeuvres of both independents and Royalists would be swept into oblivion; and the whole plan of D'André and his colleagues would be ruined.

The Royalists could hardly have failed to appreciate this danger, in some degree. A movement was, however, in train which gave them some chance of parrying it. How far D'André was involved in this is not clear. It seems almost certain that he knew of it and took some part in it; but it may well be that he thought it impossible for a person in his position to assume the leading part in it.[2]

[1] Although the Anciens rejected the resolution inspired by Gibert-Desmolières on the reorganization of relations between the Treasury and the Directory, it soon became clear that Desmolières and his friends in the Five Hundred had not abandoned the game of starving out the Directory. The very day after the Anciens threw out the bill on the Treasury, a move was made in the Five Hundred to frame a new bill forbidding the government to proceed with the sale of the nationalized properties in Belgium, and thereby cut off a source of its 'extraordinary expenditure' (Buchez & Roux, op. cit., tome 37, pp. 282–4). The prospect was thereby opened that the Anciens would once more, and perhaps repeatedly, hold the government, on vital questions of finance, at their mercy; and the conduct of the Anciens in other respects had already shown that it was not a wholly dependable mercy.

Indeed, the acceptance by the Anciens of the bill to repeal the vital clauses of the law of 3 brumaire had already come as a very heavy blow to the government. If the elections of year V had gone so heavily against the government, when the law was still supposedly operative, what was to be expected in year VI, when it had been repealed? (Meynier, Le 18 fructidor, p. 192). The independents might be quite innocent of any love for the 'absolute' counter-revolution; but this act of repeal was enough to show that, from the standpoint of the government, they were a very unreliable buttress against the open enemies of the established order.

[2] As will appear in the text, what was involved was a negotiation between some of the opposition deputies and certain of the Directors. D'André certainly had indirect, if not direct, connections with one of the Directors in

Certain representatives, both of the Right and of the independents, were, in the first two months of the session, attempting to persuade the Directors to consent to change some of their Ministers and to appoint others who would bring about easier relations between the Directory and the new legislative majority. Both the independents and the men of the Right hoped thereby to weaken the government and to make it more dependent, even in the executive sphere, on the legislature; and we must always bear in mind that the independents were no more the unconditional supporters of the Directory than the Right, however much they might differ from the Right on the ultimate issues.[1] Both Barthélemy and Carnot were willing to agree. Carnot no doubt saw in this suggestion another means of rallying the *honnêtes gens*. The next step was to win over Barras, whose lack of firm principles of any kind was universally assumed. It was a critical moment. If Barras had finally consented to desert Reubell and La Revellière on this issue, it would have split the Directory, no longer in the proportions of two more or less friendly to the legislature and three hostile, but of three more or less friendly and two hostile.[2] And it would have engendered such ill feeling between the Directors, not only on this issue alone, that the Directory might

question, Barthélemy, as appears from Wickham's Private despatch no. 12, 27 June. In the same despatch occurs the passage, printed in Wickham's *Corresp.*, vol. II, pp. 40–1, beginning: 'Mr Berger has seen Carnot frequently . . .' D'André in his letters to Wickham occasionally claims 'inside' knowledge of discussions in the Directory, e.g. in the letter of 29 June, where he refers to the (temporary) *rapprochement* between Barthélemy and Barras. But these indications do not show, or even suggest, that D'André took a leading part in the matters now about to be discussed.

[1] Lefebvre, *Directoire*, p. 66; Pariset, op. cit., p. 340. We have already seen Wickham's account of the stipulation made by Dumas, in his *rapprochement* with Carnot, that three Ministers should be replaced. The effect of such changes, if motivated, as Carnot suggested, by regard for 'le voeu du Corps législatif', would, constitutionally, have been to convert the regime from a 'presidential' system to a 'parliamentary' one.

[2] Lefebvre, op. cit., p. 66; Pariset, tome cit., p. 340. Reubell appears to have been far more clear sighted, both as to the political and as to the constitutional issues involved, than Carnot, who was pursuing his dream of reconciling the bulk of the conservatives to the Directory and to the established system, quite oblivious of the evidence that they were, in his sense of the word, already proved to be irreconcilable, and who could appeal to nothing in the constitution to support his proposal to make the regime parliamentary.

well have fallen into a state of virtual paralysis: a situation almost ideal from the point of view of D'André and his friends.

In the earlier part of June it seemed possible that Barras would indeed facilitate this development; and it is possible too that the Royalists understood the magnitude of the advantage which might fall to them. Barras certainly seemed to respond with complacency to his suitors from the legislature. But, at some point in the latter half of June, Barras decided to disappoint them and to rejoin Reubell and La Revellière in strenuous defence of the existing status. One of the factors which is said to have decided Barras was the evidence of Pichegru's earlier treason, supplied to him privately by Bonaparte in mid-June.[1] Why this revelation should in itself have made much difference to the Director's outlook on the current situation is not obvious. It only reduced to black and white what the government had long suspected of Pichegru. Why should we not suppose that Barras, concerned for his fortune and his head if not for the system, was becoming anxious rather over the progress and tendency of the Right in the legislature? We must remember, too, in the midst of our concern with the doings of the Councils, that there were other contemporary developments, not unconnected with them, which were steadily forcing themselves on the attention of the government. Since the elections, the government had not only lost its grip on the legislature; it was visibly losing its grip on the provinces. Emigrés and non-jurors were re-entering in greater numbers than ever, and promoting their affairs, often by violent means, quite unchecked by the local authorities.[2] The Prince de Carency had long since been in touch with the government, and it is quite possible that he had by this time revealed to the Directory some view of the whole design which D'André and his friends had constructed against the government.[3]

At all events, Barras not only at last turned his back on his tempters from the Right, but joined with Reubell and La Revellière in the decision to make an end without further delay. Barras addressed a secret appeal to Hoche, Commanding in Chief the

---

[1] Lefebvre, op. cit., p. 66; Pariset, tome cit., p. 341.

[2] Lefebvre, op. cit., pp. 63-4.

[3] Pariset, tome cit., p. 341. (According to the *Mémoires* of Barras, it was only at a much later stage that Carency informed the Director of the plans and the progress of the *Institut philanthropique*: Meynier, *Le 18 fructidor*, p. 193.)

Army of the Sambre et Meuse. On 13 messidor (1 July) Hoche ordered some of his troops and part of his staff to move towards the capital.[1] The crisis of July had begun. The struggle for the control of the Councils was now to be merged in a wider and more immediately critical conflict.

The story of the crisis of July, on the plane of the public history of the time, can be summarized as follows. Though it was set in motion by Hoche's orders of 1 July, it was realized as a crisis only in the third week of July. Its realization was immediately preceded by the announcement, from the government, of certain changes in its Ministry. The changes in question had been settled, by the Triumvirs, at a meeting of the Directory on 26 messidor (14 July). They were publicly known on 28 messidor (16 July). The changes were of a character quite different from those which had recently been suggested to Barras and from those wished by Barthélemy and Carnot. Two Ministers who were ill-regarded by the opposition were indeed dismissed: Delacroix and Truguet. But not only was Merlin de Douai retained, the three Ministers of whom the opposition most approved were also dismissed: Cochon (in charge of Police), Bénézech (at the Interior) and Pétiet (Minister for War). There were thus five portfolios to be redistributed. The names of the new Ministers were in themselves enough to show that the ruling Directors were by no means inclined to conciliate the legislative majority. They included most notably the names of Talleyrand (to be Minister for Foreign Affairs) and Hoche (to be Minister for War).

The next day, the outgoing War Minister, Pétiet, informed some of the deputies that he had indirect knowledge that certain troops, from the command of the very General who had just been appointed to supersede him, were marching through the interior, apparently towards the capital. Pétiet declared that their movement had not been ordered by himself, or by any Directorial *arrêt*. This bombshell, in the very midst of the ministerial changes just announced, quite properly threw the legislative world into confusion.

Fear and fury took hold of the nervous moderates of the centre,

---

[1] Lefebvre, op. cit., p. 66. Wickham (to Grenville, Most Secret, no. 20, 18 August 1797) believed that 'the march of the Troops to Paris was settled at a private conference between the Director Rewbell' (not Barras) 'and General Hoche, where nothing was reduced to writing'.

just as much as of the deputies of the Right. The independents, as has been seen, had no taste for what they suspected to be the ultimate aims of the Right; but they had, almost equally, no wish to assist at a new version of the 2 June 1793, especially as many of themselves had already gone far enough in opposition to be among the possible victims. The fear of the *coup d'état* abruptly stopped the cleavage which had been dividing the sections of the opposition.

Deputies of the Right and independents of the centre came together in informal gatherings to discuss the obvious and common peril. It was, apparently, such men as Lacuée, the friend and confidant of Carnot, and Portalis, and Tronçon-Ducoudray, who now urged that the Councils could not afford to wait on events, but must at once adopt drastic counter-measures: the arrest of Barras, even the outlawry of the Triumvirs. The men of the Right appear to have acted wisely, in effect if not in intention, by leaving the bold proposals to these. In fact, no decision was reached. The opposition was now facing, with its heart in its boots, an agonizing choice: was this the moment to reach for the pistol? Even if it were, what guarantee of success could there be?

The next day (18 July) the issue was discussed in formal session. Doubt and hesitation still hung over the proceedings. The Five Hundred at last resolved on a portentous, but for immediate purposes useless, gesture; they ordered an immediate report on the question of the re-establishment of the Paris National Guards. As Thibaudeau sensibly remarked two days afterwards, if a military *coup* were really intended, there would be no time to embark on such a measure.

On 19 July, the crisis reached its height. The Inspectors of the Hall were informed that detachments of Hoche's command had arrived at La Ferté-Alais, near Corbeil, and, being there, were in contravention of the limits of proximity to the seat of the legislature laid down in the Constitution (12 leagues).[1] Pichegru (who now naturally came into his own) and other members of the opposition went off, on their own discretion, to beard the Government in its den and to ask it to explain what, exactly, was in progress. The President *pro tem.* of the Directory was Carnot, who had been as discontented by the ministerial changes as anyone,

[1] Article 69.

and who was quite as much in the dark about the movement of Hoche's troops as his interrogators. Carnot said frankly that he could not explain the troops' arrival; he promised, what he certainly must have hoped would be performed, that orders should be given at once for their withdrawal from the constitutional limits.

The following day, 20 July (2 thermidor), the Five Hundred voted an urgent message to the Directory, placing these unofficial enquiries on a formal footing. They asked by whose orders the troops had been brought beyond the legal limits, and what steps were being taken to deal with those who were responsible. Needless to say, this gesture of energy and confidence on paper did not tend in any degree to win the battle. But unofficially, a few of the opposition were trying to find a more realistic approach to the heart of the problem. Pichegru and Vaublanc were not content simply to complain to Carnot, who was, on his side, quite as unhappy, for reasons both personal and political, as the deputies. They had negotiated a private understanding with Carnot. As soon as Carnot had clear evidence that a *coup d'état* was in progress, he was to appear at the bar of the Five Hundred in person and denounce the Triumvirs. The House would then, it might with confidence be presumed, vote their immediate impeachment.

In fact, while the deputies debated, and some few planned, the crisis was already at an end—for the time being. Hoche, arrived in Paris, found to his astonishment that it was not a united Directory whose orders he had hastened to obey, and that Carnot the organizer of the great military machine of the Republic was bitterly opposed to the plan which Hoche had been summoned to execute. The young General drew back; so—if only to await another opportunity—did the Triumvirs.

The legislators did not yet know anything of this when they received the Directory's reply to their urgent enquiry. The reply was, in itself, not a very reassuring one. The government might well have sent exactly the same answer if it had still intended to make an immediate stroke. The troops, it was said, were proceeding, in accordance with their proper duties, to 'une destination éloignée'. Their journey was legitimate, but it was admitted that they should not have taken a route which approached so nearly the seat of the government. An error of routing had been committed by some subordinate. The opposition found it even less reassuring that this vague message was signed, on behalf of the Directory, by Carnot. The Five Hundred expressed their misgivings and irritation by voting, on the proposition of Doulcet de Pontécoulant who was himself a Republican, though one of the most moderate, the establishment of a special commission to investigate the issue of responsibility for the unlawful infringement of the limits. The commission included Doulcet himself, but also Pichegru and Willot, the obvious men of action, should matters still come to a head.

In fact, the governmental message did not mean what it might well be feared to mean; nor did Carnot's signature mean that he had (in the sense that was suspected) gone over to the Triumvirs. But it was the case, though the legislature could not guess it, that Carnot had been given a shock, which induced him to join with the Triumvirs in trying to cover the traces of the *coup manqué*. Carnot had just received, from Barras, the proof of Pichegru's earlier treason. Whatever his colleagues might think, Carnot was no Royalist. He realized that the evidence just given to him threw a sinister light on the current behaviour of the legislative Right wing, and he now saw that there was indeed reason to fear that the moderate Republic was in danger from this side, as well as from the Jacobins.

During the few days following, the tension perceptibly relaxed somewhat on both sides. Hoche resigned his new Ministerial portfolio (for which, it had been—a little pedantically—argued, he was about six months too young)[1] and left the capital. His troops, or at least some of them, displayed reassuring signs that their journey had not reached its termination; and they presently moved onwards towards Brest. On its side, the special commission, reporting to the Five Hundred by the mouth of Pichegru, recommended the cessation of enquiries, and the public signposting of the *rayon constitutionnel* round the seat of the legislature, to prevent any possibility of such a military blunder, if indeed it were a blunder, in the future. Such a report was, in the circumstances, an olive branch from the Five Hundred to the government. The Council accepted it on 26 July (8 thermidor). By

---

[1] According to the Constitution, Ministers must not be appointed 'below the age of thirty years'. Hoche was in his thirtieth year, but was six months short of completing that year.

the end of the month, the Elders had concurred. In early August, the *Journal de Paris* was able to claim that a *rapprochement* had been reached between the Councils and the government.[1]

We have now to see what D'André thought of the crisis, and how he tried to determine his party's reaction to it. A hasty message to Wickham, dated 17 July, shows that D'André recognized the Ministerial changes as marking a critical conjuncture, before any news of the proximity of Hoche's troops had reached him.[2] From this moment, D'André moved, for more than two weeks (longer than the ostensible state of crisis lasted) through a difficult period of conflicting hopes and fears, calculations of caution and impulses towards a bold initiative. If his appraisals appear to be sometimes discordant with each other, this is not necessarily in the least discreditable to him, and we may say at once that in all his observations and suggestions, whatever the occasional marks of inconsistency, there are clear traces of an active mind, busily looking—even in different places—for the largest and most realistic policy.

D'André never lost sight of the fact that, in the conditions of that moment, organized force was entirely in the hands of the Triumvirs; and he saw clearly that, if matters indeed came to an

---

[1] For the history of the crisis of July, see Lefebvre, *Directoire*, pp. 66–7, 85–6; Pariset, op. cit., pp. 341–2; Buchez & Roux op. cit., tome 37, pp. 295–319, 322. Cf. the interpretation of the crisis afterwards offered by Wickham (Most Secret no. 20, 18 August). Wickham had derived some, though apparently by no means all, of the 'secret information' embodied in this despatch from D'André's reports to him. The explanations offered by Wickham in this despatch should be carefully compared with D'André's comments on the same events, examined below.

[2] A short note to Wickham, dated 17 July and written, not by D'André but on instructions from him, announces laconically: 'Kilien me charge de vous marquer que Cochon, Petiet, Benezech La Croix et Truguet sont renvoyés et remplacés par le Noir la Roche, Talleyrand et Pleville, tous detestables. Nous sommes très mal (*sic*). Repondés de suite, et des fonds nous avons le plus grand besoin.'

Lenoir-Laroche, noted as a violent Republican and anti-clerical, was the newly-appointed Minister of Police; Pleville Le Pelley, the newly-appointed Minister for the Navy.

In the light of subsequent letters in this correspondence, the brief reference made here to the need for immediate *funds* suggests that D'André already feared that the ministerial changes heralded a grave crisis and that he wanted to be in a position to organize force against force (Wickham Papers, bundle 67).

issue, the Triumvirs would probably emerge triumphant. For this reason, his original line, with which his collaborators in the legislature agreed, was to avoid this issue if possible. But he also, and very understandably, felt that a policy of simple passivity in face of the threat from the other side was not adequate. This alone would not avert the danger, it was far more likely to confirm the Triumvirs in their hostile intentions. The opposition, he thought, must display the will to resist, and must do what it could, even in this admittedly not very promising situation, to mobilize the public support which it believed it had, by reconstituting the National Guard of Paris. It did not escape D'André that such a course was as much open to objection as a policy of strict passivity; the Triumvirs might be confirmed by this, too, in their intention to strike. There were, however, he thought, complementary factors, which inclined the balance in favour of a policy of resolute resistance. The division within the Directory itself was an embarrassing, perhaps even paralysing, fact for the Triumvirs; equally important might be the obvious change of attitude which had now occurred in the minds of the independents in the senior Council. These had hitherto been inaccessible to the solicitations of the Right; but they had now become as much afraid and indignant about the conduct of the Triumvirs as the Right wing itself. The Triumvirs, with all the advantages of available force in their hands, might well shrink from a final conflict with an opposition which (on these issues) had a clear majority in both Houses, and which was prepared to show all the fight it could show. How could the Triumvirs feel sure that this majority, if pressed, would not raise the stakes higher still, and risk a vote of impeachment? And if so, how could the Triumvirs feel sure that the Councils would not win? There could be no certainty, but the Triumvirs were no more immune to doubt and misgivings than their opponents.

If the final conflict were reached, D'André was anxious that his party should meet it in as strong a position of force as its admitted material unpreparedness would allow. In the circumstances, he was anxious to draw, as soon as possible, on the resources which were to be made available by the emergency credit for which he and his friends had asked Wickham, but which had not yet been arranged. D'André seems to have thought that these 'milliers de louis d'or' might, if it came to a final issue, conceivably, even in these unpropitious conditions, turn the scale; and he urged Wickham to expedite the credit.[1]

Such were the implications of the brief and rather cryptic comments which D'André made on the crisis down to the 21 July. He wrote at greater length about it all on 27 July, by which date Hoche had resigned his portfolio and the Five Hundred had accepted Pichegru's very moderate recommendations. The crisis was then in fact at an end, though we must bear in mind that the legislative opposition still felt a good deal less than sure that this was so. Whatever D'André himself expected in the immediate future (we defer consideration of this for the moment) it is clear from his letter of 27 July that he had been very much disappointed by the behaviour of his party, and indeed of the Councils generally, in the days immediately preceding.

We have already made use of this letter in showing how disappointed D'André had become, by this date, in the whole state and prospects of the renewed Councils, on which, at the time of the elections, he had set his hopes so high. We must now view the letter with greater regard to its immediate context, which is of course provided by the conduct of the Councils during the crisis of July. It repays, for several reasons, extensive quotation:

[1] A note to Wickham, once again written not by D'André but on his instructions, and dated 19 July, indicates very briefly the mixture of hopes and fears with which D'André then regarded the crisis. On one side, the writer observes: 'Les affaires ne vont pas si mal qu'on le dit. La division du Directoire est forte. Les sottises rameneront le Conseil des anciens. Dupont de Nemours va être President aux anciens et Dumolard aux 500.' On the other, he refers to the need for the emergency credit which D'André and his allies had long since demanded: 'Le tems approche ou les milliers de Louis seront nécessaires' (Wickham Papers, bundle 67).

On 21 July, D'André himself wrote to Wickham in the following terms, which hardly need further comment: 'Les Papiers Publics vous ont appris la Division du Directoire. Elle existe de plus en plus. Elle est telle qu'elle ne peut finir que par un eclat. Les anciens épouvantés du danger, se sont réunis aux 500... Ainsi nous voilà à la veille des plus grands évenemens. Le Directoire a les troupes pour lui. L'assemblée a l'opinion, mais point de force, ce qui me fait craindre l'issue du combat. Ainsi nous recommandons la prudence. Aujourd'hui on prendra vraisemblablement un parti relativement à l'approche des troupes; demain la Garde Nationale; le Bureau Central (de Paris), objet très important, est en bonnes mains. Seulement qu'on nous donne le tems. C'est bien le moment ou les milliers de louis d'or auroient été plus que nécessaires. J'attends avec impatience votre réponse à ce sujet . . .'

Il y a grande apparance que la crise qui— (?) ne se décidera pas et (*que*) les affaires s'arrangeront. Je dis que c'est un bien, parce que nous n'étions pas en mesure de lui faire prendre une tournure utile au succès des nationaux. L'assemblée n'est pas assés forte pour suivre de grandes mesures. Si on alloit directement au but, le Parti Constitutionnel, qui est encore très nombreux, se réuniroit aux Jacobins; et nous retomberions dans la terreur. Il faut donc temporiser et attendre, ou que nous ayons propagé l'institut dans la majorité des Départements, ou qu'une nouvelle Election dont nous serons certainement les maitres nous donne une majorité assurée dans l'assemblée.—Vous desirés sans doute connoitre a fond l'esprit du Corps Législatif. On doit y compter environ 80 francs Royalistes des deux tiers aux cinq cents. Les Jacobins sont aussi nombreux. Ainsi le reste est constitutionnel, mais dans la majeure parti hait... tellement les Jacobins qu'elle se tourne plutot vers les Royalistes. Par contre ceux des Orateurs Royalistes qui se trouvent aux cinq cents nous assurent une majorité plus constante.

Aux Anciens les Parleurs sont tous constitutionnels. Cela met les Royalistes en minorité. Cependant le renvoi des Ministres aimés dont nous sommes servis... ramenera une partie des Anciens que le Directoire avoit trompée. Je ne peux pas dire si cela durera, car les Orléanistes ont un très fort parti dans les anciens. Si on pouvoit trouver parmi ceux-ci deux ou trois Orateurs, les choses changeroient de face. Mais le seul sur lequel on pourroit jetter les yeux, Portalis, est poltron et si ambitieux qu'il n'y a rien à esperer de lui.

Le mal de l'Assemblée vient ce de qu'au milieu de beaucoup de gens d'esprit et de courage il n'y a pas un *satisman*; que plusieurs de ceux sur lesquels on pourroit le plus compter sont paresseux et qu'il n'y a pas une confiance établie. *Thibeaudeau* nous a échapé, ainsi que *Siméon* et *Emmery* par la maladresse des Clichiens qui n'ont pas voulu les porter aux places. *Pastoret* et *Dumolard* qui dominent les Clichiens se donnent pour Royalistes, mais ils ne sont qu'ambitieux. *Lemerer* dont on pourroit tirer un grand parti n'aime que l'argent et les plaisirs. Ce que nous avons de mieux c'est avec Jourdan du Rhone, Jordan de Lyon. Je ne parle pas de quelques uns du nouveau Tiers, qui sont excellens, mais qui ne se mettent pas en avant. Je suis d'avis qu'ils doivent se réserver car d'apres l'exemple du Parlement d'Angleterre, il ne faut pas multiplier les Orateurs si on veut centraliser la force.

Dans le choc qui vient d'avoir lieu, on a été trop vite, ou trop doucement. Trop vite parce qu'on a attaqué sans être sur du succès. Trop doucement parce qu'on n'a pas suivi assés vivement après avoir attaqué. On n'a pas poussé l'attaque jusqu'à la victoire.

Vous me dirés pourquoi nous n'avons pas empêché d'agir ainsi.

C'est que quand on n'est pas dans le Corps Législatif on n'a pas de moyens de direction...[1]

We need not consider again here, what we have already considered by anticipation, the bearing which much of this has on the *general character* of the legislature of year V. What concerns us now is what D'André expected of the Councils in the particular conjuncture through which they had just passed, and what he made of the conduct which they had in fact displayed. It seems clear that D'André's own point of view had moved somewhat since 21 July. Then he had identified himself with a policy which was to be cautious, though firm; the Councils were to stand up to the sabre-rattling of the Triumvirs, and to proceed with the reconstitution of the National Guard, but were not to take a direct initiative for an immediate final settlement. On 27 D'André implies that he had in the meantime himself changed his mind about this, so that though the Five Hundred had, in fact, acted in accordance with his earlier view, he was now dissatisfied with them for doing so: he had come to feel that this policy was a dangerous half-measure, and that if the Councils were to stand up to the government at all on this issue, they should have played boldly for complete victory. The inference clearly arises that he was disgusted by the proposal which Pichegru had made, to call off enquiries and to be content with signposting the constitutional limits. His conclusion (expressed at the beginning of the letter), however, was that, since no 'grandes mesures' could be expected of this legislature, it was just as well that *both* sides were recoiling. The only possible course was to 'temporize' for a much longer period, perhaps till the next elections.

In another letter, written about a week later, there is evidence which clearly confirms these implications in the letter of 27 July.

Les preuves que l'on a acquises rélativement à la marche des troupes sur Paris ne sont point assés positives contre les Directeurs pour les mettre en accusation, mais elles peuvent suffire pour compromettre violemment Hoche. Plusieurs Députés parmi lesquels est Avre croyent que rélativement au défaut de forces extérieures il faut éviter d'en venir à une affaire. Quant à moi j'ai pensé (*que la Fortune?*) n'aide que les Audacieux. J'aurois voulu qu'on la poussa (*sic*) à bout. Et je suis persuadé que malgré l'apathie des Parisiens, si le Corps Législatif sortant un peu de la Constitution que le Directoire ne respecte pas, avoit mis les

---

[1] Wickham Papers.

Directeurs hors de la Loi et fait une proclamation vigoureuse, li réussiroit complettement...[1]

It is, then, perfectly clear that D'André changed his mind in the very midst of the crisis, and decided that, so far from running away from it, or even seeking with dignity and firmness to ward it off, the Councils, having once in any sense faced the danger, should have gone the whole way, and should have tried to pluck both safety and complete victory out of it. And this leaves us in a very real difficulty. In the very letter of 27 July, in which he first reveals his new ambition to drive the opposition to all lengths, D'André offers a good deal of evidence to show that, in his own words, the existing legislature was not capable of following through great measures. It is quite clear, from the terms of the letter itself, that the various weaknesses which he identified in the legislature were not weaknesses which had only appeared within the past few days; and if there were any doubt about this in the words of the letter, that doubt would be cleared completely by reference to D'André's own remarks during the previous two months. It had long since been apparent that his own party lacked discipline, cohesion and his own leadership in the Five Hundred; that it lacked almost everything in the Elders; that the independents were afraid to back the Right too far, and that it was proving impossible to win them over to closer alliance. D'André had filled his earlier letters with expressions of the need to conciliate the fearful, to restrain the over-bold, and to hasten slowly. How, in the face of all this which he had felt and had been urging for weeks, could D'André have conceived the hope that the legislative majority might acquire a different soul in the very midst of an immediate crisis, and rise abruptly to the greatest possible occasion? How, especially, could he have supposed that the independents would have been willing to join his own party in a bold act

[1] Wickham Papers. Wickham, in his account of these matters (Most Secret no. 20, 18 August, *quoted above*) makes reference to D'André's abrupt conversion, in the midst of the crisis, to the policy of a bold and decisive initiative by the Councils, and takes sides with D'André on this point: 'It seems indeed to have been the opinion of most thinking men (Mr Berger alone excepted) that all offensive measures ought ... to be ... avoided, until the National Guard should be completely formed and armed ... Mr Berger has indeed been uniformly of the same opinion, excepting at that moment when he was persuaded (in my mind upon solid grounds) that the blow would have succeeded.'

of impeachment? That they were solidly opposed to the dark designs of the Triumvirs is obvious enough; but to vote their impeachment, on what D'André confessed was inadequate evidence, and at the bidding of the Right, the independents would have needed not only great steadiness and daring, but also great confidence in the character and ulterior intentions of the Right. How were the independents to acquire these, having, only too clearly, never possessed them before?

We can only suppose that, as the crisis came to its height, D'André's mind was torn in contrary directions and that he was unable, in the stress of the moment, to prevent himself thinking and even planning on two really incompatible levels. With his normal sense of caution and realism he continued to observe and to set down the shortcomings of his legislative allies and the far from unconditional support offered to them by the independents; and on this level, he could still feel and express relief when signs appeared that the crisis was going to pass over without need for any 'grandes mesures'. On a different level, D'André saw the facts about the legislative personnel rather less clearly, but this was because he could see another range of facts much more clearly. It was by no means intrinsically absurd to argue, as D'André began at some point just after his letter of 21 July to argue, that in the circumstances in which the Councils then appeared to be, a policy of *l'audace* was the only course which offered any good prospects, and that the line of resolute defence, without a counter-initiative, which he had himself hitherto favoured, was much inferior to it. We can see his point, that an attitude of resolute defence involved the Councils in all the risks of the action, without any of the advantages. If the Triumvirs were too bold, or too desperate, to be impressed by the bluff of the resolute defence, the Councils might be hurried into ruin without any chance to strike back. If the Councils accepted the admittedly great risks of a bold stroke on their own part, however, they might not only ward off the Directors' blow, but dispose of these enemies for ever.

The difficulty obviously was to find means of adjusting two lines of policy which started from different premises. On one side appeared the well substantiated fact that the legislative majority was incapable of rising to a grand stroke; on the other, the argument that the choice might well lie between this seemingly impossible grand stroke, and sheer disaster. It is not surprising that D'André should have shifted his ground between these obviously incompatible views and have found no completely coherent appraisal of the situation.

There is evidence that, for several days after Pichegru had done his best to disengage the Councils from the battle, D'André continued to think, at least intermittently, in terms of the grand stroke.[1] What made it the more natural that he should do so, was his suspicion that the government's placatory gestures were insincere and that the attack on the Councils might at any moment be resumed.[2] If this were indeed to be the case, all the arguments in favour of the grand stroke would obviously recover their attraction. And it seems clear that, under the pressure which this suspicion placed upon him, D'André's combative instincts came strongly to the fore. Even when he was professedly resigning himself to a *détente* and to a policy of playing for time, he was at the same moment planning a further programme of legislative measures for the current session, which do not in the least express a determination to temporize until the next elections; they express rather a strong, if unadmitted, desire to take the initiative in a decisive resumption of hostilities with the government. The very man who had so recently complained that his party was pushing on its policy of 'sapping and mining' rather

[1] It is necessary to say 'at least intermittently', for D'André's comments to Wickham during these few days are not easy to bring into complete harmony. We quote in the text of the chapter a number of remarks which clearly show D'André's disposition to regret the appeasement of the quarrel and to force on a revival of it; but it has to be said that there are other passages in his letters which seem to show that he was, at certain moments, inclined to revert to his former policy of caution and restraint.

[2] In his letter of 31 July, D'André refers to the famous addresses from the troops of the Army of Italy, calling for the extermination of the Royalists in the Councils. He also reports that the orders for retreat from the metropolitan area, which had been given to the troops of Hoche's command, have been countermanded; that Paris is surrounded by these troops on every side, and that its food supplies could therefore be cut at any moment. Again, he states that some of these troops are being allowed to enter Paris, in plain clothes and in small numbers, and that a divisional commander, Lemoine, has been busy in the city, arranging accommodation and apparently collecting information. The government, he says, denies all responsibility for this activity (Wickham Papers, bundle 67). D'André's allegations were probably not wholly unfounded, though it did not in fact prove to be the case that any revival of the plan to use Hoche's troops in a *coup d'état* was involved.

too rapidly and too boldly now wants to conduct 'sapping and mining' even more boldly and even more vigorously. This appears in another passage, which we have not yet quoted, of the letter of 27 July, the very letter in which D'André expressed his conviction that his party was unable to sustain a decisive encounter, and his relief that both sides were disposed to avoid a decisive encounter at that stage:

Maintenant, si on peut se remettre dans le calme,... je désire qu'on suive cette marche: 1. Difficulté extrême pour les finances 2. Révocation du délai fatal pour les Réclamations des emigrés. 3. Renvoi de leurs causes aux tribuneaux ou aux départemens. 4. Destruction des Passeports, cartes civiques. 5. Garde Nationale à cheval et artillerie Nationale.[1]

Two days after this, D'André wrote again, in terms which express not only his satisfaction with the latest successes of the 'sapping and mining' policy, but also his hitherto smothered desire to reopen the crisis, this time at the initiative of the opposition.

Sans doute vous êtes satisfait de la marche que nous suivons. Plus de coup de tête, mais de la suite et de la fermeté. La clôture des clubs, la garde nationale, la délivrance des amis echoués, la rentrée de ceux de Toulon, voilà bien des avantages en peu de jours... Je voudrois tacher que le Corps législatif s'attribue la police de la Commune de Paris en entier. Ce seroit un coup mortel pour le Directoire.

In another part of this letter, D'André adverted to the 'desperate' financial straits of the government and expressed the hope that this could be exploited in the form of 'une attaque formelle' upon the government, as soon as the re-establishment of the National Guard had reduced the obvious danger of this particularly provocative move.[2]

---

[1] Wickham Papers.

[2] Wickham Papers, D'André's letter of 29 July. A note is required to explain the reference to recent opposition successes contained in this letter. A bill 'provisionally' prohibiting 'toute société particulière s'occupant des questions politiques' had been read to the Five Hundred by Duplantier on 12 July (before the crisis became apparent). It was the opposition's crushing retort to the founding of the so-called 'Club de Salm' and other new Republican societies, the seemingly pro-Jacobin character of which had made them as offensive to men of Dumas's type as to the deputies of the Right. It was, on the other hand, constitutionally open to question; but it passed the Five Hundred on 24 July (during the critical period) and was endorsed by the Elders, then

One of the considerations which encouraged D'André thus to incline once more to the policy of a bold seizure of the initiative, with only a short delay, was the impression that he received from the behaviour of the Elders. The deputies of the Upper House were extremely and obviously aggrieved by the recent behaviour of the Triumvirs. Even after the crisis had receded, they continued to show favour to the opposition in the Five Hundred. D'André was emboldened by their attitude to build up, what he evidently needed if his present policy was to make sense, the hope against hope that sooner or later these independents could be induced to throw in their lot decisively with his own party, and so make possible a final settlement of scores with the Directory.

---

at the height of their anger with the Directory, the very next day. The Triumvirs had already decided to avoid an immediate collision with the opposition, and made no comment on this new law.

The bill to re-establish the *compagnies d'élite* of the National Guard, i.e. the grenadiers and the chasseurs, as a force in the hands of the *honnêtes gens*, had, as has been seen, appeared as one of the measures in D'André's programme for the work of the session. It was actually brought forward, in the Five Hundred, as an obvious, but not (in the moment of crisis) very apposite response to the danger of a military stroke. It was finally put through the Five Hundred between 27 and 30 July. At the time of D'André's letter, therefore, it was still only a bill, and not a law. It was in fact accepted by the Elders only on 12 August. For obvious reasons, the Triumvirs regarded this law with great repugnance. They delayed its publication for as long as possible; thereafter they delayed its implementation for long enough to make possible their successful *coup d'état* without the complication which this force would have involved for them.

The *délivrance des amis échoués* no doubt refers to the efforts of the opposition on behalf of the fifty or so émigrés in English service, shipwrecked off Calais in November 1795. There had been much dispute as to their standing in law, and as to the appropriate treatment to be meted out to them. The opposition was now trying to carry a law (actually completed on 2 August) providing that they should enjoy specially favourable treatment, namely re-embarkation to a neutral port. This was a very minor victory for a party which was trying to rescue the *émigrés as a whole* from penalties; even as such, it remained a paper victory, for the *coup d'état* arrived in time to frustrate this measure also.

D'André also refers to a measure to readmit freely into France the *Toulonnais* who had been evacuated from that port in British vessels in 1793, another piecemeal contribution to the problem of the émigrés. This measure passed the Five Hundred, but was destined to be left in suspense by the Anciens. On these points, see Lefebvre. *Directoire*, pp. 64, 86, 63; Pariset. tome cit., pp. 344, 339.

Le plus grand (*avantage*) peut être est d'avoir su profiter de la faute du Directoire pour nous rallier les Anciens. Je ne promets pas de les tenir pour toujours, mais il peut arriver telle circonstance qui les rende inséparables, et c'est (*ce*) à quoi il faut travailler.[1]

In letters of 2 and 3 August D'André expressed in set terms his new determination after all to work for a decisive encounter during the course of the session then current. 'La cession (*sic*) actuelle', he notes with dramatic clarity, 'ne finira pas sans une accusation contre les Triumvirs.' [2] He now openly says that he is trying not to lay the recent crisis finally to rest, but to reopen it. 'Tout ceci n'est pas fini... J'espere faire forcer les Inspecteurs à faire leur rapport, et cela peut amener une crise.' [3]

Whatever we may think of D'André's wish to believe, in the teeth of his own evidence, that it might after all be possible to rally a solid majority of the legislature behind a 'grand coup', at least it has to be said that he did not intend to face a renewal of the crisis with nothing but moral force to rely on. Nor was he simply working on the presumption that the National Guard would be re-formed in time to neutralize the government's appeal to the Army; he was exerting himself meantime to build up a secret emergency defence force at Paris, in case the point of explosion were reached before the Guard was ready for action. And he also realized that the new crisis, for which he was so anxious, must at all costs be delayed for long enough to permit this emergency force to be organized.

If we thus see the champion of *l'action légale* preparing to improvise civil war, by methods which at other times and in other hands he had severely discountenanced, again it is fair to point out that D'André adopted this policy with reluctance and with emphasis upon the point that the initiative which he was so anxious to seize was not to be sought by the means of physical force; the armed bands which he was trying to bring upon the

[1] Letter of 29 July, cited above.
[2] Wickham Papers: D'André's letter of 2 August.
[3] Wickham Papers: D'André's letter of 3 August.

D'André was hoping to persuade the Inspectors of the 500 to embody in a new formal report to the House the disturbing evidence which suggested that the military threat had perhaps not after all been withdrawn. It seems that he rather hoped for a new and more violent legislative reaction against the Triumvirs, and for a decisive encounter without further delay—even *before* the National Guard was re-formed.

scene must be employed only to counter the expected use of force by the government, which, D'André thought, might well again be attempted before his own side was in any sense ready. His own remarks on these subjects place all these points in a clear light:

Les milliers de Louis ne furent jamais plus necessaires. Nous faisons la guerre d'affiche. Tous les jours nous en faisons une. Si le Directoire nous donne le tems, il sera perdu; mais le tout c'est d'avoir le tems. Heureusement il semble qu'il a peur. Je crois qu'il ne cherche qu'à mieux prendre ses mesures; et je ne cesse de le répéter afin qu'on ne s'endorme pas dans une fausse sécurité... Malgré ma répugnance à lever des armées, je vais faire venir ici des jeunes gens des départemens. Il faudra peut être se battre, et il faut avoir des batteurs.[1]

... Je forme ici des Compagnies d'hommes surs et braves. Depuis deux jours je suis à cinq cents; je le porterai à deux mille et plus. Dans les départements (sic) environnants on se prépare à la guerre civile, mais nous avons peu d'armes et point de munitions. Que Preçy ne s'eloigne pas?[2]

... Voici... le détail de ce que j'ai fait depuis trois jours. Trois divisions sont formées. La premiere est chargée de suivre les jeunes gens qui commencent à devenir nombreux; à leur parler dans le bon sens. Elle est composée de gens en état de prêter le collet en cas de besoin. La seconde, composée d'anciens militaires, doit s'insinuer parmi les troupes et y répandre le bon esprit. Elle travaille déja avec quelque espérance de succès. La troisième réunit les jeunes gens qui pensent bien et les forme en compagnie. Ce qui m'embarrasse le plus pour ces derniers, c'est de leur fournir des armes et de la poudre. Je vais en faire acheter autant que possible. Les agens ont bien ici quinze cents fusils et trois cents livres de poudre, mais ils ne veulent pas les donner. Si vous ne connoissies pas déja ces hommes, cela vous en donneroit la mesure.[3]

... Nous n'avons pas intention de guerroyer à moins de la derniere extrêmité, mais de nous mettre en défense et de nous préparer à tout évenement. Je ne m'aveugle point sur les chances défavorables, mais je ne désespère pas du succés... J'aime mieux parvenir surement et lentement que de retomber dans les malheurs que nous avoit (sic) attiré la précipitation et l'étourderie.[4]

Such were D'André's rather complex reactions to the situation on the immediate morrow of the crisis of July. On 3 August, there took place an important discussion between D'André and Pichegru,

[1] Wickham Papers: D'André's letter of 31 July.
[2] D'André to Wickham, 2 August 1797.
[3] D'André to Wickham, 3 August 1797.
[4] D'André to Wickham, undated, but placed between papers dated 1 and 2 August 1797.

which marks an important turning-point, both in D'André's relations with the General, and also in his attitude to the political problems of the time. From this moment, D'André, who had hitherto been much less than enthusiastic about Pichegru, began to speak of him in terms of considerable regard; and from the same point, D'André gave up his recent inclination to force on an early renewal of the crisis. He now fell back into the same attitude of watchful but cautious and unprovocative truce with the government as Pichegru had been recommending and practising for the past week. The two leaders agreed that it would be unwise, as things stood, to press any direct (political) offensive against the Triumvirs, but that it was nevertheless necessary to continue preparations for (physical) defence, in case the Triumvirs should again attempt to overpower the opposition by military means.[1] Was it Pichegru's arguments that impressed D'André, or was it rather that, in conversation with the General, his mind reverted without pressure to what had, after all, been his own original impression, that the deputies were much too divided and too flabby to play the part which he so much wished to cast them for? At all events, it seems clear that D'André thus quietly gave up his hankerings for an early attempt at a *grand coup* even before the Inspectors raised in the Council the business which D'André had recently been hoping would bring about an immediate resumption of the crisis. This business was, of course, the persistence of suspicious military activity in and around the capital. The Inspectors actually raised it on the day after D'André's *tête à tête* with Pichegru.[2] The Council sent them on another errand of enquiry to the Luxembourg; and Carnot produced a very conciliatory response, which the House adopted with obvious signs of relief.[3]

[1] D'André to Wickham, 4 August 1797. 'Nous avons eu hier une conférence de deux heures avec Avre dont j'ai été parfaitement content. Il a été convenu entre nous qu'il n'étoit pas prudent d'attaquer dans ce moment; mais qu'il falloit se préparer du moins à une vigoureuse défense.' It will be remembered that early in June D'André had commented rather coldly after his first meeting with the General: 'J'ai été content d'Avre, mais sans excès.'

[2] Pariset, tome cit., p. 244.

[3] These developments are illustrated in D'André's letter to Wickham of 6 August, in which D'André quotes some of the written questions which Murinais, on behalf of the Inspectors, put to Carnot, and goes on to speak very feelingly about the willingness of the deputies to be lulled asleep by the reassurances of the government: this part of the letter is quoted on p. 267.

In view of the deputies' attitude on this occasion, D'André no doubt congratulated himself that he had already given up his recent dreams of pushing them into any kind of strenuous action. What struck him now was that too many of them—not, indeed, Pichegru—were so comfortable, or so cowardly, as to be unwilling even to face the fact that the *rapprochement* with the Luxembourg was unreal, that the danger of a *coup* by the Triumvirs was just as great as it had ever been. In the circumstances, D'André thought, his party would be fortunate indeed, if the insincere truce lasted long enough to permit some of the more realistic and energetic of the opposition leaders to redeem the time, and mobilize sufficient means of armed resistance to make the next executive stroke even more difficult to carry through than the first. This was now the best that he could hope for.

Tout cela [wrote D'André to Wickham on 6 August, referring to the latest exchange between the Inspectors and Carnot] nous amenera peut être une paix platrée dont beaucoup de gens seront les dupes. Car je suis sur de ce que vous avés vu dans les papiers, que le Directoire manigance une conspiration sortie du Portefeuille de d'Antraigues; et que s'il recule dans ce moment, c'est que d'un côté Hoche a eu peur, et que de l'autre il n'est pas parfaitement sur des troupes. Je ne cesse de (? *le*) répéter à nos amis, et de les exciter à une salutaire méfiance, non que je veuille les porter à une attaque qui seroit peut-être imprudente, mais afin qu'ils ne se laissent point endormir. Imbert-Colomes, Pichegru, et quelques autres sont bien persuadés de cela. Mais vous connoissés mieux les hommes que moi, et vous savés combien il est difficile de donner du courage à un poltron, et de l'éveil aux endormis... Enfin je profiterai de ce calme apparent pour nous mettre, du moins s'il est possible, en état de défense.[1]

We have now followed the political activities of D'André down to the point at which, belatedly and rather reluctantly, he acquiesced in the establishment of the very hollow truce which followed the crisis of July. At this point, there still lay ahead of his party, and of himself, another month of manoeuvres, of growing excitement, and of final crisis, before the verdict of the 18 Fructidor swept his cause once more into ruin. But we may conveniently pause before entering into the discussion of these develop-

[1] Wickham Papers, D'André to Wickham, 6 August 1797. It was the capture of d'Antraigues's papers which had given the Directory its first positive evidence of Pichegru's treason.

ments, and turn aside to consider first the many other activities
and relations which, in spheres outside of the scene of government, were meantime claiming a share in the busy days of the
resourceful ex-Constituent.

IX

'Any other Business'

D'ANDRÉ regarded it as his chief personal contribution to his cause, that he should lead the campaign in the legislature to undermine and finally destroy the Republican system. But he had set himself to take part in other developments besides, of scarcely smaller importance. It will be remembered that, among other points, he had agreed with Bayard on the need for a carefully organized press campaign, and had written, in this connection, of the papers which he and Bayard were going to have. Accordingly we find him, in mid-May, preparing to assume direction of a journal, chiefly with a view to the needs of the *Institut philan-thropique*.[1] The paper in question was the *Mémorial*,[2] D'André duly embarked on this work, but without much success. At the end of June he confessed to Wickham that he had 'tant d'occupations et de soucis' that he could not give enough attention to the paper. It lacked *ensemble*, he felt; but he still hoped that all would come right.[3] It didn't; he finally despaired of managing 'his associates, being *men of letters*' on this paper; but he then transferred his editorial zeal (with how much better success does not appear) to *L'Europe politique et littéraire*. Here he had the aid, not only of his own colleague Bayard, but also of Peuchet; the collaboration of the latter was approved by the great Mallet du Pan. On the eve of the *coup d'état*, D'André was hoping for occasional contributions for his paper by Mallet du Pan himself.[4]

[1] Wickham Papers, D'André's letter of 15 May.

[2] Wickham's draft, Most Secret no. 22 of 1797 to Grenville, 27 August. La Harpe and Fontanes wrote for this paper (Lefebvre, *Directoire*, p. 57) but D'André does not appear even to have mentioned them in his correspondence with Wickham.

[3] Letter of 29 June.

[4] Wickham to Grenville, 27 August, cited above; Wickham to D'André, 1 August; D'André to Wickham, 6 August. D'André and Bayard seem to have used their system of *voitures* to convey this literature to their 'frères et amis' of the *Institut* in the provinces, as they had planned before the elections. The *voitures* are mentioned as just about to set out again in D'André's letter of 4 June.

A good deal of D'André's attention was of course given to the development of the *philanthropie*. He himself took over responsibility for its impulsion in the South, as his own origins and detailed knowledge made evidently advisable, leaving Des Pomelles to conduct it in about sixty other departments.[1] In his reports to Wickham, D'André repeatedly expressed the greatest satisfaction over the progress and prospects of this movement, especially in the area where he was himself directing it.

Tout va très bien dans le Sud. La Société Philanthropique y prend a merveille...[2]

Il y a trois mois, que rien n'étoit fait, aujourd'hui une correspondance active et sure est établie entre le Nord et le Sud. L'opinion, si elle ne gagne pas à Paris, fait de grands progres dans les Departemens...[3]

Cette philanthropie va bien; ce sera un excellent moyen. Elle nous servira pour l'établissement de la Garde Nationale; et à moins que nous ne succombions d'ici à l'année prochaine, elle nous rendra absolument maitres des elections.[4]

D'André appears to have been rather less than satisfied, after short experience, with the conduct of his colleague Des Pomelles. He told Wickham in mid-August that Des Pomelles was 'un peu mou', something of a drinker, and not good for much after lunch time. He inferred, though quite mildly, that the Institut would have progressed even better under more efficient management than Des Pomelles provided.[5] It was, however, only in Paris that D'André felt the fortunes of the Institut to be seriously disappointing; and he does not appear to have attributed this chiefly to the failings of Des Pomelles.

All this work of secret enlistment, propaganda and organization, from which the ex-Constituent, perhaps justifiably, expected so much, was being promoted on a remarkably modest budget. D'André was stipulating with Wickham for a subsidy of only 2,000 louis a month for the operations of Des Pomelles in sixty Departments. He even insisted that this was ample:[6] though Des Pomelles, it is true, claimed that it was inadequate.[7] It does not

---

[1] D'André's letters of 29 July and 4 August.   [2] Letter of 27 June.
[3] Letter of 1 July.   [4] Letter of 29 July.
[5] Letter of 18 August.
[6] D'André's letters of 29 June and 2 August; cf. Wickham's draft, Most Secret no. 23, to Grenville, 27 August.
[7] Wickham's draft to D'André, 26 August.

appear how much of his own subsidy from Wickham D'André proposed to spend on the needs of the Institut in his own Southern province; but even if we assume that he planned to spend as much in that area as Des Pomelles in all the rest of the territory, we are left with the inference that the great engine for the final overthrow of the Republic was calculated by its chief director to run at no more than about £4,000 a month.

If D'André had had to fight only against the Republic, his task would evidently have been heavy enough. Unhappily, he had to fight also against the high direction of his own party. The Court of Blankenburg had at last accepted his policy; but it did not even then accept his plea to be allowed to conduct that policy without the danger and embarrassment of interference from Royalist headquarters, or from men who claimed superior authority from thence. When Bayard went, after the elections, on his mission of report to Wickham, he brought also a message from D'André to the exiled Court. The burden of this was, that D'André would keep up regular communications with only one of the all too numerous persons in the interior, who professed special powers from the Pretender: namely, Des Pomelles. He 'would have nothing to do', as Wickham explained to Lord Grenville, 'with a correspondence to which several were privy.' But Bayard, 'to his great surprise and disappointment', learned on arriving at Berne that he had been 'crossed on the road by a person going from Blankenburgh to Paris, who carryd with him an *order* for the regular establishment (*at Paris*) of a Council of twelve Persons, the whole in as due form as if the King were actually on his Throne'.[1] If this ambitious project had been fulfilled, D'André would have found himself required to accept investigation and control of all his doings by twelve masters on the spot—quite unsuited, by their numbers, their ignorance, and even perhaps their lack of discretion, to the needs of the situation.

Thanks to the joint efforts of the Pretender's counsellor La Marre and of Wickham, this scheme was countermanded;[2] and some time in June Bayard set off to Blankenburg to entreat the Pretender, in D'André's name, not only (as we have already seen) to make no further statement about the political future, but

[1] Wickham's draft no. 12 of 1797 to Grenville, 24 May.
[2] Wickham's draft to D'André, 8 June; no. 12 of 1797, and no. 19 of 1797, to Grenville, 24 May and 30 June.

also to 'form no new Council, give no new powers . . .'[1] until
D'André's current designs had been worked out.

The plan for a 'Council' sitting in state in Paris was thus at
least deferred; but D'André continued to be troubled by numerous Royalist agents, great and small, meddling and indiscreet,
attempting to question, interfere with, modify or even control his
various operations. They caused him, he said, with an almost
Royal gesture of complaint, 'more work and worry than the
whole of France put together'.[2] He thought it wise, so far as
possible, to avoid them.[3] But that was not the appropriate remedy
in some instances—when, for example, certain of them tried to
intervene in the organization of the Institut far away in the
South.[4]

Meantime, his deliberate decision to have nothing to do even
with the members of the Agence de Paris, with the exception of
Des Pomelles, inevitably brought him into difficulties of its own.
Since he would not share his secrets with them, they—from their
own point of view very naturally—refused to place their own
resources, such as they were, at his disposal when he needed
them. We have already quoted the terms of bitter contempt in
which he reported their refusal to hand over to him, at the turn of
July to August, their supplies of small arms and ammunition.[5]
But why were they so deeply in the wrong to hesitate to strip
themselves at the bidding of a man whose objectives were largely
obscured from them, whose reserve inevitably offended their
vanity, and whose very position in the movement seemed unofficial at best?

The crisis of July had hardly subsided when D'André and his
legislative collaborators found themselves facing another interference on a high level from the side of the pure Royalist emigration. The Prince de la Trémoille arrived in Paris, claiming new
and superior authority over all the servants of the King, and also
in some sense the authorization of the British government. This
threw both D'André and the deputies into great concern and

[1] Wickham's draft to Grenville, no. 19 of 1797, dated 30 June and noted:
'dispatched Sat. 8 July 1797'.
[2] D'André to Wickham, 4 June.
[3] Letter of 4 June.
[4] D'André to Wickham, letter of 2 August.
[5] D'André to Wickham, letter of 3 August. Cited ch. VIII above.

annoyance. D'André hardly knew what line to take with an emissary who claimed the authority both of Blankenburg and of London. Hitherto he had been able, with some success, to take the line that, though working for the exiled King, his direct responsibility was only to Wickham. This line would hardly serve if it were really true that de la Trémoille had the confidence of Wickham's employers. D'André wrote off to Wickham in terms of misgiving and (conditionally) of deep regret: 'La Trémouille (*sic*) est arrivé ici. A-t-il des Rélations directes avec votre Gouvernement? Je ne sais quelle conduite tenir avec lui. J'aurois bien désiré que tout vint de vous.' [1] What D'André and his allies disliked about de la Trémoille was not only that he claimed to come between D'André and Wickham, but also that he was a notorious émigré, and therefore might be very dangerous company, and moreover that for other reasons too he was a doubtful friend to their plans. Pichegru, as Wickham later explained to Lord Grenville, flatly refused to have anything to do with the Prince, no matter what claims to authority he advanced:

Baptiste has peremptorily refused to see the Prince de la Trémouille, giving for reason that the latter is an Emigrant, but I know that he has also been put upon his guard by the late Minister of Police who has assured him, what I have long known, that the best agents and spies of the Government are among the old chiefs of the Chouans, with whom, as it appears, Mr de la Trémouille is chiefly associated. [2]

Other 'leading deputies' found a further subject of complaint about the Prince: they regarded him as the champion of a rival Royalist project rather than as a loyal fellow-worker of their own, and felt his arrival indicated the King's lack of serious support for their policy. These were so disgusted by his intervention that they abandoned the King's cause completely. [3] D'André could do nothing but watch helplessly the development of all this mischief.

In all his difficulties, D'André could rely with absolute confidence upon the aid of Wickham. The British envoy could not, of course, resolve all the problems of D'André. But the efforts which

[1] Letter of 2 August. The Prince had, in fact, been commissioned by Louis XVIII to direct the Agence de Paris.
[2] Wickham's draft Most Secret no. 22, to Grenville, 27 August. Cf. D'André to Wickham, 14 August.
[3] Wickham's draft of 27 August, cited above.

he made, in particular, to supply, in what proved difficult circumstances, the financial needs of D'André's campaign make up an impressive feature of the whole episode.

It will be recalled that towards the end of May, Wickham passed on to Lord Grenville the request of D'André and his associates for a regular allowance of £10,000 monthly and also for powers to draw a sum of not more than £50,000 *en bloc* in case a sudden emergency were forced upon them. D'André himself, much to Wickham's admiration, soon proposed a reduction of the suggested monthly allowance. He explained in June that all the operations of himself and his allies might be adequately supported at a cost of only 8,000 louis a month. This would include 2,000 louis a month for Des Pomelles's undertakings. Des Pomelles would thus receive his funds, not from London *via* the Agence but from Wickham, *via* D'André. Des Pomelles would thus be freed from the difficulties of contact with England, and also from the danger that his colleagues at Paris would misappropriate his moneys[1] (for if he received them through D'André, who had no dealings with other members of the Agence, these other members of the Agence could not even try to interfere with what they would know nothing about). As for the saving, involved in the reduction of the whole budget from £10,000 monthly to 8,000 louis monthly, D'André proposed that Wickham should allocate this to Précy, who could conveniently use it separately, on Wickham's 'side of the country', to influence the development of local politics there.[2]

While Wickham's French ally was thus demonstrating his financial honesty, care for the interests of the British Government, and willingness to share resources with Précy, Wickham was already conceding, on his own discretion and without waiting for Grenville's approval, a first monthly subsidy to the full extent of what had originally been demanded, that is, £10,000. He also undertook, again upon his own discretion, to release further money, for immediate use in an emergency, on the strength of a written assurance from D'André of its absolute necessity. Wickham regarded with understandable complacency the efforts which he thus made for D'André on his own respon-

---

[1] D'André to Wickham, 4 June, 29 June; cf. Wickham's draft Most Secret no. 23, to Grenville, 27 August.

[2] Wickham's draft, Most Secret no. 23 of 1797, 27 August.

sibility. 'Je suis sur que vous en êtes content. Si vous aviez lu les ordres que j'ai recu [*sic*] vous series même étonné que je me sois aussi avancé.[1] But Wickham was to do far more than this upon his own responsibility in this matter before the summer was over.

Wickham expected Lord Grenville's reply to the financial demands of D'André and his allies before the end of June.[2] But that reply was destined not to arrive, even by the end of July.[3] Grenville had in fact sent a favourable reply, dated 30 June;[4] but the ship carrying both the Foreign Secretary's despatch, and the special courier charged with it, was captured in the narrow seas and taken into a Dutch port. It was not until 1 August that Wickham was able to give this news to D'André,[5] and even then the envoy did not know what Grenville's answer had been; all he knew was that the messenger had been captured and had presumably destroyed his messages before the enemy could take charge of him. As yet, Wickham had not received approval even for the advance of the sums he had made available to D'André at the time of the elections.[6] Yet in the meantime, that is to say

[1] Draft to D'André, 8 June.

[2] In his draft of 8 June, Wickham told D'André that he expected the return of his courier, with the reply, in three weeks or a month. But more than a fortnight had already elapsed since the demand had been sent off (on 24 May).

[3] Wickham's drafts to D'André, 27 July, 1 August.

[4] Wickham Papers, Grenville to Wickham, no. 4 of 1797, dated 30 June: *duplicate*, with postscript dated 5 August. The reply was not, indeed, unconditionally favourable. The Foreign Secretary's mind was now taken up by the prospects of Lord Malmesbury's mission to Lille (then just about to occur) to treat for peace with the Republic. He 'authorized' Wickham 'to proceed in the payments of the ensuing month (i.e. *July*) on the scales, and for the purpose, stated' . . . 'but . . . the Line of Conduct to be pursued hereafter must depend upon the event of the negotiations. You must therefore . . . decline giving any assurance . . . beyond the period of this monthly payment, and of one more, if you should not hear to the contrary from me.' This meant that Lord Grenville was giving a conditional approval to a further monthly subsidy for August, and was tacitly approving Wickham's earlier payments to D'André; but he would not commit himself even provisionally to pay subsidies beyond the month of August, and he said nothing at all in reply to the request for powers to draw a sum of £50,000 in emergency.

[5] Wickham's draft to D'André, 1 August: 'Enfin nous avons la clé de l'énigme... mon courrier a été pris en revenant avec le Paquebot et conduit dans un Porte (*sic*) de Hollande. Ces dépêches ont été sans doute jettés a la mer. Du reste vous pouvés être tranquille, personne n'y aura été nommé.'

[6] Letter of 1 August, cited above. Wickham resumes: 'Cette affaire du courier est bien malheureuse pour moi, vu qu'il m'apporte beaucoup de

during July, he conceded to D'André on his own discretion sums amounting to D'André's whole demand for the month of July, namely 8,000 louis, with the stipulation that 2,000 of these were to be passed on to Des Pomelles.[1] 'Vous serez étonné d'apprendre que mon courier n'est pas encore de retour, et que j'ai pris tout ceci sur moi.' [2] But while Wickham was undertaking this, to cover the campaign's regular expenses for the month, D'André and his friends were moving into the crisis of Hoche's march, and, as has been seen, pressed Wickham from 17 July onwards for the immediate, and already long delayed, establishment of the large emergency credit, which, they felt, the current situation urgently called for. Could Wickham, still acting, of necessity, upon his own responsibility, rise to this occasion? He could and did.

On 26 July, Wickham announced to D'André the arrangements which he was making to complete the payment of the 8,000 louis demanded for the regular expenditure of that month. The next day, he wrote to D'André again to grasp the much larger nettle of the emergency credit. He declared that he was making available a further immediate draft of 8,000 (2,000 of which were again allocated to Des Pomelles). The effect of these concessions would be to give D'André an immediate spending power of 12,000 louis—six thousand being the belated satisfaction of his requirements for July, the second six thousand being primarily for the possible needs of the crisis. Wickham next explained that he was prepared to go much further still. 'Lors que vous et Avre seres d'accord de frapper un coup, ne craignes pas d'outrepasser les pouvoirs que je vous donne aujourd'hui, de les doubler, de les tripler meme, s'il est necessaire. Je prends tout sur moi.' [3] Wickham does not say, in figures, to what sum he was prepared to let D'André and Pichegru draw; but his subsequent account to

---

lettres particulières, et que je n'ai pas encore reçu d'approbation de la grande remise que je vous ai fait (*sic*) lors des Elections.'

[1] Wickham's drafts to D'André, 16 July (explaining that he had authorized an advance of £2,000, pending the return of the courier, and requesting that £500 of this should be passed on to 'vos amis', i.e. Des Pomelles); 26 July (repeating the former announcement, and stating that a further advance of 4,000 louis was authorized that day, of which 1,500 were for Des Pomelles, while 2,000 more would shortly be credited to D'André at another (a Genevan) bank).

[2] Wickham's draft to D'André, 26 July.

[3] Wickham's draft to D'André, 27 July.

Lord Grenville makes it clear that he had arranged to concede them the full amount they had originally asked to meet the 'case of an extreme emergency'—£50,000.[1] No higher demonstration of the envoy's entire commitment to D'André and Pichegru could have been provided.

Their response to the efforts he thus made for them gave Wickham great satisfaction. D'André at first seriously demurred to Wickham's offer of the subsidy for July, feeling that it would be wrong to work, perhaps, at Wickham's personal loss: 'pour tout au monde je ne voudrois pas vous exposer personnellement'.[2] He soon tacitly withdrew this objection,[3] doubtless in view of the fact that Wickham was meantime offering much larger sums, still at his personal risk; but he and Pichegru won the envoy's special appreciation by their abstention from any attempt, during the crisis of July and the doubtful days which followed, either to wring any large sum from Wickham's bankers before receiving his letter of 27 July, or to take advantage of the large offers contained in that letter when it was received. D'André indeed several times urged Wickham for 'thousands of louis', but he seems to have been genuinely unwilling to draw on his patron except with the agreement of London, and when he received the letter of 27 July his situation was simplified in that he had now accepted the 'patched up peace'; so he responded to Wickham's offer of emergency funds at Wickham's own risk with the simple statement that he did not think they would now be needed.[4] Wickham was astonished and delighted by the forbearance of D'André and Pichegru:

The conduct of these persons [he informed Lord Grenville] has been so extremely honourable and of a nature so new to me that I feel it a duty to particularize it . . . they declined making any use of the credit for

---

[1] Wickham's draft, Most Secret, no. 23, to Grenville, 27 August.

[2] D'André's letter to Wickham, 2 August.

[3] In his letter of 4 August, D'André says that he does not think there is any immediate necessity for emergency funds, but adds: 'Les huit milles (sic) sont suffisans pour le travail actuel.' These *huit milles* must be the money which Wickham had already offered him for the month of July; and his expression suggests that he is now prepared to accept them.

[4] D'André to Wickham, 4 August. 'Je ne vois pas, je ne crois pas que nous faisions usage de l'excédent que vous accordés en cas de nécessité.' In this same letter D'André reports his conference with Pichegru on 3rd, and their agreement that it would be unwise to press an immediate attack on the Triumvirs.

£50,000, though there were certainly moments at which, under the strictest construction, . . . they might fairly have drawn for the whole.[1]

Yet all Wickham's exertions to keep D'André financially supplied were more valuable to D'André in a moral sense—as proof of Wickham's support for him—than in a material manner. The fact remains that D'André was in considerable difficulties of supply throughout the time under review in this chapter. The subsidies for the month of June, announced to him by Wickham early in that month, appear to have been the only moneys which he actually received, from the time of the elections to about the middle of August. All the operations in which he was concerned were meantime being conducted on a basis far more modest than even his own revised estimate of what they would cost: £10,000 in all. A certain amount of D'André's 'other business' unavoidably consisted in worry over the delay of supply, and in expostulating about it with Wickham. His anxiety naturally reached its height in the July crisis, when he lacked not only the agreement of London to the provision of the emergency credit, but also the subsidy for the expenses of the current month.

The chief cause lay in the non-arrival of Grenville's reply to the financial demands made in May. Wickham arranged the subsidy for June on his own discretion. When July was half over, and he still lacked the expected authority from London, he began to take steps to provide the July subsidy, again on his own discretion. The hour was already late. Other causes intervened to make the fulfilment of this provision later still. Wickham arranged for the payment of this July subsidy in three portions. The second and third portions were authorized only towards the end of the month.[2] It is not suggested that Wickham could have managed matters more speedily than he did; how anxious he was to do everything possible, in view of the crisis at Paris, is shown, as we have said, by his conferment, still before the end of the month, of emergency powers upon D'André and Pichegru at his own risk. Nevertheless, the delay of the greater part of the July subsidy till near the end of July was a misfortune for D'André, and to make matters worse, there were delays—not for the first time—on the part of one of the bankers, so that it was not until

---

[1] Wickham's draft, Most Secret, no. 23, to Grenville, 27 August.
[2] Wickham's drafts to D'André, 16 and 26 July, cited above.

12 August that D'André was able to acknowledge receipt of even a part of the subsidy for July.[1]

With these explanations it becomes clear that when D'André at several points during the July crisis stressed his need for 'thousands of louis' he was pointing not only to the unfulfilled demand for a large emergency credit, but to a grave shortage even of far more modest spending power; and it seems rather surprising that at the beginning of August he should have been able at all to enlist men or to purchase arms and ammunition.

No more must be said, in the text of this chapter, about the financial provision of D'André's operations. We must turn now to the observation that Wickham, besides giving D'André the fullest possible moral and financial backing, was also finding him a good deal of work, in matters which lay somewhat apart from the immediate and proper aims which D'André was trying to achieve. These matters of course related to the needs of British policy, needs which D'André and his allies had necessarily, and (in the case of D'André himself, at least) no doubt willingly, agreed to serve, so far as they were not inconsistent with the interests of France. About this aspect of D'André's work in the summer of 1797, we have as yet said nothing.

An element of special difficulty for D'André characterized this part of his activity during the time in question. There was no doubt that Wickham wanted to secure the same solution to the problem of French politics as D'André; there was no doubt that Wickham believed this solution could be achieved, if at all, only by the methods which D'André was using, and under the direction which D'André was trying to supply. But in summer 1797, it was the case, more obviously than at any previous moment, that

---

[1] D'André to Wickham, 12 August: 'Prenés les arrangemens convenables avec Baboin pour que les sommes du mois d'Août arrivent en leur tems, puisque celles qui sont arrivées sont natives de Juillet' ('Baboin' was a banker, cf. Wickham's draft to D'André, 6 July). The sums which D'André thus acknowledged on 12 August did not represent all that he was due to receive in respect of July, as appears from Wickham's draft to D'André, '16 et 17 aout 1797': 'Baboin doit venir sous deux jours; et j'espere faire en sorte que vous aurés au moins tout votre argent pour le moi (sic) de Juillet avant le 30 du courant.'

D'André's subsidy for the month of June had suffered similar delay at the hands of the banker—perhaps the same; he is referred to on the former occasion, however, as Dorothée (Wickham's draft to D'André, 8 June).

British policy in French affairs was concerned with other issues besides those nearest the hearts of French Royalists. England faced a situation of appalling difficulty, both on the continent and at home. British Ministers unavoidably devoted their attention, not to the possibilities of encompassing the downfall of the Republic by movements within its own territory, but to the preservation of England's surviving interests from the clutches of the conquering Republic while that Republic still lived. They could not afford to bank too heavily on the outcome of the political struggle for mastery in France; they were more concerned to guard against invasion of the British Isles, to limit the scope of French domination in central Europe, and to achieve a peace, on terms short of disastrous, with the Republic for fear of worse evils. In these conditions it was only natural that they should value their connections with French Royalists inside France, not chiefly for their chances of overturning the Republic, but for their possible services in providing information about Republican plans, and in mobilizing French opinion to put pressure on the Directory to moderate its external ambitions.[1] Wickham's correspondence with D'André clearly illustrates the dominant place which these considerations now held in the mind of the envoy at Berne, as much as in the thoughts of Pitt and Grenville. And thus it occurred that during the critical summer, while D'André tried to concentrate all his attention on the campaign for the overthrow of the Republic, Wickham was ceaselessly urging him to promote objects of a lesser, and indeed essentially different kind. However fully D'André and his collaborators had accepted in advance the stipulation that they should try to promote the more immediate interests of England, as well as their own more radical objectives, they must have found this situation in practice very provoking. What seems most remarkable is the very great willingness which D'André displayed to satisfy the exigencies of Wickham in these matters; his extant letters to Wickham show no trace of impatience, and he seems to have given sustained atten-

[1] In his despatch no. 4, 30 June (the despatch which was captured by the enemy, or the courier of which, at least, was captured by the enemy) Lord Grenville, advising Wickham of the proper limits of his expenditure on the activities of D'André and his allies, added the further direction, to guide him in his future relations with these persons: 'Such influence as you can in any manner direct to that object should be employed in compelling the Directory to peace with Great Britain.'

tion to the points which Wickham pressed on him. But it is, of course, obvious even before we look at some of the evidence, that here also D'André was condemned to labour with only very imperfect success. It was chiefly as an agent of secret information about the further designs of the Republican government that D'André was able to give any satisfaction to the wishes of the British authorities. To force the Directory to moderate its external policy and to agree to peace on any terms which England might, even with reluctance, accept, were objectives which proved unattainable.

Passages in the envoy's drafts for Lord Grenville show clearly how much Wickham's attention was concentrated, from the beginning of the new session onwards, upon the prospect of turning the efforts of the enlarged opposition towards restraining the ambitions of the Directory, and how entirely he relied upon the willingness and ability, not only of D'André himself, but of the opposition deputies generally, to pursue this line.

The Directory is as averse as ever to a peace with England. I have, however, the utmost confidence . . . in the efforts . . . the new members . . . will make to bring about so desirable an event. Those efforts can hardly fail, if they be directed, as it is intended that they should, upon principles as well of Morality and Justice, as upon those of the strictest economy in the public expenditure . . .[1]

Mr Berger has . . . engaged himself to me in the most solemn manner that nothing shall be left undone . . . to check the progress of the Revolution in other countries, . . . that the business of Genoa and of Venice, if not of Ireland, shall be immediately brought forward . . .[2]

Wickham added on this occasion, but subsequently deleted from his draft, some further words, which show, if possible even more plainly than those just quoted, that he was now so deeply concerned to secure the limitation of the Directory's expansion, as to have practically lost sight of the prospect of overthrowing it:

It is most evident to me that there are no means of preventing . . . the most terrible calamities (*from falling*) upon every surrounding state . . . but by forcing the French Government (*through its own people*) to a system of Justice and Moderation.[3]

How far Wickham's hopes of all this were fulfilled will be

[1] Wickham's draft, no. 13 of 1797, 24 May.
[2] Wickham's draft no. 17, 27 June.   [3] Ibid.

illustrated in due course. Meantime, the envoy was also pressing upon D'André the importance of information regarding the future intentions of the Republic towards its neighbours, and urging him to remember—thus admitting some fear that he and his party might forget—that every foreign success of the Republic must strengthen its position at home.

On me charge de vous exhorter... de faire passer votre Journal... en Angleterre par Calais... d'avoir un correspondant a Brest qui marquât (comme font les Gazettes Angloises) l'arrivée et le départ des Escadres, destination..., noms des Capitaines, pour combien de temps ils sont ravitaillés...[1]

And Wickham went on to ask for a similar service, in respect of naval or of military developments as the case might be, 'pour Dunkerque, Toulon, etc., et même pour Cologne, Dusseldorf, &c., du côté de l'Hanovre'. He concluded:

Il faut absolument... écrire souvent vos notions sur les liaisons du Directoire avec l'étranger et ses projets hors de la République... Il vous importe tout autant qu'à nous. Encore deux mois, et le Directoire est établi sur son trône d'une manière inébranlable. Ses ressources et ses moyens sont dans l'étranger.[2]

D'André was already doing what he could. At the beginning of June, he had sent his agent Foy to Berne with reports of the Directory's intention to occupy the North German ports and so deal a crushing blow to England's European export trade.[3] He seems, in fact, to have had good sources of information and to have tried to use them intelligently. Thus in a very few words he gave to Wickham, at the end of June, an excellent forecast of the fate of Lord Malmesbury's second negotiation for peace, then just about to begin at Lille, and also of the line of French policy towards Austria on the morrow of Leoben:

La paix ne se fera pas, je crois. Les pretensions du Directoire sont trop fortes. *Restitution entière.*

Tout n'est pas fini avec l'Empereur.[4]

D'André claimed he had received this information from a man 'qui fait des affaires pour les Directeurs et qui a toute leur con-

---

[1] Wickham's draft to D'André, 11 June.   [2] Ibid.
[3] D'André to Wickham, 4 June.   [4] D'André to Wickham, 27 June.

fiance'.[1] At the cost of conducting, himself, 'affaires' of a different kind with this person, D'André gathered the further information that the Directors, though not seriously interested in the possibilities of a peace with England, were quite prepared to go through the forms of negotiation with Malmesbury, among other reasons because they hoped to line their own pockets. D'André referred to the intention of asking, what was, it seems, indeed asked during the negotiations at Lille—'cinquante mille livres sterling pour chaque Directeur'.[2] At the same moment, he claimed the information that the Republicans had planned an occupation of Lisbon, as well as of the North German ports, and that both these operations had been temporarily suspended, though not wholly given up; he also asserted that an invasion of Ireland, on the other hand, had been resolved upon, and claimed to know that this decision had been reached only by a divided vote in the Directory, Barras and Barthélemy, who, he understood, had latterly been working together, protesting strongly against it[3] (at this date, the end of June, Barras was, as has been seen, veering between the opposing parties, and this report is therefore not intrinsically incredible).

It is possible that by 'un homme qui fait des affaires pour les Directeurs' D'André meant no less a person than Talleyrand, his old fellow-member of the Constituent, and now the Directory's new Secretary for Foreign Affairs. There is, at all events, no doubt that D'André resumed his connection with Talleyrand at some point during the session, and shortly before the *coup d'état* he certainly received information from Talleyrand about the Lille negotiation, and enjoyed, apparently under Talleyrand's protection, some kind of back-stairs *entrée* at the Ministry of Foreign Affairs.[4]

There is evidence that D'André enjoyed, and did his best to exploit, even closer connections with the hostile government. He seems to have had frequent direct personal communication with Carnot,[5] and he had access to the private views of Barthélemy

[1] D'André to Wickham, 29 June.   [2] Ibid.   [3] Ibid.

[4] D'André to Wickham, two notes dated 24 August. In the first, he writes: 'Je recois un billet de Talleyrand. Il n'y a point de paix.' In the second: 'On nous annonce la paix signée avec l'Empereur. J'ai été deux fois aux affaires Etrangères sans voir personne.'

[5] A passage in Wickham's draft Most Secret no. 12, 27 June, beginning 'Mr Berger has seen Carnot frequently' is publ. in Wickham's *Corresp.*, vol. II, pp. 40–1.

through that Director's personal confidant, the former postal Intendant D'Aubigny. Towards the end of June, Wickham was able to pass on to Lord Grenville D'André's assurance that Barthélemy was bitterly opposed to his colleagues' 'hostile intentions with respect to Switzerland and to Hamburgh, and their determination to humble England'.[1] Wickham attributed the postponement of the attack on the North German ports partly to the influence of Barthélemy,[2] and rejoiced to report that the Director had expressed his anxiety to work with the conciliar opposition in frustrating any further developments of 'the nefarious system of the Committee of Public Safety'.[3]

But, however valuable might be the sources of information which D'André enjoyed, and the intelligence which he collected through them, this could not be the most important field of the services which Wickham now expected from D'André. Even more important than knowing where the next blows were to fall, was to prevent them from falling, and to force the Directory to adopt less terrifying courses. Even two out of the five Directors, however moderate their inclinations, could do nothing of themselves to secure this; only the legislative opposition could attempt an effective contribution to the problem. Wickham had the assurance of D'André and his collaborators, before the session began, that everything possible should be done, to ensure both the interests of England, and the safety of the rest of Europe. There is no reason to doubt that D'André sincerely intended to fulfil these promises and did what he could to that end. But it also seems clear that in the event he found it all much more difficult than Wickham wanted to believe. When, apparently some time in the second half of June, D'André repeated his assurances to Wickham on these points, he did so in terms so heavily qualified by conditions and cautions as to amount rather to a withdrawal than to a confirmation of his promises. This need involve no reflection on D'André's good faith, it illustrates, more probably, his good sense and caution in the light of sad experience since the session began. But it certainly shows what formidable difficulties this part of the programme incurred. Wickham's account of D'André's fresh assurances reads as follows:

[1] Wickham's Most Secret no. 12, 27 June.
[2] Wickham's draft no. 17, 27 June.
[3] Wickham's draft Most Secret no. 12, 27 June.

Mr Berger has desired me to say that if H.M. Ministers can point out
. . . any line that can be taken, or any arguments that can be used, with a
reasonable appearance of fairness and without shocking too openly the
national prejudice . . . which still exists in its full force against the
English nation, he and his friends will do their utmost to give them full
effect, and that . . . though the intentions of the Directory with respect
to England cannot perhaps as yet be openly censured, yet as they have
followed the same line of conduct with respect to other states, the
principle on which that conduct is founded may and shall immediately
be attacked.[1]

What do all these carefully guarded expressions really amount
to? D'André's collaborators in the Five Hundred are quite prepared to criticize the aggressive foreign policy in general terms.
But they find it impracticably embarrassing to champion in particular the needs of the traditional enemy, England. They can speak
for England only under the cover of a general attack on Republican aggressions; unless, of course, the English authorities can do
for them, what they confessedly cannot do for themselves, namely,
find them ingenious arguments whereby to defend England without appearing to do so.

The realities behind these bland but hardly promising words
were even more depressing. A month of the new session had
elapsed before the opposition had produced any serious contribution to the subject of foreign policy—even in respect of its
developments in central Europe, leaving aside entirely the question of England. The new deputies had already incurred the
wrath of Mallet du Pan, who was meantime publicly reproaching
them for their supine negligence of the common interests of European civilization.[2] It is true that Mallet had been badgered to

[1] Ibid. In the phrase 'as they have followed the same line of conduct with
respect to other states', *they* apparently means the Directory.

[2] Mallet du Pan's *Lettres à un membre du Corps Législatif*, published in the
Quotidienne, end May–June 1797. Mallet had already predicted that the new
deputies, and the moderate public which they represented, would be dazzled
and silenced by the conquering peace which the Republic was now in a position to dictate on the continent (to Ste Aldegonde, 29 April, in Sayous, op.
cit., tome II, p. 300). In the first of the *Lettres*, he savagely condemned Bonaparte's cynical assault on the Venetian Republic, and turned to upbraid the
French legislature for allowing itself so tamely to be fobbed off with a bland
official apologia for the crime. In a subsequent *Lettre*, he dealt in a similar
manner with the feeble attitude of the Councils towards the French sub-
version of the Republic of Genoa. 'Est-ce là, se dit-on..., ce corps législatif

U

write his *Lettres à un membre du Corps législatif* by certain deputies who wished to stir the question of the unprincipled imperialism of the government, and wanted public discussion of it before they opened their campaign.[1] But these deputies must have felt themselves to be both few and untypical in their own country, if they had felt it necessary to seek the aid of a famous foreign journalist to rouse the national consciousness on the subject before themselves venturing to speak on it. In fact, it was only with Dumolard's famous discourse of 5 messidor (23 June), denouncing Bonaparte's piratical attack on the Most Serene Republic,[2] that any branch of the opposition seriously confronted this subject; and Dumolard's attack does not seem to have owed anything, either to D'André or to his legislative collaborators.[3] Moreover, Dumolard's initiative cannot even be said to have given rise to a belated turn of serious attention to this subject on the part of the opposition speakers generally.[4] The most evident effect of his speech was to inflame the already formidable enmity of the generals against the opposition.[5]

---

qui s'annonçait avec un éclat consolateur, et qui devait ramener sur la terre paix, justice et bienveillance?' Extracts dealing with these parts of his subjects are given in Sayous, tome cit., pp. 302–6.

[1] Mallet to Ste Aldegonde, 1 July, in Sayous, tome cit., p. 313. Dumolard was presumably one of these deputies; the *Lettres* were addressed to him, and it was he who, on 23 June, finally launched a philippic against the conduct of the Republic towards Venice.

[2] Lefebvre, *Directoire*, p. 82.

[3] It will be remembered that Dumolard was a member of Dumas's group, though he was one of those who had refused, after the disconcerting turn taken by the elections, to return to alliance with the Directory. D'André, in his letter to Wickham of 27 July, described Dumolard and his friend Pastoret as dominant figures at Clichy, who gave themselves out to be Royalists, though they were, in fact, merely men of ambition. It is quite clear that D'André did not reckon Dumolard in the number of his 'friends'.

[4] It is true that Pastoret supported his friend Dumolard, and that they procured the establishment of a legislative commission of enquiry into the issues of foreign policy which had thus been raised. But this was practically the end of the subject.

[5] Dumolard's outburst was one of the causes which gave rise to Bonaparte's proclamation to his Army on occasion of 14 July, with its open menace of military intervention against the 'Royalists', and to the even more violent addresses subsequently adopted by various divisions under his command. It also probably helped to induce Hoche to lend his support to the Triumvirs in the (abortive) plan for a *coup d'état* against the legislative opposition in July, and

We need not feel surprised that D'André's friends in practice left unfulfilled his promises that they would exert themselves in the interests of 'other states'. Even if they seriously wished to take up these issues, they must have seen weighty reasons for withholding their words. The French people certainly longed for peace; but peace, at least on the continent, seemed already as good as assured when Austria bowed to the dictates of Bonaparte at Leoben. How much support, even in the legislature, would D'André's friends have had for an effort to repudiate the moral implications of the peace which the conquering Republic was now in a position to impose? Such an attitude would have seemed un-patriotic, and (in view of the feelings of the Army on the subject) positively dangerous, as the case of Dumolard showed. And we can be even less surprised that the friends of D'André never travelled beyond promises, and heavily conditioned promises, in respect of the interests of England. It seems hard to believe that most of his party can ever have cherished sincerely helpful inten-tions towards England. Not only was it, as D'André admitted to Wickham, extremely embarrassing to appear to espouse, in a French assembly, the cause of a powerful, traditional, unscrupu-lous, often victorious, but now (as it appeared) defeated enemy; it is surely doubtful whether D'André's allies really wanted to overcome this difficulty. Had not Wickham himself, in a 'moment of truth', grasped the fact that if there was one element of com-mon feeling among the French, from the Jacobins to the pure Royalists, it was enmity towards England? And, at best, was it not asking rather too much of French anti-Republican politicians, to ask them to promote an object (peace between the Republic and Great Britain) the success of which was more than likely to deprive them of English financial support in their own unfinished battle with the Directory?

We need not go into further details on these subjects here; it will suffice to say that D'André continued to assure the British envoy that whatever could be attempted in the field of foreign policy should indeed be attempted, and that Wickham retailed these assurances to the Foreign Secretary as he anxiously watched the negotiations at Lille; the envoy achieved, indeed, towards the

---

to inspire the menacing addresses adopted by the troops under Hoche's com-mand, in style similar to those from the Army of Italy.

end, a more realistic view of what could be expected as a result of such promises.[1] As for D'André, whatever efforts he made to satisfy the demands of Wickham on these points were made, to all practical purposes, in vain.

It may be argued that the legislative opposition was, in a more indirect and tacit manner, making a very real and effective contribution to the curtailment of the Directory's foreign policy throughout the session, by attacking the spending power of the Republic and by undermining in many ways the domestic prestige and security of the regime. It may be urged that the effect of these policies would, but for the occurrence of the Fructidor *coup d'état*, have been to disarm and paralyse the Republican government, long before they completely destroyed it, and that this process would have been, was already becoming, as fatal to the Directory's foreign policy as to every other branch of its policy. There is an element of truth in these arguments. It is true that the conduct of the opposition, for all its shortcomings of incoherence and lack of *suite*, presented a formidable difficulty to the governing party, and that if the opposition had been able to continue indefinitely with its policies of financial strangulation and political

---

[1] In his draft, Most Secret no. 22 of 1797, to Grenville, Wickham repeated the assurances of those who direct the 'Influence at Paris', that everything possible shall be done to induce the government to adopt a more moderate attitude in the conduct of foreign relations, and in particular to agree to peace with England. But the envoy now expresses his own expectations in these matters in the following very significant terms: 'It would be as unwise as dangerous to attempt any direct motion to . . . compel the Government to agree to peace with Great Britain . . . in either of the two Councils. It seems far better . . . that the Directory should live, as it now does, from day to day, in the dread of such an attempt, than that it should discover the weakness of its antagonists by the utter impossibility in which they would find themselves, of conducting such a motion to any precise determinate end . . . If the two Councils, supported by the cry of the whole people, are yet too weak to punish the Directory for such a wanton violation of the Law of Nations and of the constitution of their own country (*as*) . . . the affair of Venice and Genoa . . . it would be too much to hope that any effort (allways excepting such arguments as are drawn from the wants and miseries of the people in France, the frequent use of which I constantly recommend) made in favour of an open enemy could obtain even a patient hearing, particularly when all the national prejudices are taken into consideration, and when it is recollected that a very considerable party, I mean that of the pure Royalists, consider peace with England . . . the most fatal blow that could befall them.' This draft is dated 27 August.

sabotage, the results would have compromised its position on every side, even though the regime still escaped overt destruction. But the ruling party never permitted matters to reach this stage; and, at the point of the Fructidor *coup d'état*, the foreign policy of the regime had not suffered any actual set-back at the hands of the opposition. The Directory's financial embarrassments were real enough at home, but they had not yet affected the operations of its diplomacy or of its forces, and the Army of Italy, especially, had long been living at the expense of occupied areas and even winning new financial assets for the government. Indeed, Bonaparte, by breaking Austria's resistance before the session of year V began, had effectively anticipated any early possibility of the opposition's organizing decisive financial pressure against the expansionist tendencies of the regime.

As has been admitted, everything would indeed have changed if the opposition had been allowed indefinitely to prolong its efforts to enfeeble the government on every side at once. But, precisely because the Triumvirs realized that not only their foreign policy, but all their policies and indeed the very survival of their regime were eventually at stake, they could not and did not allow these threats to develop further. To suppose, as did both Grenville (at least at one point) and Wickham, that it might be possible for the opposition to hamstring the foreign policy of the Directory even though it could not, in any near future, attempt the radical destruction of the regime, was to posit a half-solution which was in practice unattainable. If the opposition had been able to criticize the foreign policy of the Triumvirs more persistently and more directly: if they had been able to bring more drastic financial pressure to bear, it is hard to see that this could have had any effect at all. The opposition were already doing quite enough to make it obvious to their rivals that everything was at stake. No doubt the opposition would have been only too pleased to be allowed to go on mining and sabotaging the regime at their own pace, until it collapsed almost of itself. But if the Triumvirs chose, as they did choose, to resist the slow extinction planned for them by the opposition, the latter would no longer be able to carry on the battle at their own leisurely pace, but would have to face the clear issue of immediate and complete success or immediate ruin. The aggressive external system of the Republic could in fact be halted and reversed only by the complete overthrow of the party which directed it. If the opposition had been able to destroy the government outright, either at the crisis of July or at the moment of the Fructidor *coup d'état*, then there would doubtless have occurred also a revolution in French foreign policy; though it would hardly have been inspired by any good feelings towards England. On no other conditions could there have been any change in French foreign policy.

It was, then, a game of 'all or nothing' which was engaged at Paris during the middle and close of the summer. If, in the negotiations at Lille and at Udine respectively, Pitt, Grenville, and Malmesbury, Thugut and Cobenzl, played a waiting game and spun out time, the contingency which justified their conduct was not the possibility that the Councils would succeed in forcing the Directory to be more moderate in its foreign policy, but the possibility that, in the much more deadly encounter which was engaged, the opposition would unseat the Triumvirs.

If these arguments are well founded, it follows that Wickham, in urging D'André and his friends to act against the foreign policy of the Republic, even if they could not as yet overtly attack the Republic itself, had been asking them not only to attempt a difficult and embarrassing task, but to attempt an impossible task. The Republican government and its foreign policy were inseparable. If D'André had been able to push his friends further along the lines which Wickham so strongly recommended, he would only have been wasting still more of his time and attention.

X

Towards the 'Explosion'

WAS there any real chance that the truce, painfully and pre-
cariously established at the end of July, could be maintained? Meynier, following Thibaudeau, considered that the Triumvirs would genuinely have abandoned their intention to make
a *coup d'état*, if only they could now have recovered, on adequate
terms, the alliance of the independents of the centre.[1] The independents would have had to give the Triumvirs security against
any further measures of reaction in the legislature, and agree to
the full re-establishment of the laws of brumaire. On this basis,
the Triumvirs might have been willing to spin out time until the
approach of the elections of year VI, when they would naturally
have reappraised the situation in the light of developments which
had occurred in the interval. But the independents were not
willing, at least in sufficient numbers, to lend themselves to this
compromise. They distrusted the ulterior intentions of the Right
as much as ever. But their distrust and dislike of the Triumvirs had
also been greatly enhanced by the recent threat of a military *coup*
against the Councils, and the addresses from the Army, illegal by
their very nature and suggesting that the danger of a military
stroke was by no means at an end, kept alive all their suspicions.[2]
The independents could find nothing better to do than to scout
the offers of both sides, to retire into a virtuous but negative and
despairing neutrality. Thereby they destroyed whatever chance
there was that the Triumvirs would seriously observe the truce.

But perhaps there was never much chance of this, even if the
independents had been willing to try it. Perhaps early in August,
when the truce was still in its infancy, Barras received, through

[1] Meynier, *Le 18 Fructidor*, pp. 192–3; cf. Thibaudeau, *Mémoires*, tome II,
pp. 242–50.

[2] Thibaudeau, tome cit., p. 250. The addresses from the Armies are
illustrated in Buchez & Roux, op. cit., tome 37, pp. 326–9. The addresses
formed a proper subject of legislative complaint, since by the Constitution
(art. 274–5) the armies had no deliberative capacity; moreover, the matter involved libels against the Councils.

the Prince de Carency, that corrupt and shifty son of the now dis-
graced Prime Minister of the exile, La Vauguyon, detailed evidence of the structure and progress of the *Institut philanthropique*.[1]
The Triumvirs thereby lost all conceivable motive to spin out
time. The Royalist conspiracy must be smashed, both in head and
in members, before it achieved such a grasp on the country that it
was invincible.

It only remained for the Triumvirs, then, to choose afresh both
the moment and the machinery of the *coup*. And, even when the
truce was in being and there was some doubtful chance that the
Triumvirs might decide to persevere in it, it is a fact that they
never altogether abandoned the stance of men who intended to
draw the sword. Hoche and his troops, for all the natural misgivings of the opposition, duly marched away. But the Triumvirs
never took any steps to prevent the adoption of menacing addresses by the Army; they were widely suspected rather of in-
citing them, even of manufacturing them.[2] And as early as 8
August they seem to have reverted with firm intention to their
decision to make a *coup*, for on that day they appointed Augereau,
who had been sent to Paris by Bonaparte with the addresses of
the Army of Italy, to the command of the 17th Division, in the
territorial area of which the capital lay; and Augereau became in
the event the military director of the *coup d'état*.

Two days later (23 thermidor, 10 August) the Directory sent a
message to the Five Hundred, which was little less than a justification of the *coup d'état* before the event. The executive message pur-
ported to reply to fresh questions, raised by the already once more
anxious Council, on the old topic of Hoche's march and on the
newer issue of the illegal, offensive, and disturbing military addresses. It offered no new explanation of Hoche's march, but it
boldly apologized for the addresses from the armies, as being
morally, though not legally, justified, by the spectacle of the
counter-revolution rampant throughout the country; and it implied not obscurely that the good patriots of the armies rightly
held the legislative opposition responsible for this state of things.[3]
From this time onwards, the governmental party hardly took

---

[1] Meynier, op. cit., pp. 193–4, citing Barras, *Mémoires*.

[2] Buchez & Roux, tome cit., p. 319. Thibaudeau, tome cit., pp. 240–42.

[3] The portions of the Directorial message dealing with the military addresses are given in Buchez & Roux, tome cit., pp. 323–5.

pains to disguise the intention to save the Republic by force.
Thibaudeau came away from a conversation on 15 August with
Benjamin Constant, Talleyrand, Debry and Poulain-Grandpré
quite convinced that this was its intention.[1] And, from that same
date, visible signs of the impending coup began to appear. Small
detachments of troops and artillery, on various pretexts and more
or less furtively, made their way into the city. Chérin, a close
friend of Hoche, was appointed commander of the Directors'
guard.[2]

It is clear then that D'André's recent protests, that the truce
would turn out to be a trap, and that the opposition, even though
it could not rise to a decisive challenge to the government, could
certainly not afford simply to relax, were soon highly justified by
events. D'André had also predicted that too many of the non-
Directorial deputies would prove unable, or even unwilling, to
act realistically. Here again, he was to be proved right.

It is easy enough to explain, in general terms, the reactions of
these deputies to the immensely difficult situation in which they
found themselves during the last four weeks of this tragic session.
The danger, which had only so recently been conjured away, now
seemed to be once more looming before them. They had no resources of physical force actually in being. Could they unite in a
consistent and constructive policy, either to ward off the danger,
or to defeat their rivals if things reached a clear issue? There were
two obvious difficulties in their way. On one side, it was hard to
feel quite sure that a governmental *coup* was certainly impending
—until it was too late; and meantime there was the formidable
risk that any efforts they might make to ward it off might in fact
precipitate it. On the other side, the difficulty which they had in
reaching agreement on this issue of tactics was intensified by their
lack of agreement and cohesion in so many other respects. As has
been remarked already, they were united in little except reproba-
tion of the existing Directory and its policies. They had throughout been divided among themselves as to their ultimate purposes,

[1] Thibaudeau, tome cit., pp. 248–50.
[2] Lefebvre, *Directoire*, pp. 86–7. On 18 August, D'André in a note to
Wickham refers to the transfer of cannon from the artillery park at Meudon
to the Ecole Militaire. On 21 August, Wickham warns D'André that Bonaparte is detaching troops to Paris, 'tous habillés en bourgeois'. On 24 August,
D'André advises Wickham that 1,200 troops have entered Paris the previous
night (Wickham Papers).

lacking in agreed leadership and mutual trust, sadly wanting in discipline. Accordingly we are not surprised to find that during the last month of their session they presented a broken front, and an incoherent response to the situation. Some tried to convince themselves that the danger was illusory; others felt that ruin was so probable that it was useless to imagine safeguards; some thought it best to disarm the Triumvirs by avoiding provocation to them; many who admitted the need for a careful, consistent and masterful policy nevertheless disagreed as to what that policy should be. A generally accepted leadership was the crying need of them all, yet they resented any effort which was made to supply it.[1]

The last point, in particular, deserves expansion. Out of the crisis of July had emerged at least a possible organ of collective leadership, in the commissions of Inspectors of the Halls, who were charged with arrangements for the good order and security of the two Councils. After the July crisis, these two inspectorates, sometimes acting jointly, tried to provide a general lead to the Houses. But their colleagues spoiled the chance by jealously insisting on frequent renewals of the membership of the inspectorate; only Pichegru ('a sort of perpetual President', as Wickham puts it) was allowed an agreed permanence, and Pichegru, as was finally proved very conclusively during these weeks, had no great gifts of political leadership. In these circumstances, the inspectors seldom reached a common mind even among themselves, despite the efforts of Pichegru and of D'André to 'influence' them.[2]

[1] Even when the opposition could be brought to agree on measures in the Five Hundred, it was far more difficult to ensure their endorsement by the Elders, where the voice of the moderates was decidedly more influential. See the bitter comments of De la Rue (*Hist. du 18 fructidor*, 1821, pp. 284–6), on the obstruction offered in the Elders to measures adopted in the Five Hundred.
Wickham, in a draft for Lord Grenville, 18 August, observed that there was reason to fear much worse of the moderates than flabbiness and timidity; once the immediate crisis of Hoche's march was past, it was only 'the perseverance of the Directory in . . . outrageous and insolent conduct' which 'prevented the majority of the Antients . . . from throwing themselves again into the arms of the Government'. In a draft of 27 August, Wickham credited one of the most influential of the moderates there, Tronçon Ducoudray, with a definite attempt to arrange a reconciliation between the Government and the opposition as a whole (Wickham Papers).
[2] Wickham to Grenville, Most Secret No. 20, 18 August. D'André himself, in his surviving letters to Wickham, hardly alludes to the Inspectors or to his own relations with them.

We are fully prepared, then, to discover that during the last
fatal month the Councils became, for all the efforts of a few determined and clear-sighted men to prevent it, little more than discordant talking shops. Wrangling and abortive discussion usurped
the place of action, and the sands ran out leaving them hopelessly
unprepared when the crushing blow descended.

D'André, still giving his chief attention to the management of
the Five Hundred, was one of those who laboured to work out a
policy for the legislature and to secure its adoption. He acted in
close collaboration with a small company of deputies, with
whom he had only recently been brought into touch: Pichegru,
Willot, for whom, on account of his *activité* and *montant*,
D'André soon professed an admiration even greater than he felt
for Pichegru, and Imbert Colomès.[1] Of these three, only Imbert
had been a member—occasional, at that—of the 'committee'
with which D'André had worked at the beginning of the
session.

Our immediate task is to analyse the contribution which
D'André made to the building of a policy for the Councils, and to
illustrate his comments on the fortunes which befell his collaborators and himself. To begin, we shall recall that at the beginning
of August, when D'André accepted the apparent restoration of
provisional 'calm', he envisaged that the Houses should make
good use of the time they had gained, by pushing on a series of
measures, involving a middle course between two extremes. On
one extreme, it was to avoid a merely negative relaxation of effort.
On the other, it was to avoid an immediate bid to impeach and
outlaw the Triumvirs. Positively, the object of these measures
was to be twofold: to erect effective barriers against a further
attempt at a *coup* by the government, and to ensure the decisive
success of the Royalist cause at and after the next elections. Among
the measures which he mentioned, D'André included the re-
embodying of the *compagnies d'élite* of the National Guard, the
transfer to the Inspectors of the Councils of full powers of police
throughout the city, complete freedom of re-entry and movement
for the émigrés, and a ruthless application of financial stringency

[1] D'André in his reports to Wickham at this period more than once groups
together the names of these men in terms which clearly imply that it was with
these that he now chiefly consorted. He also refers to them individually with
warm appreciation. See his letters of 16, 22 and 26 August.

against the government.[1] We can perhaps conveniently refer to this range of measures, and to others mentioned later by D'André and conceived in the same intentions, as the interim programme.

Now during the month preceding the *coup d'état*, D'André, working in close conjunction with his chief allies, mentioned above, did in fact give sustained attention to the achievement of this programme. And the question at once recurs—for we have already touched upon this point—whether this interim programme was wisely undertaken. When D'André first announced this programme to Wickham, he presented it as a course well suited to conditions in which the crisis had, at least provisionally, receded, and 'calm' had been restored. And we criticized it in passing, on the obvious ground, that if the opposition then seriously wanted to spin out time until the next elections, and to reduce as far as possible the obvious risk that the Triumvirs would soon once more resort to a solution by violence, this was a most unlikely means of achieving the opposition's aim; for such a programme involved 'sapping and mining' the regime even faster, even more obviously, than ever, and was therefore likely to encourage the Triumvirs to return to the policy of violence, rather than to keep them quiescent. But this objection to the interim programme no longer applies with anything like the same force from about 10 August onwards. Those who then continued to promote it have obvious justification, at least in the objective court of history. From that point onwards, it was clear that the *détente* between the governing party and the opposition was hollow indeed; the Triumvirs were almost openly displaying an intention to recur, at the earliest opportunity, to the use of force. D'André and his allies, in pressing the interim programme further, could hardly

---

[1] D'André's reports to Wickham include no mention, at this time, of the financial weapon; but Wickham, in his draft, Most Secret No. 22, 27 August, declares that 'very direct intimations have been given to the Government of the firm intention of the Assembly to grant no more *effective* supplies for continuing the war . . . every opportunity has been taken by several leading members to express their opinion upon that point in the most plain and unequivocal manner'. In a draft (No. 24) dated 6 September, but written of course before he had news of the *coup d'état*, Wickham claims that 'even those of the moderate party who are supposed to be most favourable to the Directory continue firm in their resolution of granting no further effective supplies'. He refers in particular, in this connection, to Tronçon Ducoudray and to 'Thibeaudeau' (Wickham Papers).

make the Triumvirs more hostile to the opposition than they already and openly were. The opposition had nothing to lose; and there was a chance, though in our eyes it must appear a faint one, that by pressing on with certain of the interim measures, it might have saved itself. If the Councils could have contrived to secure the formation of the *compagnies d'élite*, and the effective police of the city, before the three Directors were able actually to make the military *coup*, the Directors would probably have flinched, after all, from the difficulties which their blow would then have involved.[1]

But it is another question how far D'André is *subjectively* entitled to this justification of the further pursuit of the interim programme. For, from about the middle of August, that is to say very shortly after the governing party cast aside any hesitation it may have had, and determined to proceed with the *coup*, D'André formed the rather surprising conclusion that the Triumvirs were *not*, by any means, determined to do this. We must be very careful not to misrepresent D'André in this matter. He never doubted that the hostile Directors were *preparing* such a stroke; what he came to disbelieve was that they had the resolution, and indeed the unanimity, to translate their preparations into act. And again, D'André did not, obviously, reach this opinion because he shrank from facing the worst and became a victim of 'wishful thinking'; he was genuinely misled by reports which he was receiving from the Luxembourg. Barras, he understood, was impatient to proceed to the *coup*; but the other two were effectively deterred by anxiety over the outcome. It was not the case that the opposition had as yet secured the measures which might seriously have embarrassed the government's plans; the law to re-form the National Guard reached the statute book on 12 August, but it still had to be put into effect (and, in fact, the executive struggled successfully to defer this until it was too late). But D'André believed that Reubell and La Revellière were unnerved by the extra-legislative activities, which he and other opposition leaders were now—successfully, as he believed—pursuing: rousing the long timorous respectable public of Paris to active support of the opposition, enlisting and

---

[1] Wickham to Grenville, no. 24, 6 September: '. . . from the moment . . . the National guard . . . shall be in a state, the Directory will be incapable either of a blow against the Councils, or of preventing the . . . elections from taking place . . . If therefore the Directory act offensively at all, it must be immediately.'

arming men, in advance of the National Guard, to fight for the
Councils if it came to force. He thought, in fact, that two of the
Triumvirs feared the hour was already too late for their purpose.
They would fall back, he supposed, at a later stage, on an attempt
in some way to avoid the legally due elections; but for the immediate future, there was little chance of a governmental *coup*,
and their menacing behaviour was largely stage thunder. And to
this estimate, D'André adhered until the very end of August,
when the evidence that a *coup d'état* was, despite all this, impending
became too plain to be put aside.[1]

That D'André's estimate was wrong is evident enough, though
it can fairly be said that his erroneous belief in the timidity of two,
at least, of the Triumvirs was shared by important members of the
Councils, by Wickham (whose information did not come only
from D'André) and by Mallet du Pan.[2] But this is not, for us, the

[1] On 12 August D'André spoke of his efforts to galvanize the opposition
into enacting such measures (of the interim programme) as the assumption of
the police of the city, and the suppression of the Police Ministry; and he commented forebodingly: 'les bons Députés promettent de le faire. *Mais le tems
leur manque.*' But this note of foreboding thenceforward disappears from his
reports till almost the end of the month. On 16 August he was looking forward, without great misgivings, to the elections of year VI. On 18 August, he
observed that the legislature must now make a distinct choice of alternatives:
either to 'attaquer vigoureusement' or to 'louvoyer prudemment jusqu'aux
elections prochaines'. The precise meaning of these alternatives need not concern us here; the immediate point is that D'André was now no longer contemplating an attack by the Triumvirs on the Councils, but an attack, if any,
by the Councils on the Triumvirs. In the same letter, he explains his change
of front: 'Ce qu'il y a de certain, c'est que le Directoire paroit effrayé. Barras a
inutilement tenté il y a deux nuits de faire faire un coup de force. Les deux
autres, moins audacieux, ont craint avec raison le résultat.' Only in a report of
30 August did D'André accept the probability that a governmental *coup*
might, after all, be imminent.

[2] Wickham, informed by others besides D'André, declared about the middle of August that some of the best informed Deputies shared D'André's
doubts about the likelihood of an early appeal to force by the Triumvirs;
Wickham himself cherished some doubt whether 'a resumption of active
hostility' could 'be staved off for as long as . . . both . . . factions desire'; but
he certainly had no clear prevision of what was so soon to happen (Wickham
to Lord Grenville, Most Secret no. 20, 18 August). Near the end of August,
Wickham observed again: 'The same uncertainty and timidity continue to
mark the conduct of both the Councils and the Directory, the nearer one
views both the one and the other, the more one is persuaded that these are
not the men before whom the House of Austria ought ever to have trembled'

main point at the moment; what matters in our argument is the
inference, which surely imposes itself: while D'André believed
that the Triumvirate was in fact *not* resolved to strike, his pursuit
meantime of the interim programme is once more exposed to
grave objection; for to pursue that programme in these circumstances could only encourage the government to master its fears
and nerve itself, after all, for the blow. Prudence surely required
him, and all those members of the opposition who shared his estimate, rather to slacken the pace of legislative proposals, and thus
maximize the temptation of the government to leave well enough
alone. If the Triumvirs, or two of them, really feared the opposition was already too strong to attack, the best means of keeping them in that state of mind was surely not to rouse the more
dangerous fear, that the opposition would soon grow strong
enough to attack the government.

But there is evidence that, during this same period, the second
half of August, D'André was pushing boldness even further. He
was not content to pursue the interim programme. The aggressive
instinct, which he had with difficulty repressed at the beginning of
August, seems now once more to have reasserted itself in his
normally cautious and realistic mind. It appears, indeed, that
D'André's sense of caution, so obvious in circumstances where he
was able to think calmly and disinterestedly, was wont to play him
false in the midst of exciting and provoking events. He now
cherished the hope that, if the legislature could once be fairly embarked on the tasks of the interim programme, it would prove
possible, thanks to the support of a now friendly and excited public, to screw up his party—despite all its shortcomings—to an
even more 'intense'[1] pitch of action—to an immediate and direct
counter-offensive against the Triumvirs.[2]

(to Grenville, 27 August). Mallet du Pan's impression, in mid-August, that
the Directory was afraid to strike, is recorded in a letter to Ste Aldegonde
(Sayous, op. cit., tome II, p. 316).

[1] 'donner plus d'intensité à notre parti dans l'Assemblée' (D'André to
Wickham, 28 August).

[2] Reporting to Wickham on 16 August, D'André observed that the full attention of his party ought to be given to ensuring that it 'lived through'
(parvenir) to the elections of year VI. Though he now thought an early attack
by the Triumvirs unlikely, there is nothing in this letter to suggest that he
contemplated a direct attack by his own side. On 18 August, however, he not
only asserted that the Triumvirs seemed afraid to attack the Councils, but

Here again, it must be said that other leading spirits on the side
of the opposition shared this idea; it is indeed quite as possible
that D'André received it from others, as that he originated it.
Mallet du Pan, about the middle of the month, reported a plan,
among the *gens de bien* of the Councils, which was presumably the
very same as D'André hoped to see: to propose a decree against
the Triumvirs, and, in the same stroke, to place Pichegru in the
saddle for a grand gesture of appeal to the people, and for a
spontaneous effort to 'emporter le Luxembourg de vive force'.
Once again, if D'André erred in cherishing this design, he erred in
company.[1]

---

abruptly revealed that he was now working to push his party into a bold
offensive against the government. 'L'Opinion publique se prononce de mieux
en mieux... et si l'Assemblée vouloit agir, elle seroit certaine d'un puissant
secours. Je suis sans cesse aux trousses des Députés. Mais les uns croyent
qu'ils n'auroient pas la majorité pour des mesures vives, les autres qu'il faut
laisser le Directoire attaquer le premier. Je n'ai rien à dire contre la premiere
objection, si ce n'est que la majorité va où est la force. Quant à la seconde, je
ne pense pas comme eux, et je crois que quand on a une force suffisante, il y
a un grand avantage à attaquer les premiers... Je voudrois que l'Assemblée
prit un de ces deux partis: ou d'attaquer vigoureusement et pendant que nous
avons le vent, ou de louvoyer prudemment jusqu'aux Elections prochaines;
mais il faut qu'on se décide bientôt pour l'un des deux, car la marche à suivre
est absolument différente, soit au dedans, soit en dehors de l'Assemblée...
Chaque jour je distribue des fusils en mains très sures... tout cela n'est qu'une
mesure de précaution, et pour soutenir l'Assemblée si elle veut agir.'

Such expressions as '*attaquer* vigoureusement', 'attaquer les premiers', 'si
L'Assemblée vouloit agir', etc., can, in these contexts, hardly refer merely to
efforts to enact and apply the interim programme; they must appertain to
something much more ambitious and decisive even than that. It seems, rather
—taking into account the whole drift of D'André's remarks to Wickham
during these weeks—that it is 'louvoyer prudemment', which means 'to vote
the interim programme, but go no further', while 'attaquer vigoureusement',
etc., means to attempt a direct and frontal attack on the Triumvirs.

As late as 26 and 28 August, D'André still cherished plans for provoking
this 'vigorous attack', and the hope of placing the *honnêtes gens* who were to be
its supporters in the streets 'dans une telle mesure qu'ils *ne puissent reculer*'.

[1] Sayous, tome cit., pp. 317–21. Mallet attributed such a plan to Pichegru
himself and to Willot, among others; here he was misinformed, as appears
from D'André's letter of 26 August to Wickham (see p. 303 below). Nevertheless, Mallet is not likely to have been entirely unfounded in believing that
such a design was canvassing among the men of the Right. Mallet added that
it was the inability of the *gens de bien* to carry with them the wavering moderate leaders, such as Thibaudeau, Emmery, and Vaublanc, which doomed these
hopes to frustration.

But that he did, once more, err, is surely beyond question. If he cherished this plan at all, then it follows that there would have been little point in weighing the wisdom and unwisdom of the interim programme, for the interim programme was evidently to be nothing more than an interruptable curtain raiser for a piece of far more urgent dramatic quality. But all our instincts of political sense revolt against this. The interim programme, considered by itself, made perfectly good sense—always provided that the Triumvirs would tolerate its passage and application. There, of course, lay its peculiar difficulty. But to plan a sudden switch from an interim programme on which progress had hardly begun, to a direct parliamentary and popular onslaught on the Triumvirs, was to throw away all the advantages which the interim programme *might*, with luck, have yielded, and to accept mortal battle with the Triumvirs in conditions in which all the advantages were likely to be still on their side. Granted that D'André now felt that he was winning important successes in his campaign to enlist the active support of the *honnêtes gens*, to recruit and equip a private opposition force, and to suborn Republican units to the side of the Councils, it seems clear enough that on a realistic estimate, the support to be expected from these quarters would be nothing like the support which a more prudent policy could have anticipated from the *élite* of the National Guard, reconstituted, not simply on paper but in reality, and embodied for long enough to have found some degree of cohesion, discipline and steadiness.[1] And to achieve these conditions would have required several months. Again, the interim programme involved the attempt to secure control by the Inspectors of the whole police of the city,

---

[1] Wickham, in his despatches home, showed a far more realistic appraisal of the importance of the National Guard. On 18 August, after expressing his own doubts whether it would be possible to 'stave off . . . a resumption of hostilities' very long, he commented: 'In that case, *provided the explosion do not happen . . . before the guard of the Councils be formed* (Wickham's marks of emphasis) it is my firm and entire persuasion that the popular party will be successful.' And he expressed, though without naming 'Berger'—or indeed anyone else—his misgivings of 'some imprudent and premature attempt by the Royalists'. On 7 September (when it was in fact too late) Wickham addressed to D'André some very weighty words about 'l'époque ou les Compagnies de Grenadiers et de Chasseurs de la Garde Nationale seront en état d'agir': 'c'est le moment, selon moi, qu'il faut saisir comme le pivot sur lequel tout doit tourner, et celui vers lequel toutes vos opérations doivent être dirigées'.

x

which again involved the abolition of the Police Ministry, necessarily the creature of the government,[1] and the removal of Republican units which the government was once more furtively bringing into the city.[2] And these measures would have been a matter of
very great advantage to the opposition, if it came to a trial of
strength with the Triumvirs. But, at the time when D'André
began to press once more his plan of an immediate stroke against
the government, this great advantage was as much a paper project
as the re-embodiment of the National Guard; it required time, not
only to enact its necessary conditions, but even more to bring it
into actual effect.

Even more basic is the objection that D'André, and the other
exponents of an immediate bold stroke, had no serious reason to
hope that the mass of the non-Directorial deputies would agree to
join in such a seizure of the initiative. If these deputies, with all
their suspicions of each other, their different hopes for the future,
and their want of common organization, could ever have been
placed at a point where, on the one hand, they knew beyond doubt
that the Triumvirs were launching a *coup* against them, and where
they had, on the other, a clear opportunity to take drastic action to
prevent that *coup*, it is certainly to be supposed that they would
have united to carry a decree against the three Directors. They
might well have felt that they had nothing to lose, and everything
(perhaps) to gain, and have wielded their weapon with the courage
born of desperation. But it was not for this kind of reaction that
D'André (and others) were now pressing. They wanted the deputies to pass a decree against the Triumvirs on presumption, and
seize the initiative for their own side. Yet D'André himself, during

[1] As recently as 12 August, D'André had expressed his anxiety that 'les
bons Députés' should secure legislation on these points, Wickham Papers,
bundle 67. In his Most Secret no. 20 to Grenville, Wickham referred to the
'common committee' of the ablest and best members of both Councils (i.e.
the two Inspectorates) as having the prospect of absorbing 'the whole police
of Paris into their hands' (18 August).

[2] On 26 August—in the midst of his plans to bring about a *vigorous attack*
on the Triumvirs—D'André adverted to the need to secure this element of
the interim programme: 'Ensuite nous travaillerons à renvoyer tout à fait les
troupes, qui seroient déja dehors sans la défection de Vaublanc. Nous allons
travailler du moins à faire supprimer l'Etat Major de la 17eme. Division.
C'est un coup de parti que je tacherai de conduire avec prudence, mais qui ne
pourra gueres avoir lieu que dans trois ou quatre semaines' (Wickham Papers,
bundle 67).

the earlier crisis, had correctly judged that they were incapable of
such a step; and at this very time, they were dawdling endlessly,
even over the various prearranged measures of the interim programme, and driving D'André and his collaborators nearly to despair by their lack of business and energy.[1]

For all this, D'André seems to have clung with a hope that was
beyond reason to the plan to push the Right into a *grand coup*.
We see him pestering some of the deputies of the Right to make up
their minds to 'a vigorous attack'; and even when these deputies
replied that there would be no chance of rallying the legislative
majority behind such a course, and that it was better to leave the
initiative in mortal combat to the other side,[2] D'André's only reaction was to pour out to Wickham the solemn reflection that the
deputies really must make up their minds whether or not to
'attaquer vigoureusement pendant que nous avons le vent', since
the planning of legislative strategy greatly depended upon the
choice they made: as though they had not already, repeatedly and
clearly made known what their choice was.[3]

It is a fact of considerable interest that although D'André's
hopes of a *grand coup* by the Councils were shared by some few of
the deputies of the Right, they were not shared by the three men
with whom he was now most closely connected.

Le Général Willot est, ainsi que le Général Pichegru et M. Imbert
Colomès et autres, d'avis que, les moyens d'attaque étant trop peu de
chose, et ceux de defense tout au plus (*suffisans?*) au danger, il faut
louvoyer jusqu'en Germinal, et d'ici là nous serrer de plus en plus.[4]

It is no surprise to learn that this was the attitude of Pichegru,
who had leaned on the side of caution during the crisis of July and
in the doubtful days which had followed; though there is something rather wry in the thought that the general whom some
wanted to hoist into the saddle at the critical moment was himself
opposed to the whole scheme which involved that act of glory. It

---

[1] D'André complained bitterly of these things throughout the second half
of August. Sometimes his grievance is that he cannot induce the Deputies to
follow up the measures of the interim programme, sometimes that they will
not listen to the case for a *vigorous attack*; on one or two occasions it is uncertain which, but it is always clear that the Deputies are far below whatever is
expected of them.

[2] D'André to Wickham, 18 August.

[3] Ibid., 18 August.   [4] Ibid., 26 August.

is rather surprising, however, to find his cautious attitude shared
by such bold adventurers as Imbert and Willot; and their view of
this question speaks more loudly than that of Pichegru of the
hopelessly impracticable nature of the scheme which D'André so
much longed to see attempted.

It is fair to add that, much as D'André hoped for and pressed
for the expedient of the *grand coup*, he realized clearly enough that
his wish might not be fulfilled; and he was prepared throughout
to acquiesce in the alternative, that the opposition should, as he
put it, 'louvoyer prudemment', or 'filer le cable', 'jusqu'aux Elections prochaines'.[1] By these phrases he meant, not that the opposition should simply lie low, and attempt nothing, until the
Elections of year VI, but rather that it should work away at the
interim programme, without however seeking an opportunity in
the meantime to try decisive conclusions with the government.
This was, in effect, the policy of his three chief allies.

---

[1] D'André uses the expression 'filer le cable' in his letter of 28 August. In
that same letter he restates the alternatives, which he had said lay before the
opposition in his letter of 18 August; and on this latter occasion, he is evidently more than half resigned to the probability that the Deputies will prefer
to follow the line of the lesser risk: 'la patience et la longanimité doivent être
notre partage.'

It is, moreover, a fact of great interest, and deserving the strongest emphasis
here if not in the text, that D'André himself sometimes realized, even in the
midst of all his concern with the interim programme and with the more
ambitious and incompatible plan for a *vigorous attack*, that the best and wisest
course was different from either of these, and consisted simply in pressing on
with the development of the *Institut*, the infallible means of winning a crushing success at the elections of year VI. Only two days before writing the
report of 18 August, with its evident *penchant* for a *vigorous attack*, D'André
had observed: 'Je persiste toujours à penser que rien n'est meilleur que
l'Institut, parce qu'il nous fait travailler avec sureté; et que si on nous laisse
le tems d'arriver en Germinal, l'effet est immanquable. Tous... (*nos*)... efforts
doivent tendre à... parvenir... (*aux*)... Elections, et d'ici là à serrer et à coaliser les honnêtes gens' (16 August). In the same letter, he claimed that the
work of the *Institut* was still absorbing a very large share of his own attention
('les Voyageurs, et l'immense correspondance').

It seems, however, very ironical that D'André, formerly the great exponent
of a 'long-term' policy and the great adversary of sudden and risky attempts
at complete victory, should at this stage have given only intermittent attention to the *Institut*, and devoted so much more of his effort to the impossible
policy of *vigorous attack*—at the very time when it was, precisely, the progress
of the Institut which was finally inducing the Triumvirs to drop their last
scruples and make a *coup d'état*.

In discussion and effort of these kinds, the last few weeks before the *coup d'état* ran swiftly and fruitlessly through. Then, at the end of August, an abrupt change came over the attitude of all those concerned with the fortunes of the opposition. The stroke of military power, long since envisaged, constantly expected by some, discounted as a serious danger by others, was at last generally felt to be absolutely imminent. D'André and his friends now attempted the only possible course, short of outright surrender: to rally the Councils in an effort, no longer to take the initiative against the government, but to anticipate the initiative of the Triumvirs against the Councils.

But before we can follow the fortunes of D'André and his colleagues in this, the final phase of the strange story, we must first gather up the material which remains regarding D'André's activities outside the legislature during these closing weeks. Here we shall find matters of importance for the history of the time, as well as details of interest in the career of D'André.

We shall recollect that during the crisis of July and the uneasy lull which followed, D'André had reported efforts which he and his friends were making, to mobilize public support for the Councils, and to gather the nucleus of an armed force to fight their battle if battle became immediately necessary. D'André had also, at that time, shown interest in the possibilities of winning over Republican soldiers to support the Councils rather than the government. Moreover, we recollect that when, on 3 August, D'André had rather reluctantly agreed with Pichegru to abandon the idea of an immediate bold stroke by the legislature against the government, the two leaders had also agreed that work of this kind must be continued, as a necessary defensive precaution against an early resumption of the government's plan for a military stroke.[1] During the following month, activities of this sort were in fact pushed on; and when the *coup d'état* was finally recognized to be imminent, the opposition, though still lacking the resources of the National Guard, did nevertheless have some means —though they proved to be totally inadequate—of meeting force with force. D'André's reports to Wickham during August give some impression of the progress which was made.

On 10 August, D'André confessed in desponding terms the difficulties which he was experiencing; and incidentally this letter

[1] Ch. VIII, pp. 264–7.

is in itself a sufficient comment on the imprudence of the scheme
which he had latterly cherished, and which he was so soon to take
up again, of attempting a bold initiative against the Triumvirate.
The Paris public, he wrote, received his propaganda with 'frighten-
ing apathy'; he had enlisted only five hundred volunteers in the
city; he was equally short of arms; the allies who had been summoned from the provinces, 'petits chouans', were troublesome
supporters, 'anxious only to scrap' or, still worse, to frame plans
for mad adventures in order to attract funds.[1] D'André, even at
his most bellicose, thought as a politician, not as a militarist
adventurer; physical force must be prepared, but only to back up
the decisions of the legislature, and it was always, for him, an
instrument subordinate to the direction of political authority. He
was seriously afraid, however, that the *chouans*, backed by the
formidable authority of de la Trémoille, would take the bit between their teeth, brush aside the politicians, and turn his long-
matured plans for the capture of the Republic by its constituted
authorities into a vulgar and futile guerrilla *putsch*.[2]

Soon, however, D'André found himself able to cherish much
more optimistic views of these matters. The apparent dearth of
small arms yielded to persistent search; 20,000 cartridges had
already been manufactured.[3] Propaganda produced more encouraging results, both among the public and with Republican
units,[4] near and far.[5] Police agents dismissed by Cochon's successor were recruited by the Inspectors;[6] D'André's own activities

---

[1] '... un tas de petits chouans qui ne veulent que guerroyer. Ces gens, qui
n'ont pas de soldats, présentent sans cesse des plans militaires pour attraper
de l'argent.' A number of the best known *chouan* leaders were now in fact
at Paris: besides La Trémoille, there were Frotté, Bourmont, Autichamp, La
Rochejaquelein, etc. (De la Rue, *Hist. du 18 Fructidor*, p. 288, note).

[2] D'André to Wickham, 18 August: 'Vous savez que mon système n'est pas
de former une armée, ni toutes ces sottises d'état major, mais que nous devons
attendre notre salut des autorités constituées...' 14 August: 'La Tremouille...
s'est jetté entre les bras de ces petits Chouans qui ne veulent que plaie et
bosse, et qui ne voient de succès qu'au bout de leur épée.' Cf. 10 August: 'Ce
qui me fache c'est Monsr. de la Tremouille qui me paroit avoir donné dans
leur sens' (i.e. 'dans le sens des petits chouans').

[3] D'André to Wickham, 12 and 10 August.   [4] Ibid., 14 and 18 August.

[5] Ibid., 14 and 22 August. The reference in the former letter to the fact that
D'André and his friends 'had no one with the Army of Italy' seems to imply
they *had* 'someone' with *other* field Armies of the Republic.

[6] Ibid., 10 August.

in enlisting and arming volunteers began to move faster.[1] The *jeunes gens* became bolder in the war of scuffling,[2] and towards the end of August D'André claimed that they had won it.[3] D'André subsequently claimed that his party had, by the date of the *coup d'état*, secured the armed services of a thousand auxiliaries (five hundred *jeunes gens*, five hundred *chouans* and émigrés) as well as those of five hundred Republican troops.[4] These claims can to some extent be confirmed by independent evidence.[5]

Needless to say, Wickham gave D'André his warmest support and best assistance in all this. He exerted himself to speed up the full settlement of D'André's arrears for the month of July, and to ensure a more prompt payment of the subsidy for August.[6] Before the end of August, he had, much to D'André's advantage and ease of mind, achieved both of these objectives. 'Finances . . .' wrote D'André on 26 August, 'vous n'aves pas l'idée de l'aise et de l'indépendance ou vous me placés en mettant cet objet au courant.' Wickham also confirmed the arrangement which he had made towards the end of July, whereby D'André, with Pichegru's concurrence, could draw up to £50,000 in emergency.[7] D'André, who did not believe that the Triumvirs really meant to use force, repeated his former gesture and declared that he and Pichegru could not foresee the necessity to use this fund. With the prompt payment of the monthly subsidies, he reiterated, he would be perfectly content.[8]

Such remarks help us to appreciate the extremely modest scope of the preparations for the use of force, upon which D'André and his allies were now engaged; and, in view of what was soon to occur, we must naturally raise the question whether D'André would not have been wiser to spend British funds more lavishly on the recruitment and arming of auxiliaries, and on the winning

---

[1] Ibid., 18 August.   [2] Ibid., 16 August.   [3] Ibid., 28 August.

[4] D'André's claims on these points are quoted by Pariset, op. cit., tome II, p. 346—from a document which does not appear to be included in Wickham's papers at Winchester. Note that no more Parisians were enlisted.

[5] De la Rue, op. cit., p. 294 says, that General Willot, the evening before the *coup d'état*, gave 'stand-by' orders to the *jeunes gens* and officers who had agreed to defend the Councils, and that these numbered between 1,200 and 1,500 men.

[6] Wickham's draft to D'André, 15 August.

[7] Ibid., 16 and 24 August.

[8] D'André to Wickham, 26 and 18 August.

over of Republican officers. Probably it would have made no difference in the outcome, for when the government's blow was descending, the cause of the opposition failed because of faulty leadership on the side of armed action, before it had even a chance of failing from an insufficiency of armed support. Nevertheless, it seems clear that there would have been a hopeless insufficiency of armed support, had the leadership been effective in the highest degree. What, after all, could have been done with fifteen hundred men, even under the most clear-sighted and fortunate direction, against the force then commanded by Augereau? It seems difficult to resist the conclusion that D'André and his friends had worked on far too small a scale,[1] and that D'André's claims of growing success in these undertakings, in the second half of August, must be interpreted in the light of that fact. There is evidence, indeed, that before the end came the opposition belatedly realized that they had not attempted enough in these respects. D'André reported that they were speeding up their efforts to arm the *honnêtes gens;*[2] Rovère and other deputies were, rather pathetically, collecting subscriptions to pay for the establishment of a 'police'.[3]

But, if D'André was involved in miscalculation here, it does not at all follow that he carries the chief blame. It was, surely, for Pichegru and Willot to form the estimate of the numbers of men which the opposition should try to enrol; if they had given D'André a more realistic and more timely idea of the appropriate target, there is no reason to doubt that he would have been willing to spend, and demand, larger British funds for these purposes. There is, however, no evidence that the Generals ever tried to convince their paymaster that more should be done. And there is a little evidence, in D'André's correspondence with Wickham, which suggests that Pichegru was sadly lacking in energy and initiative, even in these things which properly pertained to him as a military man.

Pichegru naturally made himself responsible for negotiations

[1] De la Rue (op. cit., p. 294) claims that the leaders of the good cause had more than ten thousand men at Paris who were willing to be called, over and above the 1,200–1,500 actually alerted; but this seems suspiciously vague and grandiose.

[2] D'André to Wickham, 28 August. 'Nous travaillons avec plus d'activité ... à connoitre ceux qui doivent armer les bons citoyens.' The phrase seems rather obscure, but its general bearing is clear enough.

[3] Thibaudeau, tome cit., p. 263.

with promising Republican officers. It seems that towards the middle of August, Pichegru's aide-de-camp sent a message to Wickham, advising him that Pichegru had no funds with which to carry on this work, but could not bring himself to mention to D'André anything so indelicate as his need of money.[1] Wickham was horror struck, for he felt that it was chiefly to the winning over of Republican troops that the opposition ought now to look.[2] He obtained Pichegru's own confirmation of this startling news, and then addressed to D'André the following urgent admonition:

Il me semble que vous aves manqué de perdre ici le *plus puissant de tous vos moyens*. Il faut donc, cette lettre vue, en ménageant la délicatesse de Pichegru, lui remettre quelques fonds, en l'exhortant à les employer pour le travail en question. Le meilleur de tous à mon avis.[3]

D'André replied, in terms of probably sincere surprise:

Ce n'est pas ma faute si Baptiste n'a pas tout ce qu'il lui faut en fonds. Je vais tacher de lever cette difficulté de mon mieux.[4]

And a little later he reported that he had advanced 1,500 louis to the General—all that he could spare for the moment.[5] But it was then the third of September. In the light of this correspondence, we can only wonder what exactly Pichegru was really good for. If it were really a sense of delicacy which deterred him from asking D'André for funds for this work, on the importance of which both were agreed, this would be quite sufficiently discreditable to Pichegru; for such delicacy would be evidence only of extraordinary weakness of mind. But one cannot help supposing that 'delicacy' was not the real reason, but only an excuse, and that the real reason was simply inertia and lack of grasp.[6]

[1] Wickham's draft to D'André, 26 August.

[2] The British envoy had often been allured by hopes of gaining over a substantial Republican force; now that D'André's plans for the capture of the legislature had run into difficulties before they were fully ripe, these hopes readily sprang up again in his mind. In a draft to D'André, 15 August, Wickham congratulated D'André on his now cordial relations with Pichegru, and reflected: 'C'est par cet homme que vous arriverés le plus surement aux troupes.' He added, at the conclusion of this letter, 'Les troupes! les troupes! Tout dépend des troupes!' [3] Wickham's draft to D'André, 26 August.

[4] D'André to Wickham, 1 September. [5] Ibid., 3 September.

[6] De la Rue (op. cit., p. 289, note) asserts that Pichegru (for whom he felt unbounded admiration) was achieving great things in this matter of winning over Republican forces, apparently without any question of bribery being involved: he says that about a week before the blow fell, Pichegru showed him

In an attempt to be perfectly fair to the opposition leaders, we must add that they were throughout under the impression that they could be sure of one body of Republican soldiers, without need for complicated negotiations involving considerations of cash. This, of course, was the Guard of the Councils, which they confidently and not wholly unreasonably expected to stand by the authority which it was specially under orders to protect.[1] It is only too clear that Pichegru and Willot made a sad hash of things on the fatal night when they allowed themselves to be arrested *in the Tuileries* (naturally the first objective of Augereau) instead of placing themselves at some point not known to the enemy and thus safeguarding the opportunity to rally their armed supporters round them.[2] But the Generals made this capital blunder partly in the mistaken belief that the conciliar Guard would ward off, at least for a time, any violence which might be attempted at the Tuileries. Unfortunately for them, this belief was proved to have no foundation; the Guard made no attempt to defend the site of the legislature, and even suffered meekly the arrest of its own commander Ramel. A few hours later the victorious Triumvirs kindly received a deputation of these troops, and allowed them to return to duty, to stand guard over the miserable rump which the three Directors now allowed to masquerade as the legislative body of France.[3] But, having stated this extenuation for the leaders of the opposition, it is difficult to say how far it seriously benefits their case. Was it not their business, the business of Pichegru and Willot especially, to make quite sure that the Guard could be trusted to stand by the Councils, before risking their safety, and

---

a letter from one of the 'leading generals', who disposed of 30,000 men, and who declared himself ready to march to the aid of the good cause in the Councils at the first appeal. This 'leading general' was, one supposes, Pichegru's friend Moreau. In fact, this incident illustrates the uselessness of Pichegru rather than anything creditable to him. Granted that the other General sincerely meant what his letter promised, how could Pichegru build serious hopes on a promise of aid from an army far distant, against a danger on the spot and likely at any moment, and without warning, to be realized? Unless, indeed, Pichegru had taken steps to ensure that detachments of this army were made available *in advance* of a stroke by the Triumvirs; which there is no reason to think Pichegru had taken, or was able to take.

[1] De la Rue, op. cit., p. 289, *init.*

[2] Ibid., pp. 295–7 and note to p. 296.

[3] Pariset, tome cit., p. 346.

the whole remaining chances of their movement, on the supposition that its loyalty and steadiness were certain?

As for D'André's fears that his party's *chouan* allies would get out of hand and seek a solution in violence too early, these fears were natural, but as the event proved quite unnecessary. There seems to have been far more bark than bite here; on the night of the *coup d'état*, when Pichegru and Willot had been eliminated, the *chouans* would have had a good opportunity to indulge their taste for independent action, and for desperate encounters; but they did not take it. Perhaps while we are at this point we may go on to explain the outcome of D'André's kindred fears about the Prince de la Trémoille. Wickham gave D'André sympathetic and careful advice about this problem, which D'André in fact acted upon. Wickham assured him that he was 'morally' certain that the British authorities, in extending recognition to the Prince as the French King's chief representative in the interior, had not intended to countenance any interference by the Prince with the operations with which D'André and Wickham were concerned.[1] He encouraged D'André to resist, if it came to the point, any such interference.[2] But he also counselled him to try to win the confidence of the Prince by personal attentions, and predicted that D'André would by this means win as much influence with de la Trémoille as his *chouan* adviser Frotté had hitherto had.[3] Everything fell out exactly as Wickham proposed; before the *coup d'état*, D'André enjoyed excellent relations with de la Trémoille, who, so far from trying to dictate to him, was glad to have his advice.[4] Thus, if the

[1] Wickham to D'André, 8 August.

[2] Ibid., 8 August.

[3] Wickham to D'André, 8 and 15 August.

[4] D'André to Wickham, 22, 24 and especially 30 August. The mission of La Trémoille was not the only embarrassment which the Court of Blankenburg brought upon D'André during the closing weeks of his ill starred venture. The Court revived its earlier plan to establish at Paris a formal Council, to direct all the Royalist operations there, and to subordinate to itself the activities of all its servants in the interior. (Wickham's draft to Grenville, Most Secret No. 23, 27 August; Wickham to D'André, 15 August, and D'André to Wickham, 22 August).

Moreover, it appears that the Blankenburg Court was now expressing dissatisfaction with D'André, and causing him irritation and anxiety by its seeming lack of confidence in him. See his outpourings to Wickham on this subject in his report of 24 August. D'André, though worried and vexed, declined to haul down his flag: 'Berger... prouvera par ses oeuvres et par le

Prince was of no help to D'André and his party in their final trial, he was at all events no cause of additional difficulty.

The review of D'André's interests outside the legislative arena, which we have now attempted, forms a well-matching counterpart to our immediately previous discussion of his interests within it, during the same four weeks. The reports of this single man of course do not present a complete and undistorting image of the whole political scene; but there is no doubt that they embody a substantially true portrayal of the contemporary position and prospects of the opposition, both in the Councils and beyond. And they portray a scene which is, despite the sanguine and combative temper of the man who wrote them, depressing in the last degree. Whatever grounds for hope D'André may have found in that scene, to us it presents all the possible auguries of certain ruin for the cause of the opposition. There are some revolutions in history, of which, despite all the distorting influences deriving from our knowledge of how the event actually turned out, we cannot help remarking how strange it seems that the winning side should in fact have won; that the odds seem to have been all in favour of the losers. The event of 18 fructidor is most conspicuously not one of these. It is all too obvious that the legislative opposition was virtually defenceless before its enemies. Its nominal majority in the Councils counted for little indeed, since its internal divisions, want of cohesion and lack of agreed plans even to deal with the immediate tactical situation rendered that majority almost a fiction. And, even if the majority had indeed become the united force, agreed at least on the destructive aspect of its pro-

témoignage d'Imbert et de Pichegru, que non seulement il a fait beaucoup, mais que s'il y a quelque chose de fait, c'est lui qui l'a fait... Berger est décidé à faire parler les faits pour lui, et à n'en parler que par eux.' Wickham replied (31 August) with words of praise and encouragement; he supported D'André to the end against all comers.

It may be that D'André had at least an exaggerated impression of the exiled Court's displeasure towards him; for, whereas D'André in the letter of 24 August had complained, among other things, of the fact that the exiled Court had sent him no powers, Wickham, in a draft to D'André dated 7 September, referred to D'André's 'nouveaux pouvoirs', as now available to be shown to certain of the moderate Deputies, to lend greater authority to D'André's arguments to win them over. The powers, then, which D'André had so recently said had significantly been denied to him, had in that short interval been granted.

gramme, which D'André had hoped to make it, it would still have needed much more than parliamentary votes—even of impeachment or of outlawry—to win the battle against military power, which was now being forced upon it. It would have needed resources of physical force far greater than it actually boasted, and it would have needed military and insurrectional leadership of a quality different indeed from that of Pichegru.

What is to be our judgement, then, of the combative and hopeful spirit which D'André kept up despite all the evil auguries which accumulated round him? It is, perhaps, at this stage that we can best attempt to construct a general judgement of the political qualities, and defects, which D'André had displayed during the period covered by this study. The materials for this judgement are already before us. It is clear that D'André's talent lay chiefly in the fields of political criticism and (what we may call) political strategy at the high level. His analyses, in 1796, of the political condition and tendencies of France, of the weaknesses of the Republican regime and of the lines along which Royalist policy should accordingly be directed, were, though not entirely original, nevertheless strikingly discerning and realistic. His planning, in what we have called the 'great design', involved the combination of many ideas and expedients, which, once more, he cannot be said to have produced entirely from his own head. But he certainly brought to the work the gifts of careful and versatile elaboration; and he combined its elements together in a logical, coherent, and promising manner. We can, surely, with confidence attribute to him the qualities of a great chief of general staff.

In the tactical execution of a political design, however, it is equally obvious that D'André was much less gifted. It is true that, when the 'great design' was actually attempted, D'André had to face the consequences of serious misfortunes not of his making. In particular, a 'coalition of parties' built upon only an ambiguous programme produced disappointing and perplexing results, largely because of the blunders, both past and persisting, of the Pretender and of the more *intransigeant* pure Royalists. The chances of success were (it may be) still further diminished by D'André's inability to lead his party in the legislature. But making allowances for such misfortunes as these, the fact remains that D'André does not show to unmixed advantage in the tactics of the campaign. His powers of political criticism certainly did not wholly desert him; he recognized clearly enough the weaknesses of his party in the Councils, and the almost insurmountable difficulty presented by the attitude of the independents. But D'André, once on the scene of operations, proved himself to be not only a political analyst and a careful planner, but also a man of almost unlimited devotion to success, a man to whom disappointment and failure were almost intolerable, a man of immense combative and aggressive spirit. Such qualities are not, in themselves, disadvantageous in a politician. But in the situation with which D'André had to deal they were of doubtful benefit, either to the cause he was trying to serve, or to his own reputation. His reason and his will to success dragged him in opposite directions, and in this conflict it was his will to success which prevailed. It led him, against the verdict of his own critical judgement, twice over to push his party towards a decisive initiative against the Triumvirs, despite its moral inability to sustain this role, despite the uncooperative attitude of the independents and despite the almost complete lack of physical force on the side of the opposition. It led him, after the July crisis, to a strange and inconsistent use of what we have called the interim programme. It presumably helped to form his oddly unrealistic view of the extent of armed assistance which his party would require in the event of a final crisis, however that crisis might be reached: though, as has been remarked above, the generals on the side of the opposition do not seem to have given him any help to escape from this strange delusion.

Being to this extent the victim of an over-wilful and over-ardent temperament, D'André was clearly not an ideal leader in the tactical execution of his own design; and we cannot but reflect that his failure to secure election, and consequent inability to assume the public and responsible leadership of his party in the Five Hundred, may not, in fact, have been the great misfortune for his cause, which he naturally felt it to be. Yet, though all this has to be said, the impression remains that his persistent courage and over-optimism in the face of a situation so difficult and discouraging has about it something that is rather splendid; and though his policies were often in themselves unworkable, it may well be that his general influence had some good effect in the counsels of his party, and helped to give it such sense of direction, such energy and persistence as its character and circumstances permitted.

For all his tendency to overboldness in the tactical sphere, D'André appears in another respect to have suffered rather from undue timidity and diffidence. He seems to have had little confidence in his personal influence over other individuals, and little also in his ability to judge their characters. An obvious instance is his attitude towards the Prince de la Trémoille. He gave himself (until he was prompted thereto by Wickham) no opportunity to judge the Prince by personal experience, still less to influence him, but accepted a rather defeatist attitude towards him, which was founded on nothing but second-hand reports and his own natural fears. More important for the outcome of the work on which he was engaged was D'André's behaviour with the military men of the opposition. Here, his diffidence and passivity in personal dealings united with his excessive overconfidence in political matters to rob him of the chance of rendering an important service to his cause. D'André's original impression of Pichegru was unenthusiastic, and to this extent it was sound enough. But, instead of pursuing his first impressions, and testing them by close personal observation, D'André surrendered himself, with very little further evidence, to the popular view, which was also that of Wickham, that Pichegru was the ideal leader for the hour of action: modest and retiring, perhaps, but competent to all occasions and deserving unlimited trust.[1] Towards the end, it seems that D'André's misgivings about Pichegru began to revive.[2] But he did not act on them, and it would in any case have been too late. It would have been better by far if D'André had followed his own earlier judgement, and worked, both on his own collaborators and with Wickham, to secure the relegation to the background of this singularly shallow and inept military adventurer. It would have been better still if D'André had meantime discovered someone else, professional soldier or otherwise, who might have filled

---

[1] e.g. D'André to Wickham, 22 August: 'Vos Réflexions sur Pichegru sont extrêmement justes. Je me rapproche de lui de plus en plus. Ses principes et sa conduite sont conformes aux miens, et c'est un grand bonheur pour nous d'avoir cet homme.'

[2] On 26 August, D'André told Wickham: 'Je suis extrêmement content de... Willot... Je vous assure que dans certains moments il vaudroit mieux que le Général Pichegru. Il a plus d'activité et de montant.' No direct criticism of Pichegru is involved, but the *certains moments* are evidently the moments for 'action', and the implication is clear that D'André felt Pichegru to lack something on this side.

more effectively than Pichegru the place of the man of action. D'André might then have spared his party the unwisdom of trying to face Augereau and his troops with only a handful of men, and the fiasco of its military leaders' arrest before that handful could be brought into action. But D'André found no such man, does not seem even to have contemplated looking for him, further than the obvious, but by no means good choices, Willot and Imbert; and these behaved rather as seconds to Pichegru than as his supplanters.

It now remains only to follow the events of the closing days, and to relate to these the final reflections and efforts of D'André. At the end of August, the impression began to force itself upon the minds of all concerned, that the government was indeed about to strike. 'Il était difficile,' says Thibaudeau, 'de ne pas... voir partout le présage... d'une très-prochaine explosion... L'orage s'annonçait par l'état de l'atmosphère politique.'[1] Behind the feeling, there were facts: on 10 fructidor (27 August) La Revellière, in an address to delegates of the Cisalpine Republic, openly threatened action against 'the enemies of the Republic';[2] on 30 August, the troops in the metropolitan area embarked on military exercises, which seemed the natural and obvious cover for an impending operation inside the city.[3] As early as 29 August, the fear had gained ground among the deputies of the Right that the Triumvirs would strike in the hours of darkness and arrest eighty of the members in their beds, when resolutions of impeachment and decrees of outlawry would be out of the question. On that night, a similar number of the opposition deputies assembled together, in order to frustrate this purpose, at the house of Imbert Colomès. They planned that, if any hostile attempt were in fact made, they would at once take to horse, summon their prepared auxiliaries, appeal to their wider, though as yet unorganized, public support, and march boldly against the Luxembourg. D'André refers to this development in a note of 30 August.[4]

In this note, D'André no longer discounts the danger of a *coup*

[1] Thibaudeau, tome cit., pp. 260–61.   [2] Lefebvre, *Directoire*, p. 87.
[3] Thibaudeau, loc. cit. supr.
[4] 'Toute la nuit 80 Députés de bon coin ont été assemblés chez Imbert-Colomès. On nous menace d'une attaque pour la nuit prochaine. Ils seront encore assemblés, et nous prêts. Si le Directoire tente quelque chose, nous attaquons le Luxembourg, et j'espère...'
Cf. Mallet du Pan to Gallatin, 5 September: 'Le Directoire . . . projette

d'état; and he regards the conduct of these deputies, so far as it goes, with approval. But, in his opinion, it did not go far enough. The deputies were, apparently, leaving the initiative strictly to the other side. They would fight (physically) if attacked; they did not contemplate any attempt to anticipate the hostile act of the government, probable as they thought it, by an act of the legislative body. This did not satisfy the ex-Constituent. He had great faith in the power of legislative thunder at the vital moment, and this faith inspired him now. To borrow the expressions of Mallet du Pan, he thought that to raise the city against the Triumvirs, it would need a 'decree' as well as 'Pichegru';[1] and that the deputies should have been exercising their vigilance and energy, not simply in preparations to take to horse, but also in the legislative halls. This, again, appears from his note of 30 August. Unlike the mass of his own party, he still hoped, against evidence, that it would be possible to win over a sufficient number of independents, to vote the adoption of permanent session, and to place the Councils in a position to fulminate a decree against the Triumvirs at the first sign of illegal violence. He says, in that note, that although verging on despair of the deputies, he had nevertheless worked with some success upon Emmery, and now hoped that this well-known member (one of the Inspectors at this time)[2] would agree to make a solemn denunciation of the 'infâme discours' of La Revellière, and thereby give a decisive impetus to the independents. No doubt D'André hoped that the Councils would then agree to sit in permanence and would rise, at last, to their proper stature.

Though most of the deputies, both of the right wing and of the centre, seem to have lacked faith in the possibility or value of this, a small number of them, especially some of those who then occupied the function of Inspectors of the Five Hundred, were thinking in terms similar to those of D'André; and during the last few

l'enlèvement nocturne de quatre vingt députés... Depuis le 29, ces députés menacés découchaient,... réunis dans une maison' (Sayous, tome cit., p. 319). Mallet added: 'Ces députés se tenaient prêts à monter à cheval et à rassembler leur monde,' pp. 319–20.

[1] Mallet remarked in his letter of 5 September, cited above, that 'un décret et Pichegru entraîneront nécessairement la masse, et décideront l'engagement s'il a lieu' (Sayous, tome cit., p. 319).

[2] The Inspectors of the Five Hundred at that moment were Pichegru, Thibaudeau, Vaublanc, Emmery and De la Rue. De la Rue, op. cit., p. 291.

days he worked with these to give effect to a variant form of his own design.

The immediate author of this, the last plan which the opposition was ever able to form, appears to have been De la Rue. One of the Inspectors at this time, De la Rue had hitherto scouted any suggestion that the Councils should fire the first shot, unless there were definite evidence that the Triumvirs were in the act of proceeding to violence.[1] But on 14 fructidor (31 August) De la Rue received information from the other camp, of an 'alarming and positive' kind, which seemed to him to be sufficient evidence that the Triumvirs were in fact in that situation.[2] He felt that the independents and the waverers would find this evidence convincing, and that the Right therefore should and must present it to the Houses, and make a great effort to capture a majority, and vote drastic measures to anticipate the blow. He proposed to his fellow Inspectors, Pichegru, Vaublanc, Emmery and Thibaudeau, that they should present a report, embodying De la Rue's secret information, to the Five Hundred.[3]

However little chance we may think this proposal had of final success, it was surely well worth attempting. Here was a situation in which even the non-Directorial deputies of the year V should have found it possible to agree, and to use their power of legislation to some really decisive purpose. There was evidence—of less than certain value, it is true, but still evidence which appeared to confirm the meaning naturally attached to the ominous signs now accumulating—that a *coup d'état* was indeed actually being prepared. It had come from the hostile quarter to one of the Inspectors. Why should this not have been enough to galvanize the ragged ranks of the anti-Directorials into an energetic bid to destroy their enemies, and to save themselves? And, granting that a decree of impeachment, or of outlawry, might not alone suffice to rout the hostile array; granting that the independents still felt the gravest suspicions that they might hereafter find themselves in the hands of an excessive reaction—still it was better, surely, to run all the risks involved with these points than to wait helplessly for the ruin of the constitution and the unlimited triumph of the Three and of the Army. And there was (with good fortune) still time for the Inspectors to present their evidence, and to ask for drastic measures.

[1] De la Rue, p. 289.   [2] Ibid., p. 291.   [3] Ibid.

De la Rue and his colleagues talked cautiously over his plan. They decided to follow caution as far as they possibly could, and to wait a little longer, for further and more precise information of the Triumvirs' plan, which De la Rue had been promised.[1] Presumably Vaublanc, Emmery and Thibaudeau were all extremely anxious to make as sure as possible that a *coup d'état* had indeed been arranged, and that they were not being made the victims of a Right wing manoeuvre. Nevertheless they agreed that, so soon as De la Rue's further warning arrived, they would without delay present a report to their fellow deputies. Vaublanc was selected to present it, expressly because he seemed the man best fitted to make an effective appeal to all sections of the legislature, outside of the government's party.[2] They also agreed to embody in the report three distinct and practical propositions: that the Councils should go into permanent session, that all the troops latterly called to the area of Paris should be placed under the commander of the legislative Guard, and that the Directory should be summoned to explain its recent suspicious conduct.[3] It will be noticed that they did not propose to include an accusation against the Triumvirs—another concession to caution, but still there might yet have been time to attempt that if the Directors refused explanations.

What mattered much more than the precise proposals to be embodied in the report was the decision to wait for further details of the government's plan before presenting it. In fact, De la Rue's further information came to hand only on 17 fructidor (3 September). It was quickly followed by a further report, that the government had actually given the fatal orders to its troops.[4] Whatever the reasons may be, it is clear that the Inspectors now completely mismanaged the situation. Vaublanc's report was not ready for immediate presentation, if only because it lacked the new information which had only just come to hand. The Inspectors attempted, it seems rather feebly, to persuade the Councils to prolong the session of that day, so that his report might be read that same evening.[5] No one, it seems, was prepared to improvise the last touches of the report on the spot, and to make a valiant attempt to drive the Councils into immediate action. Nor can the appeal for a prolongation of that day's session have been very clearly or

[1] Ibid.   [2] Ibid.   [3] Ibid., p. 293.
[4] Ibid., pp. 291-2.   [5] Ibid., p. 292.

cogently expressed. The Councils closed their sittings without sign even of serious attention to the hints of the Inspectors.[1] The Inspectors consoled themselves by deciding that Vaublanc should present his report the next day, and that, in view of the grave character of the new information, he should ask for nothing less than a decree of impeachment against the three Directors.[2] But the next day, in that sense, never arrived.

D'André's last note to Wickham before the *coup d'état* was written on the same day as the Inspectors unsuccessfully tried to prolong the session so that Vaublanc's report could be read that evening. D'André does not mention, in his few and hasty lines, the plan of the Inspectors; but it seems clear that he knew of it, and he certainly expected the resolution to sit in permanence to be adopted that day—the more so in view of the fact, which he mentions, that the Inspectors' observers in the city had now been arrested: 'Cela nous amenera vraisemblablement aujourd'hui la permanence. L'explosion s'approche... Je me rends à la salle.' There can be no doubt that he went to the hall still hoping and planning for 'great measures'.

Of course he, like the Inspectors, was doomed to disappointment. And that disappointment did not arise only from the attitude of the independents; the deputies of the Right were by this time in a state of moral collapse. Only a few days before, they had felt that a *coup* was almost certainly imminent, and they had been ready to remain assembled, at least privately, and to resist the *coup* on horseback if not in the legislative chambers. But by 3 September, both their sense of the danger and their courage were ebbing away. Their belief in the reality of the danger had faded, no doubt because day had succeeded to day and the attack had still never been made. In these conditions, they had started to clutch at hopes, founded on counter-reports purporting to originate with Carnot, that no *coup d'état* was after all intended. When, on 3 September, more alarming reports were abruptly renewed, they went to pieces completely. Some declined to believe that the danger was any more real than the earlier threats had been: others fell into simple panic. Not only would they take no strong line during the meeting of the Houses, they cut an even sorrier figure when they met that evening, for the last time as it proved, at the house of Imbert Colomè. De la Rue urged them to demand a special session

[1] De la Rue, p. 292.   [2] Lefebvre, *Directoire*, p. 88; Pariset, tome cit., p. 345.

and hear Vaublanc without delay; their reaction was strongly negative. Moreover, it seemed doubtful to De la Rue whether they were prepared even to remain assembled and ready for action that night, in case (as his information suggested) that was to be the night of the attack. They finished, in fact, for the most part unwilling either to vote or to fight, half believing there was nothing to fear, and more than half convinced that, if there were, it would be useless trying to resist it.[1]

A mere handful of the men of the Right tried to face the contingencies of the night (3-4 September) with realism and activity. Willot and his aide-de-camp Angibault alerted and prepared the auxiliaries enlisted by D'André to meet force by force.[2] Pichegru, though his attitude at this last moment seems to have been characteristically less than clear—he professed nearly a certainty that the attack would not occur *that night*, though there were already plain reasons for thinking that it would[3]—was nevertheless prepared to do something; he made a tour of inspection in the city, and decided to keep vigil, in case his hope of a quiet night should nevertheless be disappointed, in the Inspectors' room at the Tuileries. There, he was eventually joined by about a dozen deputies, including Willot. But the only effect of this was, as has already been remarked, to secure the elimination of the military leaders of the opposition before they could bring their armed followers into action. They seem to have been taken completely unawares by the advance of Augereau's troops (which implies that they had made no adequate preparations for a timely warning) and their trust in the legislative Guard proved to be quite misplaced.

About the same time, D'André and a few other bold spirits of the opposition set out to do what the military leaders of their party could no longer do, and what most of their parliamentary friends had no heart to attempt: to rally the armed strength of their side, and make a fight of it. It is not surprising that this last

---

[1] On all this, see De la Rue, p. 293, and the comments of Thibaudeau on the curiously confused state of mind of the Right wing Deputies, especially during these last few days, *Mem.*, tome II, pp. 263-5, 267-8.

[2] De la Rue, p. 294 and note.

[3] Ibid., pp. 295-6. It is only fair to point out that De la Rue himself—the very man who had received the secret information of the Directory's intentions—was also inclined to believe that the stroke must have been postponed at the last moment, since the city was so quiet.

desperate gesture proved another deflating failure. The government troops had carried out, with complete success, a masterly design. They had silently entered the city, closed the barriers, seized the Tuileries and the surrounding areas. The walls were plastered with the government's proclamations.[1] The deputies were, for the most part, conspicuous by their absence. It is not wonderful that only about a dozen of D'André's auxiliaries responded to his call.[2]

For D'André there now remained only to attempt a furtive escape from the city, and the country, which he had re-entered with hopes so high little more than six months earlier. In this, at least, he was to be successful.[3]

[1] Pariset, tome cit., p. 345.

[2] Ibid., p. 346: citing, as remarked above, a document by D'André, which does not appear to be included in Wickham's private papers.

[3] D'André's next notes to Wickham are dated from Berne, in November and December of that year. They give no particulars about his return journey to Switzerland, nor his views on the final episodes of the fiasco in which all his efforts had ended.

Bibliographical Note

Something has been said about the scope, and the documentary bases, of this book in the Preface and the Introduction. The object of this note is only to supply in convenient form the necessary bibliographical details of the sources and references upon which I have chiefly relied.

Unpublished material

'The Private Papers of the Right Honourable William Wickham' (property of Lady Bonham Carter of Binsted Wyck, near Alton). The Papers are deposited at the County Record Office, Winchester. The following references must be noted:

(a) Correspondence with M. D'André, bundle 67.

(b) (Draft) Dispatches to Lord Grenville, (1795) bundle 20; (1796) bundle 22; (1797) bundle 29; Correspondence with Lord Grenville, bundles 21, 25, 27.

(c) (Original) Dispatches from Lord Grenville, (1795) bundle 26; (1796) bundle 23; (1797) bundle 24; Lord Grenville to Mr. Wickham, 1795, bundle 28.

(d) Correspondence with:
    Mr. Bayard, bundle 64
    the King of France, 1796, 1797, bundle 60
    Count d'Avaray, 1795–7, bundle 69
    Le Duc de la Vauguyon, 1796–7, bundle 94
    MM. Brottier & Duvergne, bundle 105
    Mr. Imbert Colomes, 1795–9, bundle 104
    General Pichegru, 1796–9, bundle 83
    M. Mallet du Pan, 1794–9, bundle 79

Published sources and references

References are given, where available, to the published version of parts of Wickham's correspondence, edited by his grandson as *The Correspondence of the Rt. Hon. William Wickham*, 2 vols., London, 1870.

The following correspondence and memoirs of contemporaries have been extensively used, sometimes as sources, and sometimes as providing useful illustrative material:

DE LARUE, CHEVALIER I.-E., *Histoire du 18 fructidor, ou Mémoires . . .* Paris, 1821.

MICHEL, A., ed., *Correspondance inédite de Mallet de Pan avec la Cour de Vienne*, 2 tomes, Paris, 1884.

SAYOUS, A., ed., *Mémoires et Correspondance de Mallet du Pan*, 2 tomes, Paris, 1858.

THIBAUDEAU, A.-C., *Mémoires sur la Convention et le Directoire*, 2 tomes, Paris, 1824.

The general political narrative sections of the book have been based on, or illustrated from, the following works chiefly:

AULARD, A., *Histoire politique de la Révolution française*, Paris, 1901.
BUCHEZ & ROUX, *Histoire parlementaire de la Révolution française*, tome 37, Paris, 1838.
LEFEBVRE, G., *Les Thermidoriens*, Paris, 1937; 1946.
—— *Le Directoire*, Paris, 1946.
MEYNIER, A., *Les Coups d'état du Directoire: le 18 fructidor, an V.*, Paris, 1928.
PARISET, G., *Histoire de France contemporaine* (ed. E. Lavisse), tome II, Paris, 1920.

The activities of the exiled princes and their adherents have been illustrated from:

DAUDET, E., *Histoire de l'émigration pendant la Révolution française*, 3 tomes, Paris, 3e, édition, 1907.

For details of the French legislative personnel and for the procedure of French legislative elections during this period, reference has throughout been made to the volume of:

KUSCINSKI, A., *Les Députés au Corps Législatif . . . de l'an IV à l'an VII: Listes, Tableaux et Lois*, Paris, 1905.

Published materials for the career of A.-B.-J. d'André are detailed in the Introduction above, p. xiv, note 1.

Index

Agents, Royal, 18, 87–98, 123, 167
n.2, 172, 190–1, 270–3, *see also*
Brottier, Des Pomelles, Du-
verne, La Trémoille, Lemerer,
Moreau
Anciens (Elders), Council of the, 53–
54, 161 n.1, 208, 243–5, 257,
263–4
André de la Lozère, 231
Angoulême, Louis-Antoine, Duc d',
133, 207–8
Antraigues, Comte d', 16, 17 n.1,
267 n.
Apathy of French public, 141–5,
202–3, *see also* Public Opinion
Artois, Charles-Philippe, Comte d'
(later Charles X), xviii, 38, 71–2,
205
Augereau, General, 292, 310, 316,
321
Avaray, Comte d', 99–101, 189–90
Avre (Pichegru), 233 n.2
Aymé, J.-J., 54, 56, 57 n.1, 63 n.2,
231, 242

Bailleul, J.-Ch., xvii
Baptiste (Pichegru), 100 n.1
Barbé (de) Marbois, 53, 56, 231
Barras, P. (de), 56, 75, 213–14, 226,
248–50, 283, 291–2
Barthélemy, Fr., 162 n.1, 187, 237
and n.2, 248, 283–4
Bayard, 45 n.3, 61 n.1, 154 n.2, 163–
165, 215–16, 218–20, 222–3
Bénézech, 84 n.2, 250, 254 n.2
Berger, (D'André), 134 n.1
Besignan, 18 n.1
Boisgelin de Cucé, 4
Boissy d'Anglas, 50, 141 n.1
Bonaparte, General, 213, 228–9, 249,
285 nn.2,5, 286, 292
Bonaventure, N.-M., 231
Bonnières, 195, 202, 205
British policy towards France, 19–24,
Mallet du Pan on, 7–9, 36–7,
restoration by force, 24, 35, 38,
112–14, 149–51, 160, amnesty,
25–31, and Paris sections, 45–50,

and Pichegru, 103–4, 108–9, and
Orleanism, 68, 114–15, 117–18;
and electoral methods, 119–20,
D'André and, 124–39, 159, 173–
174, 177–8, 195–6, 214–20, 273–
279, peace with Republic (1797),
279–81, 290, *see* Coalition of
Parties
Brottier, (Brotier), Abbé, 18, 83, 88,
90–95, 97–8, 101–3, 105–8,
116–18, 172, 177, 183, 189–90,
196 n.3
Brumaire, laws of, year IV: purpose,
56–7, opposition and, 59–60, the
'friends of D'André' and, 132
n.4, 140, attack on, 152, repeal,
161 n.1, 243, 247 n.1, Dumas
and, 230, the 'Triumvirs', independents, and, 291

Cadroi, or Cadroy, P., 153, 204 nn.1,
2, 231–2
Calonne, Marquis de, 4
Carency, Prince de, 171 n.1, 249, 291–
292
Carnot, 75–8, 204 n.1, 213–14, 247
n.2, 248, 251–2, 283
Castries, Maréchal-Marquis de, 16
n.1, 185 n.2
Cercle constitutionnel, 227 n.4
Champion de Cicé, 4
Charette, Fr. de, 48
Charles, Archduke of Austria, xviii,
117, 149–51
Chouans (Royalist insurgents), 56, 74,
Paris Agents on, 90, 95, 98,
D'André and the, 265, 273, 306–
307, 311
Claret-Fleurieu, 205
Clergy, non-juring, 42, 57, 90, 145,
161 n.1, 163, 177–8, 243–4
'Clichy, Club de', 234–6
Clubs, pro-Jacobin, 59, 75, Direc-
torial, 227 n.4
'Coalition of Parties', British policy
and, 30, 32, 47–8, 100–1, 110–20,
124–9, 137–9, legislative opposi-
tion and, 78–9, Pichegru and,

325

ST. MARY'S COLLEGE OF MARYLAND LIBRARY
ST. MARY'S CITY, MARYLAND

DUE

PRINTED IN U.S.A.